Drone Aesthetics
War, Culture, Ecology

Technographies

Series Editors: Steven Connor, David Trotter and James Purdon

How was it that technology and writing came to inform each other so extensively that today there is only information? Technographies seeks to answer that question by putting the emphasis on writing as an answer to the large question of 'through what?'. Writing about technographies in history, our contributors will themselves write technographically.

Drone Aesthetics

War, Culture, Ecology

Edited by Beryl Pong and Michael Richardson

O
OPEN HUMANITIES PRESS
London 2024

First edition published by Open Humanities Press 2024

Copyright ©2024 Beryl Pong and Michael Richardson, and respective authors.

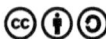

This is an open access book, licensed under Creative Commons By Attribution Share Alike license. Under this license, authors allow anyone to download, reuse, reprint, modify, distribute, and/or copy their work so long as the authors and source are cited and resulting derivative works are licensed under the same or similar license. No permission is required from the authors or the publisher. Statutory fair use and other rights are in no way affected by the above. Read more about the license at creativecommons.org/licenses/by-sa/4.0

Cover Art, figures, and other media included with this book may be under different copyright restrictions.

Sections of chapter 10 have appeared in Adam Fish, *Oceaning: Governing Marine Life with Drones*, © Duke University Press 2024. Reproduced with permission.

Cover Illustration © 2024 Navine G. Dossos

Print ISBN 978-1-78542-103-7
PDF ISBN 978-1-78542-102-0

OPEN HUMANITIES PRESS

Open Humanities Press is an international, scholar-led open access publishing collective whose mission is to make leading works of contemporary critical thought freely available worldwide. More at http://openhumanitiespress.org

Contents

Acknowledgements		7
Introduction: Drone Aesthetics – An Open Proposition Beryl Pong and Michael Richardson		9
1.	Becoming (Im)Perceptible: From Scopic Regimes to the Martial Gaze Antoine Bousquet	32
2.	Me and My Predator(s): Tactical Remembrance and Critical Atonement Joseph DeLappe	46
3.	PillCam and Drone Warfare's Redemptive Refrains Sophia Goodfriend	64
4.	Parasitoid Drone [UAV/UAS/AWS/D-IED] // Naugahyde Barcalounger Boola-Boola Tom Sear	78
5.	Everyday Militarisms: Drones and the Blurring of the Civilian-Military Divide During COVID-19 Caren Kaplan	98
6.	On Feminised Digital Media Users and Drone Operations J. D. Schnepf	115
7.	The Drone's Other Target: The Generative Aesthetics of Drone Hobbyists' Love Amy Gaeta	128
8.	Imaginational Metaveillance: Revelations in the Drone Age Kathryn Brimblecombe-Fox	145

9. The Swarm: Drone as Composite Technology
   and Neo-liberal Fantasy   160
   Mitch Goodwin

10. Posthuman Photorealism: the Science
    and Art of Seeing Living Whales with Drones   178
    Adam Fish and Edgar Gómez Cruz

11. Asymmetrical Cinema – Dawn of the Drone
    through Film, Cartography and Interspecies Relations   191
    Jack Faber

12. Computing Hallucinations: How Drones Read Oceans   213
    Simon M. Taylor

13. Drone Error: From Event to Structure   230
    Madelene Veber

14. ecologies of duration: a visual essay on thinking-imaging
    novel space-times with drones   244
    Michele Barker and Anna Munster

Coda: Post-Visual Images   254
   Yanai Toister

Contributors   268

Acknowledgments

We are immensely grateful to the contributors to this volume and especially their patience as it took shape and evolved from the very beginnings of the pandemic to the present day. Their generosity, creativity, and insight animated this book from the beginning and we are truly privileged to have guided this work to publication.

This volume collects chapters that grew from presentations at two conferences independently organised by the editors: the Aesthetics of Drone Warfare, convened by Beryl at Sheffield University in February 2020, and Drone Cultures, hosted at the University of New South Wales but gathered online in December 2020. We are both thankful for the presentations at those events and the rich discussion they occasioned. While we could not publish extended versions of every presentation in this book, we might easily have doubled the number without running short of fascinating contributions. These events and the subsequent editorial work of compiling this book were supported by a UK Research and Innovation Future Leaders Fellowship (MR/W010429/1) held by Beryl and an Australian Research Council Discovery Early Career Researcher Award (DE190100486) held by Michael, respectively. Research funding is increasingly stretched in the UK and Australia, and we are both extremely fortunate to have received significant support.

Open Humanities Press is a rare and remarkable institution in academic publishing that is driven by the passion, labour, and generosity of its directors Gary Hall, Sigi Jöttkandt and David Ottina, and the various series editors. Our deepest thanks to Sigi for her enthusiastic support for this project and to Steve Connor, David Trotter, and James Purdon for bringing this book to fruition in the Technographies series. Our added appreciation goes to James for undertaking the copyediting of this volume – no small task at the best of times, but harder still at a time when the UK academy is stretched to breaking.

If it weren't for Amy Gaeta, who saved us in the final stages through diligent and attentive work managing the proofs, and Madelene Veber, who assisted us throughout the process in tracking edits, fixing references, compiling the manuscript file, and countless other tasks large and small, this volume might never have seen the light. Their chapters in this volume are two of its highlights and both will no doubt shine ever brighter in the years to come.

Finally, we are both forever in the debt of our partners, families, and the communities of friendship and scholarship in which we are enmeshed.

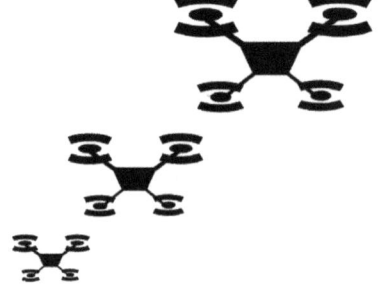

INTRODUCTION

Drone Aesthetics – An Open Proposition

Beryl Pong and Michael Richardson

There can be little doubt of the canonical drone aesthetic: a flattened aeriality that moves with an inhuman smoothness, drifting, and pitching to capture an uncanny vantage. News reports, leaked videos, and Hollywood movies have all made a decidedly militarised drone vision all too normal: grayscale environments seen from above, punctuated by the white intensity of body heat as figures move beneath the targeting reticule. Such images are a recreation in pixels for the eyes of human operators of the forward-looking infrared sensor, or FLIR, that forms an essential component of the surveillance payload of most large military drones. The product of a complex sensory apparatus that registers infrared radiation and transmits its measurements through multiple systems, signals, and satellites, the images pored over by sensor operators and military analysts are but one narrow instance of drone aesthetics. In cinematography, drones generate hyper-real environments. In art, they are both an object of aesthetic investigation and an instrument for aesthetic production.

Yet aesthetics – *sensing* and *making sense of* the stuff of the world – concerns much more than imagery. Navigation itself involves its own aesthetics, as the drone senses its environment, maintains stability, and provides flight data to pilots. Autonomous swarms sense for and between one another, generating a collective grasp of environments as relational phenomena. Even the simplest consumer quadcopters register the air around them and make sense of remote control commands. Aesthetics, then, are not separable from drones but constitutive of their operation. Nor are drone aesthetics pregiven. They arise through drone practices and help shape what drones become. Just as the drone itself is an unstable object – vehicle or system, aerial or marine, autonomous, or piloted – so too are its aesthetics always in process, always doing, always both sensing and making sense.

The past two decades have seen an efflorescence of scholarly work about drones, particularly in relation to drone warfare and practices of 'targeted killing' during and after the war on terror (Benjamin 2012; Cockburn 2015; Gusterson 2016; Tahir 2017). Our volume differs from the field, however, in its critique of a rapidly and radically changing drone landscape, and in its concern with both drone presents and drone futures. Although drones gained prominence during the post-9/11 US security state, the idea of a drone, and what counts as a drone, has since moved beyond the military sphere to fields as wide ranging as journalism, visual arts, wildlife conservation, oceanography, advertising, agriculture, and climate activism, among others. Drones have now taken to the skies across multiple sectors such that, in Michael J. Boyle's words, there is a 'Wild West atmosphere in the field' (2020: 14). War spurred more research into drone technology, which has created new expertise and new applications for drone use in countless fields. Not all drone propositions will take flight; many will fail. But what seems beyond question is that drones will remain in a state of constant and unstable evolution for some time to come.

Our challenge as editors and writers throughout this project has been to attend to the fast-moving field of drone scholarship and the unfolding, contested landscape of drone development and drone use – a landscape that altered not-so-quietly with COVID-19, which saw the use of 'pandemic drones' for transport (Hildebrand and Sodero 2021) and, as Caren Kaplan writes in this volume, the use of drones as vehicles for 'everyday militarisms' which blur the civilian-military divide. Other developments, like the repurposing of a Predator drone for domestic surveillance during the Black Lives Matter protests in Minneapolis, have further expanded the use of drones in this manner during the conception and writing of the volume itself (Holt 2020). *Drone Aesthetics: War, Culture, Ecology* considers how a once-military technology has become a 'disruptive technology' in the broader sense of the term: 'an innovative technology that triggers sudden and unexpected effects' (Dunn 2013: 1238). It examines the role that aesthetics plays: not only in drone operations, but in creating, as well as challenging, issues arising from the proliferation of drones in the past, the present, and thus, the future.

In this collection, there are at least four approaches to understanding drone aesthetics: as visual culture and the arts; as the body and its relationship to the material environment; as the machinic capacities for sensing and sensemaking that constitute drone systems themselves, and as the very foundation for how we understand politics and what makes politics possible – a question with increasing urgency, given the way drones erode boundaries between the military and the domestic. To explore aesthetics in this pluralistic manner, *Drone Aesthetics* features contributors from a range of fields, including cultural anthropology, disability studies, critical war studies, international relations, media studies, literary studies, and cultural studies, to offer new ideas and arguments about the technology, logics, and systems with which drones are intertwined. But this book is not limited to critical arguments, either. To more fully account for the unique politics of drone perception, it also features three visual essays by visual and multimedia artists who not only reflect upon drones in their art, but whose work in turn demonstrates what others have called a 'practical aesthetics' – aesthetics as practice or praxis – which intervenes into the worldmaking operations of drones in warfare and beyond (Bennett 2012). According to Jill Bennett, the work of art is not just to replicate an event, but 'to draw bodies into sensations not yet experienced'; the artists in this volume address and reflect on the opportunities, challenges, and politics of this particular dimension of their art (63). Collectively, the essays in this volume scrutinise how the aesthetics of drones are fundamental to their ethics, and how drone aesthetics are impacting the way we relate to one another and to human and more-than-human worlds.

An aesthetic approach to drones is fundamentally political because it foregrounds how drones reshape experience through their capacities to sense and be sensible, to produce both knowledge and death. Drones are not separable from regimes of power, nor from broader histories of colonial control, such as in early British aviation in the Middle East and Afghanistan (Satia 2014), in the contemporary production of peripheries (Akhter 2019), and in American forms of what Madiha Tahir (2021) calls the 'distributed empire' enacted through drone violence, disappearances, and other forms of clientelism in Pakistan. For drone pilots conducting lethal strikes from Creech Air Force Base outside Las Vegas, the mediated aesthetics of high definition and infrared video can heighten the trauma of killing (Edney-Browne 2017). But for those who live and die under drones, their aesthetics are more fundamentally transformative of how the world itself is felt. One man who lost both legs to a drone strike in Waziristan told human rights researchers: '[e]veryone is scared all the time. When we're sitting together to have a meeting, we're scared there might be a strike. When you can hear the drone circling in the sky, you think it might strike you. We're always scared. We always have this fear in our head' (International Human Rights 2012: 81). Drone aesthetics, then, is not simply about what a drone senses, what it looks like, or how it is depicted, but about how drones themselves are felt and registered, about how they transform how the world is sensed and what sense is made of the world in deeply political ways.

In their article, 'Drone Power: Conservation, Humanitarianism, Policing and War', Adam Fish and Michael Richardson discuss some of the areas that have now been altered by drones, arguing for a more capacious understanding of 'drone power' as '[n]either reductively biopolitical nor purely statist', but as an effect of their 'capacity to act as existential technologies' (Fish and Richardson 2022: 6). Drones now 'not only make *live* in the sense described by Foucault… they make *life* through acts such as conservation and humanitarianism' (18). The drone is an existential technology that changes how we see and engage with others, and our relationships to both life and death. Each of the essays collected here examines the existential power of drones across a diverse range of domains, from drone warfare to pillcams to swarm cultures to pandemic drones. To do so, each also addresses in direct and indirect ways the question of aesthetics, which signals both the vibrancy of this line of inquiry and the generative potential that resides in refusing to foreclose the nature of ethics itself. Therefore, before discussing the essays and their relation to one another, we will first delineate how aesthetics, variously conceived, has been understood within drone criticism to date, and consider why the politics of aesthetics matter in relation to the cultures of security, pre-emption, and risk management with which drones are imbricated.

Drone Theories

In the essay 'Drone Aesthetics', Eugenie Shinkle responds to Lisa Barnard's photographic artwork about modern technological warfare, suggesting drone aesthetics as a 'modern idiom, a shorthand for new modes of representing war from the extraterrestrial perspective of a machine' (Shinkle 2014). Although one tends to associate aesthetics with ideas of taste or beauty as described in Alexander Baumgarten's eighteenth-century use of the word, aesthetics is derived etymologically from the Greek *aisthetikos*, meaning 'sensitive, or per-taining to sense perception', and it is linked to *aistheta*, 'perceptible things' (Manovich 2017: 9). With this focus on situated embodiment and on how the world is sensually experienced, felt, and perceived, Shinkle argues that mod-ern technology has brought new ways of seeing, making, and experiencing war: 'as the boundaries of human perception shift, so too does the nature of aesthetic experience' (Shinkle 2014).

A brief survey of drone criticism to date shows how this broad under-standing of aesthetics, as the subject's material-affective encounter with the sensory world, has been a recurring concern in drone technology as it devel-oped within the military sphere. While drones, or unmanned aerial vehicles, date back to the First World War, it was only after the emergence and normal-isation of drone warfare that a wave of drone scholarship began. Central to this first wave is Derek Gregory's article, 'From a View to a Kill: Drones and Late Modern War', which identified one of the key aesthetic dimensions of drone warfare, the 'scopic regime', a term which Antoine Bousquet reassesses in his contribution to this volume (Gregory 2011). Borrowing from Martin Jay and Christian Metz, Gregory writes that scopic regimes 'denote a mode of visual apprehension that is culturally constructed and prescriptive, socially structured and shared' (190). The scopic regimes of drone operations – in par-ticular, the god's eye view and the conduct of war from a distance through the ocular intimacy of a computer screen – suggested to Gregory that 'the death *of* distance enables death *from* a distance' (192). This is a contention shared by

Gregoire Chamayou's influential *Drone Theory* (2015). Approaching the question of drone warfare from the perspective of moral philosophy, Chamayou examines how drones enable a mobile battlefield, and how physical distance goes hand in hand with the rhetoric of precision – drone strikes are also called 'surgical strikes' – which indicates a radical departure from the traditional idea of warfare to something asymmetrical and post-heroic, closer to the practice of manhunting (Chamayou 15: 30-5). For both critics, the politics of drone warfare are intertwined with the aesthetics of drone warfare. Does killing from a distance and a screen make killing easier? Do the aesthetics of drone warfare make this form of violence more or less just? How do the aesthetics of drone warfare change the lives of those knowingly or unknowingly targeted, who can't see but can hear the whirring of the drone, and who live with the sustained fear of sudden death from above?

Following from Gregory and Chamayou, drone scholarship focused on other aesthetic readings of militarised drones that studied certain aspects of the drone as object. In addition to scopic regimes, scholars examined the drone's weaponisation of sight, particularly through 'operational images'. Harun Farocki (2004: 17) described operational images as images that do rather than represent, as images that activate, detect, track, and identify, for instance – images not necessarily meant for human eyes, but that are part of an operation. Various critics have examined how drone vision relates to machinic vision, to 'images made by machines for other machines', especially as drones are operating increasingly autonomously with the aid of algorithms (Paglen 2014; see also Holert 2016). A significant body of critique that emerged over the last decade also focused on aesthetics as artistic representations which respond to and critique drone warfare (Braunert and Malone 2016; Stubblefield 2020). From Trevor Paglen's photographs of Reaper drones, captured as tiny specks against the Nevada sky, to James Bridle's life-sized *Drone Shadows* installations drawn around global metropolitan streetscapes, many now-canonical drone artworks sought to address the invisibility of drones, both in the skies and in terms of publicly available information and discourse, as military drone use was (and remains) shrouded in secrecy. Both drone art and art-historical criticism about drones have been integral to surfacing the political and ethical issues of remote warfare.

Much of the scholarship which focused on these aesthetic dimensions of militarised drones centred on the Predator and Reaper drones flown by the United States over Afghanistan, Pakistan, Yemen, Somalia, Libya, and other countries in the Middle East and North Africa, or they focused on the use of drones by Israel for surveillance, population control, and targeted assassination in Gaza. This first wave of drone scholarship thus tended to concentrate on the aesthetics of large, lethal drones, which left relatively unexamined a parallel development: the rapid diffusion of smaller drones that are now, from the perspective of this book's publication in 2024, a part of many areas of everyday life. From the humanitarian drones used by the United Nations for crisis mapping and search and rescue operations to the agricultural drones used for crop monitoring; from the drones used for real estate marketing and advertising to the swarm drones which are replacing fireworks at mass celebrations; from experimental commercial drone delivery programmes to the hand-held surveillance drones used to enforce lockdown rules during the COVID-19 pandemic: everyone everywhere now seems to be using drones, to be seeing drones, or to have been subjected to the drone's gaze in some way.

Even in military contexts, drone forms have become radically differentiated: the hand-launched, fixed-wing Raven is used by almost every active US combat force, while Ukrainian resistance to Russia's 2022 invasion shows how prosumer drones can be used to drop small munitions without being detected. All of these developments can be attributed to the increased accessibility and relatively low cost of drones, and the fact that drones are now in the hands of enormously varied communities of users far beyond the state. In tandem with the democratisation of drones, a wider range of motivations underpinning drone use has meant that the core functions of drones – collecting and recording data and images, and delivering payloads – has also expanded in terms of what is being recorded and what is being delivered.

The emergence of drones as a disruptive technology has spurred a second wave of scholarship in which critics have increasingly shifted attention away from the drone object to a broader range of drone systems; in doing so, they have been attending more to aesthetics as both a process and logic within wider drone assemblages. Key to this shift was the publication of the widely read collection *Life in the Age of Drone Warfare*, edited by Lisa Parks and Caren Kaplan (2017), which expanded the ambit of drone studies to capture affective, discursive, and technopolitical dimensions that continue to shape its application. Meanwhile, reflexive critiques of 'good drones' (Sandvik and Jumbert 2017) were supplemented by nuanced accounts of small drones whose positive applications remain 'bound to, and entangled with, an *inverse potential for exploitation*' (Jackman 2019: 363). Further work is being done on drone hobbyists (Hildebrand 2021), drone conservation (Fish 2021), home security drones (Jackman and Brickell 2021), civic drone visualities (Serafinelli and O'Hagan 2022), and drone mediation (Parks 2017). In addition, historical genealogies which offered more longitudinal archival studies of the politics of the aerial view (Kaplan 2018), and which have traced the long and stuttering history of military drone development and its failures (Chandler 2020), have also shown how, despite the tendency to fixate on the 'newness' of unmanned aerial vehicles, drones are part of a long lineage of unmanned technologies being used for the 'disavowal of politics' (Chandler 2020: 3). For Kaplan and Chandler, the politics that are disavowed often have to do with race, colonialism, and neo-colonialism. In this regard, the work of Ronak Kapadia (2019) has brought to light a new archive of contemporary drone art by Arab, Muslim, and South Asian diasporic artists which acts as a reckoning.

These and other works reflected a shift in emphasis away from the drone as object or system and towards the drone as logic and process. For Mark Andrejevic, the drone is not seen as singular or unique, but an avatar for broader social-cultural practices and imaginaries while shaping them in turn. In particular, he sees drones as part of a logic of ubiquitous, always-on networked sensors for the purposes of automated data collection, processing, and response' permeating contemporary societies' (Andrejevic 2016: 21). Not unrelated to the disavowal of politics, Andrejevic argues that the drone cultivates and represents the cultivation of 'passive interactivity' across wider areas such as digital media platforms, personalised advertising, security and policing, and even electoral canvassing and voting. His approach might chime with what Andreas Immanuel Graae and Kathrin Maurer have called 'drone imaginaries' – a term which 'designates negotiations between personal, emotional experiences and the broader social imagination in the form of collective imaginings including affects, desires and fantasies' which undergird the rapid development of drone technology (Graae and Maurer 2020: 2). In turn, the essays in Graae and Maurer's book have brought the field back to examining drone artworks and aesthetic representations of drones, but with a view to exploring the broader political and social worlds, beyond the martial, of which drone technology is a part. In a similar vein, Daniela Angostinho, Maurer, and Kristin Veel's special issue on 'The Sensorial Experience of the Drone' collects a number of incisive essays that show how interrogating drone sensing helps to 'critically address the blurry boundaries through which drones become more pervasive across social life' (2020: 254). There are valuable confluences and alliances between these recent interventions in the field and the present book, which we see as extending this critical line of inquiry into the constitutive relations between drones, materiality, and aesthetics.

Drone Aesthetics: War, Culture, Ecology embraces an interdisciplinary approach to drone aesthetics as a contested terrain. 'Drone aesthetics', in this second wave of scholarship, extends Shinkle's original idea to examine not only how technology is imagined or how it impacts upon sense perception – including and beyond the military – but how aesthetics relates to, and constitutes, our very practices of knowledge and our very existence in the world. In this way, the essays in this volume extend the field towards an understanding of drone aesthetics where aesthetics is understood not only as particular formal dimensions of the drone object or view, or as artistic representations of drones, but as the very basis for political life and for what makes politics visible and possible. To further explore the worldmaking power of drone aesthetics, the next section turns to Jacques Rancière's idea of political aesthetics, and to other thinkers who have sought to address aesthetics in the contexts of war and technology, to discuss how aesthetics entangle military and civilian, body and machine, distance and proximity, and life and death in drone assemblages, particularly in relation to cultures of security.

Towards Drone Aesthetics

In Rancière's writings on the politics of aesthetics, he describes the workings of politics through the 'distribution of the sensible'. By this he means politics manifests through:

> the system of *a priori* forms determining what presents itself to sense experience. It is a delimitation of spaces and times, of the visible and the invisible, of speech and noise, that simultaneously determines the place and stakes of politics as a form of experience. (2004: 13)

Politics operates aesthetically, because aesthetics concerns nothing less than how humans perceive and sense, and thus inhabit, their world. Crucially, for Rancière, who draws from Aristotle's conception of citizenship, the distribution of the sensible establishes 'what is seen and what can be said about it, around who has the ability to see and the talent to speak' (2004: 13). Politics, as the aesthetic distribution of the sensible, demarcates lines of inclusion and exclusion regarding 'who [can] have a part in the community of citizens', therefore shaping who has voice, authority, and legitimacy (2004: 12). Aesthetics, then, can not only be understood in expansive terms as the interplay between sensing the world and making sense of it; between the impingement of the world on the sensor and the sense-making through which the world becomes knowable and graspable (Fuller and Weizman 2021: 35). Following Rancière, we can understand the politics of aesthetics as the distribution of the sensible, in which the 'sensible' pulls double duty as both that which can be sensed and that which is made coherent through sensing. For Rancière, the critical question is how sensing and sense-making are arranged within political cultures and what forms of authority, hierarchy, and knowledge operate within and through that arrangement.

Rancière's writings have been influential to the 'aesthetic turn' in international relations and political sciences over the past decade (Bleiker 2018; Shapiro 2013). But pursuing such an aesthetics into the technicalities of drone assemblages, in particular, requires us to reckon with the incompleteness of those systems and with their necessary contingency. Drone aesthetics is thus not a project of the Kantian sublime, but rather an ever-evolving and continually contested enterprise that can't ever transcend the messy, complicated stuff of life – or of the fraught environments in which drones are so often found in practice.

Taken in this processual sense, aesthetics don't presuppose or prefigure distinct norms and values but rather contribute to their production in, through, and in response to power. For even while collapsing distinctions between military and civilian, body and machine, distance and proximity, life and death, drones reify such distinctions as devices that themselves distribute the sensible. For instance, there is an aesthetics to the perception that is drone warfare within the military apparatus: the array of screens, the latency of imagery, the multispectral capacities, and the narrow fields of view afforded by the 'soda straw' camera of the drone, all layered over by the algorithmic apparatus of target identification via pattern analysis. Such an aesthetics presents itself as precise and hyper-technical but is remarkably prone to errors, and as Madelene Veber's essay in this volume shows, error drives, rather than being an unintended phenomenon of, the drone's functioning. Like the processes of violent mediation to which it is yoked, the sensing and sense-making mechanics of the drone apparatus shape the knowledge claims that authorise drone violence. This authorisation is self-justifying because drones not only distribute the sensible: they make sensible and perceptible things that might otherwise not be sensible or perceptible yet, or at all.

The history of drone development is in many ways intertwined with the logic of mitigating or preparing for an uncertain, as-yet unrealised, future: early drones from the interwar period were conceived as target practice for anti-aircraft training, and during the Cold War, the pursuit of unmanned reconnaissance methods gained traction because, in the event that a manned plane is shot down, a drone presented less risk to national security (Chandler 2020). But the terrorist attacks on the World Trade Center led to another level in this logic, when the 9/11 Commission judged the event to be a failure of the imagination, attributed to a 'mindset that dismissed possibilities' (2004: 344). The response became 'a new security paradigm that was all about evoking images of imminent threats from an imaginary pool of virtual futures', Graae and Maurer write. 'In this paranoid hunt for future insecurities, armed drones soon became an important military technology, which could not only see but also "foresee" and pre-empt future threats' (2020: 4). The birth of the Predator drone, and the rise of drone use for surveillance and targeted killing, is motivated by the idea of pre-empting terror from happening and becoming sensible in the first place.

In drone warfare, this logic of securitizing and mitigating the risk of what isn't yet perceptible led to the use of 'signature strikes' – attacks against individuals whose identity remains unknown, but whose behaviour suggests one's belonging, or susceptibility to belonging, to a terrorist organisation (Chamayou 2015: 47). With drone operations aided by the use of databases and algorithms which search for and bring a target to the surface, data helps to *produce* the risk that it purportedly helps to eliminate, thereby 'in circular fashion justif[ying] the boundlessness of drone violence', since potentialities are construed as inevitabilities (Stubblefield 2020: 39). '[A]esthetics does not exclusively refer to a property or capacity of humans', Matthew Fuller and Eyal Weizman write, because 'sensing is also found in material surfaces and substances, on which traces of impact or slower processes of change are registered, including in digital and computational sensors, which themselves detect, register and predict in multiple novel ways' (2021: 35). As such, drones, and the politics of aesthetics which inform their use, are both the catalyst and the prophylaxis for the targetable bodies which are 'uncovered'. This is why Brian Massumi calls security's logic of pre-emption 'ontopower', or 'an operative logic of power': security has to constantly stage and make present an absence in order to maintain claims of that absence, which in turn consolidates security's *raison d'être* (2015: 5).

The interplay of sensing and sense-making equally animates violence unleashed from above as well as the resistant art that has arisen in response. Rancière considers how another realm of aesthetics – artistic practices – are themselves '"ways of doing and making" that intervene in the general distribution of ways of doing and making' (Rancière 2004: 13). He argues that the aesthetic arts can redistribute the sensible within the prevailing modes of perception within society, operating 'as configurations of experience that create new modes of sense perception and induce novel forms of political subjectivity' (9). We now turn to two artworks about drones and their aesthetics, to help illustrate the possibilities and issues arising from their interventions into drone logics and sensibilities, and to understand why the politics of aesthetics necessarily means that drone aesthetics will be evolving, unstable, and open to contestation.

First, consider the viral art project *#NotABugSplat* (2014), in which a group of artists, local villagers, and (oddly enough) BBDO advertising strategists spread huge prints of children across fields in Waziristan. Taking its title from the BugSplat collateral damage software used by the US, it refigures the space in which it is situated, shifting the relation between the military view from above and the land, people, and communities it surveils. Designed to critique the dehumanising scales of visuality that enable drone warfare, the image is intended to shock the conscience of an imagined drone pilot, thus refiguring the logic of pre-emption which underpins the military drone gaze. It disrupts the dehumanising technical architecture of the drone assemblage by replacing the narrow and flattened view from 5,000 feet with the returned gaze of the innocent victim as a demand for recognition of the humanity of those racially othered by the military drone apparatus. As Jennifer Rhee points out in her analysis of the project, 'drone vision, with its aerial perspective and its narrow classificatory choices, works to evade the scale at which such recognition of the other's humanness can take place' (Rhee 2018: 163). In other words, the aesthetics of drone warfare delimit the capacity for sensing (top-down, limited field of vision, high latency in transmission) and sense-making (prescribed classification for bodies caught in its field, functionalist meaning within parameters of military missions and rules of engagement) into a narrow field that conditions what can be rendered sensible – in both senses of the word – within the drone warfare apparatus.

#NotABugSplat deploys its own aesthetics of sensing (blown-up photographs, pixels readily discernible) and sense-making (refiguring what can be made visible) as a kind of counter, troubling both the capacity of the apparatus itself and seeking – through its intended virality – to bring those sensory

capacities under close scrutiny. Indeed, at times the scrutiny has been more critical than approving: because the location of the installation is further away in Khyber Pakhtunkhwa, which has endured far fewer drone strikes than Dande Darpa Khel, the Northern Waziristan village where the photographed girl's family was killed, critics have queried the efficacy of this aesthetic intervention (Pearl 2014; Stubblefield 2020: 129). Others have pointed out that the artwork's virality intervenes on another level – not on the level of the individual drone operator, but on the level of the networks which undergird drone warfare in the first place. Countering the way that drone warfare operates through 'kill chains' – a dispersed apparatus of 'actors, objects, practices, discourses, and affects' involved in the act of targeting (Gregory 2011: 196) – the circulating aerial images of #*NotABugSplat* on the internet (taken by a consumer drone), can be seen to engender a 'collective witnessing' on the part of 'networked subjects', thereby intervening in the silence and secrecy upon which the US conducts the drone war (Hoyt 2014). This project can be understood as an aesthetic engagement with drone warfare but also, and more importantly, as an intervention into the aesthetic logics and processes of the military drone apparatus itself, even while it submits the politics of its own aesthetics and intervention to dialogue and scrutiny rather than foreclosure. This is a theme that J.D. Schnepf takes up in this volume through an examination of the resonances between social media logics and digital kill chains.

A second work of art, Ai Weiwei's documentary film *Human Flow* (2017), is also an aesthetic intervention into drone logic, but beyond the space of drone warfare. Filmed in over twenty-three countries with a crew of a dozen cinematographers, it uses videography from drone quadcopters to capture the scale of what some in Western media have called the 'refugee crisis' of 2015. The camera hovers over many scenes documenting an enormous number of migrants as they traverse difficult and oftentimes inhospitable terrain, or as they stay deadlocked at refugee camps outside of the countries that they have travelled so far to enter. Critics have commented on the aesthetic beauty, some might say sublimity, of the drone's eye view here: the 'drone views help give "Human Flow" a velvety smooth look' (Dargis 2017), and its visual poetry rests on 'beautiful aerial drone shots of landscapes, refugee camps, and migrants on the move' (Zimanyi 2019: 377). Ai's use of drone videography, however, also attempts to repurpose the gaze of surveillance drones. Frontex, the European Border and Coast Guard Agency, has been using drones to monitor and pre-empt attempted migrant crossings in the Mediterranean since 2015, and the UK Border Force has been deploying surveillance aircraft – including Tekever drones and, since 2021, a Thales military Watchkeeper drone – as part of the effort to 'secure' the English Channel against migrant boats from Calais (Cockerell 2021). The refiguring and humanising of the drone's gaze are clearest mid-way through the film, when the drone camera descends from the sky and down into a circle of displaced children in a camp in Turkey, foregrounding their disenfranchisement but also wonder at the potentials of drone journalism.

Still, the vistas afforded by the drone do not sit comfortably with the subject of the film, which is the mobile immobility of refugees. The film's aesthetics of sensing (the aerial views visualise the scale of refugee hardship that one otherwise might not see) and sense-making (the drone's mobility makes perceptible the borders that are invisible and inconsequential for some, but visible and unsurmountable for others) draw scrutiny to the power differential of the filmmakers too. There is a scene of Ai himself and his drone crew at the US-Mexico border; he is given a light reprimand for the trespass, where others without his passport or stature would have of course met a very different fate. The scene can be construed as both self-conscious and tasteless, and one might argue the same of the use of drone videography itself in a documentary about forced migration. In Georges Didi-Huberman's reading, the drone represents the ease and freedom of movement which the refugees cannot have. '[W]hat dignity does the image here potentially seek to *give back* to the people being filmed… under the very conditions of their greatest distress? …[N]othing is exchanged and nothing is given back. Despite the fact that drones can be used, as we know, as deadly weapons of war, the device itself cannot be ethically evaluated: rather, it is how it is used – whether it serves a humanitarian aesthetic or a military tactic – which reveals the *degree of honesty and justice* of its user through the images it takes' (Didi-Huberman 2018) Drone aesthetics, here, intervenes into the material manifestations, as well as the concept, of the border; but it can also be an act of looking down on vulnerable others who have been deprived of fundamental rights, as it does not require vulnerability or the ceding of power in return.

Both *#NotABugSplat* and *Human Flow* are works which disrupt drone assemblages and logics through a redistribution of the sensible. Both also raise a host of questions – about the ethics of drones more broadly, and the politics of the aesthetic views that drones enable – which cannot be easily answered, because their redistribution of the sensible continues to reveal who is deemed to have a part in the community who does the looking and the seeing. Both show how drones can also produce different modes of witnessing and accountability, and different ways of construing the politics of vision and embodiment more generally. Who do drones empower, and whose agency and power do they constrict? Where do we draw the lines of responsibility between the people operating the drone, the people deciding on the use of drones, the people seeing through drones (whether directly or by proxy through other media), and the sensors which increasingly automate and guide where drones can go and how they fly? What are the ethics of seeing from a drone, and how do the aesthetic registers of the drone's eye view affect the viewer's relationship to what, or who, is being seen? Furthermore, as drones are becoming a conflicted and conflicting presence among themselves – as these artworks show, military, civilian, and nonstate actor drones are operating at the same sites, and subjecting them to different visual regimes – how do we assess 'the degree of honesty and justice of the [drone] user'? According to whose understandings of those terms do such assessments occur?

While the emergence of the drone age is inseparable from the technology's co-option into cultures of security and pre-emption by the post-9/11 security state, this volume takes flight into the openness of the field of drone studies that flows from drone proliferation well beyond the military and security spheres. In qualifying the interventions of works like *#NotABugSplat* and *Human Flow*, we are not attacking their intentions but rather gesturing to the necessity of working against the logic of foreclosure and inevitability which spurred the rise of military drones in the first place. As the essays collected here reveal, drones can be generative companions in imagining other worlds – and even preserving lives in this one – as well as devastating tools of violence and control. In pursuing regimes of the aesthetic and sensible as they take flight far from the battlefield, our collective aim in this volume is to seek new ways into ethics and justice in the face of expansive drone futures.

War, Culture, Ecology

Organised into three themes – *War*, *Culture*, and *Ecology* – the essays collected in *Drone Aesthetics* both resist easy categorisation and share an insistence on pursuing the embedding of drones, in all their diversity, in the life of the planet. All recognise the ambivalence of drone technologies; all look to unsettle the shibboleths of much drone scholarship by pursuing the drone into cloudy skies and deep waters. Resonances abound between essays with very different foci, imperatives, and even politics. But rather than converge on something like a consensus of what constitutes drone aesthetics, these essays together make abundantly clear that drone aesthetics and the political and ethical issues they raise cannot be reduced to what takes place in military applications, conflict zones, or even borders. Drone aesthetics possess different dynamics when traced through the swarming microdrones of *Black Mirror*, or the mesospheric zone of conservation drones, or the bodily intimacy of Israeli PillCams. While the specificities of context, application, technology, and technics all render distinct kinds of aesthetics, a shared interdependence with radically distributed sensory apparatuses, nonhuman agencies, and lively mediations makes it vital that diverse drone aesthetics be considered in conjunction with one another. In the essays collected here, the discrete object of the drone becomes a node through which to examine a constellation of broader issues about prosthetic subjectivities, sensor-mediated experiences, algorithmic reliance, and socio-cultural practices surrounding how intrusive technologies have become assimilated into everyday life.

The essays organised under the banner of *Part I: War* seek to trouble the frames of both public and critical understanding of martial drone violence. In the opening essay, Antoine Bousquet argues that the concept of the 'scopic regime' of cultural theory needs to be completed by the 'martial gaze', an apprehension of the world and its phenomena emergent from the technologies and techniques of militarised perception. Through an examination of drone camouflage – and especially the anti-surveillance art of Adam Harvey – Bousquet shows how the martial gaze necessitates making aesthetics a site of resistance. If Bousquet questions the dominant interest in drone visualities, Tom Sear bookends Part I by reading the drone against the grain of much critical-theoretical scholarship. Sear's drone is parasitic, inseparable from the emergence of a particular mode of warfare that is itself en route to an all-encompassing capture of techno-cultural life. To reckon with drone aesthetics, Sear insists, drone scholarship must discard its reflexive tenets in favour of an empirical conception of the technology's own contingencies, dependencies, and technological necessities.

Between these two theoretical interrogations of the relation between drone aesthetics and drone war, Joseph DeLappe and Sophia Goodfriend delve into drone practices. The first of three visual essays, DeLappe's contribution sees the activist-artist reflecting on more than a decade of critical projects that trouble the distancing of drone war from the American public. Proposing the necessity of critical atonement through what he calls 'tactical remembrance', DeLappe's contribution traces the many relations between Predator and Reaper drones and everyday American life pursued in his multimodal art practice. By contrast, Goodfriend probes the limits of drone technology, war, occupation, and the body through an ethnographic investigation of the Shimon Peres Centre for Peace and Innovation in Tel Aviv and one of its primary exhibits, the PillCam. Charting the convergence of biomedicine, the occupation of Palestine, and the self-mythology of Israel as a centre of technological innovation, Goodfriend shows how – through the miniaturisation of remote missile guidance in the surgical PillCam – drone warfare becomes the possibility of life, rather than death.

The five essays grouped into *Part II: Culture* pull focus on to the tense yet ambivalent cultural dynamics of drone aesthetics, but militarism is never far from view. Targeting appears here as the primary aesthetic relation, one in which both sensing and sense-making are pre-empted by the militarised perception of the drone. Caren Kaplan's opening essay on pandemic drones charts how the drone imaginaries of the early months of COVID-19 drew from and reproduced militarised logics and processes. From hoaxes of wine delivery by drone to stranded cruise ships and the purchase of military-grade drones by coast guards to the drone-led 'flash war' between Azerbaijan and Armenia, Kaplan argues that the pandemic saw an acceleration and intensification of drone applications in new domains. Proliferating from the peripheral wars into policing and celebratory spectacles, drones become not only an instantiation of everyday militarism but a site of innovation in which new techniques are invented and normalised. Adopting a sympathetic yet critical orientation towards hobbyist drone practices, Amy Gaeta examines the 'dronie' or drone selfie from a feminist disability standpoint that centres vulnerability and interdependence between drone, operator, and subject. Gaeta shows how drone hobbyists often have an intimate, playful relationship with their drones that works against the cold detachment typically associated with military drones and the view from above. But while these embodied relations can produce generative relations of vulnerability, they also work to normalise – and even make playful – the re-articulation of the self as target.

Cultural invocations of future war and violence occupy the other three *Culture* essays. Reading the 'Hated in the Nation' episode from the science fiction television series *Black Mirror*, J.D. Schnepf explores how drones operate as a crucial node for the transmission of logics between emergent forms of national security violence and the everyday practices of social media. For Schnepf, this near future constitutes an intensification and convergence of the targeting logics that underpin both social media and drone warfare: microdrones carry out targeted assassinations by accessing social media data to find, fix, and finish targets. Targeting also figures prominently in the collection's second visual essay, by the painter Kathryn Brimblecombe-Fox. Working with the materiality of paint and canvas, Brimblecombe-Fox investigates how life itself comes to be captured within the targeting reticule. In response, the artist engages in what she calls 'imaginational metaveillance' – an aesthetic method of making visible the electromagnetic, signaletic, and material architectures of drones and other forms of networked warfare. Networked warfare and its re-imagining as autonomous swarm occupy the final essay of Part II, in which Mitch Goodwin pursues the strange intersections of military theory, research, and industry with cultural imaginaries of the swarm. Even as initiatives by the Pentagon's Defence Advanced Research Projects Agency (DARPA) seek to make autonomous swarming drones a reality, Goodwin points to the cultural anxieties that have already existed around this kind of decentralised technology in film and television. It is not too late, he suggests, for those anxieties to galvanise into refusal.

Part III: Ecology features meditations on drone aesthetics that further complicate militarised conceptions of drone technologies. Here, the authors seek to understand the aesthetic entanglement of drones with nonhuman animals and environments. In the opening essay, Adam Fish and Edgar Gómez Cruz ask what it means for both conservation and photography to operate in the elevated but proximate space they term the 'mezzo' – an aeriality to which the nonprosthetic human does not have access, yet which remains intimate to the earth and its creatures. Combining critical investigation with ethnographic observation of drone use in whale conservation, the authors propose that drone practices attuned to the more-than-human can open up the mezzo as a zone of seeing and sensing that allows new ways of thinking and engaging with the ocean and its animals. Similarly interested in the connections between oceans and sensing, Simon Taylor's essay considers the aquatic drones used in the transnational search for MH370, the disappeared Malaysia Airlines flight from 2014. Reflecting on the limitations to remote sensing systems imposed by the deep ocean, Taylor argues that the strange spatial and environmental knowledges produced by sonar backscatter simultaneously make the ocean a site of systematic knowledge and system error with distinct aesthetic qualities. Error also occupies Madelene Veber in her essay on the tendency of drone systems to misidentify, misfire, and malfunction. Reading the Drone Crash Database of the activist organisation Drone Wars UK, Veber shows how error is not simply something that must be resolved within drone systems but rather is constitutive of their distributed and contingent nature. Error is therefore inseparable from the difficult question of where responsibility and agency lies in drone systems, and in what Lisa Parks calls their 'mediating' work: the way drones 'materially alter or affect the phenomena of the air, spectrum, and/or ground' (Parks 2017: 135).

The other two essays in Part III engage in ecological explorations of the perceptual potential of the drone. Jack Faber proposes an alternative history of the drone, one rooted in cultural imaginings of interspecies relations between humans and avians. Conceptualising filmic operations of drones as 'asymmetrical cinema', Faber argues that thinking about drones as arising from enmeshed art practices constitutes a valuable experiment in articulating a distinct aesthetics. Oscillating between Greek myth, Hitchcock's *North by Northwest*, and early military drone experiments, Faber insists that thinking with drones as the product of interspecies commingling offers powerful ways of escaping militarised logics. For artists and theorists Michele Barker and Anna Munster, drones also offer generative potential to rework systems of planetary sensing and control. In the third visual essay of this volume, Barker and Munster reflect on their in-progress video work *ecologies of duration*, and show how bringing drones into close contact with surfaces – water, rock, vegetation – can produce messy, embodied, and ecologically entangled perceptions that refuse the familiar god's-eye view. Against remoteness, Barker and Munster explore how drones can produce proximity, felt through the intensity of 'percepts' that bear witness to the co-existence of incommensurate yet coexistent forms of matter in the more-than-human world.

Finally, in the book's provocative coda, Yanai Toister pursues the operative images of drone aesthetics into a seemingly inevitable endpoint: postvisual images in which the image exists only as code, invisible to the human and yet imagistic nonetheless. Reading Harun Farocki alongside Wolfgang Ernst, Friedrich Kittler, and others, Toister calls for a recognition of aesthetics that does not depend at any point on the human sensorium – and that in fact loses its defining qualities as soon as it is rendered for our perception. In this sense, then, the post-visual image signals a potential future for drone aesthetics in and beyond war, culture, and ecology: drone aesthetics as a defining form of sensing and sense-making in futures in which political struggles over drone logics and their entanglement with life become ever more vital to the distribution of the sensible.

Conclusion: Drone Technographies

In relating the drone to narratives of power like the 'God's eye view', studies of particular aesthetic dimensions of drones have at times painted them with a theological brush: one that risks prioritising the drone as object and that obscures the human labour and imperial and military apparatuses undergirding drone development and innovation. Benjamin Noys calls these responses 'drone metaphysics': 'Drones inhabit a field of theological metaphysics, embodying dreams of transcendence and destruction that have haunted the Western imagination' (2015: 2). The scales examined in this collection do at times invoke ideas of sublimity – whether the miniscule, in the case of the pillcam, or the vast, in terms of drones' indexing of the mezzo. But by focusing on aesthetics, instead of fetishizing the technological object or assemblage, all of the essays are grounded in examining the affordances of the drone as a kind of optic or language that shapes the world around it. What paradigms do drones present for understanding surveillance, sousveillance, and metaveillance? How does the drone create new vocabularies for the way we perceive and relate to one another, to animals, and to the planet? How does the rhetoric of drone logic alter long-standing concepts like the parasite and the swarm, autonomy, and error?

If we think of the drone as something that creates, and operates through, its own discourses, one can understand drones as both a technology and a technography – the latter of which names the book series in which this volume appears. Technography, the series editors write, concerns the interrelationship between the 'writing *of* techne' and 'the writing *in* or *through* techne' (Connor, Purdon, and Trotter 2016). A technography is both a description of a technology and its socio-cultural contexts, as well as a reflection of the way that aesthetics and imaginaries have informed the development of that technology, and vice versa, in a kind of virtuous cycle. According to Sean Pryor and David Trotter, 'Technographies attend equally to the rhetoric sedimented in machines, to machines behaving rhetorically, to rhetoric that behaves mechanically, and to rhetoric behaving in pointed opposition to mechanism' (2016: 16). Drones are systems and objects that are themselves attuned to what makes their technological condition possible, both inscribing and reinforcing the logic enabled by their own being in the first place. Comprised of essays that identify, each in their own ways, the tensions underlying the technological, social, philosophical, and artistic dimensions of drone systems, *Drone Aesthetics* is offered as a technographic intervention into how drones have already altered how we think of war, culture, and ecology, as well as a technographic way forward into understanding new ways of reading and interpreting, and new normalities of taking and giving, life itself – nothing less than what Michel Foucault calls the 'aesthetics of existence' (1990: 49).

Works Cited

9/11 Commission Report: Final Report of the National Commission on Terrorist Attacks Upon the United States. 2004. London: Norton.

Agostinho, Daniela, Kathrin Maurer and Kristin Veel. 2020. 'Introduction to the Sensorial Experience of the Drone'. *The Senses and Society* 15: 251-8.

Ai Wei Wei, director. 2017. *Human Flow*. AC Films and Participant Media. 2hr., 20 min.

Akhter, Majed. 2019. 'The Proliferation of Peripheries: Militarized Drones and the Reconfiguration of Global Space'. *Progress in Human Geography* 43: 64-80.

Ali Rez, Saks Afridi, Assam Khalid, Akash Goel, Insiya Syed, Noor Behram, Jamil Akhtar, and the JR Inside Out Project. 2014. *#NotABugSplat*. https://notabugsplat.com/

Andrejevic, Marc. 2016. 'Theorizing Drones and Droning Theory'. In *Drones and Unmanned Aerial Systems: Legal and Social Implications for Security and Surveillance*, edited by Aleš Završnik, 21-43. Cham: Springer.

Benjamin, Medea. 2012. *Drone Warfare: Killing by Remote Control*. London: Verso.

Bennett, Jill. 2012. *Practical Aesthetics: Events, Affects and Art After 9/11*. London: I. B. Tauris.

Bleiker, Roland. 2018. 'Aesthetic Turn in International Relations'. *Oxford Bibliographies*, 27 June. DOI: 10.1093/obo/9780199743292-0236.

Braunert, Svea and Meredith Malone. 2016. *To See Without Being Seen: Contemporary Art and Drone Warfare*. Chicago: University of Chicago Press.

Boyle, Michael J. 2020. *The Drone Age: How Drone Technology Will Change War and Peace*. Oxford: Oxford University Press.

Chamayou, Gregoire. 2015. *Drone Theory*. Translated by Janet Lloyd. London: Penguin

Chandler, Katherine. 2020. *Unmanning: How Humans, Machines, and Media Perform Drone Warfare*. New Brunswick: Rutgers University Press.

Cockburn, Andrew. 2015. *Kill Chain: Drones and the Rise of High-Tech Assassins*. London: Verso.

Cockerell, Isobel. 2021. 'A blanket of surveillance covers Calais, but more migrants are dying at sea than ever before'. *Coda Story*, 30 November. https://www.codastory.com/authoritarian-tech/surveillance/surveillance-borders-calais-migrants-drones-police-boats/

Connor, Steven, James Purdon, and David Trotter. 2016. 'What is Technography?' *Literature, Technology, Media Research Group, University of Cambridge*, September 12. https://www.english.cam.ac.uk/research/ltm/?p=912

Dargis, Manohla. 2017. 'Review: Ai Weiwei's "Human Flow" Tracks the Global Migrant Crisis'. *New York Times*, October 12. https://www.nytimes.com/2017/10/12/movies/human-flow-review-ai-weiwei.html

Didi-Huberman, Georges. 2018. 'From a high vantage point'. *Eurozine*, 12 October. https://www.eurozine.com/high-vantage-point/

Dunn, David Hastings. 2013. 'Drones: Disembodied Warfare and the Unarticulated Threat'. *International Affairs* 89: 1237-46.

Edney-Browne, Alex. 2017. 'Embodiment and Affect in a Digital Age: Understanding Mental Illness Among Military Drone Personnel'. *Krisis* 1: 18-33.

Farocki, Harun. 2004. 'Phantom Images'. *Public* 29: 12-22.

Fish, Adam. 2021. 'Crash Theory: Entrapments of Conservation Drones and Endangered Megafauna'. *Science, Technology, & Human Values* 46: 425-51.

Fish, Adam and Michael Richardson. 2022. 'Drone Power: Conservation, Humanitarianism, Policing and War'. *Theory, Culture & Society* 39: 3-26.

Foucault, Michel. 1990. 'An Aesthetics of Existence'. In *Michel Foucault: Politics, Philosophy, Culture: Interviews and other Writings, 1977-1984*, edited by Lawrence Kritzman, 47-53. New York: Routledge.

Fuller, Matthew and Eyal Weizman. 2021. *Investigative Aesthetics: Conflicts and Commons in the Politics of Truth*. London: Verso.

Graae, Andreas Immanuel and Kathrin Maurer. 2020. 'Introduction'. In *Drone Imaginaries: The Power of Remote Vision*, edited by Andreas Immanuel Graae and Kathrin Maurer, 1-16. Manchester: Manchester University Press.

Gregory, Derek. 2011. 'From a Kill to a kill: Drones and Late Modern War'. *Theory, Culture & Society* 27: 188-215.

Gusterson, Hugh. 2016. *Drone: Remote Control Warfare*. Cambridge: MIT Press.

Guyer, Paul. 2005. *Values of Beauty: Historical Essys in Aesthetics*. Cambridge: Cambridge University Press.

Hildebrand, Julia. 2021. *Aerial Play: Drone Medium, Mobility, Communication, and Culture*. Basingstoke: Palgrave Macmillan.

Hildebrand, Julia and Stephanie Sodero. 2021. 'Pandemic Drones: Promises and Perils'. *Transfers* 11: 148-58.

Holert, Tom. 2016. 'Sensorship: The Seen Unseen of Drone Warfare'. In *Image Operations: Visual Media and Political Conflict*, edited by Jens Eder and Charlotte Klonk, 101-17. Manchester: Manchester University Press.

Holt, Kris. 2020. 'CBP Flew A Predator Drone Over Minneapolis Amid George Floyd Protests'. *Forbes*, May 29. https://www.forbes.com/sites/krisholt/2020/05/29/cbp-predator-drone-minneapolis-george-floyd-aclu/?sh=2bd2e70c40fa

Hoyt, Kate Drazner. 2014. 'Ethics of Network Subjectivity'. *Technoculture* 4. https://tcjournal.org/vol4/hoyt/

International Human Rights and Conflict Resolution Clinic at Stanford Law School and Global Justice Clinic at NYU School of Law. 2012. *Living Under Drones: Death, Injury, and Trauma to Civilians From US Drone Practices in Pakistan*. https://www-cdn.law.stanford.edu/wp-content/uploads/2015/07/Stanford-NYU-Living-Under-Drones.pdf

Jackman, Anna. 2019. 'Consumer drone evolutions: trends, spaces, temporalities, threats'. *Defense & Security Analysis* 35: 362-83.

Jackman, Anna and Katherine Brickell. 2021. '"Everyday droning": Towards a feminist geopolitics of the drone-home'. *Progress in Human Geography* 46: 156-78.

Kapadia, Ronak. 2019. *Insurgent Aesthetics: Security and the Queer Life of the Forever War*. Durham: Duke University Press.

Kaplan, Caren. 2018. *Aerial Aftermaths: Wartime from Above*. Durham: Duke University Press.

Manovich, Lev. 2017. 'Aesthetics'. In *Keywords for Media Studies*, edited by Laurie Ouellette and Jonathan Gray, 9-11. New York: NYU Press.

Massumi, Brian. 2015. *Ontopower: War, Power, and the State of Perception*. Durham: Duke University Press.

Noys, Benjamin. 2015. 'Drone Metaphysics'. *Culture Machine* 16: 1-22.

Paglen, Trevor. 2014. 'Operational Images'. *E-Flux* 59. https://www.e-flux.com/journal/59/61130/operational-images/

Parks, Lisa. 2017. 'Vertical Mediation and the U.S. Drone War in the Horn of Africa'. In *Life in the Age of Drone Warfare*, edited by Caren Kaplan and Lisa Parks, 134-57. Durham: Duke University Press.

Parks, Lisa and Caren Kaplan, eds. 2017. *Life in the Age of Drone Warfare*. Durham: Duke University Press.

Pearl, Mike. 2014. 'The #NotABugSplat Art Piece in Pakistan Won't Be Making Drone Pilots Feel Empathy'. *Vice Magazine*, April 8. https://www.vice.com/en/article/dpwyvx/this-giant-art-piece-in-pakistan-wont-be-making-drone-pilots-feel-empathy

Pryor, Sean and David Trotter. 2016. 'Introduction'. In *Writing, Medium, Machine: Modern Technographies*, edited by Sean Pryor and David Trotter, 7-17. London: Open Humanities Press.

Rancière, Jacques. 2004. *The Politics of Aesthetics: The Distribution of the Sensible.* Translated by Gabriel Rockhill. London: Continuum.

Rhee, Jennifer. 2018. *The Robotic Imaginary: The Human and the Price of Dehumanized Labor.* Minneapolis: University of Minnesota Press.Satia, Priya. 2014. 'Drones: A History from the British Middle East'. *Humanity* 5: 1-31.

Sandvik, Kristin Bergtora and Maria Gabrielson Jumbert. 2017. *The Good Drone.* London: Routledge.

Serafinelli, Elisa and Lauren O'Hagan. 2022. 'Drone views: a multimodal ethnographic perspective'. *Visual Communication.* 16 May.

Shapiro, Michael J. 2013. *Studies in Trans-disciplinary Method: After the Aesthetic Turn.* New York: Routledge.

Shinkle, Eugenie. 2014. 'Drone Aesthetics'. In *Hyenas of the Battlefield, Machines in the Garden*, by Lisa Barnard with essays by Julian Stallabrass and Eugenie Shinkle, 200-6. London: GOST Books. http://lisabarnard.co.uk/essays/drone-aesthetics-by-eugenie-shinkle-2014/

Stubblefield, Thomas. 2020. *Drone Art: The Everywhere War as Medium.* Berkeley: University of California Press.

Tahir, Madiha. 2017. 'The Ground Was Always in Play'. *Public Culture* 29: 5-16.

Tahir, Madiha. 2021. 'The Distributed Empire of the War on Terror'. *Boston Review*, September 10.

Zimanyi, Eszter. 2019. '*Human Flow:* Thinking with and through Ai Weiwei's defamiliarizing Gaze.' *Visual Anthropology* 32: 377-9.

Part I: War

I

Becoming (Im)Perceptible: From Scopic Regimes to the Martial Gaze

Antoine Bousquet

Scholars have recently turned to the notion of 'scopic regimes' in seeking to make sense of the visual practices prevalent in the conduct of war, most notably in the prominent employment of drone aircraft. Originating in cultural theory, the concept of the scopic regime was originally advanced to outline historical alternatives to the 'Cartesian perspectivalism' often held to be synonymous with modern visual culture *tout court*. Such a disruption of dominant ways of seeing is especially appealing to critical scholars keen to contest the military God's eye view that has become associated with drone operations. Artistic expression that contests hegemonic scopic regimes rather than reproduces them is accordingly valorised. Crucially, visuality is primarily apprehended within this approach in terms of its discursive and rhetorical dimensions and the role it plays in the production of truth claims.

Notwithstanding the genuine insights provided by this engagement with the visual in war, the purpose of this chapter will be to argue that there exists an alternative approach that, while also emphasising the crucial influence of Renaissance perspective, distinguishes itself by its close attention to the technical operation and functional integration of military perception. Beyond a mere interpretative or philosophical divergence, this alternative lens is most consequential for the forms of counter-veiling praxis that follow from it. In the following section, I will review the theory of scopic regimes as formulated within cultural theory and survey how it has been adopted in subsequent writings on drone warfare. I will then proceed to outline the notion of the 'martial gaze' developed in my recent work on the logistics of military perception (Bousquet 2018) and detail the treatment of linear perspective it rests upon, contrasting it with its interpretation as a scopic regime, particularly as it bears upon the question of military perception. Finally, I will consider the field of counter-conduct suggested by the analysis of the martial gaze, as illustrated by a corresponding mode of artistic engagement found in the work of Adam Harvey. Indeed, through systematic engagements with specific technologies of perception and surveillance, these exemplary projects participate in a becoming-imperceptible that evades, subverts, and overwhelms their mechanisms.

Scopic Regimes of War

While earlier references to scopic regimes in the context of war and security can be found in the work of Feldman (1997, 2004) and Saint-Amour (2003), it is arguably Derek Gregory's influential article 'From a View to a Kill: Drones and Late Modern War' (2011) that has done most to popularise the term in association with the most emblematic weapon system of our time. Subsequent invocations have appeared in a range of contributions within the abundant scholarship on drones produced in the last decade, including Coward (2013), Edney-Browne (2019), Grayson (2012, 2017), Grayson and Mawdsley (2019), Lee-Morrison (2015), Maurer (2016), and Zuev and Bratchford (2021). Although the term of the 'scopic regime' does not receive a singular conceptualisation across this literature and tends to be variously mobilised in service of the authors' specific lines of argumentation, these uses nonetheless all express the common notion that the military appropriation and marshalling of the visual field is a key aspect of contemporary military violence. We thus find the term diversely but congruently defined as the 'mode of visual apprehension' of 'a militarised regime of hypervisibility' (Gregory 2011: 193), the 'grid of intelligibility' through which militaries 'en-vision the battlespace' (Coward 2013: 99) or the 'visual practice' that 'operationalises the kill chain' (Grayson 2017: 153).

It is important to underline here that the scholars invoking scopic regimes have been typically less concerned with understanding the technical armature and functional operation of military perception than analysing the processes of meaning-making that the attendant visual practices both divulge and participate in. Gregory (2011: 190) thus states that a scopic regime is first and foremost 'a mode of visual apprehension that is culturally constructed and prescriptive, socially structured and shared', as well as 'uncoupled from any specific forms, displays and technologies'. For their part, Grayson and Mawdsley (2019: 3) are keen to establish visuality as a 'discursive practice with material effects' and accordingly claim that attention to scopic regimes can help us understand 'how particular fields of vision are constructed such that their representational properties are perceived as truthful'. They approvingly cite Feldman's own account of scopic regimes as 'the regimens that prescribe modes of seeing and object visibility and that proscribe or render untenable other modes and objects of perception. A scopic regime is an ensemble of practices and discourses that establish truth claims, typicality, and credibility of visual acts and objects and politically correct modes of seeing' (1997: 30).

This culturalist and discursivist conception is entirely consistent with the scopic regime's origin in the field of cultural theory, at a remove from the military considerations it presently finds itself applied to. The coining of the term is usually attributed to the film theorist Christian Metz (1982) but its most recognised formulation is undoubtedly that of Martin Jay in 'Scopic Regimes of Modernity' (1988). In this brief but illuminating text, Jay posits that the alleged dominance of visuality in modern culture – its ocularcentrism, in other words – is attributable to a conjunction of Renaissance perspective art and René Descartes's foundational epistemology, which he dubs 'Cartesian perspectivalism'. He proceeds to argue that this scopic regime is less hegemonic and uncontested than is usually presumed, suggesting two alternative, if subordinate, 'ways of seeing' (Berger 1972) also present in the early modern period. The first of these is found in Dutch seventeenth-century painting and its 'art of describing' (Alpers 1983) with, as its philosophical correlate, Baconian empiricism's characteristic resistance to abstraction. According to Jay, this Northern movement distinguished itself from its Southern counterpart in foregoing the monocular spectator and privileging the representation of surfaces rather than objects and space, textures rather than forms. A second, even more radical, alternative scopic regime is identified in the seventeenth-century baroque with its 'dazzling, disorienting, ecstatic surplus of images' (16). Its 'tactile, haptic quality' and 'fascination for opacity, unreadability, and the indecipherability of the reality it depicts' is seen as both an inherent disruption of Cartesian ocularcentrism and a rejection of Dutch art's faith in legible surfaces and material solidity (17).

Among the drone scholars who have adopted scopic regimes as a key analytical lens, Grayson and Mawdsley (2019) hew most closely to Jay's original scheme. While they argue for the value of a more general application of scopic regimes as part of a 'visual turn' in the discipline of International Relations, they primarily illustrate this in relation to the practice of targeted killing via drones. In so doing, they contend that both Cartesian perspectivalism and Baconian empiricism are implicated in the production of the drone strike. The former finds its expression in the 'disembodied immersion into the visual field from the perspective of an all-seeing eye' associated with the drone (12). The latter manifests as a faith in 'the collection and transmission of details that expose the real nature of what is being observed' (13). Through their respective claims to visual omniscience, both scopic regimes support the idea of a privileged access to truth which serves to legitimise political violence. In this way, the visual does not merely reflect the political but actively produces it, the authors contend.

It follows from Grayson and Mawdsley's analysis that any fundamental resistance to drone violence must mount a challenge to the scopic hegemony that subtends it. They draw particular inspiration from Jacques Rancière's call for a 'redistribution of the sensible' (2006) in seeking aesthetic expressions that might be able to undercut these truth claims. Certainly, there have been numerous attempts by artists, advocacy groups, and media content producers to make visible and (re)contextualise the military use of drones through their own visual practices (Bräunert and Malone 2016; Stubblefield 2020). However, Grayson and Mawdsley find fault in those approaches which, however otherwise well intended and useful in drawing attention to drone violence, remain caught within the dominant scopic regimes. James Bridle's *Dronestagram* (2012) – a project posting Google Earth images of drone strike sites on social media

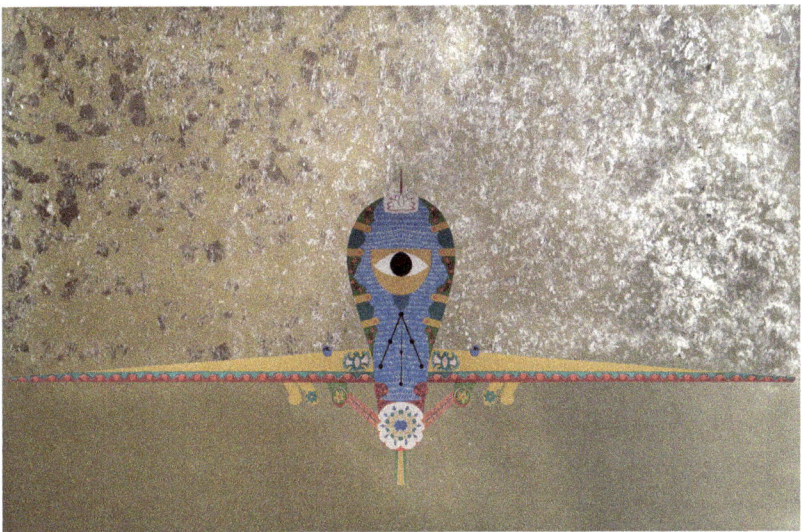

Figure 1.1. Mahwish Chishty, *Reaper* (2015). Courtesy of the artist.

– is thus found to share a similar aesthetic to 'the abstract battlespace of contemporary droning', beholden to the visual certainties of both Cartesian perspectivalism and Baconian empiricism (15). An analogous judgement is delivered on the work of Goldsmith's Institute for Forensic Architecture whose 'attempts to invert the gaze upwards towards the drone' continue to work unwittingly within existing scopic regimes (16).

In contrast, Grayson and Mawdsley favour those efforts which genuinely attempt to disrupt the distribution of the sensible associated with drone warfare by producing an 'immanent critique of Cartesian perspectivalism and Baconian empiricism' and proposing 'an alternative way of seeing' (18). As emblematic of such an approach, they put forward the work of American-Pakistani artist Mahwish Chishty whose paintings represent the drone in the visual idiom of talismanic ornaments found on trucks in Pakistan (see Figure 1.1). This decolonising move 'provincialises' the drone, challenging its 'claim to potential visual omniscience' by allowing it to 'be understood as a product of cultural presuppositions rather than universal truths' (20). In so doing, such interventions also serve to highlight the 'constitutive power' of the 'invisible' – that which cannot be seen, not merely as a function of its exclusion within a regime of visibility but as a necessary co-constituent of the 'visible'.

There is much to commend in the contribution of Grayson and Mawdsley, notably in working out in the most systematic fashion to date how the concept of scopic regimes might be applied to the study of warfare. It is not my intention to dismiss the important work of artists like Chishty that serves to challenge the representational registers in which highly asymmetric projections of violence are usually depicted. However, I want to query the potential limitations attached to the notion of scopic regimes inherited from cultural theory and whether we might not need to complement its insights with an alternative approach that engages with military perception at the level of its technical operation and functional entanglements. Such an approach carries with it corresponding lessons for the kind of artistic and political counter-conduct we should strive for.

The Martial Gaze

In *The Eye of War*, I advance the notion of a 'martial gaze' in reference to 'the general disposition and various sociotechnical means accreted toward the rational organisation of perception for the ends of military domination and control' (2018: 15). The study endeavours to show how the articulation of technologies of sensorial perception, imaging, and mapping has become central to today's war machine and underpins the increasingly granular conduct of a practice of global targeting which the drone exemplifies. In common with the theory of scopic regimes, I begin my account with the invention of linear perspective, identifying a clear lineage running from the Quattrocento to the contemporary 'logistics of perception' (Virilio 1989). However, my primary focus lies not with the rhetorical and discursive dimensions of perspective but rather with its technical features and functional relations to various fields of human activity.

In essence, linear perspective is a procedure for representing upon a flat surface a three-dimensional scene whose objects should appear in terms of relative size, shape, and position as they would to a beholder occupying a determined, singular point of view. Achieving this illusion rests upon the establishment of a rigorous mathematical correspondence between objective physical space and subjective visual space. The critical movement initiated by perspective is thus that of an intertwined process of mathematisation of space and rationalisation of vision that has continued to unfold until the present day. From this standpoint, linear perspective matters less for its cultural legacy as an artistic movement encompassing some of the most famous and celebrated paintings in the Western canon than for the historical convergence it realised between the fields of geometrical optics, pictorial representation, and land surveying. At the heart of linear perspective is a geometric conception of vision that accounts for the natural ocular estimation of spatial distances and that begets an array of mathematical techniques and associated instruments for precise measurement by the human eye. A rigorous procedure for the rule-governed (and thus automatable) construction of images that convey an optically convincing depiction of physical space logically follows from it. And in common with the field of cartography which emerged concurrently, perspective employs a system for the geometric projection of a three-dimensional space upon a two-dimensional surface in a manner that preserves the space's relative proportions and the objects contained within.

While I cannot rehearse here the fuller account I propose in *The Eye of War*, it is crucial to note that each of these strands corresponds directly with the three functional constituents of the martial gaze as it operates presently: *sensing* (the acquisition of sensorial information), *imaging* (the representation of sensorial information), and *mapping* (the correlation of sensorial information with geospatial frameworks). Profoundly entangled with each other through mutual dependencies and systemic complementarity, the instantiation of these three functions within a profusion of sociotechnical assemblages underpins the practical exercise of armed force today. The longer-term significance of perspective (and the general projective geometry issued from it) is therefore that it bequeathed both specific techniques and a generalised ambition for the realisation of a wider 'visual nominalism'. Following Lev Manovich, the latter can be defined simply as 'the use of vision to capture the identity of individual objects and spaces by recording distances and shapes' and 'create detailed maps of three-dimensional reality' (Manovich 2002: 383). This means that even where perspective has today given way to other perceptual techniques that do not rest upon classical optics and extend across the electromagnetic spectrum of light, such as radar, infrared, or laser, these still remain fundamentally tributary to that original crucible.

It is certainly true that the technical and scientific foundations and implications of perspective have long been established in the rich scholarship on perspective (Ivins 1973; Edgerton 1976). These occupy a central place in Jay's account (1988) of Cartesian perspectivalism with its 'geometrically isotropic, rectilinear, abstract, and uniform' conception of space (6) and privileging of 'an ahistorical, disinterested, disembodied subject entirely outside of the world it claims to only know from afar' (10). Somaini's own formulation of the concept (2006: 36) is a particularly good summation: 'a reduction of perceptual space to mathematical and homogeneous space, with an understanding of vision as monocular, static, fixed and immediate, distant and objectifying, purely theoretic and disincarnated'. However, Jay also appears to treat perspectivalism as a distinct historical moment, foundational for modern Western culture and its scientific tradition, but one that nevertheless has been displaced, subject even to a 'radically dethroning' by a century of artistic and philosophical developments (1988: 19). This poses a genuine problem for analysts applying scopic regimes to military affairs and positing Cartesian perspectivalism (or Baconian empiricism, for that matter) as central to contemporary war-making. At the very least, some account of how an artistic movement from the Renaissance can still underpin military epistemology today seems necessary. The puzzle of perspective's enduring influence disappears, however, if we no longer make the crux of our analysis its rhetorical role in the cultural reproduction of a certain conception of unreflexive truth but rather its technical legacy in powerful technologies for the domination of space and people.

In so doing, a new light can be shone on some long-established analyses within culturalist interpretations of perspective. For instance, it is commonly asserted that perspective's optically rigorous representations implied an arrangement of the visible world 'for the spectator as the universe was once thought to be arranged for God', exalting the human subject as its new sovereign (Berger 1972: 16). As noted above, this humanist pretence to a totalising and universalising survey of the world has been critiqued extensively within both philosophical thought and artistic practice (Jay 1993). However, the original perspectival moment is a far more ambivalent one than the simple critique of its transcendental pretensions would suggest. For at the very same time as the human subject was being elevated to a vista previously held by divinity, it was simultaneously being rendered as a new object of rational knowledge, its embodied perception now subordinated to abstract laws of vision. From this initial abstraction, the deracination of perception from the site of the living organism and its corresponding relocation into mechanical apparatuses has incrementally but inexorably advanced to the present era, with its cornucopia of perceptual prostheses and gathering of autonomous vision machines.

When Jay posits that the Dutch art of describing anticipates photography in the fragmentariness and arbitrary framing of its images and their displacement of the human subject through their automatic capture of nature (1988: 15), he revealingly neglects a vital relationship between perspective and photographic technology. Indeed, for Joel Snyder (1980), the invention of photography must be understood as the culmination of longstanding efforts to provide mechanical assistance for the production of perspectival images, a lineage that includes such devices as the camera obscura or camera lucida. At the technical level, the projective geometry that underlies the photographic image is quite simply identical to that of perspectival construction – or as Harun Farocki puts it (2001: 188), 'a photographic image is a cut, a section through the bundles of light rays reflected off objects in a circumscribed space'. By virtue of this, it is in principle possible to recover the spatial proportions of an original scene from its photograph by applying the rules of construction in reverse. The entire field of photogrammetry ('measuring with photographs', etymologically) thus co-evolved with the technology of photography, finding its most widespread application in the context of aerial survey. The latter has itself been an essential weapon in the military's perceptual arsenal since the First World War with its evident legacy in contemporary drone vision. In sum, notwithstanding the artistic association with anti-perspectival movements such as impressionism noted by Jay, the photographic image remains profoundly tied to the perspectival moment and has correspondingly played a crucial role in the development of visual nominalism.

A similar objection can be raised to Jonathan Crary's treatment of the stereoscope in his *Techniques of the Observer* (1992), a seminal work in cultural theory which does not explicitly refer to 'scopic regimes' but is commonly associated with them, including by Grayson and Mawdsley. By presenting a slightly different image of the same scene to each eye, a stereoscopic device engenders in the viewer the perception of a single three-dimensional image. Emerging in the mid-nineteenth century, stereoscopes were both central to establishing a scientific understanding of binocular vision and a popular craze within a new consumerist visual culture. For Crary, the stereoscope stands as one of the paradigmatic technologies of a new understanding of subjective, embodied vision in the nineteenth century, marking an epistemic rupture with the disincarnate perspectivalism associated with Renaissance painting and the monocular camera obscura. The rise of modern bourgeois subjectivity and its associated cultures of consumerism and spectatorship are thus held to have accompanied the establishment of physiological optics. Crary's assertion that 'stereoscopic relief or depth has no unifying logic or order' and that 'if perspective implied a homogeneous and potentially metric space, the stereoscope discloses a fundamental disunified and aggregate field of disjunct elements' may well hold at the level of the observer's phenomenal experience of these images (125). But it occludes the fact that stereoscopy was simultaneously assimilated into a general regime of rationalised vision and geometrical optics, supplementing rather than undercutting the visual metricisation of space advanced by the perspectival image. The photogrammetric use of stereoscopic images to extract measurements of physical distances, notably for the purpose of aerial photographic interpretation, and the coexistence of monocular and stereoscopic models of artillery range finders illustrate this complementarity in the military context (Bousquet 2018: 51-2, 94-6).

These rejoinders are not intended to dismiss the above interpretations altogether – they remain insightful in their own right – but to underline that they rest upon particular analytical and philosophical commitments, namely a focus on the symbolic and discursive domain in their treatment of technologies of perception and representation. These commitments are frequently justified by their proponents as necessary for warding off a defective 'technological determinism' (Crary 1992: 8). Yet the resulting work all too often commits the opposing sin of entirely evacuating any trace of material agency from its analysis. As I have argued elsewhere (Bousquet 2015, 2017), we can, with the right theoretical resources and conceptual bounding, absolutely give technical objects their due without lapsing into reductionist accounts. As I am endeavouring to show here, different accounts emerge when we do so, with significant implications at the level of both theory and praxis. In particular, I want to suggest in the final section that we can identify another 'immanent critique' of military perception than that proposed by Grayson and Mawdsley, one that finds itself instantiated in its own mode of artistic practice.

Becoming-Imperceptible

As visibility on the battlefield has become increasingly synonymous with a fatal vulnerability, so ever greater efforts have been dedicated to evading, misdirecting, or blinding the martial gaze. Reflecting on the experience of the First World in which the systematic use of camouflage was first employed, the German war veteran Ernst Jünger noted that 'the endeavour to make oneself invisible grows' (2008: 39). Since camouflage is in its essence an anticipation of perception, its exercise is constituted through a dialectical relation with the logistics of perception it seeks to foil. We can therefore speak of an entire field of counter-conduct – a pursuit of invisibility, a purposeful becoming-imperceptible that enacts its own immanent critique of the martial gaze through a praxis that identifies and exploits the inherent biases, lacunae, and blind spots of technicised perception. It typically draws on the same bodies of knowledge and technique, leveraging its shortcomings and gaps into opportunities for concealment and dissimulation.

The history of perceptual countermeasures is a rich and varied one, encompassing mottled motifs, disruptive patterns, decoys, netting, smoke screens, infrared-reflecting paint, chaff, stealth aircraft, and cloaking metamaterials. Most of these efforts have been expended during the last century under the aegis of military institutions in their contests with each other. Yet as the boundaries between conditions of peace and war erode ever more and the instruments of military surveillance turn themselves on civilian populations, it is likely to fall ever more on civil society to acquire, devise, and disseminate the means to imperceptibility, however precarious and transitory. Such an endeavour, I would contend, must necessarily pass through a deeper and wider understanding of the technical armature and functional operation of the martial gaze.

In this spirit, I want to highlight the various works of Adam Harvey, an artist whose preoccupation with questions of computer vision, privacy, and surveillance have led him to develop a practice that is exemplary of such a counter-conduct. His projects are all premised on a systematic engagement with specific technologies of perception and an uncovering of their underlying principles, particular operation, and inherent vulnerabilities. The artistic production is generated in direct struggle with the technology's capabilities of perceptual capture so as to devise through a painstaking process of trial and error the means towards a becoming-imperceptible. In the presentation of his work, Harvey is careful to underline that his creations are tailored to only counter distinctive incarnations of perceptual technologies, such as a particular computer vision algorithm. While this means that individual motifs or designs cannot serve as all-encompassing solutions, their underlying principles and methods of elaboration are nevertheless generalisable. Similarly, if Harvey's somewhat playful designs and their high-fashion aesthetic can be charged with being too impractical and inaccessible to be widely adopted as

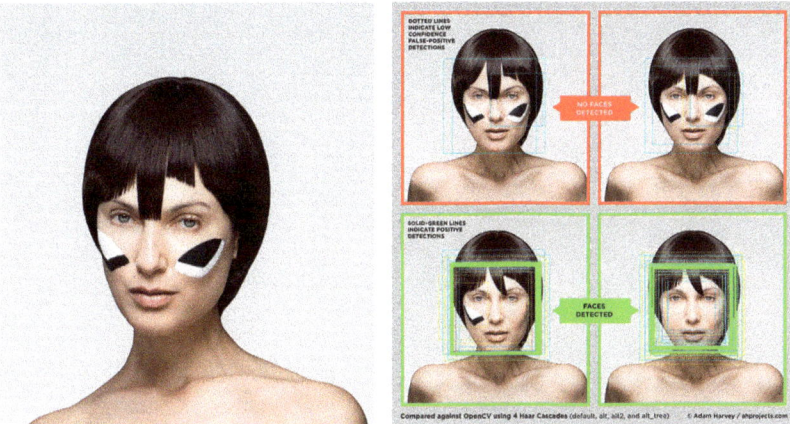

Figure 1.2. Adam Harvey, *CV Dazzle* (2010). Courtesy of the artist.

counter-surveillance measures, they remain nonetheless valuable interventions for outlining a rigorous counter-conduct that can inspire replication and emulation.

One of Harvey's first projects was *CV Dazzle* (2010), presented as 'a concept and a strategy' for the evasion of automated facial recognition. The term 'dazzle' references an unusual type of camouflage applied to ships in the first half of the twentieth century to reduce their vulnerability to submarine attack. Rather than attempt to blend ships into their surroundings as with conventional camouflage, dazzle involved painting them with bold geometric patterns and colour contrasts so as to generate the illusion of a false perspective that would impede shape recognition and create uncertainty about the outline, size, orientation, and speed of the masqueraded ships. *CV Dazzle* proceeds analogously in defeating the pattern-seeking algorithms of facial detection software through a 'form of expressive interference' judiciously arranging stylised make-up, hair styling, and fashion accessories to break up the expected features of the human face. As Harvey puts it, 'because computer vision is always based on probabilistic thresholds, these can be exploited by altering the key visual features to appear one step below the threshold of detection'. Crucially, 'evading face detection requires prior knowledge of the algorithm' and a practice combining logical inferences and empirical trial and error – a process very much akin to the design of the original dazzle camouflage (Bousquet 2018: 165-68) (see Figure 1.2).

With *Stealth Wear* (2012), Harvey turned his attention to designing fashion for countering surveillance technology in the infrared spectrum. Having acquired a thermal camera, the artist explored thermal-reflective materials that could be shaped into wearable garments able to conceal their wearer's heat signature. Alongside an 'anti-drone hoodie', he produced a burqa and a hijab with the same properties, explaining the choice of traditional Islamic

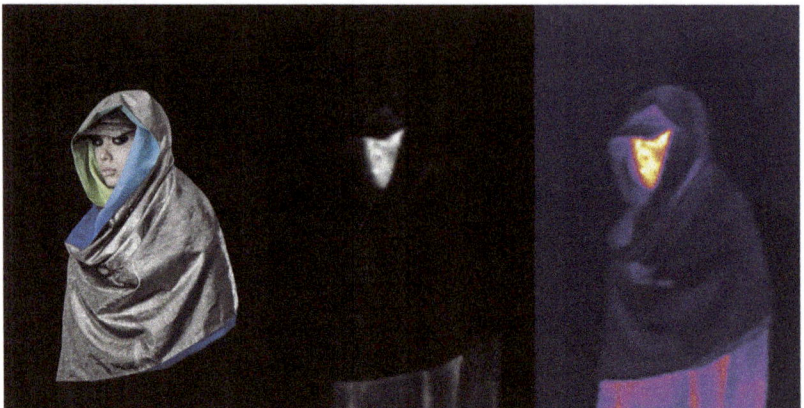

Figure 1.3. Adam Harvey, *Stealth Wear, Anti-Drone Hijab* (2012). Courtesy of the artist.

dress as motivated to provide 'a separation between *man* and Drone' – an unambiguous gesture to the populations most likely to find themselves caught in the crosshairs of the FLIR (Forward-Looking Infrared) cameras that equip military aircraft (see Figure 1.3).

Finally, whereas *CV Dazzle* entails the production of an 'anti-face' that escapes altogether the recognition of facial detection algorithms, *HyperFace* (2017) adopts the obverse strategy in producing images containing 'maximally activated false faces based on ideal algorithmic representations of a human face'. The intention here is to conceal actual human faces by overwhelming computer vision with adjoining arrangements of geometric shapes purposefully designed to trigger its pattern recognition routines. Once again, such a counter-measure requires an intimate understanding and patient testing of the specific facial detection algorithms being targeted. This approach corresponds directly to the military approach of decoying in which target signatures are simulated so as to fool optical, infrared, or radar sensors (Bousquet 2018: 177-83) (see Figure 1.4).

In summation, I have sought in this chapter to interrogate the recent adoption by critical scholars of the notion of 'scopic regime' to apprehend the visual practices of the drone – understood as a microcosm of contemporary military perception more generally – and to theorise the forms of aesthetic resistance that can be opposed to it. Contesting the epistemological certainties legitimising military violence and bringing to the fore non-Western ways of seeing our deadly weapon systems are undoubtedly worthy endeavours. One is forced to admit however that over a century of philosophical and artistic challenges to Cartesian perspectivalism has done little to interdict the quotidian operation of the logistics of military perception. For that purpose, we may instead need to break open the black box of its mechanisms so as to devise the most effective means to thwart, subvert, and distract them. Life in

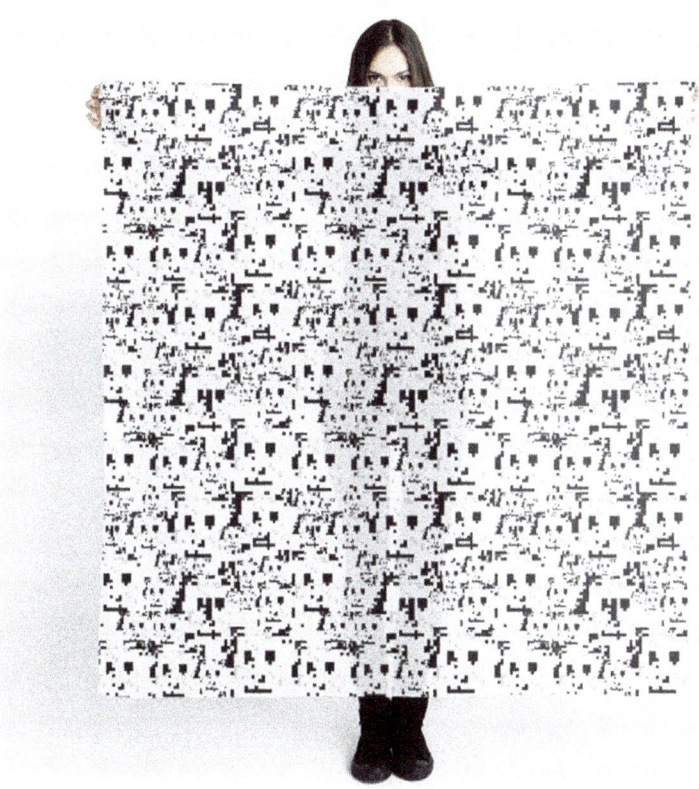

Figure 1.4. Adam Harvey, *HyperFace* (2012). Courtesy of the artist.

the interstices of a martial gaze that is itself spurred on by the obstacles and resistances it seeks to overcome offers no definitive solution to the problems of globalised targeting and the extending reach of the war machine in the twenty-first century, to be sure. Yet where else can effective resistance to our contemporary condition be forged than at the confluence of art, engineering, and politics? Or as Gilles Deleuze once put it, 'there is no need to fear or hope, but only to look for new weapons' (1992: 4).

Works Cited

Alpers, Svetlana. 1983. *The Art of Describing: Dutch Art in the Seventeenth Century*. Chicago: Chicago University Press.

Berger, John. 1972. *Ways of Seeing*. London: Penguin.

Bousquet, Antoine. 2015. 'Prolegomena to Post-Anthropocentric International Relations: Biosphere and Technosphere in the Age of Global Complexity'. In *World Politics at the Edge of Chaos: Reflections on Complexity and Global Life*, edited by Emilian Kavalski, 189-208. New York: SUNY Press.

Bousquet, Antoine. 2017. 'A Revolution in Military Affairs? Changing Technologies and Changing Practices of Warfare'. In *Technology and World Politics: An Introduction*, edited by Daniel R. McCarthy, 165-81. New York: Routledge.

Bousquet, Antoine. 2018. *The Eye of War: Military Perception from the Telescope to the Drone*. Minneapolis: University of Minnesota Press.

Bräunert, Svea, and Meredith Malone, eds. 2016. *To See Without Being Seen: Contemporary Art and Drone Warfare*. Chicago: University of Chicago Press.

Coward, Martin. 2013. 'Networks, Nodes and De-territorialised Battlespace: The Scopic Regime of Rapid Dominance'. In *From Above: War, Violence and Verticality*, edited by Peter Adey, Mark Whitehead, and Alison J. Williams. 95-118. London: Hurst Publishers.

Crary, Jonathan. 1992. *Techniques of the Observer: On Vision and Modernity in the Nineteenth Century*. Cambridge: MIT Press.

Deleuze, Gilles. 1992. 'Postscript on the Societies of Control'. *October* 59: 3-7.

Edgerton, Samuel. 1976. *The Renaissance Rediscovery of Linear Perspective*. New York: Harper & Row.

Edney-Browne, Alex. 2019. 'Vision, Visuality, and Agency in the US Drone Program'. In *Technology and Agency in International Relations*, edited by Marijn Hoijtink and Matthias Leese, 89-112. New York: Routledge.

Feldman, Allen. 1997. 'Violence and Vision: The Prosthetics and Aesthetics of Terror'. *Public Culture* 10: 24–60.

Feldman, Allen. 2004. 'Securocratic Wars of Public Safety'. *Interventions* 6: 330–50.

Farocki, Harun. 2001. *Imprint Writings*. New York: Lukas & Sternberg.

Grayson, Kyle. 2012. 'Six Theses on Targeted Killing'. *Politics* 32: 120–28.

Grayson, Kyle. 2017. *Cultural Politics of Targeted Killing: On Drones, Counter-insurgency, and Violence*. New York: Routledge.

Grayson, Kyle, and Jocelyn Mawdsley. 2019. 'Scopic Regimes and the Visual Turn in International Relations: Seeing World Politics Through the Drone'. *European Journal of International Relations* 25: 431-57.

Gregory, Derek. 2011. 'From a View to a Kill: Drones and Late Modern War'. *Theory, Culture & Society* 28: 188-215.

Ivins, William M. 1973. *On the Rationalization of Sight*. New York: Da Capo Press.

Jay, Martin. 1988. 'Scopic Regimes of Modernity'. In *Vision and Visuality*, edited by Hal Foster, 3-23. Seattle: Bay Press.

Jay, Martin. 1993. *Downcast Eyes: The Denigration of Vision in Twentieth-Century French Thought*. Berkley: University of California Press.

Jünger, Ernst. 2008. *On Pain*. Translated by David C. Durst. New York: Telos Press.

Lee-Morrison, Lila. 2015. 'Drone Warfare: Visual Primacy as a Weapon'. In *Trans Visuality: The Cultural Dimension of Visuality, Vol. 2: Visual Organizations*, edited by Frauke Wiegand, Anders Michelsen, and Tore Kristensen, 201-14. Liverpool: Liverpool University Press.

Manovich, Lev. 2002. 'Modern Surveillance Machines: Perspective, Radar, 3-D Computer Graphics and Computer Vision'. In *CTRL (Space): Rhetorics of Surveillance from Bentham to Big Brother*, edited by Thomas Y. Levin, Ursla Frohne, and Peter Weibel, 382-95. Cambridge: MIT Press.

Maurer, Kathrin. 2016. 'Visual Power: The Scopic Regime of Military Drone Operations'. *Media, War & Conflict* 10: 141–51.

Metz, Christian. 1982. *The Imaginary Signifier: Psychoanalysis and the Cinema*. Translated by Celia Britton et al. Bloomington: Indiana University Press.

Rancière, Jacques. 2006. *The Politics of Aesthetics*. Translated by Gabriel Rockhill. London: Continuum Books.

Saint-Amour, Paul K. 2003. 'Modernist Reconnaissance'. *Modernism/modernity* 10: 349-80.

Snyder, Joel. 1980. 'Picturing Vision'. *Critical Inquiry* 6: 499-526.

Somaini, Antonio. 2006. 'On the Scopic Regime'. *Leitmotiv* 5: 25-38.

Stubblefield Thomas. 2020. *Drone Art: The Everywhere War as Medium*. Berkley: University of California Press.

Virilio, Paul. 1989. *War and Cinema: The Logistics of Perception*. Translated by Patrick Camiller. London: Verso.

Zuev, Dennis, and Gary Bratchford. 2021. *Visual Sociology: Practices and Politics in Contested Spaces*. London: Palgrave MacMillan.

2

Me and My Predator(s): Tactical Remembrance and Critical Atonement

Joseph DeLappe

Introduction

My creative practice explores the development of experimental, activist approaches to memorialisation, utilising digital and analogue processes, video games, online platforms, crowdsourcing, and real-world cooperative-making in community-based settings. For the past two decades, much of this work has focused on considering the human costs incurred as a result of the reaction of the United States of America to the 9/11 attacks and the ensuing 'war on terror'. This is evident in works such as *iraqimemorial.org* (2007), a crowdsourced open call and repository for participants to share their creative proposals for imagined memorials to the many hundreds of thousands of civilian casualties from the Iraq war, and *dead-in-iraq*, (2006-2011), an online intervention into the *America's Army* computer game, which is a recruiting platform developed by the US Department of Defence. In this work, I entered the game as a US soldier, dropped my weapon, and used the game's text messaging system to type in the names of America's dead soldiers from the war in what was an act of remembrance and protest. These and other projects adopt an experimental and critical approach to respond to issues surrounding memorialisation, militarism, violence, and warfare (see Figure 2.1).

Much of my work engages the concept of the 'counter monument' as developed by historian James E. Young in his consideration of Holocaust memorials in Germany. I first encountered his writings while conducting research for the aforementioned *iraqimemorial.org* project. Young examines various German artists' approach to memorialising the Holocaust: 'Ethically certain of their duty to remember, but aesthetically sceptical of the assumptions underpinning traditional memorial forms, a new generation of contemporary artistic and monument makers in Germany is probing the limits of both their artistic media and the very notion of a memorial' (Young 1993: 27). The artists and works described by Young are focused on memorialising the past crimes

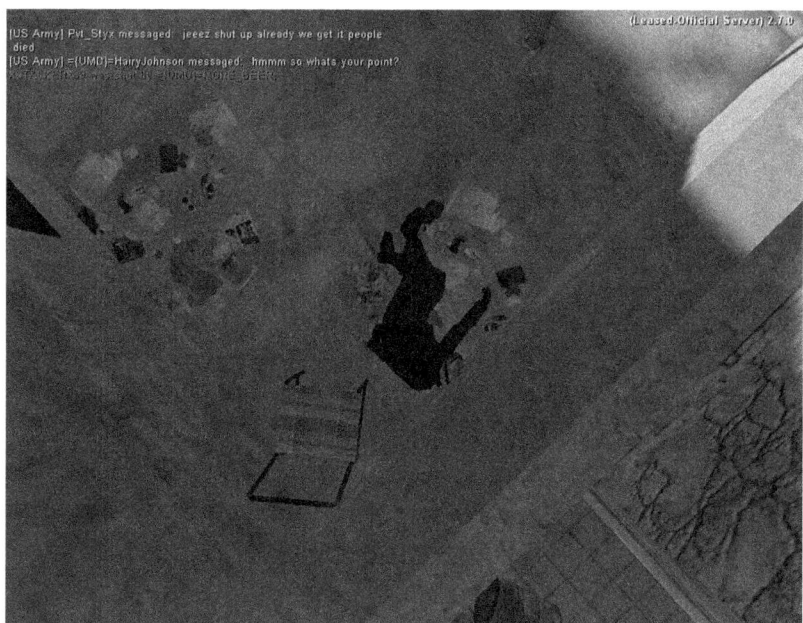

Figure 2.1. Joseph DeLappe, *dead-in-iraq* (2006-2011). Courtesy of the artist.

of their nation. Key to their approach is a recognition and a reckoning with the fact that most of them did not experience the Second World War directly. In contrast, the works I've detailed here focus on conflicts and deaths happening in the here and now, albeit at a distance. Key to my approach has been to combine aspects of memorialisation, activism, and protest in reaction to the immediate.

Following on from these earlier projects, for nearly a decade now a significant focus of my work has been engaging drones and the costs of drone warfare from a perspective of critical atonement. I question the use of these new remote weapons and seek, as an American citizen, to call attention to and memorialise the invisible and forgotten victims of our remote, foreign incursions. In the works described I've engaged in projects ranging from individual acts of tactical remembrance to collective memorials which include processes of counting and naming the dead from America's drone wars. The various projects purposefully incorporate ephemeral materials and processes such as paper, rubber stamps, GIFs, performance, and computer games and perhaps most significantly to invite and involve others to participate, make, and share in processes of intervention and critical reflection. The works explore methodologies for expanding thinking and practice surrounding the role of the contemporary artist by looking at the context of creative activism in the digital age and the attendant complexities surrounding remembrance and memorialisation.

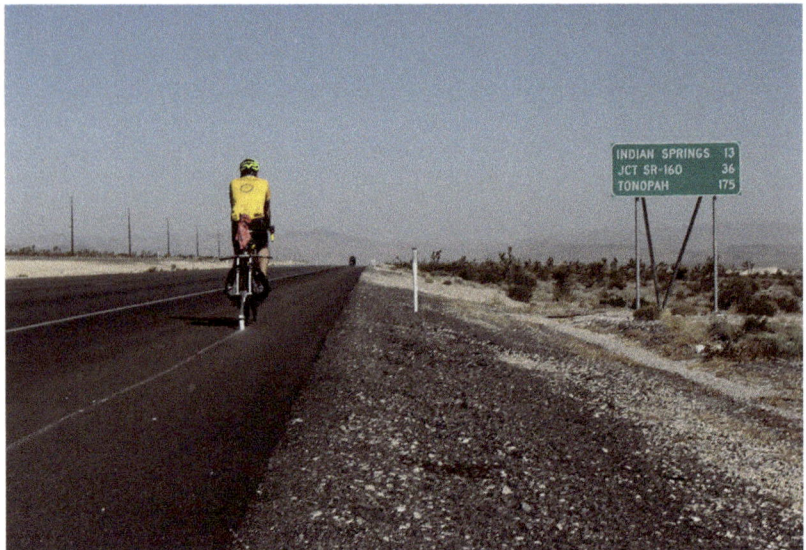

Figure 2.2. *Project 929: Mapping the Solar* (2013). Photo by Laurie A. Macfee. Courtesy of the artist.

Military drones became a focus of my work in 2013 when I enacted an artwork in the desert of southern Nevada entitled *Project 929: Mapping the Solar*. *Project 929* was a durational performance involving a 460-mile bicycle ride, using my bike to drag pieces of chalk attached to a mechanical device which trailed behind me to physically and symbolically draw a circle around the Nellis Test and Training Range. The Union of Concerned Scientists estimates that a 100 by 100 square mile solar farm in the American Southwest would be 'more than enough to meet the country's entire energy demands' (Choi 2009). This military base comprises an area roughly equal to 100 square miles and could be fit for purpose to create the world's largest solar farm. Beginning May nineteenth, 2013, I began riding a 'long-tail' touring bicycle specially equipped with a custom-built chalk drawing mechanism to draw a circle around the perimeter of the base. Nellis is enormous and the largest peacetime military base in the world. It includes: the Nevada Test Site; Groom Lake a.k.a. 'Area 51'; the proposed Yucca Mountain Nuclear Waste Storage Facility; and Creech Air Force Base. Ten days later, riding a total of 420, through heat, cold, dust, and winds, the ride – and the chalk outline – was complete (see Figure 2.2).

In conducting the background research for *Project 929*, I learned more about the various uses for Nellis. The aforementioned Creech AFB in particular interested me as it is one of the central command, control, and training facilities for America's use of military drones overseas. Furthermore, it was at the secret base at Groom Lake 'Area 51' where America's secret military aircraft are involved in test flights, including the now ubiquitous Predator and

Reaper drones. Starting in 2009, the Obama administration's growing reliance on drones to assassinate America's enemies was very much in the news. There had been a lack of accountability over the civilian deaths as a result of the Iraq and Afghanistan wars under the regime of President George Bush. The Obama administration appeared determined to carry such disregard for civilian deaths over to its embrace of drones, including claims that there had been 'no' or 'single-digit' civilian deaths as a result of America's 'targeted killings' via drones (Pilkington 2013). In further researching the use of these remote weapons of war, I was filled with a deep anger and sadness at the untold pain being foisted upon distant civilian populations by my government, and at the ethics or lack thereof surrounding the effects of these weapons on such populations.

The works described herein represent a chronology of responses to America's enthusiastic embrace of the use of drones, aka armed, unmanned aerial vehicles (UAVs) as weapons of choice in conflict zones which include Pakistan, Iraq, Afghanistan, Yemen, Somalia, and Libya among others. Central to these works is the question: how can I, as an artist, respond to the ongoing killing of innocents in the 'war on terror' and the seeming passivity of my fellow citizens of the West in regard to the very real, yet distant, consequences of our use of weaponised drones? How can one develop creative agencies that encourage others to engage, understand, and empathise in regard to what are new forms of killing that hide behind a veneer of slick technologies and exceptionalist American beliefs? Is it possible, if not crucially necessary, to find ways to memorialise the victims of our wars and in so doing, question the efficacy and moral implications of America's hyper militarised stance in the world? And perhaps most importantly, is it possible, through art and creative action, to develop works that encourage people, through experience and participation, to move from a place of abstracted distance to one of empathy, action, and atonement?

Cowardly Drones (2014)

My first drone works were designed to serve as subtle interventions into the Google image search algorithm to call direct attention to the problematic nature of weaponised drones. The process for creating these works first involved conducting an extensive online Google image search for the top results of photographs of various UAVs in use by America's intelligence and military in operations overseas. Resulting image search downloads included General Atomics's MQ-1 Predator Drones, MQ-9 Reaper Drones and Global Hawk Drones. Each image was then slightly augmented using Adobe Photoshop to include the realistic marking of the word 'COWARDLY' using a standard military font upon the drone's fuselage (see Figure 2.3). The saved image files were then strategically uploaded to my website, shared via Facebook and posted to a dedicated Tumblr site. In the months following

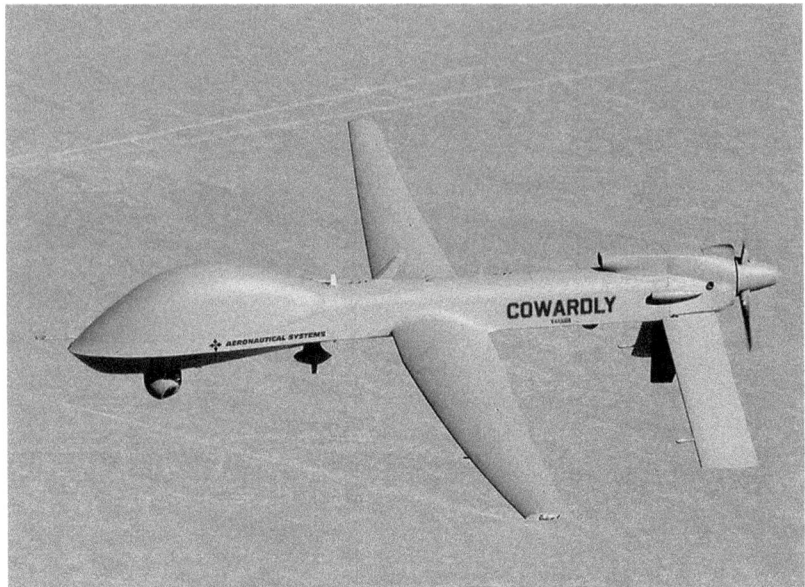

Figure 2.3. Joseph DeLappe, *Cowardly Drone* (2014). Courtesy of the artist.

the posting and sharing of these images online, several of the created images began to appear in the top twenty Google image search results respectively for 'Predator Drone', 'Reaper Drone', and 'Global Hawk Drone'. The simple digital alteration of drone imagery and the 'intelligence' of the Google search algorithm are exploited here for a subtle intervention into the media stream of US military power. The intention here was to cut to the core of what is one of the many problematic aspects of the use of militarised drones in the war on terror, its ability to unleash harm without any risk to the drone pilot. Weaponised drones are painted grey to blend with the skies above, circling unseen overhead – by literally branding each drone with a pejorative and sharing these images online, their essence is revealed and made hypervisible through the Google algorithm. These works are further the first to engage an approach that involves the subversion of the familiar and iconic image of drones in a public context (see Figure 2.4).

Me and My Predator (2015)

While working at a Pier Nine Autodesk Artist's Residency in San Francisco, I built a 1/72nd scale plastic model from a kit of a Predator Drone which I then suspended on a carbon fibre rod connected to a custom-made aluminium c-clamp/head band attached to my head. *The Personal Drone System* is a performative sculpture designed for insecurity and discomfort – to simulate using analogue technologies what it might be like to live under droned

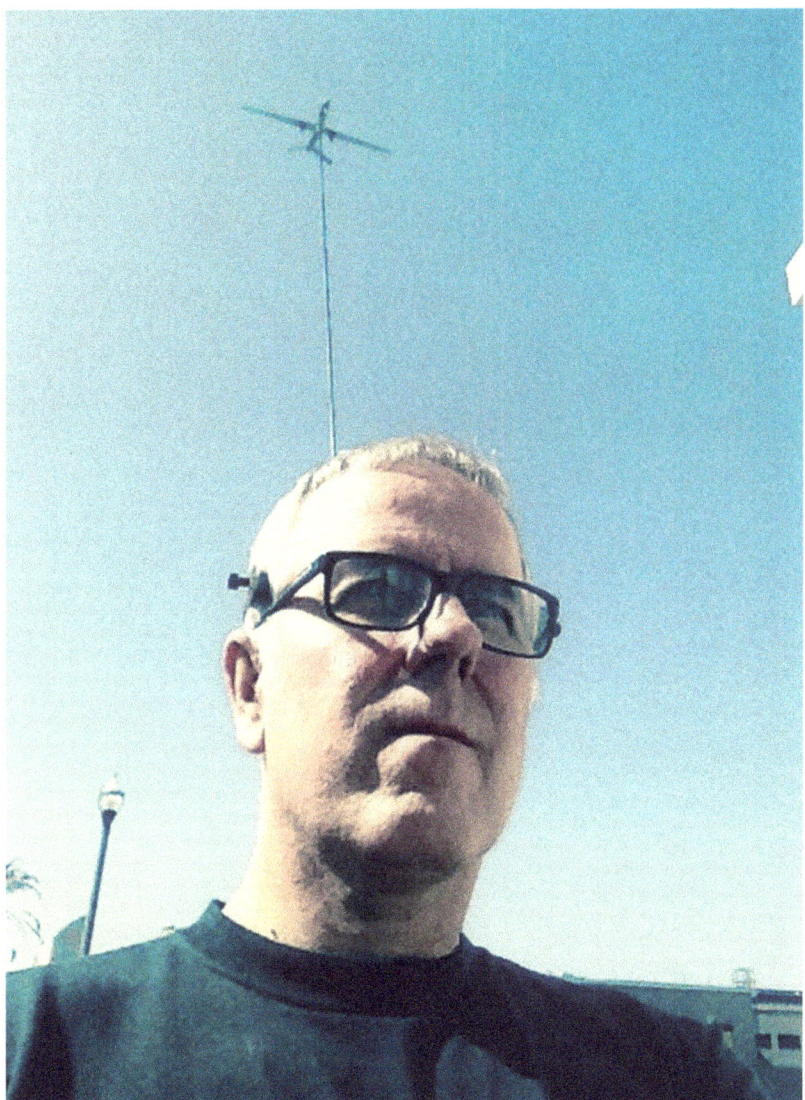

Figure 2.4. Joseph DeLappe, *Me and My Predator* (2015). Courtesy of the artist.

skies. I performed walks around San Francisco with this device attached to my head. The work was informed by reports of drones circling invisibly above warzones and the resulting stress placed upon civilian populations below. The intent was to make visible the invisible in a direct and very public fashion. One could consider this performance as a manifestation of the connection between these distant weapons of war directly to my person. In doing so, the

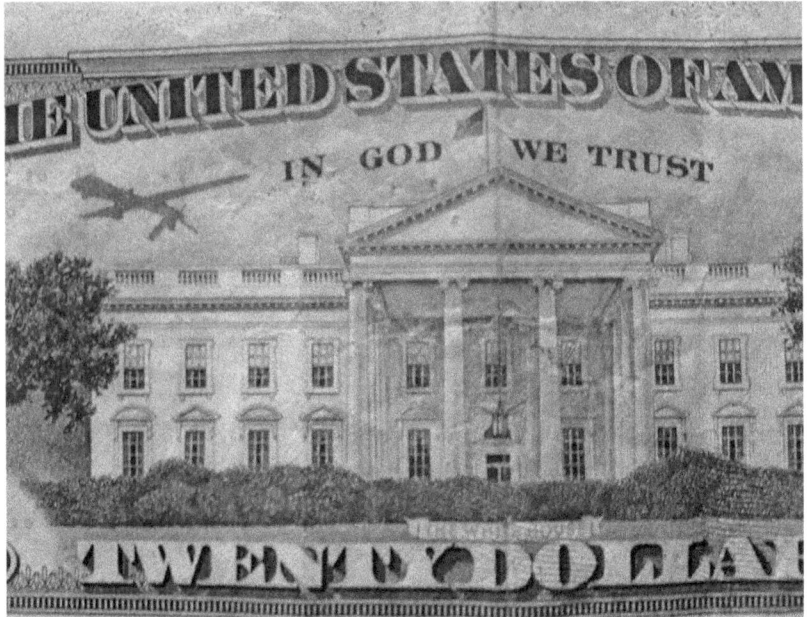

Figure 2.5. Joseph DeLappe, *In Drones We Trust* (2015). Courtesy of the artist.

surveillance and destruction of our enemies as identified by the state, done 'in our name', is made real in a direct and absurdist public gesture.

In Drones We Trust (2015-16)

Also created while on residency at Autodesk, this was a participatory project inviting volunteers across the USA to rubber stamp a tiny image of an MQ-1 Predator Drone on the back of their paper money. The idea came after closely examining US currency – all but the $1 dollar bill feature peaceful, pastoral depictions of notable government buildings or monuments on the back of the bills, albeit with lonely, empty skies (see Figure 2.5). It was while paying for a meal near the residency, looking at the back of a twenty-dollar bill with its depiction of the White House, that I imagined President Obama sitting in his office and thought to myself, 'he needs a drone!'

Considering the USA's unfettered use of drones in foreign skies, to bring them home, symbolically, to fly over the USA's most notable patriotic structures seemed wholly appropriate. As well, the work closes the gap between the USA's financial system and the larger systems of political and military power that are intrinsically connected to foreign policies, including the use of drones.

Over several months I created and shared hundreds of laser etched, hand-assembled rubber stamps, which were sent via the post to volunteer participants throughout the world. To date, over 2,500 stamps have been distributed. Participants are invited, in exchange for being provided with a drone stamp, to send me at least one image of a stamped bill, noting location and date where the bill was stamped and put back into circulation. The resulting images were shared on a dedicated Tumblr account. I shared this project as well on *instructables.com* with detailed instructions on how to make your own drone stamps on a post entitled 'Laser Etch Rubber Stamps for a Drone Stamp Revolution!'. As with other works that I shared via this platform (including the aforementioned *Personal Drone System*), the intent is to bring conceptual, critical and overtly political projects into the geeky realm of this maker's website as a way to extend the reach of the work beyond the contemporary arts milieu. The comments shared by others as a result of these drone related *Instructables* posts unexpectedly resulted in quite thoughtful debates regarding the political and moral issues surrounding America's drone policies. Thus, an online platform for hacking and making becomes a vehicle for sharing activist content and political debate.

Drone Strike Visualisation (2015)

A trope of war movies is the command centre with an enormous map and moveable models representing the field of battle. Online searches for maps of drone strikes result in a number of graphic representations of documented bombings, usually as a map of a region with a staccato pattern of concentrated dots noting each recorded attack. These are abstract visualisations where dots replace killings, that, similar to body counts, can be less than effective in truly relaying the extent of America's drone attacks around the globe. This project adapted a drone strike map into a large-scale physical visualisation and memorial that documented drone strikes in North Waziristan. A collaborative project developed with media artist Pete Froslie using sculptural and electronic components, the work depicted here is a proof-of-concept installation including twenty-five 3-D printed paper reproductions of MQ-9 Predator Drones, arranged in a pattern of documented drone strikes around the town of Mir Ali (see Figure 2.6). This is a prototype for a much larger installation to feature over 400 paper drones – each representing a documented drone strike in Pakistan. The drones would be arranged to create a map of drone strikes, and the detritus from the 3-D printing process is scattered below the stands to create the landscape. Each drone is individually lit by an addressable LED light which goes off in a staccato pattern creating dramatically intertwined shadows on the ceiling and walls of the installation space. We envision visitors to the installation walking through and among the physical map and the mounted paper drones. In the final installation, which to date has not been realised, the staccato pattern would be interrupted over time by individual strikes being highlighted with red light and the incorporation of an LED panel on the wall that would note the drone strike location, date and number of people killed. Our intention is to create a visceral space for remembrance

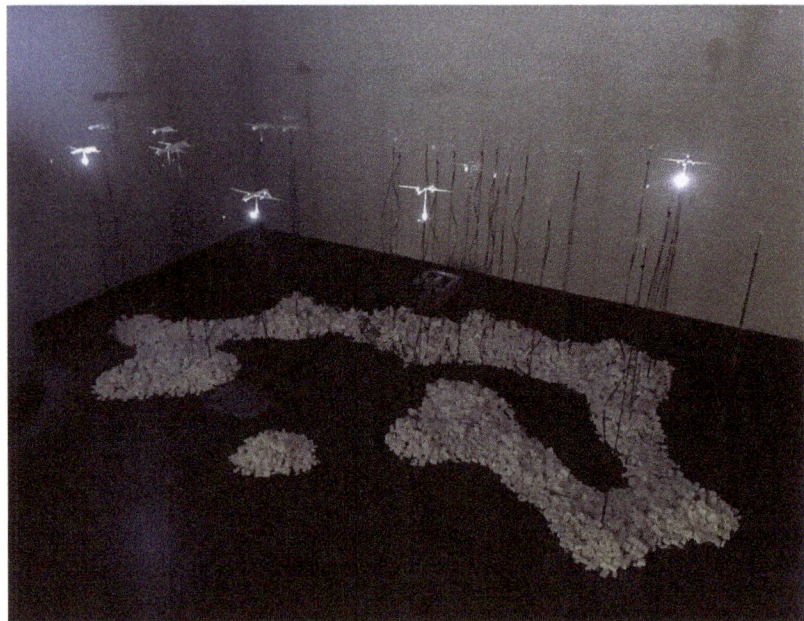

Figure 2.6. Joseph DeLappe, *Drone Strike Visualisation* (2015). Courtesy of the artist.

that immerses visitors in a silent installation that is filled with changing patterns of light and shadow created by real-world data.

Bierstadt Drones (2016)

This is an ongoing series of internet-based works that update Albert Bierstadt's iconic paintings of America's west by inserting animated GIF flybys of Predator and Reaper drones. Bierstadt's highly idealised paintings are the representation of the nineteenth-century idea of 'manifest destiny' in their fantastic, virtualised representations of bucolic mountains, pioneers on the move and rapidly vanishing native cultures. Bierstadt's work historically played a key role in attracting 'settlers' to tame the 'savage' American West. The regions depicted here of the wide-open frontier were once considered exotic, distant, and open to exploitation. His scenes of western rapture have now been invaded by the iconic image of weaponised drones flying overhead (see Figure 2.7). Idealised, imagined landscapes are reified with the addition of our latest technologies of colonisation, imperialism, power, and destruction. Bierstadt's depictions of the Western regions of nineteenth-century America were curiously absent of any evidence of the conflict and genocide being wrought upon indigenous populations. It is wholly appropriate to reimagine these images as backdrops for contemporary weapons of imperial conquest which represent nothing if not the continuation of America's violent, expansionist impulses. America's drones

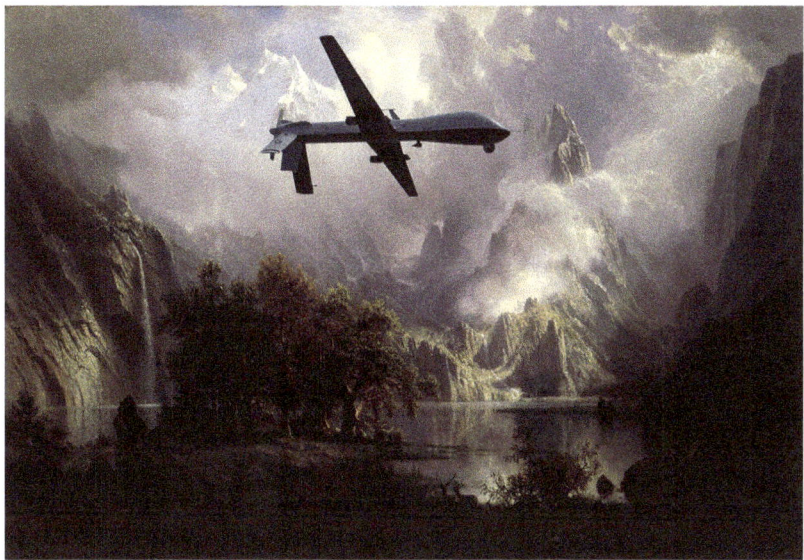

Figure 2.7. Joseph DeLappe, *Bierstadt Drone* (2016). Courtesy of the artist.

represent a new imaginary for exerting our power abroad. Bringing these two disparate and time distant icons of expansion together creates a disconcertingly cohesive combination. These works have been designed for online distribution as GIFs as well as being realised in video installation format for flat screen displays.

The 1,000 Drones: A Participatory Memorial (2014/2017)

The Bureau of Investigative Journalism estimates that in the North Waziristan region of Pakistan, between 2004 and 2020, 430 CIA-operated drones killed an estimated 2,515-4,026 people; of these, it is estimated that between 424 and 969 civilians have been killed, including an estimated 172-207 children (Bureau of Investigative Journalism 2021). The *1,000 Drones: A Participatory Memorial* (2014 & 2017) is an installation first developed as a commission on-site for the exhibition 'Making Now: Open for Exchange' at the Florida State University Museum of Fine Arts (MOFA) in 2014, followed by a second updated version created for the Sonoma Valley Museum of Art (SVMA), California, USA in 2017 (see Figure 2.8).

Volunteer participants were provided with printed paper templates which they cut out and folded to make small-scale, papercraft replicas of General Atomics's MQ-1 Predator drone aircraft. Upon the wings of each paper drone the participants were invited to write the name, age, and date of death of a civilian drone casualty. The names of the 355 civilian casualties were gathered from deaths recorded in Pakistan and Yemen as documented by the

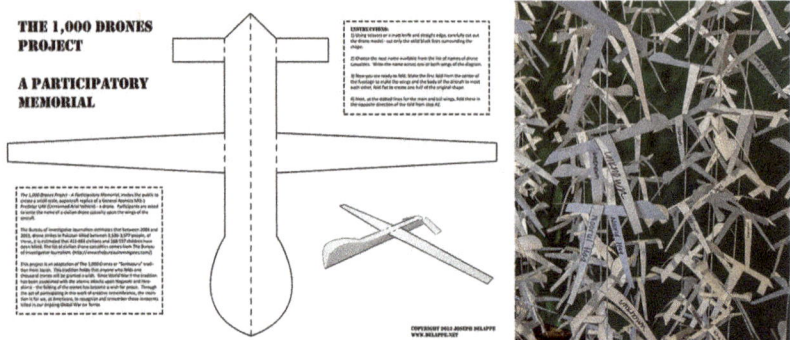

Figure 2.8. *The 1,000 Drones* (2014/2017). Photo by Robert Holmes. Courtesy of the artist.

Bureau of Investigative Journalism; the names of the remaining 645 deaths were marked 'unknown'. The annotated papercraft drones were then strung together to form a large-scale installation in the shape of a chevron. This project is intended to function as an experimental work of participation, memory, and atonement.

The 1,000 Drones was inspired, in part, by the tradition of Japanese 'Senbazuru', commonly referred to as 'The 1,000 Cranes' wherein origami cranes are made and strung together. The tradition holds that anyone who folds one thousand origami cranes will be granted a wish. Since the Second World War the tradition has been associated with the atomic attacks upon Nagasaki and Hiroshima – the folding of the cranes has become a wish for peace. Through the act of participating in this work of creative remembrance, the intention is for us, as Americans, to recognise and remember those innocents killed in our ongoing Global War on Terror.

The project uses the approach of making with others, and the process and realisation of the final work was designed to create an opportunity for cooperative, shared action and remembrance. This process of making was crucial to the overall impact of the work and intentionally designed to draw attention to individual victims who are collectively often forgotten as part of larger, abstract casualty counts.

The Drone Project (2014)

This was a commissioned project by the Center for Creativity and the Arts at California State University Fresno where I was the Visiting Artist in Residence in 2014. I worked on-site for two-plus weeks with over 100 students, interns, and local volunteers to create a full-to-scale sculptural reproduction of a MQ-1 Predator drone created using a digital 3-D file that was processed using Pepakura Designer and adapted for large-scale low polygon construction using yellow corrugated plastic. The forty-seven-foot-wide sculpture was constructed on-site and resulted in a final, performative event where local

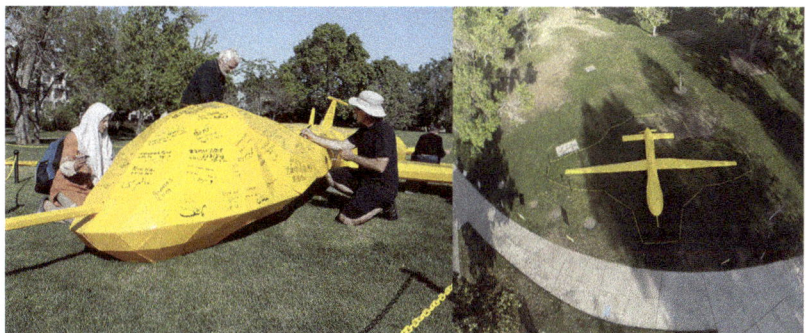

Figure 2.9. *The Drone Project* (2014). Photo by Robert D. Iyall. Courtesy of the artist.

Pakistani immigrants read aloud from individual cards the name, age, and date of death of 334 known drone strike victims from Pakistan. The cards were then provided to volunteers who were invited to write the casualty details upon the surface of the drone (written both in English and in Urdu, as translated by the Pakistani volunteers). The placement of the drone, as if it had fallen from the sky and crash-landed on the site, was inspired by an extraordinary real-life YouTube video of Afghani villagers stoning a crashed drone (see Figure 2.9). *The Drone Project*, like James Bridle's *Drone Shadow* series where a simple outline of a life-sized drone is painted on the ground, and like the 2021 sculpture by Sam Durant *Untitled (drone)* shown as if flying over the Highline in NYC, share an approach towards making drones real via scale and placement in what are decidedly not warzones. The project was temporarily installed for three months on one of the primary quad areas of the FSU campus and was visible through Google Earth, and located underneath the flight path of jet fighters from a neighbouring Air National Guard base.

Killbox: A Game About Drone Warfare (2016)

Killbox is an interactive installation and downloadable computer game that critically explores the nature of drone warfare, its complexities and consequences. It is an experience that explores the use of technology to transform and extend political and military power, and the abstraction of killing and culpability through virtualisation. *Killbox* involves players and audiences in a fictionalised interactive experience in virtual environments based on documented drone strikes in Northern Waziristan, Pakistan. The work is an international collaboration between myself and the UK-based Biome Collective, including artists and game developers Malath Abbas, Tom Demajo and Albert Elwin (see Figure 2.10).

In the public imagination, drones often represent the ultimate 'gamification' of warfare. That said, it is curious that there are relatively few games or interactive experiences that actually attempt to address the subject of drones.

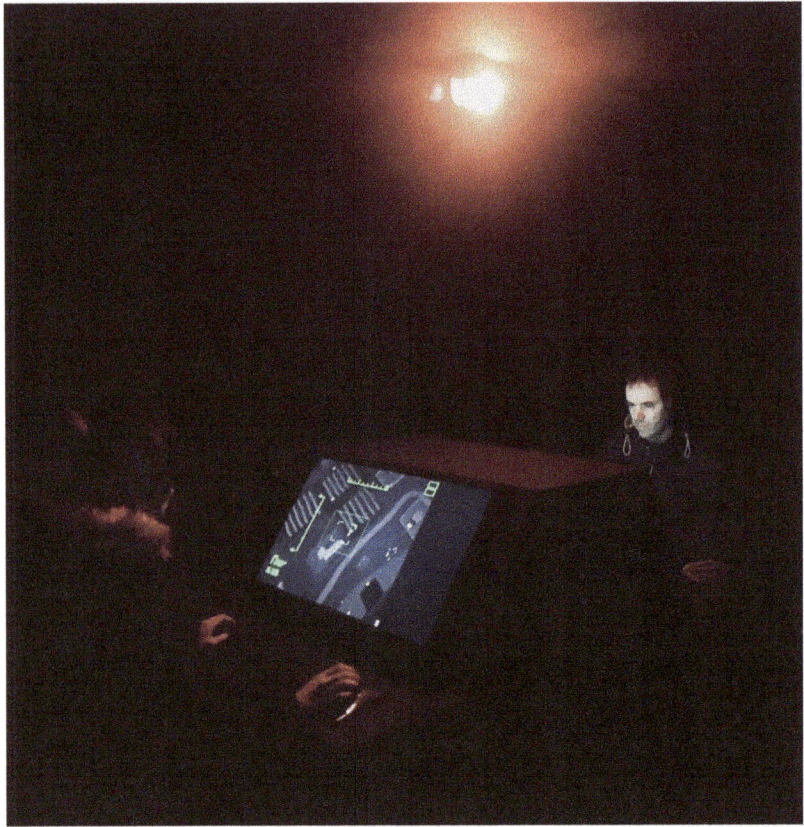

Figure 2.10. Joseph DeLappe, *Killbox* (2016). Courtesy of the artist.

It is ironic that a weapon system that is so conceptually connected to computer games has seen so little serious treatment in the world of computer gaming and interactive media. This is likely due to the asymmetrical nature of drone warfare – in most computer games, for the sake of dynamic and challenging game play, there exists a balance between opposing forces. A drone pilot faces zero threat from those on the ground, while those living under drones are completely lacking in agency. Through simulative gameplay and interactivity, we can engage with this very unequal and asymmetrical aspect of drone warfare to make for a compelling and meaningful artwork. This is a central tenet of the ideation process behind the development of *Killbox* – to develop a simulative interactive experience that focuses players upon the moral, ethical, human, and technological conditions surrounding drone warfare.

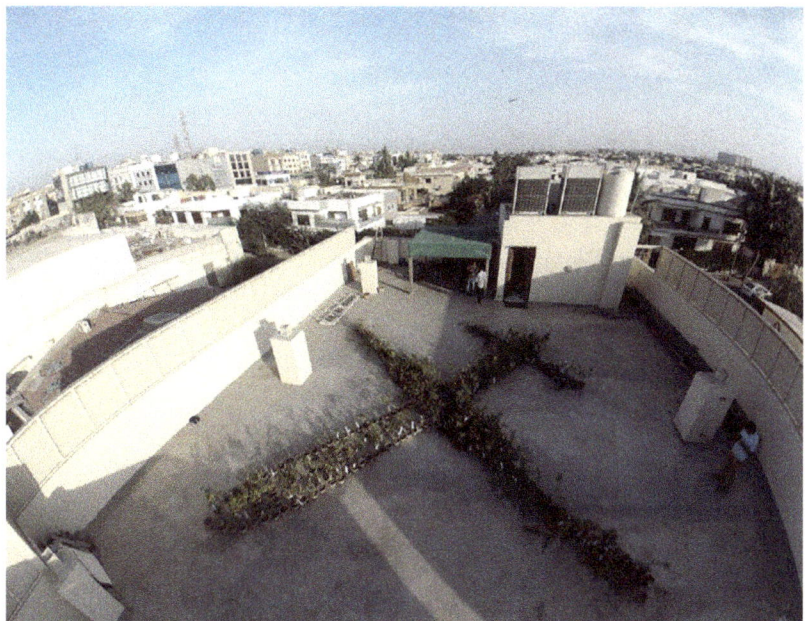

Figure 2.11. Joseph DeLappe, *Jasmine: A Drone Memorial* (2017). Courtesy of the artist.

Jasmine: A Drone Memorial (2017)

This project involved the creation of a temporary rooftop installation at Studio 7 Gallery, Karachi, Pakistan for the exhibition *May We Not Go Up There?* curated by Iftikhar Chohan and Mehreen Hashmi. The installation was a participatory memorial to the civilian victims of drone strikes in North Waziristan. The memorial was created on-site by arranging 360 Jasmine plants in ceramic pots to form the shape of a full-sized Predator drone (see Figure 2.11). Jasmine is the national flower of Pakistan. At the end of the exhibition, the plants were gifted to gallery visitors, which allowed the memorial to be scattered throughout the city's many homes and gardens. It is important to note that this work was created remotely by the curator and gallery staff – I was unable to travel to assist with the creation of the project on-site. Here there is an intentional repurposing of strategies of engagement from a distance, the peaceful use of contemporary communications technology to facilitate the creation of a temporary memorial that is further a community-based gesture of gifting and atonement. There is as well a life beyond the memorial sculpture as represented by the nascent futurity of the gifted, growing plants and the hope that when the recipients of the Jasmine encounter the plants in their daily lives the memorial gesture and the meaning behind such is remembered and further enhanced.

This is the first of what I hope will be a series of memorials to be staged in the various countries currently and historically bombed by UAVs/weaponised

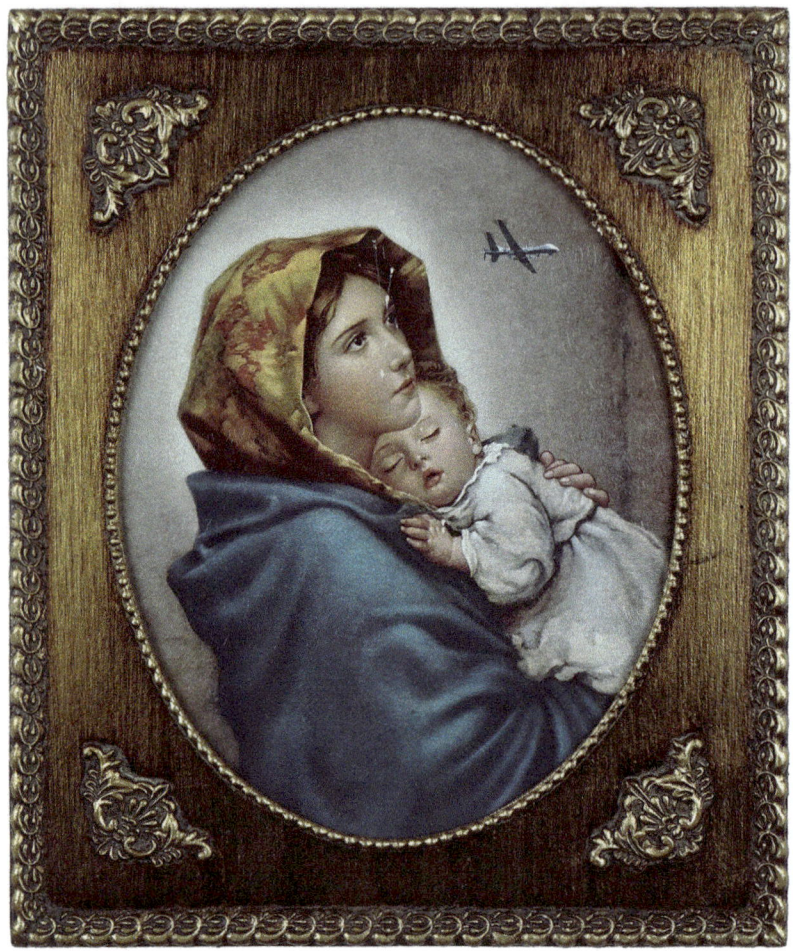

Figure 2.12. Joseph DeLappe, *Thrift Drones*. (2016). Courtesy of the artist.

drones. My concept is that each memorial will incorporate the national flower of the country, for example: Iraq = Roses; Yemen = Arabica Coffee Blossom; Syria = Jasmine; Afghanistan = Tulip and Somalia = The King Protea. The intention is, where possible, to create permanent drone-shaped flower bed memorials within these countries.

Thrift Drones (2016-ongoing)

These works are purchased thrift store and second-hand shop artworks which are then changed with the addition of collaged images of Predator and Reaper drones (see Figure 2.12). This project flows directly from the impetus behind such works as the *Bierstadt Drones* and *In Drones We Trust*, seeking to reimagine and subtly subvert discarded, everyday paintings, prints and photographs procured in the first instance from thrift shops in Reno, Nevada. I started collecting images for this series in 2016, making 135 droned works just prior to relocating to the United Kingdom in January of 2017. I had thought this series was completed once I had left the United States; however I found myself inspired by the plethora of second-hand shops and the diversity of artworks to be found while also learning more about the RAF's growing utilisation of drones for foreign incursions and surveillance. Images of these works, which serve as reminders of droned skies, have been widely shared using social media, primarily Instagram, Facebook and Twitter.

To date, I've made over 275 of these works in total. The larger concept behind the project involves the creation of the works, the sharing of images on social media, followed by the eventual re-donation of the physical works to thrift stores in the USA and second-hand shops in the UK in or near cities that are home to major drone command and control bases (Las Vegas Nevada/Creech and Nellis AFB in the USA, Lincolnshire's RAF Waddington Airbase in the UK). The intent is to re-donate the droned artworks back to thrift stores in order to facilitate the public re-distribution of the works. I see this as a long-term effort to place drones into the skies of hundreds of pieces of thrift store art, and to document, share, exhibit, donate, and so on. Through these works, and the sharing of these for resale through charity shops, the intention is to continue to draw attention to the use of drones. While placing a cut and pasted image of a Predator drone in the skies above a group of ballet dancers or behind a portrait of a child may have humorous undertones, there lies within these works the potential to provoke surprise that then hopefully leads to questions such as: 'Why is this here?' Perhaps this then becomes, 'Why are these there […] in the skies above Pakistan?' Plans for the distribution of the works have been postponed temporarily by the COVID-19 pandemic and will commence in late 2021 and early 2022.

Conclusion

It is now 2021. America's drone wars continue unabated, albeit now faded into the background of the distant hum that is our forever war. News reports during the Trump years that noted a significant increase in the use of weaponised drones (Larison 2020) and the relaxation of Obama era controls for launching drone strikes, all seemed to barely register with a desensitised and distracted American public. The proliferation of UAVs as weapons of warfare has as well seen an increase worldwide (Sayler 2015: 3) Unmanned fighter planes are now being tested and soon to be produced (these have proven more than a match for manned fighter pilots). Our automated future of war at a distance appears to be a certainty.

How, in this context, might I consider the efficacy of the works described here? I can cite those interactions where I find my work directly connecting

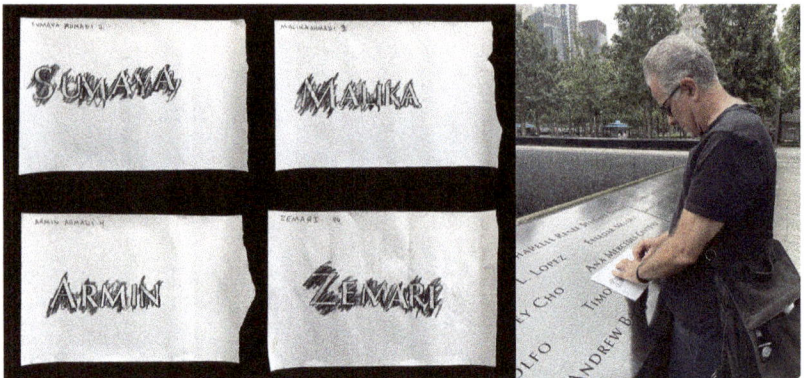

Figure 2.13. Joseph DeLappe, *The Atone Project* (2021). Courtesy of the artist.

with and thus affecting individuals. The young college student coming upon our drone construction site at CSU Fresno, with whom I had a conversation, noted that they had not been at all aware of America's drone policies prior to stumbling upon our site and volunteered to help build the memorial. Or a story as related to me by a fellow drone researcher/activist who actually had US Air Force personnel play my video game *Killbox* and noted the reaction of one drone sensor operator who commented that they had not, prior to playing the game, held any empathy for those being on the receiving end of a drone strike. Or those who would email me excitedly when they came across a drone stamped five-dollar bill when buying a coffee. It is my goal to reach audiences, overtly, and at times subversively, through a kind of quiet activism, to build one project upon the other in the hope of affecting change, cumulatively over time. It is often not direct or clear, yet, as Rebecca Solnit notes in her book *Hope in the Dark* (2016): '[…] if your activism is already democratic, peaceful, creative, then in one small corner of the world these things have triumphed' (Solnit 2016: 61).

Postscript
The Atone Project: Remembering the Ahmadis (2021)

I completed this essay in early August of 2021. It was a few weeks later that America's war in Afghanistan came to an ignoble and unexpectedly rapid end. On August twenty-ninth, three days after a double suicide bombing at the Hamid Karzai International Airport which killed thirteen American soldiers and 170 Afghan civilians, the US military unleashed a Reaper drone attack on suspected suicide bombers in the center of Kabul. The US government insisted their target was a group of ISIS-K terrorists planning further bombings at the airport. Reports soon emerged that in fact they had killed a civilian aid worker, Zemair Ahmadi, and nine members of his extended family, including seven children.

On Friday, the seventeenth of September I visited the 9/11 memorial site in New York City. It was just over twenty years since the 9/11 attacks. Family members visiting the national 9/11 memorial were invited to make rubbings of the inscribed names of loved ones, using provided black wax crayons and commemorative paper. I went to the memorial site on this day to make, instead, rubbings of the names of the Ahmadi family. I made a rubbing of each family member's first name, taking letters from the names inscribed on the memorial to create composite names in honour of this family of innocents murdered in the last days of the Afghanistan withdrawal (see Figure 2.13). It was later on this same day that the Pentagon announced that the 'over the horizon attack' that killed the Ahmadis was a mistake.

I conducted this action as an American citizen to remember the Ahmadi family as an indication of critical atonement, remembrance, and sorrow. The action links the memorialisation of the 2,983 civilians named at the 9/11 memorial and the estimated 71,000 civilians who have been killed in the Afghan and Pakistan war zone since 2001. Peace.

Works Cited

Bureau of Investigative Journalism. 2021. 'Drone Warfare.' https://www.thebureauinvestigates.com/projects/drone-war.

Choi, Charles Q. 2009. 'The Energy Debates: Solar Farms'. *Live Science*. https://www.livescience.com/3115-energy-debates-solar-farms.html.

Larison, Daniel. 2020. 'Trump Escalates Killer Drone War and No One Seems to Care'. *The American Conservative*. https://www.theamericanconservative.com/articles/trump-escalates-killer-drone-war-and-no-one-seems-to-care/.

Pilkington, Ed. 2013. 'Does Obama's 'single-digit' civilian death claim stand up to scrutiny?' *The Guardian*. https://www.theguardian.com/world/2013/feb/07/drones-obama-single-digit-civilian-deaths.

Sayler, Kelley. 2015. 'A World of Proliferated Drones: A Technology Primer'. Report from *Center for a New American Security*. http://drones.cnas.org/wp-content/uploads/2016/03/CNAS-World-of-Drones_052115.pdf.

Solnit, Rebecca. 2016. *Hope in the Dark: Untold Histories and Wild Possibilities*. Chicago: Haymarket Books.

Young, James E. 1993. *The Texture of Memory: Holocaust Memorials and Meaning*. New Haven: Yale University Press.

3

PillCam and Drone Warfare's Redemptive Refrains

Sophia Goodfriend

The Shimon Peres Center for Peace and Innovation lies in the heart of Jaffo, Tel Aviv (see Figure 3.1). The Center was built in 2010 and opened to the public in March of 2019, fifty-one years after Jaffo was annexed by Tel Aviv's Jewish municipality and many of its Palestinian residents forcibly displaced with the foundation of the State of Israel. Out of place amidst the neglected infrastructure that marks the unequal allocation of resources in a deeply stratified settler colonial city, the square, four-story structure emerges awkwardly from a hillside facing the Mediterranean Sea. The façade, made from green concrete and glass compressed into thin strips, was designed by Italian architect Massimiliano Fuksas to evoke 'time and patience, the stratification of the history of two peoples' (Rose 2009). 'It is the representation of an emergency', Fuksas says of his masterpiece (Rose 2009). Yet the promise of redemption whispers through architectural details. While the concrete and glass mar views of the now gentrifying Palestinian neighbourhood to the north and the Palestinian graveyard lying just south of the Center, the clear glass composing the front beckons visitors to gaze out towards the sea, towards the future.

If the building is at once a museum, a research institution, and a monument to Shimon Peres, it is also a sanctuary that promises salvation. Peres was a contradictory figure: a refugee, a soldier, a president, and winner of the Nobel Peace Prize. A staunch Zionist who called for reconciliation with Palestinians, Peres was the first Israeli official to endorse illegal Jewish settlements in the occupied Palestinian territories, a leading figure in the Oslo Accords, and largely credited with the peace plan that, critics say, enabled Israel's military rule over the occupied Palestinian territories to drag on. Yet the Center focuses on neither the ironies of the past nor the messiness of the present. 'Peres was a man of the future', an opening video playing on loop in the lobby announces as visitors enter. 'He was the founding father of Israeli innovation. A man who knew that in order to overcome existential threats and challenges, you had to dream'.

Exhibition rooms scattered throughout four levels literalise this narrative of salvation. Interactive displays of Israeli inventions – Elbit Systems missiles, the Orbit satellite, the USB stick, among others – are overlaid on a timeline

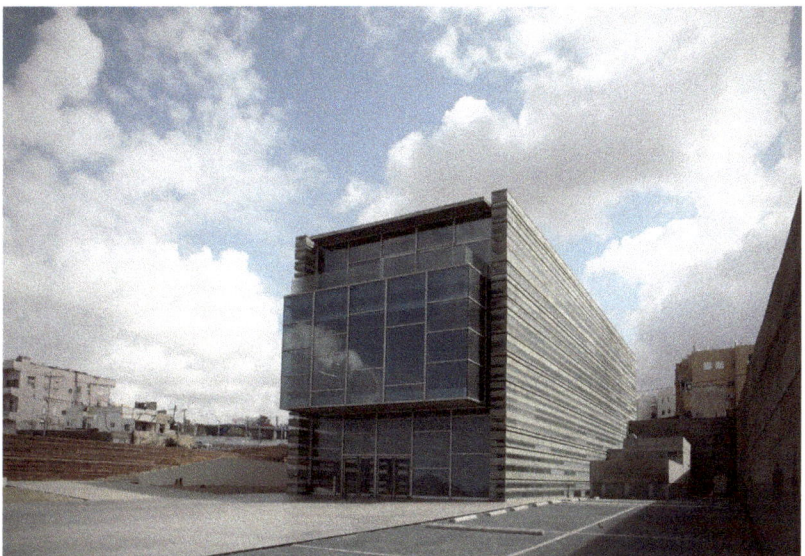

Figure 3.1. Roi Boshi *The Peres Center for Peace*, Tel Aviv, Israel (2010).
Source: Wikimedia Commons CC-BY-SA 3.0.

of Israel's founding. A room with life-sized holograms of Israeli innovators biographise the start-up nation. Prize inventions are illuminated alongside archeological artefacts on the ground floor. And each guided tour climaxes in the Virtual Reality Tunnel: a white tube illuminated with blue neon lights to evoke a spaceship. Here, visitors don virtual reality goggles with surround sound headphones and experience how Israeli inventions have saved a planet vulnerable to climate change, population crises, famine, and war, twenty years in the future.

Distinct from other objects on display, PillCam, a pill the size of a tic-tac outfitted with drone missile-guiding and imaging technology, beckons to be revered repeatedly. First, in the holographic hands of its creator, Gavriel Iddan, who expounds how he transformed drone technology into a biomedical device for endoscopies. Second, on the interactive timeline explaining how Iddan founded the company Given Imaging to produce and export his invention in 2001. Third, in the Virtual Reality Tunnel, where visitors become the drone-turned pill and surveil for malicious bacteria on the gastrointestinal tract of an omniscient patient. And finally, in a display room on the bottom floor, where the eleven-by-thirty-millimetre medical device is illuminated in a glass shrine.

Biomedicine-War-Nexus

In this chapter, I describe the development and promotion of PillCam through the lens of what the feminist sociologist Jennifer Terry has called the biomedicine-war-nexus, or the way in which 'national security, warfare, and biomedical logics form a nexus in which deliberate violence – war – is bound up with far-reaching aspirations about improving life' (2017: 27). Biomedical logics, per Terry, denote how medicine's ethic of care is wielded in the service of militarism as, for example, in allegorical renderings of drone operations as medical procedures by US army generals. Following Terry, biomedical logics obfuscate violence, suturing 'attachments to war' instead – an affective relationship that binds populations to militarism as warfare promises to care for and revitalise human life.

Terry describes a biomedicine-war-nexus emerging from particular cultural values and historical developments in the United States beginning in the latter half of the twentieth century. This chapter, in contrast, turns to Israel, examining how this nexus accrues through longer histories of Israeli militarism and colonisation. Drawing from observation of three guided tours during the Summer of 2019, this chapter examines representational strategies used at the Shimon Peres Center for Peace and Innovation where PillCam is showcased. PillCam, in this analysis, is not simply a drone repurposed as a medical device; it is also an object that operationalises specific fantasies about drone warfare as a regenerative, and thus virtuous, endeavour. I show how such fantasies emerge from particular histories of Israeli state building and work to sustain affective investments in warfare, as militarism promises to vitally enhance life itself.

In so doing, I hope to productively extend scholarship critical of Israel's perceived leadership in defence and security industries (Graham 2010; Khalili 2012; Li 2006). In recent years, scholars have emphasised how Israel's ascendance as a major exporter of weapons and security expertise derives from its ongoing occupation of Palestinian lands and repression of its communities – a dynamic that allows defence and security technologies and tactics to be tested and refined before exported elsewhere (Gordon 2010; Hever 2018; Puar 2017). As Rhys Machold has argued, however, such critiques often inadvertently recapitulate the Israeli state's own claims to technological superiority. As such, they reiterate popular narratives of innovation and progress, or the notion that 'self-sufficient innovation in science and technology has allowed Israel to triumph against all odds' (2018: 89). This chapter heeds Machold's call to examine how such narratives of innovation and progress are constructed and solidified through longer histories of occupation. In what follows, I situate PillCam as part and parcel of a triumphalist narrative of technological progress: a narrative that justifies the violence of Israeli militarism through the generative potential of technological innovation. Turning to the rhetorical and representational techniques through which this narrative garners traction in and beyond the Shimon Peres Center for Peace and Innovation, I underscore how, and to what end, militarism has a hold on life itself.

Technological Salvation

The Shimon Peres Center for Peace and Innovation, like all museums, serves a pedagogical function. It consists of cultural objects, texts, and sounds that tell the history of Israel's establishment in 1948 and transformation into the 'innovative start-up nation' it is today. Tours begin with a video that recounts the tale of Israel's miraculous founding in a region where resources are limited and conflict unending. The film begins with aerial footage of barren desert, accompanied by dramatic narration: 'We faced existential challenges: a barren land and a need for security. To survive we had to face these challenges differently and create a new reality'. Soon, irrigated farmland and high-tech office parks appear on screen: 'Unique security and defense solutions were developed alongside bold initiatives for peace, inventing our own brand of innovation that has changed the world'. Warfare, from the outset, is presented as the regrettable, yet necessary, precondition for Israel's national flourishing.

In the years since the second intifada, or Palestinian uprising (2000-2005), the Israeli state has turned this triumphalist narrative into a distinct branding strategy. Launched in 2008, the Ministry of Foreign Affair's Brand Israel campaign has emphasised Israel as a hub of technological innovation rather than the center of one of the world's more notorious and enduring conflicts (Kuntsman and Stein 2015). Rigorous military training in computer science and engineering, so the story goes, cultivates the human-capital that seeds a fertile high-tech economy (Gordon 2010; Senor and Singer 2008). As Prime Minister Benjamin Netanyahu proclaimed at a cybersecurity conference in Tel Aviv in 2019, 'We took the sum-cost of war and limited landmass and invested it in human capital, military-trained workers, and programmers who could drive an IT revolution'. Indeed, today the 'start-up Nation' hosts more start-ups per capita than anywhere else in the world, with life science and digital health constituting one of the fastest growing sectors (Israel Innovation Authority 2019). Israel's growing biotech industries are increasingly intertwined with its defence and security apparatus as homeland security and surveillance technologies developed in the military are repurposed as medical devices (Gordon 2011: 159). Today, Israeli counterterrorism spyware is deployed to track civilians infected with contagious disease, VR simulators that train soldiers to deal with PTSD, and remote sensing robotics deployed to set off explosives help amputees to walk again.

In Israel, however, championing regional conflict as economically generative stretches the nation's recent promotion of its high-tech economy even further. Rebecca Stein and Adi Kuntsman describe Israel's self-fashioning as the 'Start-up Nation' as a 'classic Zionist modernising narrative' (2015: 26). To understand the centrality of technological innovation to state building, one need only turn to Theodore Herzl's science fiction novel, *Altneuland*, published in 1902 (Sa'adi 1997). The techno-utopian tract describes how a Jewish state in Palestine brings about regional peace and moral uplift through the technological ingenuity and enterprise of Jewish settlers. While written long before Herzl's dream of a Jewish state in Palestine came to fruition, historians have emphasised how this fantastic vision did, at least partly, materialise. As in other colonial contexts (Anderson 2006; Mitchell 2001), Zionism brought with it the promise of modernity. Scholars have demonstrated how scientific practices produced Jewish-Israeli claims over land (Abu el Haj 2001; Suffian 2007) while technological infrastructures (Meiton 2019; Salamanca 2016) abetted Palestinian dispossession. Such work revises popular framings of Zionism as simply an economically productive force, emphasising instead, as Edward Meiton notes in his study of electrification in mandate Palestine, the 'mutual influences running between technology, economics, and politics' (2019: 219). Technological innovation promised to 'drain the swamps and make the desert bloom', promoting Jewish settlement as a project of economic transformation (Wolfe 2006: 388). Historically and today, such narratives work to morally rationalise militarism, promising the destruction sowed by warfare might be redeemed through the innovations it breeds.

Zionism's promise to transform the region into an economically viable territory, of course, came with a price. Israeli militarism, waged in the name of generating security, economic power, and self-sovereignty, sowed immense destruction. Israeli culture has historically grappled with this paradox through a model of remorse known as 'shooting and crying' (Pappé 2006). Throughout Israeli literary texts, cinema, and songs, Israeli soldiers are often cast as figures who hate violence, and, following Karen Grumberg, only act violently in order to survive (2011: 49). Gil Hochberg argues this model is as much about 'remorse and moral dilemmas' as it is about 'self-justification and the creating of a masculine warrior subject', one who is both 'human and sensitive, but also logical and responsible' (2019). At the Shimon Peres Center for Peace and Innovation this model of remorse is grafted on to the imperatives Israel's high-tech economy. The logical and responsible warrior will alleviate guilt for the violence they inflict through innovation that will save human lives all around the world.

Gavriel Iddan, an army engineer who spent the bulk of his military and civilian career developing missiles for the Israeli Defense Forces and Israel Weapon Industries, emblematises this figure. Iddan frames PillCam (see Figure 3.2) as an invention born from the regrettable violence of necessary war: 'I was born here, I didn't choose it', he divulges in an interview with the *Times of Israel* from 2015, 'it was chosen for me' (Shamah 2015). Iddan goes on to celebrate PillCam as a fulfilment of Issiah's prophecy, that 'swords would be transformed into plowshares' (Shamah 2015). At once acknowledging the violence inflicted by the weapons he spent decades producing, Iddan frames his military background as a sacrifice that is redeemed by his invention.

The redemptive narrative Iddan articulates is at once personal and collective. Patented in the late 1990s, although conceived nearly a decade prior, PillCam positioned Iddan as one of the first and most celebrated Israeli

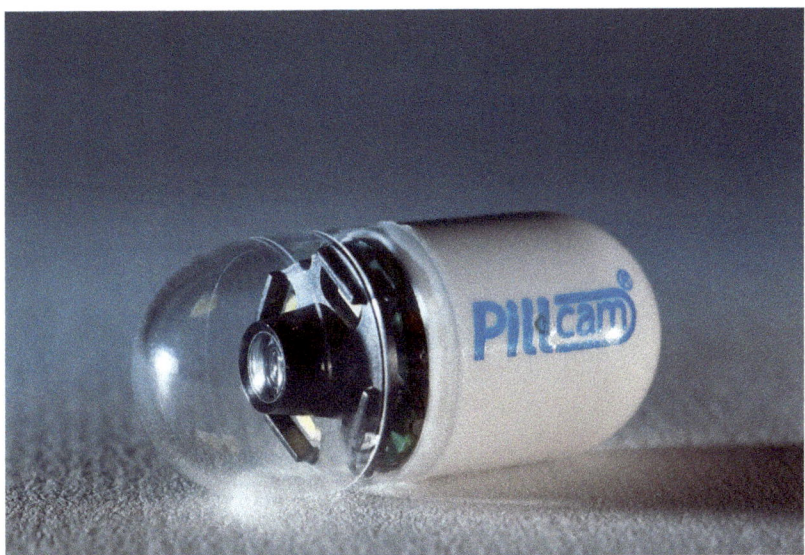

Figure 3.2 David Bleeker Photography *Gavriel Iddan's PillCam*.
Courtesy Alamy Stock Photo.

engineers who, as one Israeli commentator put it, 'proved that technology developed in the IDF could be used for civilian purposes' (Shamah 2015). Iddan conceived of PillCam in the 1980s, far before Israel became synonymous with high-tech innovation, while engineering the prototypes of what would become contemporary drone technology for Israel Weapons Industry. In his free time, Iddan filled notebooks with sketches of miniscule drones outfitted with cameras, LED lights, and transmitters – a 'mini-television studio' with the sensing and guiding capabilities of a drone (EPOfilms). Over years of friendly chats with his neighbour, a doctor of internal medicine, Iddan realised the technologies developed and refined for warfare from above – the so-called 'strategic strikes' that are, today, carried out by the IDF in Gaza's crowded urban settings – could be repurposed to make visible three to five meters of the gastrointestinal tract that had never been imaged before (EPOfilms). By 2001, Iddan founded the company Given Imaging and patented the device. In 2011 Iddan won the European Inventor Award, celebrated for revolutionising the ability to diagnose and treat gastrointestinal disease (EPOfilms). As of 2015, one-point-seven million patients had used the device in hospitals around the world (Shamah 2015).

PillCam has undoubtedly enabled significant advances in gastro-intestinal imaging. Yet its widespread celebration in and beyond the Shimon Peres Center for Peace and Innovation emblematises how the device emerges from larger cultural imaginaries and generates particular orientations towards militarism. Iddan's narrative not only recapitulates tropes of technological triumphalism, framing militarism as the necessary precondition for transformative innovation. PillCam, as the following sections demonstrate, also brings to life certain fantasies of drone warfare as a vital, and thus virtuous, endeavour.

Militarised Biomedicine

That a weapons engineer could repurpose lethal technology as a biomedical device appears, perhaps, antithetical to widespread understandings of war as that which destroys human life. Yet drones are uniquely positioned in relation to biomedical logics and practices. As Grégoire Chayamou has written, drones, more than any other modern weaponry, are construed as distinctly humanitarian. Their use is justified not only on the grounds that, as automated killing systems, they save the lives of service members no longer deployed for on-the-ground combat. Their technological precision also, if only nominally, reduces the number of noncombatants killed on the battlefields of counterinsurgency warfare. Eyal Weizman echoes such claims; interviews with Israeli drone operators from the early 2000s demonstrate how military personnel frame drones as life-saving devices that in fact 'minimise slaughter' (2006: 193). Chayamou describes this logic as a 'necro-ethics', wherein a weapon used to maim and kill is justified on the grounds that it only maims and kills certain bodies, namely those enemy combatants identified, surveilled, and taken out through a purportedly precise targeted strike (2015: 136). Killing, under this rubric, is something that can be done with care (139).

If Chayamou and Weizman turn to ethical justifications of drone strikes, disentangling the 'paradoxically vitalist' logics of contemporary counterinsurgency, others have demonstrated how such logics shape the very strategies of drone warfare (136). Military generals in the United States, the United Kingdom, and Israel not only employ medical metaphors when celebrating successful 'operations', describing enemy combatants as 'tumors' excised through 'surgical strikes'. The United States Army's Counterinsurgency Manual, heavily influenced by Israeli war doctrine, analogises drone warfare as a tripartite medical procedure. First, 'stop the bleeding'; second, 'inpatient care – recovery', and finally, third, 'Outpatient care' or 'movement to self-sufficiency' (Gregory 2008: 40). Under this model, the population under attack is framed as a diseased body whose illness must be surveilled and eradicated: death becomes justified through recourse to the biomedical logics of immunisation (Bell 2012: 235). The army general is reconfigured as a surgeon who instructs drone operators to eradicate a malicious disease; the drone is framed as a medical device that can effectively annihilate the enemy; and the weapons engineer is tasked with developing the most effective means of targeting and killing while preserving the vitality of the social body writ large. Collateral damage, under this rubric, becomes a metaphor for a side effect, an unpleasant but vital component of drone operations.

As Allison Rowland has argued, comparing drone strikes to surgical procedures conflates 'technological superiority to virtue', eclipsing the more debilitating effects of drone warfare for those who live in spaces of constant war (2016: 614). Obfuscated from statistics of targeted killings are the millions displaced by counterinsurgency warfare, the not-quite-lethal injuries sustained by those living in the vicinity of drone warfare, and the grief for lives lost to targeted killings. Instead, as Colleen Bell writes, modern counterinsurgency 'evinces a politics of life' rendering death and destruction the necessary precondition of regeneration and vitality (2011: 34). Allegorising drone warfare to a medical procedure, Bell notes, 'draws on the authority and perceived objectivity of medicine to produce a charitable understanding of the purpose and function of counterinsurgency warfare' (36). Building on Bell's insights, Jennifer Terry argues such discursive representations function as allegories not only for military personnel carrying out such operations, but also for those living far away from the battlefields of contemporary warfare. The allegory of medical intervention, like all allegories, 'tells a story for the sake of presenting a truth' (2018: 39). The tax-paying publics urged to support such interventions are made 'to find comfort in thinking that these operations are actually forms of benevolence and care' (39). Beyond sanitising militarism of the actual destruction it entails, such allegories promote warfare as a virtuous endeavour. Like any medical operation, the drone strike is framed as the necessary precondition for future vitality.

Terry, drawing on others critical of drone warfare's biomedical lexicon, argues such discursive strategies militarise biomedicine, as biomedical logics are mobilised to justify and rationalise violence. PillCam's promotion at the Peres Center for Peace and Innovation, however, goes beyond such rhetorical strategies. In what follows, I demonstrate how biomedicine is not simply militarised through recourse to analogies and metaphors. Here, biomedicine and militarism are collapsed into one in the same endeavour as visitors are made to experience drone warfare as the condition of possibility of life itself.

Communion

Guided tours of the Shimon Peres Center for Peace and Innovation march, chronologically, through Israel's history. On the first floor, immersive displays showcase particular existential challenges and pivotal events that led to Israeli innovations in various fields: society and culture, health and medicine, agriculture and environment, and defence and security. The prized inventions of 'seventy years of innovation' are showcased alongside contemporary Israeli start-ups, like the GPS application WAZE. Holograms of key innovators personalise their own stories of enterprise and ingenuity – from historical figures like Shimon Peres and David Ben Gurion to contemporary CEOs, like Gavriel Iddan. If the first floor meditates on the challenges of the past and the potential of the present, by the time tours reach the second floor they enter the future. Here, visitors enter the Virtual Reality Tunnel, a long white tube illuminated with blue LED lights and lined with plush leather seats. Donning virtual reality headsets, they are immersed, immediately, into an individualised video game platform that plunges them twenty years into the future (see Figure 3.3).

Within the VR headsets, state of the art-surround features and computer-generated simulations transform visitor's arms and legs into robotic limbs. Through headphones, a generic female voice announces: 'In just a moment we will take you twenty years into the future, there you will explore solutions to the challenges of tomorrow. Some of the most important innovations were born and developed right here in Israel. Ready? Hold on tight!' For twenty minutes, visitors can experience how Israeli innovations have solved the pressing crises of climate change, an aging population, and global hunger. Visitors must gesture their robotic arms in the direction of the 'experience' they desire: an animated PillCam dances on the corner of the screen as one of five options. When selected, the visitor is seamlessly transported into the operating room of a standard medical institution. A white man in a medical coat and mask explains how PillCam will save an aging population from rising cancer rates by catching malignant bacteria in a portion of the gastro-intestinal tract never before imaged by medical devices.

The virtual reality experience begins when the presumed doctor launches PillCam into the mouth of a patient lying on a surgical bed in the operating room. The visitor immediately acquires the visuality of the drone-turned-medical device. For three minutes, visitors travel through the gastrointestinal tract of this now-omniscient patient, surveilling for malicious bacteria by swiveling their pill-head and eradicating toxins from the body by motioning their pill-arms. While in its present iteration, PillCam captures malignant cells on camera and allows operators to target disease through treatment, in this promised future the chain of command is collapsed. The visitor animates PillCam with lethal capabilities and PillCam animates the visitor with the redemptive power of biomedical technology. Each time malicious bacteria are successfully targeted and eliminated, visitors get a point, extending the patient's life chances.

In this way, the virtual reality experience brings the biomedical analogies subtending drone warfare to life. In counterinsurgency warfare, military personnel, tasked with purifying an imagined national body from a perceived territorial threat, aim remotely guided missiles at enemy combatants discursively construed as a disease to be eradicated. At the Shimon Peres Center for Peace and Innovation, visitors, tasked with purifying an imagined body from hostile viruses, kill malicious bacteria to immunise the patient and preserve their life-chances. Here, drone warfare is not simply discursively construed as a medical operation, as it is in counterinsurgency handbooks. Metaphor becomes literal as battle unfolds on a surgical bed in an operating room.

The Virtual Reality Tunnel's PillCam experience thus brings visitors into communion with the technologies displayed throughout the center: they don VR headsets and are reincarnated as a product of Israeli Innovation. As

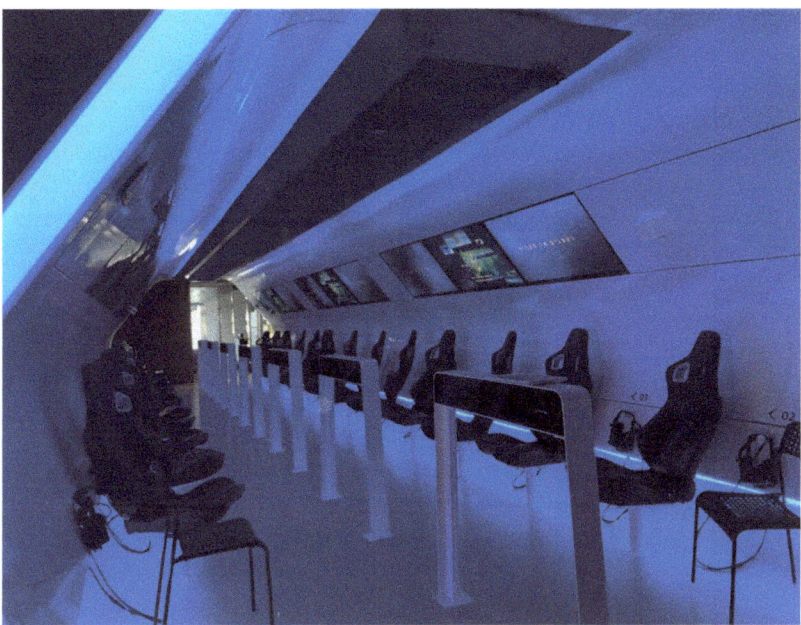

Figure 3.3. *A view from inside the virtual reality tunnel.*
Photo by Sophia Goodfriend. Courtesy of the artist.

PillCam, visitors embody a technological superiority that promises to preserve human-life. The body of the omniscient patient is a sacred body which, like Israel's national body, must be defended at all costs. The drone-turned-pill repurposes the lethal capabilities of Israel's high-tech security state, empowering visitors to turn a weapon of war into weapon of medicine. If humanitarian discourse justifies the violence of drone warfare through recourse to biomedical logics, the PillCam experience clouds any distinction between the two. Militarism and biomedicine are experienced as the same endeavour, as war is represented as the necessary precondition for life itself.

Conclusion

This chapter has presented PillCam as a technology that sutures biomedicine and militarism together through the promise of innovation. By historicising PillCam's development through the pivotal role technology has played in Israeli state-building, I have argued that innovation offers a distinct salve for the violence of warfare, in Israel and beyond. PillCam emerges from longstanding narratives of technological triumphalism in Israel. But more so, the device operationalises the biomedical logics that rationalise and justify contemporary drone warfare. At the Shimon Peres Center for Peace and Innovation, discourses of care and vitality comes to life as drone warfare is experienced as a biomedical procedure. Visitors are made to invest in violence, as militarism is presented as life's very condition of possibility.

The promise of innovation on display here is, however, as illusory as the VR platform that delivers technological communion. The reality of those living under the shadow of constant warfare interrupts any fantasy that counterinsurgency can regenerate and care for populations in places like the West Bank or the Gaza strip. Moreover, commentators in Israeli and international mainstream press have called attention to a disjuncture between Israel's self-branding as an 'innovative start-up nation' and the material conditions of everyday life for those living within the Israeli state (Goichman 2020). Overinvestments in defence and security sectors have led to long-standing underinvestment in public health, transportation, and education infrastructure. Such neglect only exacerbates socio-economic inequality within Israel. In 2017 *The Economist* went so far as to revise Israel's 'start-up nation' self-branding, suggesting the 'left-behind nation' might better account for ninety percent of the country left out of high-tech industries ('Israel's Economy Is a Study in Contrasts' 2017). Indeed, as of 2018, twenty-one-point-two of Israelis lived below the poverty line – the highest poverty rate of any OECD, (Organisation for Economic Cooperation) country (Einhorn 2018). This number is nearly doubled for Palestinian citizens of Israel – with forty-four-point-seven of the population living in poverty as of 2019 (TOI 2019). While in the occupied Palestinian territories, poverty and insecurity are far more endemic (Hever 2010). Despite the start-up nation's claims to miraculous self-transformation, investments in militarism only benefit a select few who circulate through elite military training programmes and enter Israel's high-tech industry.

As Israel's centrality in war and security industries garners robust critiques across academic and activist spheres alike, this chapter has turned the cultural imaginaries that sustain investments in militarism. PillCam's promotion at the Shimon Peres Center for Peace and Innovation offers a lens on to how the promise of innovation has long worked to obfuscate violence and justify warfare in the name of a better, more vital, future. Yet beyond the Center's walls, violence drags on throughout Jaffo's heavily policed Palestinian neighbourhoods. A short thirty-minute drive away, Israel's occupation curtails and confines Palestinian life behind border walls and checkpoints while sixty miles south, Israeli drones hum relentlessly over the debilitated Gaza strip. The concrete façade of the Center mars views of this colonial present. Inside, visitors are enclosed within a virtual reality where the pleasure of biomedical innovation congeals in the violence of a surgical strike. The only view out is towards the Mediterranean, beckoning visitors to the promise of uncharted territory lingering on the hazy horizon.

Works Cited

'1.8 Million Israelis, Half of Them Children, Live in Poverty – Government'. 2018. *The Times of Israel*. December 31.

Abu El-Haj, Nadia. 2001. *Facts on the Ground: Archaeological Practice and Territorial Self-Fashioning in Israeli Society*. Chicago: University of Chicago Press.

Azoulay, Ariella. 2011. 'Declaring the State of Israel: Declaring a State of War'. *Critical Inquiry* 37: 265-85.

Anderson, Warwick. 2006. *Colonial Pathologies: American Tropical Medicine, Race, Hygiene in the American Philippines*. Durham: Duke University Press.

Bell, Colleen. 2012. 'Hybrid Warfare and Its Metaphors'. *Humanity: An International Journal of Human Rights, Humanitarianism, and Development* 3: 225-47.

Chayamou, Grégoire. 2015. *Theory of a Drone*. New York: New Press.

EPOfilms. 2011. 'Gavriel Iddan-Pill sized Cameras for Wireless Endoscopies'. YouTube video, 5:46. March 17. https://www.youtube.com/watch?v=tSfPpO427fk.

Einhorn, Alon. 2018. '21.2% of Israeli Population Lives below the Poverty Line - New Report'. *The Jerusalem Post*. December 31.

Getzoff, Joseph F. 2020. 'Start-up Nationalism: The Rationalities of Neoliberal Zionism'. *Environment and Planning D: Society and Space* 38: 811–28.

Goichman, Rafaella. 2020 'Israel's Reputation as "Startup Nation" Is Fraying, Survey Finds'. *Haaretz*. October 11.

Gordon, Neve. 2008. *Israel's Occupation*. Stanford: Stanford University Press.

Gordon, Neve. 2011. 'Israel's Emergence as a Homeland Security Capital'. In *Surveillance and Control in Israel/Palestine. Population, Territory and Power*, edited by Elia Zureik, David Lyon, Yasmeen Abu-Laban, 153-71. New York: Routledge Press.

Graham, Stephen. 2010. 'Laboratories of War: Surveillance and US-Israeli Collaboration in War and Security'. In *Surveillance and Control in Israel/Palestine. Population, Territory and Power*, edited by Elia Zureik, David Lyon, Yasmeen Abu-Laban, 133-53. New York: Routledge Press.

Gregory, Derek. 2008. '"The Rush to the Intimate": US Counterinsurgency and the Cultural Turn'. *Radical Philosophy* 150: 8-23.

Gregory, Derek. 2011. 'From a View to a Kill: Drones and Late Modern War'. *Theory, Culture & Society* 28: 188–215.

Grumberg, Karen. 2011. *Place and Ideology in Contemporary Hebrew Literature*. Syracuse: Syracuse University Press.

Halbfinger, David, and Isabel Kershner. 2020. 'Israel, "Start-up Nation," Groans Under Strains of Growth and Neglect'. *The New York Times*. March 20.

Hochberg, Gil. 2019. 'From Shooting and Crying to Shooting and Singing'. *Contending Modernities*. https://contendingmodernities.nd.edu/global-currents/shooting-and-singing/

Hever, Shir. 2018. *The Privatization of Israeli Security*. London: Pluto Books.

'Israel's Economy Is a Study in Contrasts'. 2017. *The Economist*, May 18.

Israel Innovation Authority. 2019. 'Israel's Life Sciences Industry IATI Report 2019'. *No Camels*. July 2.

Khalidi, Laleh. 2012. *Time in the Shadows: Confinement in Counterinsurgencies*. Stanford: Stanford University Press.

Li, Darryl. 2006. 'The Gaza Strip as Laboratory: Notes in the Wake of Disengagement'. *Journal of Palestine Studies* 25: 38-55.

Machold, Ryes 2018. 'Reconsidering the Laboratory Thesis: Palestine/Israel and the Geopolitics of Representation'. *Political Geography* 65: 88-97.

Meiton, Fredrik. 2019. *Electrical Palestine: Capital and Technology from Empire to Nation*. Berkeley: University of California Press.

Mitchell, Timothy. 2002. *Rule of Experts: Egypt, Techno-Politics, Modernity*. Berkeley: University of California Press.

Parks, Lisa, and Caren Kaplan. 2018. *Life in the Age of Drone Warfare*. Durham and London: Duke University Press.

Pappé, Illan. 2007. *The Ethnic Cleansing of Palestine*. Oxford: One World Press.

Puar, Jasbir. 2017. *The Right to Maim: Debility, Capacity, Disability*. Durham: Duke University Press.

Rowland, Allison L. 2016. 'Life-Saving Weapons: The Biolegitimacy of Drone Warfare'. *Rhetoric & Public Affairs* 19: 601-27.

Rose, Steve. 2009. 'Peace Centre with a Panic Room'. *The Guardian*, February 17.

Sa'adi, Ahmad H. 1997. 'Modernization as an Explanatory Discourse of Zionist-Palestinian Relations'. *British Journal of Middle Eastern Studies* 24: 25-48.

Salamanca, Omar Jabary. 2016. 'Assembling the Fabric of Life: When Settler Colonialism Becomes Development'. *Journal of Palestine Studies* 45: 64-75.

Schwarz, Elke. 2016. 'Prescription Drones: On the Techno-Biopolitical Regimes of Contemporary "Ethical Killing."' *Security Dialogue* 47: 59–75.

Senor, Dan, and Saul Singer. 2008. *Start-Up Nation: The Story of Israel's Economic Miracle*. Toronto: McClelland & Stewart.

Shamah, David 2015. 'Pillcam's Inventor Regrets Sale of 'Biblical Tech Firm'. *The Times of Israel*. April 23.

Kuntsman, Ari, and Rebecca Stein. 2015. *Digital Militarism: Israel's Occupation in the Social Media Age*. Durham: Duke University Press.

Suffian, Sandra. 2007. *Healing the Land Healing the Nation: Malaria and the Zionist Project in Palestine 1920-1947*. Chicago: The University of Chicago Press.

Terry, Jennifer. 2017. *Attachments to War: Biomedical Logics and Violence in 21st Century America*. Durham: Duke University Press.

Veracini, Lorenzo. 2010. *Settler Colonialism: A Theoretical Overview*. New York: Springer.

Weizman, Eyal. 2008. 'Thanotactics'. In *Indefensible Space: The Architecture of the National Insecurity State*, edited by M. Sorkin, 325–50. New York: Routledge.

Wolfe, Patrick. 2006. 'Settler Colonialism and the Elimination of the Native.' *Journal of Genocide Research* 8: 387–409.

4

Parasitoid Drone [UAV/UAS/AWS/D-IED] // Naugahyde Barcalounger Boola-Boola

Tom Sear

ISR

This drop is a provocation and polemic: Naugahyde Barcalounger Boola-Boola – armchair philosophy targeting *Drone Dysphoria*.

DO-178C/DO-254

Academic cultures have developed a *Drone Dysphoria*. Academic diagnostics of the drone have inscribed the militarised UAV with a nonspecific unease which defies nosographic description, while normalising a conceptual dissolution into domestic drone anhedonia. Drone studies' dysphoric condition seeks to alleviate its sense of drone discomfort. Drone studies' conceptualisation of the drone around binaries is the area's coping mechanism for the sense of nonspecific unease the drone triggers. Externalisation as the basis for conceptualisation, which confines drone complexity to specifics, serves to ease an affectual intellectual overwhelm. Drone studies' heuristics overemphasise the spatial over the temporal; the visual and optic over the processual and the aural; the predominance of linear mechanistic and thermodynamic forces; formalism over improvisation; teleology over telemetry; *drone legalism* mechanisms of conventional jurisprudence and regulation over the irregular; the vertical over the horizontal grounded progressions; confuses and conflates borders and frontiers. Drone studies have constructed an object of extrinsic axiology wherein drone diegesis foreshadows a focused monocular line of sight narrative.

Academic drone dysphoria's conceptual coping mechanism of externalisation elevates an anthropogenic vision and internalises a Foucauldian panoptic consensus of the drone as a biopolitical condition. Such drone studies assume a fundamental ontology. Drone academic scholarship emphasises drone existence floating over essence wherein drone technical relations are

Heideggerian existentialist, eschatological, entropic energies of inevitable catastrophes devoid of cultural immanence and historical situation. Drones conceptualised as existential technologies – extended from Heideggerian philosophical assumptions to post-modern Foucauldian interpretations – emphasise power as externalised via linear lines to anthropocentric connections. *Foucauldronian* discourse analysis assumes symmetrical dominance and object singularity, not relations and the adversarial entanglement of war. Dysphoric drone discourse – ironically, perhaps – adopts a military bias, as it is unaware of its epistemic and ontological basis in a re-affirmation of the colonial and repression of the cosmotechnic.

JADC2

Academia has especially pathologised the military expression of the drone. Here the ontological nature of 'the drone' often assumes a specific phenomenological formulation. Generally, it is a western military-centric model of a Reaper or Predator drone post-2001. The result is a cultural understanding of the drone as both under and over determined simultaneously.

Of course, this is not a universal drone studies formulation. An academic consensus of the drone as an assemblage in strong drone theory has been emergent in recent years. Such an analysis troubles simplistic constructions and explores how the drone object is part of an assemblage of cultural imaginaries, lawfare, difference, affect, and postcolonialism. Critical drone studies have examined the drone from the perspective of post-structuralist, feminist, and queer theory, and exposed the importance of the drone and power, biopolitics, and perception. The drone has become a contested object in the process. This is partly because of the capacity of the object to connect and contain so many important issues of our era (Parks and Kaplan 2017). However, in scholarship the drone essentially remains an object, even when in a matrix. The assemblage is more often stated than interrogated. The convenience of the drone as an object of study in an assemblage or for an argument about the matrix of militarisation means the idea of the flying apparatus as singularity remains. Recent work has developed a concept of 'drone power'. Such an approach deconstructs simplistic biopolitical and statist drone associations. Drone power is a signal which 'migrates between biopolitics and resistance' (Fish and Richardson 2021). This contribution to drone studies differentiates how drone genealogies, performativities, and the nonhuman are co-constitutive of distributive 'sites' of drone power. But such existentialist distinctions also risk retaining a conception of the drone as an autonomous object and of human subjects as self-contained even when entrapped within discourses of 'drone power'. Overall, such meanings of drone assemblage are expressed as connections from straight lines of an exploded-view diagram, but not a schematic. While I recognise 'drone power' operates, I de-emphasise Heideggerian existentialist socio-technical assumptions and explore a biological and information-centric drone conception. I argue for para-sites of drone power.

LiDAR

'The Drone' is a system. A drone is a UAS. We need new lines of inquiry which reflect this awareness. We need a drone theory of telemetry and relays and less 'flightways' (Fish and Richardson 2021); one of oscillation, back and forth. Recent drone theory has considered connections, but not connectivity (Parks and Kaplan 2017). While drone verticality (orthogonality) has been troubled, nonetheless such theory perpetuates the drone as an individuated material object where a link – a connection – over space defines power. Drone connectivity, more complexly, however, is the quantification of an ongoing relation of communications observed over time. Drone agency derives from the ability of one entity to communicate with another. Therefore, the chapter posits an *information theory of the drone*. Theories of drone biopolitics as binary exclude a third component of the system. As Serres stated, 'there is no system without parasites' (2007: 12). This chapter – via parasite logics – argues for a more complex entity of a continuum of interactions between the inside of the drone and its outside. The process of drone individuation is more closely circumscribed by the way information operates through the drone than the material or spatial substrate. Drone dysphoria is a cognitive unease symptomatic of the uncanny reflexivity inherent to the process. The drone as a semi object and parasite has entered ecology, military, social, and academic cultures, compelling them to accept or reject the parasitic relation, but in all cases – the drone parasite changes them.

The parasitoid drone forces the issue. What we talk about when we talk about aesthetics and drones needs to be more clearly defined. The predominant representation of the US Reaper drone is dependent upon a linear, kinetic, thermodynamic form. This chapter does not avoid such forms but instead emplaces them within the specific historical context of the postmodern form of warfare specific to the Middle East 2001-2021. Exploring drone individuation, the chapter examines the adversarial entanglement of technology in warfare via the assemblage of the drone in relation to the Improvised Explosive Device (IED) of asymmetrical warfare of the Middle East. The drone is not just a vertical axis but a horizontal one. Exploring drone individuation which incorporates a *ground* both physically and philosophically assists with understanding the inside and outside of the drone.

The role of aesthetic perception in drone studies is important for how we understand militarised drones in another generalised way. The process of human perception as signals – which are understood at a level of abstraction – as ethics – has been under-interpreted in drone scholarship. Understanding a human perception of reality is fundamental to philosophical aesthetics in the Kantian sense of Judgement (Kant 2007). Kant when talking about aesthetics was considering what capacity for the conceptual understanding of an object a human could make (Kant 2007). This chapter understands aesthetics in the formal Kantian sense.

Much drone theory, as described, is unconsciously framed within the Kantian sense of the ineffable and the instrumental. Such an approach is a gimbal which ensures drone aesthetics is inordinate and tied to a specific Westernised form of ethics. Such ethical formulations from a Kantian conception of aesthetics have become a basis for ethical rules in Western thought. The reason for this is to integrate drone aesthetics with the praxis of conducting warfare. Kantian ethics is the fundamental basis of the Laws of Armed Conflict (LOAC). If we are overflying this Kantian territory, then we are also in an ethical space. Kantian conceptions of the relationship between perception and aesthetics informs post-enlightenment ethical frameworks. I'd suggest that much prior drone theory lacks philosophical ethical complexity, because of its location within a couple of narrow Kantian expressions. To grossly compartmentalise and generalise for the sake of argument, much drone scholarship is located within a Kantian instrumentalist mode (military drone as linear, tool, weapon) and ineffable (mysterious, spooky, sublime drones) aesthetic constructs. The resulting drone aestheticism is passive, fetishistic. Drone discourse is often a proxy for autonomy, a way to build an imminent bridge to a new fully Autonomous Weapons Systems (AWS) in the near future and deciding – with drones a kind of academic discursive template – for the new ethical and legal requirements for war. Without interception we risk keeping these drone conceptions aloft via a conceptual air-to-air refuelling, allowing them to overfly an emergent ethics of AWS. We need to resist such force multipliers. The risk is that we will take our poorly understood and reactive drone conceptions into a new war via a kind of academic 'probe-and-drogue' refuelling method. Current aesthetic readings I'd suggest assume a traditional Kantian 'correlationalist' model not best suited to a recursive computational conflict that is emergent. Such conceptions imply a 'human in the loop', or contextual use case discourse is sufficient to bring drones back down to Earth (Dwyer 2019).

We need a drone theory of telemetry and relays, not flightways. Telemetry empowers machine to machine connectivity, just as it delimits an anthropocentric visual horizon as the limit for drone theory. I suggest a new genealogy of speculative posthumanism which emphasises the 'Un' in Unmanned and less the 'Manned' after finitude, beyond the horizon: BVLOS (Beyond Visual Line of Sight) drone theory is required.

In addition, there is another para-site, a third component that binary-centric drone theory has excluded: warfare. Kantian aesthetics of ethics is vital, but so is consciously incorporating the role of Kant with the Clausewitzian theory of *warfare*. This chapter calls for a Clausewitzian gyroscopic adjustment. Clausewitzian irrationality introduces a further fractal third, that of nature. Clausewitzian war theory addresses the nature of war and war in nature. I suggest we explore the distinction of 'nature' in war via the drone. Extrapolating from the role of nature in the drone and the nature of warfare, I suggest that the ethnozoological co-option of chiefly – but not wholly – entomological adaptations into drone technology closes a feedback loop between biopolitical drone theory (Fish and Richardson 2021).

The drone has come to represent the ethical challenge of mutual – interconnected – ethics of human and machine. Ethical and ontological entanglements of the human with Otherness through the drone has created what I call the *parasitoid drone*. The parasitoid drone explores the node of drone dysphoria but takes the alien quality of technology and biological interface further. The UAV is *Unheimlich* and abject. Such Kristevian and Lacanian concepts of the specular are a telemetry of alienation, not just connection (Sear 2016). As the parasitoid drone is an uncanny presence, drone relationality is expressed via a media assemblage where the *Un* of its Unheimlich, the *Un* of the Unmanned, is an abject absence wherein the relationality of the parasite is emplaced. A drone studies dysphoria where abjection is exteriorised does so to avoid recursive loops. One of those is a failure to incorporate the nature of computation integral to the drone. A primacy of agencies composed of assemblages of connection and not connectivity avoids the role that the microtemporalities of disconnection play in communication. Drone theory risks misunderstanding the heuristic smoothness of computation. Computation is about discrete aesthetics, not the wave function analogue. Computational parasitoid drone logics thereby explore the ontological aesthetic impasse of incorporating the otherness of computation as a discrete process, and the problem of post-phenomenological temporality in the formulation of individuation (Ernst 2021; Fazi 2018, 2019).

MEMS CNA

Drones deceive.

Drone analysis has been binocular: both anthropocentric and ocularcentric. Scholarship has exaggerated the primacy of militarised vision in framing drone significance. Lethality and sight are overdetermined in drone analysis. Selective attention to one hominid-centric sensory drone modality has distorted drone aesthetics (Pautz 2021).

Perception – and therefore ethics – is more complex. Perception is information processing relationality between an inside and outside to formulate experience. Further, the computational parasitoid drone as a technical mediation apparatus adds further states of nonhuman perception, where who is perceptually parasitic upon whom may be more symbiotic than it first appears. It is the *visual* which has been overemphasised on drone sense and sensors.

TX

Drone is a sound. Drone is an aural sense. Drone is a sustained sound or tone/s (Sword 2022). 'Drone' has a meaning equivalent to – both – a male bee – *and* – the sound of buzz or hum which arises in proto-Indo-European language. Etymologically, entomologically, and onomatopoeically – 'drone' – was already entangled in military technological development culture that applied the nomenclature to aerial device controlled in the absence of human pilot in the craft. Remarkably, the sound of a small quadcopter drone of today is extremely sonically similar to a swarm of bees (Islam and Stimpson 2017). Drone syncopation of nature, language, semantic meaning through the sense of sound – not sight – is important because I make the case here that contrary to the broad scholarship it is 'noise' and nature intertwined in information theory which is important to understand drone transformation and change.

Noise + signal = information theory. The computation and calculation of information posits a generative aesthetics of sensors and sense-making as co-constitutive. This approach is not an aestheticisation of the drone, but where and how sense perception through and of the object of the human and machine labour produce a synthesis is knowledge (Fuller and Weizman 2021). Biological metaphors have enabled the ontological leaps of the drone. The drone arises from a particular analogous and analogue phylum of war life: specifically, a military-entomological complex executes these shifts. The drone moniker for the UAS/UAV arose from a Trans-Atlantic interwar interaction between British and US Navy engineers (Chandler 2020). The concept in translation became masculinised from the Queen bee of the British prototype to the male drone of the hive analogy in US formulations. The taxonomic cultural nomenclature drone within (male) 'nature' complexly integrated to the philosophically organicist notion of nature, was about the entomological (gendered) notion of 'the colony' (Parikka 2010). I suggest similar entomological transformations have taken place in the mutation into the archetypal post-2001 cultural and militarised drone form. One of these is incorporating the complexity of digital computational control as aesthetic discreteness, as opposed to prior analogue electro-servo mechanical first order cybernetic forms. The concretised second order cybernetic techno-social relations within the drone form – beyond cyborg – and its external relations now follow a parasitic logic.

Considering the drone within parasitic logic enables a third space of relationality to be explored. A drone as a UAV is an assemblage of subsystems composed of a triad. These are: a craft or form which moves through a state of matter(air), a C4 and computational core responsible for command, control and communication, and a hominid. A UAS would articulate such a system into other states of matter of levels of abstraction, but still a system with subsystems in relations which include a human. Typically, it is the absence of the human – the lack – which is the axial by which we focus analysis. This automatically infers a kind of negative space of an 'un'. But this 'un' is not an 'unreal', or virtualised space.

AMPXCO

The *Un* of the UAV/UAS defines the drone via negative space. What presence arises from the absence? Is the drone purely technical, or is it also a form expressed in nature? Either way, is a drone definition *a priori* from nature or do we project it upon nature? The instance to consider for relative 'droneness' which follows are triadic forms with subsystems.

P-Mode

What drone counterfactuals or thought experiments could be deployed to find the boundaries of droneness? Consider the host prey of the entomophagous parasites, the jewel wasp (*Ampulex compressa*) a drone (Arvidson et al. 2018). The parasitoid wasp targets the cockroach *Periplaneta americana* or *Periplaneta australasiae* to assist reproductive success. The wasp first envenomates the prothoracic ganglion of the cockroach temporarily and reversibly, immobilising its front legs. The wasp then digs around as a surgeon in the skull to locate and then deliver a sting to an extremely precise section of the subesophageal ganglionganglia of the cockroach to permanently eliminate the escape reflex of the neurotransmitter octopamine (Graf, Willsch, and Ohl 2021). After stripping the antennae of the cockroach, the far smaller wasp leads the roach by its antennae. The cockroach follows the wasp willingly to a protected burrow where the wasp blocks the roach in. The wasp lays eggs on the roach's legs. When the larvae hatch, they consume the still alive but immobilised cockroach, from the inside living as an endoparasitoid until the cockroach is consumed and killed. A mature wasp can then emerge by breaking out of the cockroach carcass and the burrow (Arvidson et al. 2018).

Consider then the parasitoid jewel wasp itself as a drone. Parasitoid wasps serve as hosts for the viruses polydnavirus (Weiss, Parzefall, and Herzner 2014). These viruses are multiple segments of double-stranded, superhelical DNA packaged in capsid proteins in which the full genome is endogenous and distributed within the wasp genome. The virus exists in a symbiotic state with the wasp, infecting the wasp while also preventing the host from killing the wasp eggs via immune suppression as the virus itself kills the host slowly (Jasso-Martínez et al. 2021). There is a parallel here with both information theory and UAV control subsystems. In this sense the polydnavirus is analogous to the Kalman filter incorporated in most small drones to mathematically provide position data variables: a kind of noise controlling subroutine process within a microcontroller (Condomines 2018; Lee, Lee, and You 2019).

AHRS/IMU

This ento-techno drone taxonomy example is designed to open an ontological question. The example explicates the importance of ontological individuation and for troubling the inside/outside divisions of the drone as autonomous systems. The reason for destabilising drone theory is to situate the drone more precisely in an era where epistemic insecurity is itself the armature in which information warfare spins. I suggest that the drone exists as symbiont within a military ecology where overlap may occur typologically.

Misconceptions of nonmilitary academic and popular mediatised analysis can occur where concepts are insufficiently delineated. For instance, weapons and sense systems on the military drone can be in a phoresis: where the smaller subsystem is carried by the drone, or in a mutualist dependency when intertwined to defend or avert against a missile strike against the drone. Conceptual precision of linear, thermodynamic, teleological drone elements is important because goal direction and teleology is the way automated weapons are best defined.

PWM

The year 2021 saw the drone figure in a broader future-orientated debate and formulation of norms and law concerning automation in warfare. In December 2021, the United Nations Convention on Certain Conventional Weapons did *not* agree to a resolution with reference to Automatic Weapons Systems (AWS) and/or Lethal Automatic Weapons Systems (LAWS). A key – but separate – report from a warzone concerning drones to the UN had earlier become a 'star witness' in the Convention decision process. In March 2021, a report to the UN had quoted a 'confidential source' that in 2020 during the Second Libyan Civil War, Libyan government targeted Haftar Affiliated Forces (HAF) with Turkish-made Kargu-2 ('Hawk 2') 'without requiring data connectivity between the operator and munition' (United Nations 2021: 148). This report outlined a possible drone violation of the LOAC. At the very least, the report implicated an instance of drone/AWS elision as a distinct UAS complication of the Law of Armed Conflict (LOAC).

This report was a kind of parasite to the staider Convention submission. National governments provided formal definitions to the UN of AWS in relation to International Humanitarian Law (IHL). The Kargu-2 issues enabled a more emotive debate. Politicised organisations were opposed to automated weapons systems, and the ICRC utilised descriptions such as 'slaughterbots' and 'killer robots', emphasising the role of 'human intervention' and the 'unmanned' in decisions over life and death (Future of Life Institute 2021). The resulting debate collapsed human-machine multiplicities inherent to the UAS form into an anthropomorphised singularity. Equally, the debate collapsed heuristic dichotomies which define sentient life. More broadly, an ethical context of discourse assuming a strong humanist position took place. The UN discourse primarily framed the debate through a moral lens of the Law of Armed Conflict (LOAC) (ICRC 1977). As a consequence, *drone legalism* became the key discourse to discuss the future of automation in warfare itself. Drones may in some populist and legal frameworks be perceived as devices of automation, but technically in constrained, limited ways. Populist *drone legalism* became an introject in a possibly misaligned jurisprudence-centric articulation of the control of future automated warfare risk. The question arises: if we have considered, or if we do consider, the drone in limitingly objectifying ways, what are the consequences for militaries, civilians, and future warfare, even with good intentions? I will now explain why parasite logic troubles these assumptions and why it matters.

ZIGBEE

The parasitoid drone analysis deconstructs the broadly assumed understanding of the drone as a singularity in linear anthropocentric, humanistic, and legalistic defined object and subject relations. The combative assumptions of LOAC, anti-LAWS, and pro-LAWS debates at the United Nations in 2021 were based in a broad Enlightenment moral consensus defining life and the 'unmanned'. 'Man' is a special, unique being superior in rationality amongst the species in this worldview. The drone – as it was in this 2021 debate – is also often framed as a coherent entity, even as an object in an assemblage, of sharply delineated inside and outside, as binary as the algorithmic code which, in these UN debates, is considered so alien to 'man'.

Drone theory might reflect upon another genealogy. This genealogy reconsiders all life as 'temporality and spatiality that produces subjects and objects, a genealogy of the temporality of becoming' (Grosz 2012). Grosz's reading of the genealogy of Uexküll, Simondon, and Ruyer articulates an understanding of the 'incorporeal forces' of matter's 'forces of potential sense, forces of virtual significance that living bodies, in elaborating their own ends or finality, affirm and develop'. It is via this 'concept of finalism, a goal-directedness, a design', whereby 'biology as a process of bodily form-taking that relies on the form-taking qualities of inorganic existence' (Grosz 2012). There is in this view a continuum of relations between nonlife materialism and life in a process of becoming. It is how the materialist inorganic and the organic interact in a control-independent, goal-directed reaction to environmental change which is the important process for defining individuation in biological life forms. The ethical control of a machine in a similar way in warfare is the most value-free way to consider automation of any kind from a human perspective. The chain of parasitic logic offers an insight to the relationality through this process.

POI

The drone has become a way to talk about autonomy. This is misguided. The March 2021 report to the UN on a specific military use of drones – as possibly autonomous weapons – in the debate at the Convention on autonomous weapons problematically freighted the aesthetic assumptions about drones I am troubling in this chapter within the broader AWS/LAWS debate. Unconscious adaptation of drone dysphoric heuristics in the LAWS debate has had unforeseen consequences. In defining LAWS, what is important to understand is whether in the drone object there is a continuum between automation and control, the automatic, and the autonomous. Aesthetic and mediatised assumptions from drone pop culture and academia are misplaced in such a debate about autonomy if uncritically examined. Not all drones are autonomous; but under some circumstances they could be. But just transferring a fear of drones into an AWS debate is a misrepresentation of what an 'autonomous' weapon is. The presence and intersection of three key articulations best define an AWS: adaptivity (internal rules choice), autonomy (state change), and interactivity (reflexive environment impact). It is the continuum of these factors together which is the only way to effectively define a value-free definition of the meaning of autonomy and thus an AWS (Taddeo and Blanchard 2021). The parasitoid drone formulation clarifies this distinction more clearly and allows the space for the third discourse of autonomy to be addressed. I take this further by exploring symbiosis and how drone parasitism is also creating bodily form by taking from another entity. Energy in parasitic relations is extracted from another thing rather than from the environment directly.

STANAG 4671

The parasitoid drone enables technologies of governmentality as para-sites of drone strikes to be incorporated as part of the inclusion of the dronic in the Clausewitzian triad of warfare. In turn this more complexly integrates the drone into possible future variations of targeting in IHL and LOAC.

Before 9/11, the US Air Force had no drones in its armoury. Subsequently, the United States congress authorised targeted killing with drone force in its formal declaration of the 'War on Terror': the drone has since become a 'technological response to terrorism' where the figure of the Terrorist and their targeting is the basis for the drone's existence (Chandler 2019: 822). As such, the drone 'strike' process is conceived as enmeshed with the administration of sovereignty and governmentality of western power. Typically drone theory considers the drone a subject and technique of Foucauldian articulation of state power and domination (Chandler 2020). The result is a theory of 'Drone Power' (Fish and Richardson 2021). Such theory takes Foucault's vision of Clausewitz at face value. Deleuze suggests in opposition to Foucault that war escapes an easy relation between war and politics and 'has as its object not war but the drawing of a creative line of flight' (Reid 2003: 61). Military-strategic thought, Deleuze argues, has a socio-epistemic origin which escapes such a neat correlation of war and political sovereignty. The 'war machine' Deleuze suggested is resistant to – not in the employ of – the formation of the state apparatus. The 'war machine' is 'of another species, of another nature, of another origin' to that of the state, despite the fact that the state absorbs and integrates its techniques. War is a mythical metamorphic 'milieu of exteriority' to the state. Deleuze argues that Clausewitz makes a distinction between wars of the state and the absolute acts of the nomad war machine (Reid 2003: 83). Conventionally postmodern and Foucauldian drone power theories decontextualise and generalise the Baudrillard and Virilio interpretations of the First Gulf War (1990-1991) – as an expression of statist political sovereignty as pure deterritorialisation – with a more imbricated, and yet elusive 'State', in the 'war machine' of the period 1993-2013. However, metamorphoses are in fact a defining character of such warfare (Hardt and Negri 2000: 347).

After 2001 warfare might be post-post-modern or even meta-modern in its oscillations of signal and noise, wherein modernity is a war within itself. Indeed, uncanny aesthetic conceptual reversals took place wherein states wanted to look like nonstate actors and nonstate actors sought to be perceived as states between 1993 and 2013 (Kilcullen 2020). In this way *jus ad bellum* and *jus in bello* were themselves hacked as aesthetic-ethical adversarial terrain manoeuvres. The 'view from [...]' in virtualised targeting positions and superpositions of subjectivity has encouraged drone dysphoric analysis. Deleuze draws here on Virilio's conception of the Transurban and war to unpack this aspect. While Virilio may be more Foucauldian than Deleuzian in many ways, Virilio's understanding of the return of the urban in the postcolonial wars of 1991-2021 spun around the Middle East as virtualised and real space in the era.

Even recent strong drone theory assumes the anthropogenic form of 'The Terrorist' as the primary target of the drone (Chandler 2019). However, the main target of the drone strike is infrastructure and technology. Statistically, the overwhelming majority of drone strikes are upon buildings and vehicles. Meanwhile, critical war theorists emphasise Baudrillardian disappearance, but the greatest dissimulation of terrorism is the concealment of human within machines and urban structures, not war's absence of dissolution in process. Drone dysphoria is a melancholy view of humans remote piloting semi-robots of reapers, but as 9/11 showed it is far easier to get a human to act like a robot than a robot to act like a human. 9/11 was already deconstructionist. Drone genealogy proper is from the suicide bomber transformation of terrorism: aircraft guided as missiles by suicide operatives into architectures of industry and military architecture. Human death was a by-product of spectacle.

The Twin Towers, and the 'War on Terror' expressed a 'double articulation (double pincer)' through the drone Stratum where form and substance become indistinct (Deleuze and Guattari 1987: 502). This was 'going beyond the organism, plunging into a becoming' because 'not all Life is confined to the organic strata' (503).

There is materialist media archaeology of the drone arising from terrorist originary acts which created a war ecology of trophic cascades. The Twin Towers of 9/11 paradoxically plunged into the becoming of an emergent ecosystem of war. The stratigraphic skyscraper columns – and their absence as enveloping fractal dust cloud – created a trophic vertical ecosystem of conflict: top-down drone trophic cascade, bottom-up cascade Cambrian explosion of Improvised Explosive Devices (IED). The aesthetic predominance of the unitary prey hunting General Atomics MQ-1 Predator /MQ-9 Reaper (UAV) is the phoenix which took flight from the transform of smouldering Tower ruins. Equally, a terrestrial swarm of suicide and improvised explosive terror rapidly expanded in a bottom-up trophic cascade. Whereas drone scholarship has emphasised straight lines, war ecology is one of feedback loops and non-linear dynamics.

As Parks indicates, circulations predominate in US drone targeting decision processes (Parks 2017: 141). Parks's analysis of a US DoD targeting diagram as a simple cyclical form is, however, used both out of context and without depicting granularity. Parks highlights the role of circumlocution in such cycles of return. But Parks's rhetorical, critical, return is one of closure, which sacrifices and encloses a far more insidious, productive fractal escalation of recursive power. Recursion is not closure. Recursive power is productive. It is the ontology of recursive loops – real, but not represented in the diagram Parks deploys – which spiral *off*, and fractally, *within* the process Parks's analyses which inform what is novel and significant in drone targeting decision chains (Dwyer 2021). Computational decision loops are a new, unknowable, and emergent form of warfare. Parks's argument is circular. Parks's cosy conclusions are symmetrical, enclosed. Recursive drone decision chains are part of an emergent geometry of warfare. Computational recursion loops adversarial hominids and the inhuman into a xenotic morphological topology of techno-geographic outside (Sear 2020).

CN3

Geometries of asymmetrical and broken symmetries of postmodern warfare demonstrate the third – xenosis – space of the para-site. The asymmetrical advantage of the predator UAV is what makes the drone such a stark object of warfare and aesthetics analysis. The military drone is certainly lethal. But it is not the only new weapon species assemblage which the postmodern era of warfare has spawned: the IED was responsible for the majority of coalition casualties in Iraq and Afghanistan.

The IED and the drone are entangled in a negative feedback loop of mutually assured deconstruction. Consider the IED (Improvised Explosive Device) and the drone as a new relational identity of symbiosis: the *D-IED*. The kinetic apposite of the predator drone is the IED. One high tech, one low tech. Both are loitering weapons. Both are teleological agents associated with human controllers. The IED and drone exist in a superposition of entanglement. On the one hand, the IED is the drone's asymmetrical 'Evil Twin': the drone is high tech, the IED is low tech. Equally, the IED is in symmetry with the drone: both bring death and injury. Both weapons loiter. Both are weapons that wait for their prey. Both are blind. *D-IED* 'eyes' are equally human assemblages of intelligence and long observation elsewhere in time and/or space. Both are forms latent with kinetic potential and are then triggered – initiated – by the physical presence of the Other. Both are entangled in autobiography as they are anonymous. Both are potential ontologies of the accidental and the potential error. Both are narratives of the fragmentary, the explosive, nonlinear in effect.

One side of the techno-social sophistication assemblage of D-IED fear does not have a monopoly on monstrosity. Indifferent transformations of trauma are shared potentially by each platform and are each other's counterpart in their respectively hidden element of air or earth. IEDs and drones are both tangles of constructed electromagnetic spectrums of destructive, explosive ruptures and high velocity metallic punctures of bodily flesh.

Humans walk careful labyrinths in response to both IED and drone. The IED is stationary, the drone in constant motion but human movement is triggered, nonetheless. Both the drone and the IED are agents of temporal becoming with the environment as they slow the capacity of other agents to control and move in space. If the drone is simplistically a Foucauldian panoptic measure, humans changing their internal regulations in response to *overwatch*, so the IED crudely does so with *underwatch*, beneath the earth not in the sky. Inversely IED invisibility is nonvision, which is also biopolitical in terms of power, like the drone. Equally, though in a parasitism of the human, the IED maker reproduces the IED – plants, observes, and monitors – its activity with care. Simultaneously the IED planter and the drone operator are panoptic human agents for the apparatus which is parasitic of them – as *D-IEDs* benefit from an extraction of their energy.

BARMA

Parasitic logics introduce the importance of temporality as well as space defining drone power. In informational-temporal terms the tactical effect of the IED and drone are similar. In military terms the IED operates as 'Block' effect to slow travel of a military section through a space, just as the drone above moves freely where air power is dominant, it is designed to slow and impair insurgent movement on the ground. But the process is one of feedback because the most effective way to reduce IED effects is dronic overwatch and identification when a device is being laid or investigated. These are the feedback loops dynamically akin to ecological systems. 'The IED is not a thing', Grove asserts, instead the 'IED is a condition of possibility present in almost all contemporary life; IEDs are native inhabitants of a world of global relations and things that hover on the edge between tool and weapon' (2019: 117-8). Grove suggests IEDs are an object 'at once technical and geographical' (119). This latter phrase also describes well the military drone post-2011. Where the drone has *Kill Chains*, the IED always has *Daisy Chains*. The drone and the IED operate in a parasitic chain with each other: the species of *D-IED*.

CNPC

The *D-IED* has demonstrated how rapidly a war ecology has evolved from 2001 to 2021. The drone also has its own individuated place in that ecology. Drawing upon Serres's theory of the parasite I suggest that the drone is entangled with parasite logic (Braune 2020; Serres 2007). Conceptualising the drone via the parasite enables the asymmetrical interruption of drone aesthetics to be explored through a relationality of system boundaries. The parasitic *noise* of the drone's aesthetics as a third space enables progression beyond a Kantian and neo-Kantian perception of the relation between – conception of a drone as a singularity – and as one that is understood as a multiple aesthetic-ethical entity. Deleuze and Guattari allude to this nonhuman turn in metaphysics in the example of the wasp and the orchid. A specific orchid flower deceptively imitates a species of female wasp encouraging repeated mating from the male of that species to spread pollen from flower to flower. This co-option, Deleuze and Guattari argue, is a process of 'becoming'. The symbiotic dyad of wasp and orchid is a multiplicity whereby virtuality degrades unity as it produces coherent assemblages which are expressed aesthetically as rhizomic. The *D-IED* has this quality of relation. This analogy of assemblage introduces Serres's idea of parasite, but his version extends it. Serres is similarly post-structuralist in his goal with parasite logic but offers a ternary – information theoretic – understanding of power relations which is useful to drone theory. Serres argues that communication between entity A and B requires an intermediary which is noise. While seemingly a distraction, this third space is essential to the system. This third interruption is an 'uninvited guest', simultaneously adjacent (a para 'site'), as it is an unequal exchange (it takes), and in this taking it irreversibly transforms the triad, creating a temporal differentiation – a history – as it does so. Parasitic power is relative to the position of a parasite in a chain where power is adaptation and innovation to be in the best position – the last in the chain. Topological power relations are expressed in drone parasitic chains. Al-Qaeda created a parasitoid assemblage of human suicide pilots, terrorists who in turn parasitically exploited the vulnerability of the aircraft system which flew planes into buildings in 9/11. September eleventh was a para-site of topological power transference. Terrorism topologically exploited an open subset of adjacency to create an ecological niche for the insurgence of drone form. Mathematically, topology incorporates the spatial relations of subsets which inform the larger continuous abstract space. Topologically, emergent drone supremacy was an equivalent co-homology of 9/11 tower terrorist paracompact manifold collapse. The suicide pilots of 9/11 collapsed the space between Manhattan and the Middle East, articulating an interface for drone intersection. The military drone aesthetic form undertook maturation and reproduction within US military systems and a phorotic migration within the 'War on Terror' in a third space of Middle East conflict which exploits a parasitic niche in physical boundaries of liminal national border zones both below on earth and in the air. The drone then is parasite just as it is a para-site, a space of adjacency. The specific relation between the IED and the drone is also a symbiotic host and parasite relation: the drone necessitates the IED and the IED necessitates the drone within a triad of warfare entangling humans and nonhumans.

To date, aesthetic readings in drone studies unconsciously mis-apply the ethical component of aesthetics to perceptions of the drone, and to a particular situational place of the drone within warfare ethics. Aesthetics – via perception – incorporates a more abstract discussion of teleology. Drone interception impels a parasitic logic of perception. To Grosz, 'perception requires an external perspective, and in many cases, it requires actual physical distance, as in the case of seeing and hearing; it addresses objects that can be positioned side-by-side; and it requires a delimitable field within which these objects are positioned' (Grosz 2012). The preposition para- (πᾰρᾰ́), then, is: the potentiality which arises or is generated aesthetically by the drone as 'alongside', as *para*-site? Or, more precisely, the relational question is to consider the *para*-dronic within an ecology of warfare that is not delimited to representation, nor to optic-centric forms of cognition which are simply mediations – signals – of affect. Dronic perceptual discernment is not prosthesis but catalysis of the ethics of social relations: parties change themselves as they expel or incorporate a drone intercept.

The *paradronic* catalyses information complexity. The *paradronic* also catalyses the rate of complex change. I wish to emphasise the role of temporal informational theory in framing the drone debate rather than solely those of space and power. Conceptions of drone individuation in studies which unconsciously use a traditional Enlightenment empirical taxonomy imbricate a traditional ethical entrapment for the drone. I wish to consider drone individuation of, and its delineation as, a life/nonlife form via recent temporally defined information theory approaches – which can deploy parasitism to generalise the drone in war – and the law of war (Krakauer et al. 2020). An information theoretical approach enables the inclusion of temporality's role in defining what is an individual technical object such as a drone. Such spin of angular momentum enables the drone to escape the entrapment of a

Heideggerian phronesis as a necessary basis for praxis of the human-machine assemblage. Instead, a Deleuzian aesthetic perception would consider the drone as an incorporeal surface of objects which provides a sense of internal frames from a perception of an outside. Such an approach – beyond existentialism's essentialist straitjacket of 'Being' as rigidly defined – is more conducive to more fluid human-machine interactions. Therefore, an individuation of life forms, the parasite, and the UAS as an object, are relational in informational and temporal, rather than existential, frameworks. Paradoxical complexities of drone power are not obscured but articulated at parasitoid border zones. Drones transgress borders of nation states and create a new site of governance, but moreover it is their parasitic relation to the co-constitutive inhuman in their sense of being which troubles notions of autonomous nonhuman objects and live subjects. Parasitic relations reveal the uncanny animations of subject and object divisions that drones prefigure. Grosz argues life is to be understood as a complex paradox of idealism and materialism, both outside itself whereby 'being-otherwise', and that 'becoming-other' is a reflexive teleology (Grosz 2012). Applying this conception to the drone enables a complex understanding of drone evolution from the period starting with 9/11 in 2001 to 2021, when the drone was co-opted in an uncritical deployment as pre-paradigm animate form of autonomy at the 2021 UN AWS LOAC deliberations.

Headless Mode

The drone is a remora of war. Drone phoront commensalism has not only travelled *with* postmodern warfare but has a developed a niche *of* consumer-resource interactions systems. This chapter argues for a parasitoid perception of drone evolution from 2001-2021. A parasitoid drone view locates the drone form as recursively nested within an interactive process of evolution over that era. The drone is a phoresis with post-modern warfare; the drone 'travels with' warfare. The drone is deployed within a discursive phronesis. Drones challenge and prey upon ethics, law, and the era of warfare. Beside warfare drone phoront niche has created a new ecology for ethics of conflict. Recursively drone fires catalyse an emergent *forensis* (Latin for 'pertaining to the forum') of automation and warfare in 2021 (Franke and Weizman 2014).

On the eleventh of September 2001, parasite logics and swarm topologies enabled aircraft infrastructure to be exploited from within. In the subsequent ecological shock, the military drone is a parasite which has exploited a niche to perpetuate and evolve itself, within twelve months, spawning its symbolic progeny of civilian quadcopters. Targeting the infrastructures of terror, the IED and suicide agent then embedded itself within the infrastructure that the drone created to parasitise, redirecting resources and support to its own perpetuation from 2001-2021. Now as warfare changes again and accelerates to autonomy, the drone has insinuated itself as a simulation of that assemblage to avoid being parasited itself. However, if we deploy Serres's mode of analysis, we can also more easily see the relationality of the drone even within its own internal agents of parasitism in subsystems. This will assist in defragging more effective ways to understand a new form of ethics for drone warfare and even AWS – in the emergent era of the inhuman in informational xenowarfare.

Works Cited

Arvidson, Ryan, Victor Landa, Sarah Frankenberg, and Michael E. Adams. 2018. 'Life history of the Emerald Jewel Wasp Ampulex compressa.' *Journal of Hymenoptera research* 63: 1-13.

Braune, Sean. 2020. *Language Parasites: Of Phorontology*. Baltimore, Maryland: Baltimore, Project Muse.

Chandler, Katherine. 2019. 'Making Terrorist Targets: Techniques of Power in the Horn of Africa from Drones to Anti-Terrorism Laws'. *Interventions (London, England)* 21, no. 6: 821-37.

Chandler, Katherine. 2020. *Unmanning: How Humans, Machines and Media Perform Drone Warfare*. New Brunswick: Rutgers University Press.

Condomines, Jean-Philippe. 2018. *Nonlinear Kalman Filter for Multi-Sensor Navigation of Unmanned Aerial Vehicle: Application to Guidance and Navigation of Unmanned Aerial Vehicles Flying in a Complex Environment*. Amsterdam: Elsevier.

Deleuze, Gilles, and Félix Guattari. 1987. *A Thousand Plateaus: Capitalism and Schizophrenia*. Translated by Brian Massumi. Minneapolis: University of Minnesota Press.

Dwyer, Andrew C. 2019. 'Malware ecologies: a politics of cybersecurity'. PhD diss., University of Oxford.

Dwyer, Andrew C. 2021. 'The Unknowable Conflict: Tracing AI, Recognition, and the Death of the (Human) Loop'. *Hague Cyber Norms Artificial Intelligence and International Conflict in Cyberspace*. The Hague, Netherlands.

Ernst, Wolfgang. 2021. 'Existing in Discrete States: On the Techno-Aesthetics of Algorithmic Being-in-Time'. *Theory, Culture & Society* 38, no. 7-8: 13-31.

Fazi, M. Beatrice. 2018. *Contingent Computation: Abstraction, Eexperience, and Indeterminacy in Computational Aesthetics*. London: Rowman & Littlefield International.

Fazi, M. Beatrice. 2019. 'Digital Aesthetics: The Discrete and the Continuous'. *Theory, Culture & Society* 36, no. 1: 3-26.

Fish, Adam, and Michael Richardson. 2021. 'Drone Power: Conservation, Humanitarianism, Policing and War'. *Theory, Culture & Society* 39, no. 3: 3-26

Fuller, Matthew, and Eyal Weizman. 2021. *Investigative Aesthetics: Conflicts and Commons in the Politics of Truth*. London: Verso.

Future of Life Institute. 2021. 'Slaughterbots'. YouTube video, 5:27. December 1. https://www.youtube.com/watch?v=9rDo1QxI26o.

Franke, Anselm, and Eyal Weizman. 2014. *Forensis: the Architecture of Public Truth*. Berlin: Sternberg Press.

Graf, Stefan, Maraike Willsch, and Michael Ohl. 2021. 'Comparative morphology of the musculature of the sting apparatus in Ampulex compressa (Hymenoptera, Ampulicidae) and Sceliphron destillatorium (Hymenoptera, Sphecidae)'. *Mitteilungen aus dem Museum für Naturkunde in Berlin. Deutsche entomologische Zeitschrift* 68, no. 1: 21-32.

Grosz, Elizabeth. 2012. 'Deleuze, Ruyer, and Becoming-Brain: the Music of Life's Temporality'. *Parrhesia* 15: 1-13.

Grove, Jairus Victor. 2019. *Savage Ecology: War and Geopolitics at the End of the World*. Durham: Duke University Press.

Hardt, Michael, and Antonio Negri. 2000. *Empire*. Cambridge: Harvard University Press.

ICRC. 1977. 'Protocol Additional to the Geneva Conventions of 12 August 1949, and relating to the Protection of Victims of International Armed Conflicts (Protocol I), 8 June 1977'.

Islam, Raya, and Alexander Stimpson. 2017. *Small UAV Noise Analysis: Humans and Autonomy Laboratory*. Durham: Duke University.

Jasso-Martínez, Jovana M., Alexander Donath, Dieter Schulten, Alejandro Zaldívar-Riverón, and Manuela Sann. 2021. 'Midgut transcriptome assessment of the cockroach-hunting wasp Ampulex compressa (Apoidea: Ampulicidae)'. *PloS one* 16, no. 6: e0252221.

Kant, Immanuel. 2007. *Critique of Pure Reason*. Translated by Norman Kemp Smith. London: Palgrave Macmillan.

Kilcullen, D. 2020. *The Dragons and the Snakes: How the Rest Learned to Fight the West*. Melbourne: Scribe Publications.

Krakauer, David, Nils Bertschinger, Eckehard Olbrich, Jessica C. Flack, and Nihat Ay. 2020. 'The Information Theory of Individuality'. *Theory Biosci* 139, no. 2: 209-23.

Lee, Hyukwoo, Kyunghyun Lee, and Kwanho You. 2019. 'Postural Stabilization of Quadrotor using Extended Kalman Filter and Integral Sliding Mode Control'. *IOP Conf. Ser.: Mater. Sci. Eng* 630, no.1: 12002.

Parikka, Jussi. 2010. *Insect Media: An Archaeology of Animals and Technology*. Minneapolis: University of Minnesota Press.

Parks, Lisa. 2017. "Vertical Mediation and the U.S. Drone War in the Horn of Africa." In *Life in the Age of Drone Warfare*, edited by Lisa Parks and Caren Kaplan, 134-57. Durham: Duke University Press.

Parks, Lisa, and Caren Kaplan. 2017. *Life in the Age of Drone Warfare*. Durham: Duke University Press.

Pautz, Adam. 2021. *Perception*. New York: Routledge.

Reid, Julian. 2003. 'Deleuze's War Machine: Nomadism Against the State'. *Millennium* 32, no. 1: 57-85.

Sear, Tom. 2016. "Uncanny Valleys and Anzac Avatars: Scaling a Postdigital Gallipoli." In *Beyond Gallipoli: New Perspectives on ANZAC*, edited by Raelene Frances and Bruce Scates, 55-82, Melbourne: Monash University Press.

Sear, Tom. 2020. 'Xenowar dreams of itself'. *Digital War*.

Serres, Michel. 2007. *The Parasite*. Translated by Lawrence R. Schehr. Minneapolis: University of Minnesota Press.

Sword, Harry. 2022. *Monolithic Undertow: In Search of Sonic Oblivion*. Nashville: Third Man Books.

Taddeo, Mariarosaria, and Alexander Blanchard. 2021. *A Comparative Analysis of the Definitions of Autonomous Weapons Systems*. University of Oxford.

United Nations. 2021. 'Letter dated 8 March 2021 from the Panel of Experts on Libya established pursuant to resolution 1973 (2011), addressed to the President of the Security Council'. https://undocs.org/S/2021/229.

Weiss, Katharina, Christopher Parzefall, and Gudrun Herzner. 2014. 'Multifaceted defense against antagonistic microbes in developing offspring of the parasitoid wasp Ampulex compressa (Hymenoptera, Ampulicidae).' *PLoS One* 9, no. 6: e98784.

Part II: Culture

5
Everyday Militarisms: Drones and the Blurring of the Civilian-Military Divide During COVID-19

Caren Kaplan

On February seventh, 2020, a seemingly trivial hoax pointed to the convergence of two apparently unrelated phenomena – the global circulation of a viral pandemic and the emergence of new industrial, governmental, and consumer markets for the technological assemblage often referred to as 'drones'. On that day, Jan and Dave Binskin, an Australian couple on a holiday cruise, found themselves quarantined aboard their ship as COVID-19 began to sicken passengers and crew. Bored, they claimed on a social media post that they had received a couple of cases of wine delivered by drone. The post went viral, generating news stories and the proverbial fifteen minutes of fame for the Binskins until it was debunked several days later by their own admission (AFP 2020).

The Binskins' Facebook post was hardly the first time that drones were noticeable in public discourse since the COVID-19 virus was first officially reported in China in December 2019. Perhaps most obviously, drones played a significant role in documenting the shock of the first waves of social change as the virus spread around the globe in the first months of 2020. Aerial photography of cities in lockdown, often enhanced with added soundtracks of gloomy music, crowded social media, offering images of normally busy streets emptied of traffic congestion. Yet, the spectacle of 'emptiness' revealed by drone flyovers masked the presence of numerous 'essential workers' who could not quarantine at home, as well as the homeless population along with the animals that were observed moving around in suburban and urban spaces (Zimmerman and Kaplan 2020). Rather than offering a way to 'see all', this drone imagery provided what we know to be the drone's eye view; highly selective, incomplete, and tied to discrete genealogies and visual conventions – many of them linked to the operations of air war and the targeting of groups identified through asymmetric power relations (Gregory 2011; Kaplan 2018; Parks 2018; Richardson 2018).

The Binskins' post and surrounding commentary highlighted possible new relations of distance and proximity engendered by the pandemic: relations that point to the intensified malleability and mobility of the kinds of drones now available to a wider array of customers and users than ever before. The movement of drones through cultural, governmental, and military practices during the first months of the COVID-19 pandemic demonstrates the profoundly unequal modes of power at work in the current moment of deepening authoritarianism and state violence, blurring or disturbing the boundaries between military and civilian. Thus, although Dave Binskin's first Facebook post took a jocular tone, it also raised questions about territorial boundaries, national security, and neoliberal industrial logistics under pandemic conditions: 'Naked Wine Club your [sic] incredible just got the First Drop Thank God For Drones the Japanese Coast Guard did not know what the Fuck was going on' (AFP 2020). This jokey comment speaks to the fantasy that a small hobby drone can not only relieve the boredom and inconvenience of quarantine for wealthy tourists, but that this kind of delivery service can evade or at least confound the territorial boundaries of the nation state and its security agents – in this case, the Japanese Coast Guard.

Reorganised only twenty years ago under the authority of the Ministry of Land, Infrastructure, Transport, and Tourism, the Japanese Coast Guard has seen its purview and responsibilities greatly expanded in recent years to include extensive patrolling of the enormous marine zone that surrounds Japan. To aid in this task the Japanese Coast Guard conducts its work by drone as well as by ship, plane, and helicopter. Until very recently these drones were produced in China. However, the Japanese Coast Guard announced in late 2019 that it would stop using Chinese-made drones due to concerns about 'information security' (Pollmann 2019). Not coincidentally around the same time, General Atomics – the energy and defence corporation that is headquartered in San Diego, California (and the producer of the Predator and Reaper drones), released accounts to the press of tests of the maritime version of the Reaper, nicknamed the 'SeaGuardian', for the Japanese Coast Guard (Ryall 2020).

The twinned examples of the Binskins' seemingly innocuous fantasy about drone wine delivery and General Atomics's sale of military-grade unmanned aerial vehicles to the Japanese Coast Guard illustrate some of the ways that 'everyday militarism' operates 'hidden in plain sight' (Kaplan, Kirk, and Lea 2020). The coast guard is an ambiguous entity, evoking the blurry line between police and military that plagues and arguably maintains the modern nation state. The Binskins' prank also evokes the strained political economy of consumer drone delivery – still a wistful dream even for giants like Google and Amazon – that aims to emulate the supply chains and logistics inaugurated by modern militaries (Bélanger and Arroyo 2016; Cowen 2014). The intersection of a global viral pandemic with shifts in the production and marketing of drone technologies offers the opportunity to trace power dynamics at work in transnational capitalism and neoliberal governance, particularly in relation to security and policing practices. In the midst of the terrible costs of a public health crisis, drastic inequities in wealth and social services are rendered in stark relief. In a world of transnational industrial and cultural circulations, deepening forms of racism and gender-based discrimination and greater income disparities along with rising authoritarianism generate dangerous vulnerabilities to rapidly spreading diseases such as COVID-19 (Diaz and Mountz 2020). However, drones do not just move through this landscape of inequality and precarity. They participate actively in creating the world in pandemic.

Everyday Militarisms and the 'Good Drone'

The Binskins' joke about the Japanese Coast Guard in the early days of a virulent pandemic troubles any rigid separation between leisure, commerce, policing, and the military, prompting a consideration of some of the key operations and characteristics of drones in the current moment – malleability, mobility, and ubiquity. These 'hidden in plain sight' elements both produce and disturb the dynamics of everyday militarisms. There is no question that drones today are highly malleable, the apt term applied recently to the technology by Anna Jackman (2019). Indeed, drones are extremely adaptable; they take many shapes, are differentially scaled, and their mobility and distance technologies not only bring them to seemingly infinite numbers of locations and uses but inalterably changes those sites and ways of doing and being. Drone assemblages are not just innocent or inert objects; they are active, networked participants in world making. As Lisa Parks puts it, '[...] they rewrite and reform life on earth in a most material way' (Parks 2018: 147).

If drones were first primarily associated with the asymmetric air wars of the last twenty years, they have become rapidly integrated into most sectors of society across a wide variety of scales and sites from battlefields to agricultural fields, from DIY hobbyists to oil pipeline protestors, from delivery of medical supplies to cinematic innovation, from wedding photography to human rights projects. This rise of what Kristin Sandvik and Maria Jumbert have termed the 'good drone' has inaugurated an industry that generates billions in profits for companies like DJI, Parrot, and Intel (Sandvik and Jumbert 2017). Funding for drone research (military, consumer, and industrial) at universities and their linked 'innovation incubators' (which support start-up ventures) is a relatively new, lucrative arm of the expansive post–Second World War military-industrial complex (Der Derian 2001; Napolitano 2016). The malleability, mobility, and ubiquity of a wide range of products and operational assemblages under the term 'drone' opens up many possible meanings and practices even as it masks differences that matter.

This growing ubiquity of drones has led to what Michael Richardson has referred to as 'drone culture', an 'ambivalent, intimate, and unsettling confluence of technologies, practices, discourses and affects' (Richardson 2020: 2). Indeed, the intensified integration of smaller unmanned aerial systems into everyday life begs the question of militarism; that is, the ways that society becomes structured by, for, and with military agendas and practices. Obvious forms of militarism can be observed in security discourses and operations, military recruitment and deployment, and nationalist patriotism taken to xenophobic extremes. In a militarist society, funding for homeland security as well as for overseas deployment is rationalised through the threat of war or outright warfare. But a more insidious and pernicious form of militarism that legitimates more overt operations takes quotidian, even banal, forms; the seemingly 'hidden in plain sight' institutional infrastructures of production, logistics or distribution, and cultural practices that create hegemonic consent to military dominance in supposedly nonmilitary social life (Kaplan 2006; Kaplan 2018; Kaplan, Kirk, and Lea 2020).

If we view drones as highly adaptive and differentially scaled assemblages that rely on inter-related media infrastructures, materials, supply chains, and complex discursive similarities and differences, then we must trouble the distinction between 'good' domestic and 'bad' military drones. The very division between military and nonmilitary is a manifestation of everyday militarism, requiring the relentless burial of evidence of military or security concerns, ideologies, materials, and rationales in plain sight, as it were: a process that has become normalised through divisions between domestic and foreign, good and bad, and civilian and military. These binaries of everyday militarism primarily benefit the military as an operative arm of the nation state along with its security and policing operations. That is, the military garners ideological power and political legitimation from the appearance of its separation from civilian society – despite so much evidence to the contrary. And, concomitantly, civilian society becomes exempt from responsibility for military operations to the point that it does not have to recognise the influence of or connections to the military that are distributed throughout everyday life. The costs of this learned illegibility of militarism are exacted in examples like public health projects utilising surveillance drones through research university and metropolitan policing consortiums.

Hidden in Plain Sight: Drone Policing for Public Health

The malleability, ubiquity, and mobility of drones that operationalise the technology's everyday militarism has propelled an energetic collaboration between drone manufacturers, university researchers, and police departments as they have been pressed to improvise public health surveillance practices for the United States during the pandemic. Not surprisingly, DJI, the leading drone manufacturer that is based in China, leapt swiftly into action early in the pandemic, adding to their drones the capacity to measure body temperatures remotely and to broadcast social distancing messaging. Accordingly, the police department in Elizabeth, New Jersey ordered a fleet of five DJI Mavic drones to break up 'unsafe' public gatherings (Kelley 2020). Police or governmental representatives in many countries including China, France, India, and the UK also announced that they either were or would be using remote sensing devices, primarily drones, to conduct surveillance of body temperatures and to police social distancing in public spaces.

Unsurprisingly, then, in the third week in April, the police department in Westport, Connecticut announced with some fanfare that they would participate in a pilot programme co-organised by Draganfly, a Canadian small drone manufacturer, along with researchers at the University of South Australia. Seeking to differentiate themselves from behemoths like DJI, Draganfly emphasises 'artisan craftsmanship and technical prowess'(Draganfly 2020). Teaming up with Draganfly, Professor Javaan Chahl and his colleagues at the University of South Australia explained in a press release that their algorithmic software would enable drones 'fitted with a specialised sensor' to 'interpret human actions such as sneezing and coughing' and 'monitor temperature, heart and respiratory rates'. Professor Chahl, who also holds a position at the Australian Department of Defense, is quoted as saying that the technology was originally designed for use in war zones as well as in responding to natural disasters (Green Car Congress 2020).

Public health applications of autonomous surveillance technology provide useful case studies of militarism hidden in plain sight. The urgency of pandemic conditions demands creative solutions and prompts transnational scientific and industrial collaboration. As military research and development funding moves through university innovation labs and research institutes a kind of whitewashing takes place, normalising wartime research agendas and needs. Spin-off industries and start-ups disseminate many military technologies into consumer and industrial formats. The survival of small companies and start-ups along with their networks of academic counterparts and collaborators depends on finding a wider need for technology that was designed originally for a relatively narrow military purpose. The COVID-19 pandemic opened up opportunities for innumerable start-ups, small companies, innovation labs, research institutes, public health departments, and other interested parties to address a world-wide crisis, create new products and markets, and be linked to the aura that is often generated by new technologies. Accordingly, the Westport 'Flatten the Curve Pilot Program' promised to show just what the Draganfly drones could do in collaboration with the University of South Australia's expertise while positioning Westport as a community with a cutting-edge police force. The chief of police, Foti Koskinas, stressed in his department's press release that the pandemic 'has opened up a new frontier and urgent need for the use of drones', particularly in reducing risk for police first responders as well as extending services to remote areas, along with surveillance of social distancing compliance (Westport Police Department 2020).

To be fair, towns and cities all over the United States had been left largely to their own devices, literally and figuratively, since the Trump administration failed to institute a comprehensive approach to public health and safety in general and to the pandemic most particularly (Aratani 2020). Thanks to this chaos and confusion, infection and death rates in the US in April and May of 2020 were astronomical, particularly in the northeastern part of the country. As a result of high rates of commuter connectivity to urban areas like Manhattan, in mid-to-late April the small town of Westport was considered to be 'an early epicenter' of the virus in the state of Connecticut (Nickerson 2020). Yet, a mere two days after mobilising an enormous amount of press attention for the Westport pilot programme, the town announced that it had 'scrapped' its plan. Protests by local civil libertarians had arisen quickly. Alarmed by the surveillant powers of the proposed pilot programme, the American Civil Liberties Union (ACLU) released a statement that stated, in part:

> [...] Towns and the state should be wary of self-interested, privacy-invading companies using COVID-19 as a chance to market their products and create future business opportunities. Any new surveillance measure that isn't being advocated for by public health professionals and restricted solely for public health use should be promptly rejected, and we are naturally skeptical of towns announcing these kinds of partnerships without information about who is operating the drones, what data they will collect, or how or if that data will be stored, shared, or sold (McGuire 2020).

Not unreasonably, the ACLU position paper pointed out that even if the 'drone-based remote symptom detection technology is accurate', it probably cannot detect those who are infected who are asymptomatic. Perhaps most critically, no hospitals or medical associations asked for these kinds of high-tech surveillant tactics. In April 2020, hospitals in the US were still begging for adequate supplies of basic protective gear like disposable gowns and masks and were resorting to wearing layers of garbage bags. There was a severe shortage of coronavirus test kits and very little systematic public health contact tracing (Schwellenbach 2020).

The dire situation in the United States offered fertile ground for arguments for the use of so-called 'good drones'. The capacity of drones for distanced sensing operations and the tantalising promise of efficient accuracy suggested a tight fit between the marketing of small scale unmanned aerial devices and municipalities eager to find some kind of scientific approach to containing a virulent disease. Nevertheless, it is necessary to situate the desire for what Martin French and Torin Monahan term 'disease surveillance' in the context of a sharp intensification of military-style operations, particularly the thriving relationship between police departments and all manner of technologies that perform predictive and pre-emptive tracking, targeting, and regulation (French and Monahan 2020: 1; Wall 2016). This intensification is due in large part to Section 1033 of the National Defense Authorisation Act for Fiscal Year 1997 (H.R. 3230) which authorised the Secretary of Defense to 'sell or transfer excess military equipment' to domestic police departments (Delehanty et al. 2017: 2). Consequently, just after the first Persian Gulf War, a veritable avalanche of military-grade materiel started to flood local US police departments with assault rifles, grenade launchers, bayonets, airplanes, helicopters, and even tanks. This arsenal now includes situational awareness and predictive software and small drones. Concurrently, since 2001, the 'War on Terror' has debilitated civil rights in the US, inaugurating all manner of sensing and identification programs at airports and other transportation hubs. Biometric tracking, facial identification programs, data-mining, etc. have all become increasingly normalised and integrated into activities that blur the lines between civilian and military security practices.

While it is important to focus on the increase in predictive biometric surveillance practices, we cannot lose sight of how the pandemic era is undergirded by the massive infrastructure of air power in industrialised nations and the rapidly increasing flow of unmanned aerial devices from strictly military uses into not only consumer but security and policing applications of all kinds. Aerospace corporations and, particularly, consumer drone producers have identified a lucrative niche – metropolitan police departments. A recent Bard College study found that 'at least 1,578 state and local public safety agencies' have 'acquired drones' and that the majority of those drones are 'consumer or prosumer models' (Gettinger 2020). The growing dependence of border patrol and police on drone assemblages must be situated within the biopolitical 'long-arc' of airpower in relation to so-called 'small wars', as well as 'insurgencies, civil rebellions, labour strikes, prison uprisings', border crossings, and protests against authoritarian regimes (Kaplan and Miller 2019: 420). The ideological assertion of a strict division between the military and domestic police undergirds the 'violence work' of the state, as Micol Seigel would put it, and accelerates the normalisation of everyday militarisms (Seigel 2018).

Keeping all of this in mind, it was perhaps not bizarre, even if it was unfortunate, for small-town police departments to welcome the offer of 'disease surveillance' pilot programs. Surveillance technologies propose themselves as a modern and efficient method of assessing disease prevalence and as a tool for enforcing social distancing. But these surveillant assemblages are highly restrictive and oppressive, demonising and racialising subjects, reinforcing structural inequalities, even increasing anxiety or destabilising communities, while under-delivering vital resources or failing in the primary tasks of detection and pre-emption (French et al. 2018: 67; Gershgorn 2020). For example, as French and Monahan point out, while China has been praised for containing the coronavirus swiftly and definitively, they accomplished this feat by utilising the 'same heavy-handed techniques of surveillance-based control and containment' that they have used to intern Uyghur Muslims and others (French and Monahan 2020: 6).

'Game Changers': Shifts in Battle Spaces and Markets

Drones are big business. It is impossible to analyse the economic and social cost-benefit element of disease surveillance in general without taking into account the enormous push by specific industries and corporations for the integration of drone technologies into everyday life. An annual report issued by the Drone Industry Insights group in June 2020 offered the figure of forty-two-point-eight billion US dollars for the drone market by 2025, almost double the amount for 2020 (Schroth 2020). If restrictions on airspace continue to decrease, a report by a major finance group argues that the greatest area of expansion for drones is predicted to be in the commercial arena, particularly for 3-D mapping, delivery, inspections, data transmission, cinematic production, and video patrolling (Castellano 2020). The report concludes that drones that use predictive or prescriptive analytics will be 'game changers', eliminating the need for human drone pilots and increasing profit margins (Castellano 2020).

If even a fraction of the growth predicted by industry analysts takes place, we are still going to see a lot of smaller drones in the airspace around us. COVID-19 arrived at a moment when the drone industry was both expanding and contracting and, not incidentally, battlefield operations were also in flux. The growing ubiquity of drones and the marketing of increasingly affordable smaller units that can be purchased 'off the shelf' alters the power dynamics of security and military operations. For example, DJI Matrice drones loaded with C4 explosives were involved in the attempted assassination of Venezuelan President Maduro in 2018, while three large US drones armed with Hellfire missiles were key actors in the strike at Baghdad airport in January 2020 that killed Iranian General Qassem Soleimani (Dilanian and Kube 2020; Franke 2018). The first example reflects a growing trend by non-state actors to deploy modified consumer drones for war-like purposes. The second example illustrates the kind of targeted assassination programs that have become associated with the US military and its allies throughout the War on Terror. The larger, heavy, slow-moving military drones like the Predator are becoming increasingly obsolete as newer iterations that further blur the boundaries between military and nonmilitary move into widespread use.

Concerns about who operates what kind of drone and why emerge as nation states and municipalities increase funding for security and policing in an atmosphere of growing authoritarianism across the globe. The malleability, mobility, and ubiquity of the technology across scales and price points hails numerous actors and operators and further blurs any pretense of a hard line between 'good' and 'bad' drones or between military and nonmilitary arenas. Accordingly, as Anna Jackman puts it, the drone 'remains at once both a policing assistant and one to be policed' (2019: 367).

Changes in perceptions of threat and deterrence along with the evolution of contemporary battle spaces and securitised zones are shaking up what had become a 'traditional' drone industry. For many years, General Atomics dominated the market for large unmanned aerial vehicles. Their Predators and Reapers conducted surveillance and aerial strikes first in the Balkans and then in Afghanistan and the Middle East. Purchases of drones by US Intelligence and the Department of Defense constituted a large portion of General Atomics's sales but the drones were also sold to many other countries including the UAE and Turkey. While the aging Predator was officially retired from US Air Force service in 2018, it apparently came as something of a shock for General Atomics to learn that the Air Force has cancelled orders for Reapers after 2020 (Rogoway 2020). According to some analysts, this abrupt change reflects a growing realisation by the US Department of Defense that the Air Force will need vehicles that are faster, lighter, and able to evade air defences. The Reaper is now viewed as too easy to shoot down with contemporary surface-to-air missiles. As more countries produce or purchase their own drones, greater autonomous functionality and swarm capacities are growing priorities.

So, what is a behemoth like General Atomics to do? They had expected the US Air Force to purchase Reapers for at least five more years and planned production accordingly. Fortunately for the global giant, their programme to modify versions of their military drones for civil entities like coast guards and border patrols was already well underway and could be swiftly scaled up. In addition to overseas sales to entities like the Japanese Coast Guard, General Atomics has been eying the US domestic metropolitan police and border patrol market. In the winter of 2019, right before the pandemic began to spread rapidly in the US, General Atomics announced that test flights of its SkyGuardian drone, the MQ-9B or Predator B, would take place over San Diego, California, a moderately sized port city near the border with Mexico. Responding to nervous inquiries, General Atomics sought to assure the public that they were not selling 'military-grade drones to law enforcement agencies' and that the SkyGuardian would be used only for 'mapping of critical infrastructure' and demonstrating possibilities for civilian applications like 'broader support for first responders contending with natural disasters such as floods and forest fires' (Bernd 2020).

Despite the denials offered in carefully crafted press releases, Candice Bernd's reporting for the *Truthout* blog reveals that General Atomics aims to sell SkyGuardians to US police departments across the US by 2025. As part of its efforts, General Atomics has touted the drone's persistent surveillance capacity, offering police departments the ability to 'silently monitor suspects or protests for up to forty hours and stream high-resolution video [...] from more than 2,000 feet above' (Bernd 2020). As Bernd points out, 'military-grade drone integration in civilian airspace is advancing rapidly without substantial public debate regarding the privacy and civil liberties implications of normalising military surveillance technologies over American cities' (Bernd 2020).

Unarmed MQ-9s already patrol the US borders between Mexico and Canada. Since 1953, the US Customs and Border Patrol (CBP) has been authorised to fly in a border zone that has been extended to 100 miles. But as the ACLU has noted, the Border Patrol often ignores the 100-mile limit (Rickerd n.d.). It becomes difficult to discern the difference between 'military' and 'civilian' in these 'humanitarian' operations. As J. D. Schnepf has pointed out in her discussion of drone operations during the aftermath of recent catastrophic floods in the US, the discursive positioning of 'eco-drones' as humanitarian can 'veil' their 'alignment with geopolitical objectives of the US security state' (2020: 14). Here, we can extend Inderpal Grewal's notion of the 'exceptional citizen' of the racialised and gendered imperial and neoliberal security state to an exceptional technological assemblage that targets 'black and brown Others' through 'modes of war that incorporate militarised humanitarianism and surveillance' (2017: 21). This mode of warfare operates through everyday militarism cast as humanitarianism or civilian 'peacekeeping' as well as in overtly weaponised conflicts, disturbing conventional boundaries between civil society and the military.

'Instant Air Forces': Malleable and Mobile Drones in Offensive Strikes

The shakeup in drone design, manufacturing, and marketing has intensified during a period of geopolitical instability and domestic upheaval. While the Obama administration became associated with the ramp up of drone warfare throughout the War on Terror - deservedly so - the Trump administration has relied heavily on drones in a number of ways that have received much less attention. After the Trump administration removed the regulations to ensure greater transparency in reporting civilian casualties that Obama instituted via Executive Order at the end of his presidency, drone strikes have been difficult to quantify. But watchdog groups report that targeted assassinations and heavy civilian casualties have, if anything, intensified (Democracy Now 2020, Harpootlian 2020). In part, the dearth of commentary on this widescale deployment of drones in numerous conflict zones can be attributed to the chaos and high drama of US domestic politics over the past four years - a trend that has been exacerbated by media attention directed so heavily to US electoral politics and pandemic fatalities. The lack of attention to drone strikes and casualties can also be attributed to the blurring of the conventions of a military-civilian divide. As drones at various scales have become more ubiquitous, their incorporation into homeland state violence is less remarked upon. Concomitantly, their deployment in warfare becomes normalised as well.

For close to two decades US-built, large-scale drone assemblages have patrolled and attacked communities and nations without their own air force. This advantage has reduced casualties drastically for the US Air Force while dramatically increasing damage and harm for civilians who have had no choice but to try to endure decades of US and Allied air power. What we are witnessing now is a strategy by the growing and lucrative market for unmanned aerial vehicles to produce as many as possible and to sell them to whoever can pay. Countries that want an 'instant air force' can buy quite sophisticated drones for fairly reasonable prices and shift a stagnant battlefield into a devastatingly asymmetrical conquest (Frantzman 2020). The adaptability and practical nature of a large range of drone products mean that purchasers do not need trained pilots and may launch devices from the back of trucks or from anywhere else, motivating nonstate actors to use drones to attempt self-defence or to conduct attacks.

The conflict between Azerbaijan and Armenia over Nagorno-Karabakh, a disputed territory, is a good example of a drone-supported 'instant air force'. The conflict has flared up continually since the dissolution of the Soviet Union as Armenians inside the 'internationally recognised borders' of Azerbaijan have sought to reunite their region with Armenia (Tharoor 2020). Azerbaijan, which has deep resources from its oil industry, has superior military strength and has recently acquired Israeli and Turkish drones to conduct an air war that has rained bombs on civilian sites in Nagorno-Karabakh. David Ignatius has argued that the use of drones by Azerbaijan against civilian as well as military targets has 'altered the balance' of power, providing a 'visceral demonstration of how modern weapons technology can suddenly unlock' what had seemed to be a 'frozen' conflict (Ignatius 2020). Without any significant aerial vehicles of their own, the Armenians found themselves in a very dangerous and possibly doomed position. In early November 2020, they accepted a cease-fire on terms that have been deemed nothing less than 'punishing' (Dixon 2020).

The drones that gave Azerbaijan an 'instant air force' are considered to be small and relatively inexpensive. The older Soviet defence systems used by Armenia could not defend fortified installations from the modern drones Azerbaijan deployed, like the Turkish Bayraktar TB2 and Israeli Harop kamikaze drones (which hover over an area before diving in on a target) (Dixon 2020). The Turkish drone was developed by Selçuk Bayraktar, an electrical engineer with degrees from the University of Pennsylvania and MIT, who transformed his father's automobile factory into a signature drone production facility (Farooq 2019). The Bayraktar drones have been used extensively by Turkey for patrolling the country's borders as well as to conduct warfare against the Syrian Army and Kurdish forces. Recently, the Turkish-made drones have been purchased by Qatar, Ukraine, Libya, and Tunisia as well as Azerbaijan (Crino and Derby 2020). The smaller, Harop kamikaze drones deployed by Azerbaijan were procured from Israel – Azerbaijan buys sixty percent of its arms from Israel and Israel buys a 'large portion' of its oil supply from Azerbaijan (Ravid 2020). Prized for its ability to take out air defence networks, the Harop has been purchased by Turkey and India as well as Azerbaijan. Taken together, these two kinds of drones demonstrate that national militaries are moving away from US-made products and towards a range of automated aerial vehicles. Asymmetries in air forces are being reorganised and the line between military and nonmilitary use is also being renegotiated and reshaped.

Mission Accomplished: Everyday Militarism as Innovation

I opened this discussion with the example of a jocular social media post about drone wine delivery to a couple stuck on a luxury cruise ship off the coast of Japan in February 2020 as the pandemic began its ravaging global circulation. I want to close with one last example of the drones we encountered during the spread of COVID-19 and what we can learn from their presence and activities.

It brings us to 7 November 2020, the Saturday night following the Presidential election in the US. The Trump administration was making outlandish claims of voter fraud and filing lawsuits to 'stop the steal'. The Coronavirus was raging through new areas of the country, filling hospitals to overflow capacity while the death toll was spiking to new levels. On Saturday evening, President-Elect Joseph Biden held a socially distanced outdoor celebration to announce his win. As the event concluded, the night sky lit up with exquisite constellations of little drones flying in carefully coded patterns, making patriotic shapes. They evoked celebratory fireworks which are, after all, always already military (but also not), and brought the new world of swarms, which are always already military (but also not), into the iconic mythologies of the next administration. The bittersweet beauty of munitions that light up the sky are a kind of sublime in everyday militarisms, offered as a treat at every national holiday and deployed for the most special, large occasions. The drone version for events like the global Olympics or the US Super Bowl halftime extravaganzas bring together corporations and university innovation labs around the world to offer spectacular entertainment. The Biden celebration drone swarm was designed and implemented by Verge Aero, a company spun out of the University of Pennsylvania Pennovation Labs - a research consortium that sponsors many start-up robotic and autonomous systems companies. Verge Aero has been quite successful - as their website states, they have produced drone shows for, among others, the Olympics, the Rolling Stones, Coldplay, and, now, the President-Elect (Verge Aero). Drone shows, they emphasise in bold letters, are their '**singular mission; it's all we do**'.

Companies like Verge Aero or Draganfly that position themselves as friendly alternatives to General Atomics or DJI offer not so much a different approach, as they are dynamic actors in the network of ubiquity, malleability, and mobility that is responsible for the robust health of the industry. The diversity of drone products and applications that proliferate exponentially each year distract us from the militarist relations that are generated within the mythology of individualist consumer choice as well as corporate initiative or governmental agenda. As the COVID-19 pandemic stretches on, we must consider unmanned aerial vehicles and their assemblages not only as singular panaceas for public health policing or as providing 'instant' air forces or celebratory entertainment but as part of the transnational workings of everyday militarisms; the recruitment of industries, authorities, and consumers across the civilian-military divide into support for and participation in state violence.

Works Cited

AFP. 2020. 'Did A Quarantined Australian Couple Have Wine Delivered By A Drone?' *Boom* (blog), February 23. https://www.boomlive.in/world/did-a-quarantined-australian-couple-have-wine-delivered-by-a-drone-6974.

Aratani, Lori. 2020. 'Oversight Report Calls Trump Administration Response to the Pandemic a "Failure"'. *Washington Post*, October 30. https://www.washingtonpost.com/local/trafficandcommuting/trump-coronavirus-response-failure/2020/10/29/cb58e066-1a15-11eb-82db-60b15c874105_story.html.

Bélanger, Pierre, and Alexander S. Arroyo. 2016. *Ecologies of Power: Countermapping the Logistical Landscapes and Military Geographies of the U.S. Department of Defense*. Cambridge: MIT Press.

Bernd, Candice. 2020. 'Large Military-Grade Drones Could Soon Be Flying Over Your Backyard'. *Truthout*, January 16. https://truthout.org/articles/large-military-grade-drones-could-soon-be-flying-over-your-backyard/.

Castellano, Francesco. n.d. 'Commercial Drones Are Revolutionizing Business Operations'. *Toptal Finance Blog*. n.d. https://www.toptal.com/finance/market-research-analysts/drone-market.

Cowen, Deborah. 2014. *The Deadly Life of Logistics: Mapping Violence in Global Trade*. Minneapolis: University of Minnesota Press.

Crino, Scott, and Andy Dreby. 2020. 'Turkey's Drone War in Syria'. *Small Wars Journal*, April 16. https://smallwarsjournal.com/jrnl/art/turkeys-drone-war-syria-red-team-view.

Delehanty, Casey, Jack Mewhirter, Ryan Welch, and Jason Wilks. 2017. 'Militarization and Police Violence: The Case of the 1033 Program'. *Research and Politics*, June, 1-7.

Democracy Now. 2020. 'U.S. Drone Strikes and Raids on Yemen Accelerated Under President Trump'. October 30. https://www.democracynow.org/2020/10/30/headlines/us_drone_strikes_and_raids_on_yemen_accelerated_under_president_trump.

Der Derian, James. 2001. *Virtuous Wars: Mapping the Military-Industrial-Media-Entertainment Network*. Boulder: Westview.

Diaz, Ileana I., and Alison Mountz. 2020. 'Intensifying Fissures: Geopolitics, Nationalism, Militarism, and the US Response to the Novel Coronavirus'. *Geopolitics* 25: 1037–44.

Dilanian, Ken, and Courtney Kube. 2020. 'Airport Informants, Overhead Drones: How the U.S. Killed Soleimani'. *NBC News*, January 10. https://www.nbcnews.com/news/mideast/airport-informants-overhead-drones-how-u-s-killed-soleimani-n1113726.

Dixon, Robyn. 2020. 'Azerbaijan's Drones Owned the Battlefield in Nagorno-Karabakh – and Showed Future of Warfare'. *Washington Post*, November 11. https://www.washingtonpost.com/world/europe/nagorno-karabakah-drones-azerbaijan-aremenia/2020/11/11/441bcbd2-193d-11eb-8bda-814ca56e138b_story.html.

Draganfly Website. https://draganfly.com/about-us/.

Farooq, Umar. 2019. 'How Turkey Defied the U.S. and Became a Killer Drone Power'. *The Intercept*, May 14. https://theintercept.com/2019/05/14/turkey-second-drone-age/.

Franke, Ulrike. 2018. 'The Caracas Drone Attack Won't Be the Last of Its Kind'. *The Verge*, August 17. https://www.theverge.com/2018/8/17/17703570/caracas-drone-attack-venezuela-president-nicolas-maduro.

Frantzman, Seth. 2020. 'Israeli Drones in Azerbaijan Raise Questions on Use in the Battlefield'. *The Jerusalem Post*, October 1. https://www.jpost.com/middle-east/israeli-drones-in-azerbaijan-raise-questions-on-use-in-the-battlefied-644161.

French, Martin, and Torin Monahan. 2020. 'Dis-Ease Surveillance: How Might Surveillance Studies Address COVID-19?' *Surveillance & Society* 18: 1–11.

French, Martin, Eric Mykhalovskiy, and Carmen Lamothe. 2018. 'Epidemics, Pandemics, and Outbreaks'. In *Cambridge Handbook of Social Problems*, edited by A. Javier Treviño, 2: 59–77. Cambridge: Cambridge University Press.

Gershgorn, Dave. 2020. 'Covid-19 Ushered in a New Era of Government Surveillance'. *Medium*, December 28. https://onezero.medium.com/covid-19-ushered-in-a-new-era-of-government-surveillance-414afb7e4220.

Gettinger, Dan. 2020. 'Public Safety Drones, 3rd Edition'. Center for the Study of the Drone at Bard College, March. https://dronecenter.bard.edu/files/2020/03/CSD-Public-Safety-Drones-3rd-Edition-Web.pdf.

Green Car Congress. 2020. 'UniSA Researchers, Dragonfly Working to Deploy Drone as Screening Tool for COVID-19 Pandemic'. March 27. https://www.greencarcongress.com/2020/03/20200327-unisa.html.

Gregory, Derek. 2011. 'From a View to a Kill: Drones and Late Modern War'. *Theory, Culture & Society* 28: 188–215.

Grewal, Inderpal. 2017. *Saving the Security State: Exceptional Citizens in Twenty-First-Century America*. Durham: Duke University Press.

Harpootlian, Allegra. 2020. 'Droning the World: How the President Became a Drone Operator'. *TomDispatch*, January 12. http://www.tomdispatch.com/post/176649/tomgram%3A_allegra_harpootlian%2C_droning_the_world/.

Ignatius, David. 2020. 'What's Needed for a First Step toward Peace for Armenia and Azerbaijan'. *The Washington Post*, October 20. https://www.washingtonpost.com/opinions/global-opinions/whats-needed-for-a-first-step-toward-peace-for-armenia-and-azerbaijan/2020/10/20/cd00693c-1319-11eb-ad6f-36c93e6e94fb_story.html.

Jackman, Anna. 2019. 'Consumer Drone Evolutions: Trends, Spaces, Temporalities, Threats'. *Defense & Security Analysis* 35: 362–83.

Kaplan, Caren. 2018. *Aerial Aftermaths: Wartime from Above*. Durham: Duke University Press.

Kaplan, Caren. 2006. 'Precision Targets: GPS and the Militarization of U.S. Consumer Identity'. *American Quarterly* 58: 693–714.

Kaplan, Caren, Gabi Kirk, and Tess Lea. 2020. 'Editors' Letter. Everyday Militarisms: Hidden in Plain Sight/Site'. *Society & Space Online Forum*, March 8. https://www.societyandspace.org/articles/editors-letter-everyday-militarisms-hidden-in-plain-sight-site.

Kaplan, Caren, and Andrea Miller. 2019. 'Drones as 'Atmospheric Policing: From US Border Enforcement to the LAPD'. *Public Culture* 31: 419–45.

Kelley, Alexandra. 2020. 'Talking Drones Issuing Social Distancing Warnings in New Jersey'. *The Hill*, April 9. https://thehill.com/changing-america/well-being/prevention-cures/491951-talking-drones-issuing-social-distancing.

McGuire, David. 2020. 'Statement Regarding Westport Drone COVID-19 Pilot Program'. ACLU of Connecticut, April 22. https://www.acluct.org/en/press-releases/statement-regarding-westport-drone-covid-19-pilot-program.

Napolitano, Janet. 2016. 'Why Universities Are the New Startup Incubators'. *Medium*, October 3. https://medium.com/@UofCalifornia/why-universities-are-the-new-startup-incubators-be877f3c4cc4.

Nickerson, John. 2020. 'Coronavirus Map: Tracking COVID-19 Cases Nationwide'. *The San Francisco Chronicle*, April 23. https://projects.hearstnp.com/projects/coronavirus-maps/.

Parks, Lisa. 2018. *Rethinking Media Coverage: Vertical Mediation and the War on Terror*. New York: Routledge.

Pollmann, Mina. 2019. 'The Ever-Evolving Importance of Japan's Coast Guard'. *The Diplomat*, December 12. https://thediplomat.com/2019/12/the-ever-evolving-importance-of-japans-coast-guard/.

Ravid, Barak. 2020. 'Azerbaijan Using Israeli "Kamikaze Drones" in Nagorno-Karabakh Clashes'. *Axios*, September 30. https://www.axios.com/israel-kamikaze-drones-nagorno-karabakh-azerbaijan-d3ebfd39-2cf8-4bf6-a788-b24d80a8569f.html.

Richardson, Michael. 2020. 'Drone Cultures: Encounters with Everyday Militarisms'. *Continuum* 34: 1–12.

Richardson, Michael. 2018. 'Drone's-Eye View: Affective Witnessing and Technicities of Perception'. In *Image Testimonies: Witnessing in Times of Social Media*, edited by Kerstin Schankweiler, Verena Straub, and Tobias Wendl, 64–74. London: Routledge.

Rickerd, Chris. n.d. 'ACLU Factsheet on Customs and Border Protection's 100-Mile Zone'. American Civil Liberties Union. https://www.aclu.org/other/aclu-factsheet-customs-and-border-protections-100-mile-zone.

Rogoway, Tyler. 2020. 'Abrupt End of Air Force MQ-9 Reaper Buys Points To New Focus On Survivable Drones'. *The Drive*, February 27. https://www.thedrive.com/the-war-zone/32379/abrupt-end-of-air-force-mq-9-reaper-buys-points-to-new-focus-on-survivable-drones.

Ryall, Julian. 2020. 'Japan Tests US-Built Drone "to Monitor Chinese Ships"'. *South China Morning Post*, October 16. https://www.scmp.com/week-asia/politics/article/3105664/japan-tests-us-built-drone-monitor-chinese-ships-near-diaoyu.

Tharoor, Ishaan. 2020. 'The War in the Caucasus Nears a Bloody Tipping Point'. *The Washington Post*, October 29. https://www.washingtonpost.com/world/2020/10/30/armenians-azerbaijan-clashes-nagorno-karabakh/.

Sandvik, Kristin Bergtora, and Maria Gabrielsen Jumbert. 2017. *The Good Drone*. London: Routledge.

Schnepf, J.D. 2020. 'Flood from Above: Disaster Mediation and Drone Humanitarianism'. *Media+Environment* 2: 1-18.

Schroth, Lukas. 2020. 'Drone Market Size 2020-2025'. *Drone Industry Insights*, June 22. https://droneii.com/the-drone-market-size-2020-2025-5-key-takeaways.

Schwellenbach, Nick. 2020. 'The First 100 Days of the U.S. Government's COVID-19 Response'. Project on Government Oversight, May 6. https://www.pogo.org/analysis/2020/05/the-first-100-days-of-the-u-s-governments-covid-19-response/.

Seigel, Micol. 2018. *Violence Work: State Power and the Limits of Police*. Durham: Duke University Press.

Verge Aero Website. https://verge.aero/.

Westport Police Department. 2020. 'Westport Police Department Testing New Drone Technology "Flatten the Curve Pilot Program"'. Press Release. April 21. https://www.westportct.gov/home/showdocument?id=25925.

Zimmermann, Patricia R., and Caren Kaplan. 2020. 'Coronavirus Drone Genres: Spectacles of Distance and Melancholia'. *Film Quarterly Quorum*, April 30. https://filmquarterly.org/2020/04/30/coronavirus-drone-genres-spectacles-of-distance-and-melancholia/.

6

On Feminised Digital Media Users and Drone Operations

J. D. Schnepf

Target Practice

A bathroom is the site of a gruesome drone attack in the 2017 *Black Mirror* episode, 'Hated in the Nation' (dir. James Hawes). The scene tracks a swarm of lethal microdrones as it breaches a police perimeter and a house's outer walls on its hunt for a woman who has fled into a bathroom alongside two others who seek to protect her by barricading themselves inside. The insectile swarm amasses outside the locked bathroom as if drawn by instinct to their target, emitting a buzz like the sound of a dentist drill's high-pitched whine. The scene cuts to the women inside the room, who scramble to seal every means of ingress, hastily shoving the shower curtain into the slight gap at the bottom of the door. A close-up of horizontal lines resolves into a dingy exhaust fan high on the bathroom wall, then the auditory click of metallic footfalls signals the successful entry of a solitary microdrone, its reflective body glinting from within the fan's dark recesses. Having breached the sealed room, the drone takes flight – an erratic, darting speck. It circles the hunted woman as she bats it away and falls to the floor. We cut to a close-up of the woman's face, head tilted back and cradled in another woman's hands in an effort to block the ear canals. The dark hollows of the target's open mouth and round nostrils occupy the top center of the frame. The camera moves in for an even tighter shot of the lower half of her face, from the bridge of the nose to the arch of the neck, just as the drone lands near the outer corner of the lip. With a preternatural precision, it scuttles into the nearest unobstructed nostril and out of sight. From this closer vantage, the woman's death is visceral: blood and mucus stream from her nose and mouth. The woman cries out and writhes in pain until suddenly all is quiet. The scene concludes a horrific string of attacks targeting subjects who provoke online outrage through their various failures to respect the nation's biopolitical future or, as is the case with this final attack, service to the militarised state. Detective Chief Inspector Karin Parke and her new colleague, Trainee Detective Constable Blue Colson, trace each attack back to an errant microdrone. Referred to as ADIs or autonomous drone insects, the UK government introduces the winged robots to the nation's ecosystem to address the ecological emergency of honey-bee colony collapse. While it will turn out that a hacker has programmed the robotic bees to take their murderous cues from a hashtag on social media, it's also revealed that the ADIs can target their victims because they are a part of the UK's counterterrorism security infrastructure, and thus part of the state's networked effort to achieve what Colson refers to in the episode as 'total nationwide surveillance'. In addition to accessing CCTV footage and traffic cameras, UK security services spy on citizens through the visual feed onboard each ADI in times of 'increased national security' ('which is, as I understand it, pretty much all the time', one of the episode's engineers quips).

Although the television series *Black Mirror* regularly conjures up speculative security technologies in its dystopian visions of the near-future – other episodes have featured predatory robo-dogs and invasive mind-reading devices – this particular episode achieves its unsettling effect by linking national security practices fuelled by the ongoing war on terrorism to the prosaic social networking ones of citizen-consumers through drone operations. Media studies scholars have explored how these seemingly disparate digital practices intersect. For Thomas Stubblefield, 'the integration of everyday media into military applications is also inseparable from an inverse trajectory, in which the latter are just as often folded back into civilian platforms' (2020: 3). This means that 'a shared ground of operations emerges that imbues everyday media such as the mobile device with an inconceivable simultaneity, such that the capacity to serve as both medium of civilian communication and drone targeting system is not only possible, but in fact comprises the conditions of everyday mediality' (3). Tung-Hui Hu points out that this sort of '[online] user engagement with security has disturbing consequences: when users are invited to perform or play at the sovereign's role as a "decider" (and, ultimately, the sovereign's right to kill), security and participation fuse into [...] the *sovereignty of data*' (2016: 115, emphasis in original). Hu uses the verbs 'perform or play' here to underscore that, at this historical juncture, online engagement has taken the form of target practice: 'the sovereignty of data is primarily a fantasy' – one that arises due to ideologies of boundless interconnectivity around the robust 'system of networks that pools computing power', which Hu has termed 'the cloud' (x). At once 'a single, virtual object' as well as an infrastructural entity 'comprised of millions of hard drives, servers, routers, fiber-optic cables, and networks' (x), the cloud is both 'an idea and a physical and material object' (ix). 'The cloud', Hu asserts, 'places users uncomfortably close to the mechanism of state violence. The sovereignty of data may manifest itself primarily through targeted advertisements, and through the bloodless forms of control and governmentality typically described by new media scholars, but occasionally appears as targeted killing' (115).

With killer microdrones carrying out assassinations at the behest of social media users, 'Hated in the Nation' dramatises this latter scenario: the sovereignty of data is converted seamlessly into a series of precision deaths. However, unlike Hu's case study, which centres on the effects of user adjacency to the mechanisms of state violence on geopolitical military interventions such as the 2011 NATO bombings of Libya, 'Hated in the Nation' is a cultural text that plays out the consequences of the cloud's continuity across civilian and martial digital platforms in the geographic settings of the Global North's home offices, daily commutes, kindergarten classrooms, living rooms, and bathrooms. Situated in the everyday spaces of empire's 'homeland', the human and nonhuman assemblages that make up drone operations compose the social formation of networked securitised society and its subjects. Here we might recall that the drone does not constitute merely the singular airborne object but rather 'a fluid system of relations' that includes 'the distributed nature of the kill chain and the remote relations it reproduces' (Stubblefield 2020: 10). As Derek Gregory explains, the kill chain of late modern warfare is 'a dispersed and distributed apparatus, a congeries of actors, objects, practices, discourses, and affects, that entrains the people who are made a part of it and constitutes them as particular kinds of subjects' (Gregory 2011a: 195). While the militarised kill chain is an institutionalised operation that aligns these dispersed elements 'into the same zone' in order to mete out imperial violence efficiently (195), the civilian version in 'Hated in the Nation' is unplanned and opaque to its human participants.

Moreover, the domestication of this apparatus brings the gendered uses of networked media to the fore. Gendered accounts of digital media culture often resort to what Hu calls the 'fictitious binary between participatory media practices that "fight back" and gullible, feminised media consumption' (120). Caren Kaplan updates this account of feminised consumption to address the rise of enthusiastic militarised consumerism in the wake of 9/11. For Kaplan, the mobilisation of such consumers 'allows us to move beyond the model of consumers as feminised, passive targets of unscrupulous advertisers in order to see the ways in which people participate in their construction by 'volunteering', if you will, to engage in the products generated by technoscience' (2006: 708). 'Hated in the Nation' portrays women as users of networked digital media in the age of imperial technosecuritisation by keeping both the newer and older models of feminised media consumerism Kaplan refers to in play: on the one hand, the proactive volunteerism of users for whom security doubles as a form of feminised care labour, on the other, the 'bad' media consumer depicted as the women who mindlessly take in the cultural 'garbage' that litters the contemporary digital landscape. If this chapter asks how assumptions about the gendered use of networked digital media undergird the politics of securitisation, obscuring the targeting of racialised populations abroad to protect imperial citizens at home, then we shall see that 'Hated in the Nation' implies that there is no good answer to the question of how feminised citizen subjects ought to engage such media. Under neoliberal capitalist globalisation, those engaged in productive care work that secures familial norms and those engaged in passive consumption that deviates from these norms both partake of the necropolitical drone's kill chain as targeters and targeted, respectively.

Crowdsourced Kill Chains

At the time when 'Hated in the Nation' first aired, the United Kingdom was a year into a national discussion concerning whether or not the potential social benefits promised by ramped up surveillance measures that included the police use of small unmanned aerial systems (UAS) would outweigh their panoptic implications. This latter concern was unambiguously expressed by members of the British public in a series of state-sponsored workshops hosted across five cities across the United Kingdom between the months of December 2015 and February 2016 (TNS BMRB 2016: 4). Commissioned by the UK Department of Transport, the Ministry of Defence, and the public engagement programme, Sciencewise, in response to a 2014 European Commission communication to member states entitled 'A New Era for Aviation', the workshops sought to gauge public sentiment toward the incorporation of drones into civilian airspace. Conducted by social research agency TNS BMRB, the workshops elicited strong opinions. In their executive summary of the dialogues, TNS notes that the public's 'spontaneous associations and assumptions' regarding drones were largely negative and based on 'concerns about privacy and surveillance, safety and mis-use, and fear of the "unknown"' (2013: 4). 'Invasion of privacy was a key concern early in the process, spontaneously and in response to early information about how drones work, with women tending to be slightly more concerned about this than men' stated the report (22), while the potential 'mis-use of drones (particularly hacking, terrorism, stalking and surveillance)' remained chief concerns (5).

Public statements linked invasion of privacy concerns to the technology's apparent tendency to intrude on the heteronormative space of conventional families. For instance, 'particular concern about invasion of privacy at home' cropped up when participants were told that thermal sensors positioned on a UAS outside could detect residents inside a home. The executive summary noted that, 'some participants [said this] would make them feel "violated" and that such a possibility was "outrageous"' (22). As one resident of Newry put it,

> I would hate to think that someone [...] could pick one of these things up and spy through my window and I know nothing whatsoever about it... or spy in the back garden or when I'm on holiday with my kids, you're not allowed to stand outside somebody's door with a video camera but this thing can do it and you

don't know where it is, who he is or whatever (Newry, Wave 1, Male). (22-3)

As this worried resident tells it, spying might happen through windows, in the backyard, on vacation, or at one's front door. The disorientating account of agency in the statement ('you don't know where it is, who he is or whatever'), puts into words the sense that drones have ushered in a mediatised environment of networked surveillance that obscures individual human agents who one might pin the blame on. This tendency to regard the drone as a tool for private civilians who seek to stalk and harm families reduces the threat to civil liberties posed by the state's infrastructural surveillance to the criminal work of rogue human agents seeking to disrupt families and the drone itself to a singular object. The resident's understandable mistake – to think about digital technology's threat to the social order in the narrow terms of an individual who uses surveillance technology for deviant ends rather than as a dispersed network of human and nonhuman agents of drone operations – gives us a useful way to make sense of the misreadings committed by the detective protagonists of 'Hated in the Nation' in their quest to solve the string of deaths. By contending with the diffuse dissemination of drone operations, the episode illustrates the limitations of the television genre of the police procedural when faced with a digitally networked crime ring that numbers in the hundreds of thousands.

From the outset, 'Hated in the Nation' makes plain its indebtedness to a subgenre of the police procedural television scholars have identified as the 'British female cop show' (Sydney-Smith 2009: 49). Featuring the two-person team of DCI Parke and her idealistic junior, DC Colson, the *Black Mirror* episode draws on generic tropes including '[t]he adherence to conventional gender roles typical of soap operas, the heightened emotions surrounding the battle of good and evil that characterises melodrama, and the taming and domestication of women's power found in most situation comedies – as well as the presentation of women's culture and friendships – [...] entwined with depictions of women as managers of social order and enforcers of the law' (Newcomb cited in Sydney-Smith 2009: 49). Beyond these features, the episode follows the form of the procedural insofar as it adheres to a conventional narrative arc in which detectives scan crime scenes for clues to establish the victim's social milieu. For example, investigating their first crime scene, in which the body of newspaper columnist Jo Powers is found on the floor of her home office, the detectives determine that there is no forced entry at the windows, yet find evidence of a violent struggle and confirm the victim's husband was in the home at the time of death. Given the evidence, Karin is quick to suggest that Powers's husband is the likely culprit. While it's true that the episode does track down a rogue hacker as the episode's wanted man in the end, it's significant that the hacker's work effectively transfers the sovereign decision to social media users that number in the hundreds of thousands.

By installing a software programme that not only breaches the government's digital security networks and civilian social media networks, but also conjoins them, the hacker sets in motion one massive, networked drone apparatus that functions according to Hu's account of the sovereignty of data.

The problem of conceptualising drone operations as a networked activity is compounded by the notorious challenge of conveying digital infrastructures on screen. This means the kill chain proves difficult to visualise. As Stubblefield has observed of drones in film and television, 'the remote sensing of the kill chain manifests as a distributed mode of appearance in which the drone is never simply the subject of the image but is always already the artifact of an absent martial network' (2020: 134). Stubblefield's observation is particularly interesting in the case of the police procedural where microdrones do function as 'artifacts' – objects with no visible or physical ties to the hidden networks that control them. Early on, the episode offers up only fragments or glimpses of the kill chain. Stubblefield has suggested that to perceive the kill chain 'is contingent upon an active interpenetration of the host media by the larger processes of network-centric warfare' (134). In the case of 'Hated in the Nation,' the kill chain materialises in part through quotidian digital platforms such as Facebook or Twitter, thus those 'larger processes of network-centric warfare' penetrate the episode transmedially through what appear on first sight as the benign ambience of network-centric civilian social platforms. For instance, at the crime scene in Powers's home office, the kill chain pervades the diegesis as the auditory intrusions of social media message notifications while the detectives examine the crime scene for more conventional clues. At other times, the episode points to the kill chain's invasive reach by juxtaposing close ups of the '#DeathTo' hashtag as it pops up on phones, televisions, and computer screens in and around schools, private homes, police stations, and government offices. In fact, it's only in the final moments before a mass death event is triggered that kills all hashtag users that the episode offers two visions of the kill chain in its entirety: the network's totality is portrayed as an aggregated list of 387,000 unique social media users who posted the hashtag '#DeathTo', and as a digitally rendered map of the United Kingdom that shimmers in red to signal the kill chain's final activation.

The hack's merging of military and civilian networks also has the consequence of privatising large swaths of the nation-state's surveillance and security labour. In some ways, it is not surprising that digital media users assume the work of securitisation. As Hu has explained,

> 'war as big data' produces the subject position of a user, that is, a subject that actively participates in securing the system as a whole. A cloud user is constantly enjoined to perform digital 'hygiene'; in other words, to keep their private data private. Likewise, the cloud's disaster recovery functions make disasters and security threats continuously imaginable. When users are

responsible for selecting privacy, making disaster recovery backups, and even flagging suspicious behaviour online, security becomes an everyday responsibility. (2016: 113-4)

Hu concludes that, '[o]ne of the most unique aspects of digital culture is therefore a user's ability not just to become a target, but also to defend him – or herself, "target back," and participate in a shared project of security with the state' (114). In 'Hated in the Nation,' the digital environment attended to by observant citizens points beyond online security threats to national security threats as well. Specifically, securitised practices of targeting antisocial forces within the social body fall under the purview of hundreds of the thousands of social media users who voluntarily report on perceived social transgressions online. Rather than relying on the paid labour of national security workers to perform this work, then, the process of securitisation is effectively outsourced. As Inderpal Grewal reminds us, this configuration is already common in imperial populations living under the securitisation of everyday life. Among other things, the 'ongoing and endless war on terror, as well as the impact of decades of neoliberal policies' have effectively 'naturalise[d] self-improving and self-protecting subjects working as individuals to save not just the nation but the security state [...]' (2017: 119). In the episode, the hack functions to accelerate and make visible this process of neoliberal governance through securitised volunteerism. But more than this, the outsourcing of this securitised labour to digital media users also assumes a particularly gendered form. As Kylie Jarrett explains, 'the production of social relationships that reproduce the social order [...] is a feature of "women's work" and also the labour of digital consumers' (2014: 21). Understood as 'women's work', the affective, immaterial labour undertaken by vigilant digital users manufactures and maintains 'the nonmaterial goods of socialisation and sensibilities' through consensus formation and the disciplining of the self (21). In this way, user activities as minor as using a hashtag to signal solidarity or posting an expression of dismay on a social media site can be understood as a form of socially reproductive work. In the episode, the national project of counterterrorism sanctions social relations that protect the biopolitical interests of the nation while naturalising service to the security state.

One way socialisation under securitsation on the part of diligent private citizens works in 'Hated in the Nation' is through the preservation and protection of the figure of the child. The collective affect attached to children, understood as lives deemed worth defending, is conveyed in mediated fashion, through the heavy-handed melodramatic form of the television talk show embedded within the episode. While the genre of the police procedural would seem far removed from the conventions of melodrama, television scholar Lynne Joyrich has observed how melodramatic elements have diffused across televisual forms (1992: 233). 'Police and detective drama', she writes, 'purportedly deal with the social issues of crime, drugs, prostitution, and so on, yet even while their emphasis on action seems to remove them from the domain of the melodrama, they exhibit many of its characteristics' (230). She continues: 'Although they allow their protagonists to act freely against the criminals, the heroes of TV cop shows are still trapped within a confined world in which emotional pressure, familial concerns, and gender or class position take on heightened importance' (230). As viewers, we peer over Karin's shoulder as she sits at home on her sofa so as to watch her watching the melodramatic spectacle of the talk show, at the same moment the show's host invites a rapper named Tusk to view a video made by a nine-year-old fan who dressed up to emulate the dance moves of his idol. As Tusk watches, the scene cuts to the eager child waiting backstage as his attentive mother holds him in a protective embrace. The rapper bluntly disrupts the familial moment of maternal pride, responding to the video by criticising the child's appearance and mocking his lacklustre performance. The scene cuts back briefly to catch the face of the crestfallen child and the concerned mother. Online, the moral judgement on this slight to the family is swift, with users condemning Tusk and expressing sympathy for the child. Thanks to the integration of social media networks with martial ones, Tusk will be dead within twenty-four hours. This scenario illustrates how heightened affective concerns that seem confined to genres like the melodramatic television talk show spill out to the police procedural. Moreover, the episode implies that networked drone operations facilitate this porous boundary: vigilant digital media consumers who watch the talk show share their concern for the child and vitriol for the rapper online, leading to the microdrone attack and the consequent involvement of the police.

The link between heteronormativity, gender norms, and national securitisation is reasserted by the fact that the only conventional family home featured in the episode – idyllically situated in the countryside and strewn with children's toys – is operated by the National Crime Agency as a 'safe house for terrorist informers and their families', suggesting that the institution of national security reinforces the institution of heteronormative domesticity and vice versa. Here, the presence of a child's abandoned tricycle in the corner of a room prompts one character to ask if any of the police detectives have children, to which Blue and Karin both reply, 'no plans'. This moment is illustrative of what Amanda Greer calls 'crime television's fixation with [the] maternal ambivalence' expressed by its 'female investigators' (2017: 328). The episode seeks to resolve working women's ambivalence toward traditional gender roles associated with parenthood and family by aligning their professional concerns with the broader reproductive concerns of society. This is illustrated, for example, when Blue recounts that her previous police work in digital forensics put her on the 'Rannoch Case' which she refers to as 'the child killings'. Blue articulates her recent move out of the field of digital forensics to 'the field' by surmising that 'out here in the real world, you can genuinely prevent stuff, can't you?' In other words, for Blue, becoming a detective holds the promise of escaping the grotesque corruption of the digital realm by working directly to protect children, a belief that recasts women in the police force as care labourers tasked with managing the social order.

Indeed throughout the episode paid care labour outside the home is recast as the part of the nation's biopolitical project of optimising life. One of these labourers is Liza Behar, a teacher at Colbyn Manor Primary School. Introduced to the viewer surrounded by construction paper decorations and children's books, Behar exemplifies the feminisation of this work at the same time her young charges stand in for the very sort of life and productivity that the nation-state seeks to defend. The teacher is questioned by the detectives for sending a cake inscribed with an obscene message to one of the drone victims on the day of her death – another indication that feminised activity of baking and state practices of securitisation can go hand-in-hand. At this point in the episode, the logic of police procedural overdetermines the scene, so much so that the leads furnished by physical evidence found at the scene of the crime govern the line of questioning. What the characters in this scene never quite realise is that they've inadvertently stumbled across the digital kill chain (Colson finds that Behar has posted a message reading '#DeathTo Jo Powers' but the significance of the hashtag is not yet known). The ambient presence of the kill chain here makes for extraordinary dialogue as, in at least two respects, conversations about domestic matters double as martial ones. First, Behar explains that instead of paying for the cake herself, she collected the money to purchase the cake from eighty members of a 'mums and carers message board'. 'Crowd-sourced' online, the collective manner of funding the cake provides an uncanny domestic double of the dispersed authority granted by the martial kill chain. ('I can see if I'd done it myself, then that would be a bit weird', Liza admits.) And second, the dialogue gets remarkably close to discussing the kill chain's dispersal of drone operations when Colson accusingly reminds Liza, 'You wished she was dead'. Liza dismisses it as 'a hashtag game' – but of course it turns out to be real. The dramatic irony of this freighted conversation becomes clear as Liza insists 'It's not […] real. It's a joke thing'.

Trash Inside and Out

While some women are recast as securitised care labourers working in tandem with the biopolitical imperatives of heteronormativity, social judgement falls on women who fail to use media as a tool to participate in the production and regulation of the traditional family. The episode thematises this by beginning its flashback to the drone attacks with a tracking shot of its divorced detective protagonist, Karin, as she bypasses an urban park filled with the sounds of children playing and enters the domestic sphere of her empty flat. Inside it's a futuristic wonderland of advanced technologies designed to ease the burden of domestic labour. But rather than cook, Karin only sighs at the sight of raw ingredients and the chore of meal-making they anticipate. Instead, she reaches for a cannister of potato chips, walks absently by the morning's dirty breakfast dishes, and discards the lid on to the sofa as she settles in to watch TV. Rather than '[normalise] the isolation to be endured by the female policewoman' the way feminised cop shows have tended to (Sydney-Smith 2009: 52), *Black Mirror* pathologises it. In fact, Karin and her flat function much like rubbish bins: while she eats junk food and smokes e-cigarettes, her kitchen accumulates banana peels and unwashed dishes.

Throughout the episode, Karin repeatedly belittles online culture, preferring the 'old-fashioned' media of television instead. But Karin's passive television consumption serves as an apt model for digital media use as well. For example, journalist Jo Powers comes home from a hard day to eat chocolate cake with her bare hands before spending her evening absently drinking wine while scrolling her social media feeds. The episode cuts from Jo at home at her computer back to Karin on her couch to juxtapose the two women in their similar positions, each sitting alone and bathed in the light of her respective screen. Jo sips red wine while Karin has moved on to eating ice cream directly out of the carton – a literalisation, the episode seems to insist, of decadent, passive consumption. This sort of scene crops up again later on as one of the victims named Clara Meades is introduced nervously rolling a joint while glued to her laptop. These little vignettes, of women consuming media alongside trans-fats and alcohol, nicotine, and marijuana, offer up a convenient if clichéd shorthand for passive media use as a form of bad domestic behaviour practiced by feminised imperial subjects that refuse to conform to the biopolitical mandates of the securitised nation-state.

This attention to women as consumers of trash assumes unexpected relevance in light of the imbrications of gender with domestic security culture. Writing of domestic security culture in the post-9/11 era, Rachel Hall identifies a turn in domestic visual culture toward a pervasive 'aesthetics of transparency' that aligns with the epistemological objectives of the security state and its subjects:

> Broadly, the aesthetics of transparency is motivated by the desire to turn the world (and the body) inside out such that there would no longer be secrets or interiors, human or geographical, in which terrorists or terrorist threats might find refuge. The military and security state's objection to interiority is both physical and psychological, referring as much to the desire to rid the warring worlds of pockets, caves, spider holes, and veils as it is concerned with ferreting out all secrets, stopping at nothing in its effort to produce actionable intelligence from detainees. (2015: 127)
>
> In attempting 'to force a correspondence between interiority and exteriority' or even 'to flatten the object of surveillance' to do away with the need for correspondence between visible outsides and opaque insides in the first place (127), Hall explains, this aesthetic regime brings with it 'opacity effects' that 'visualise a

body, geography, building, or institution as possessing an interior, a realm beyond what is visible' (127).

While Hall locates her analysis in the realm of national terrorist prevention programs, the police procedural, set in a time of enhanced national security, extends this logic into private realms by structuring the interiority of the securitised subject. We see this when the two detectives, Karin and Blue, discuss the difficult elements of their respective career trajectories. Referring to computers and smart phones, Blue says 'You've seen what people tuck away on these. Schemes and kill lists, kiddy porn'. But Karin responds, 'I'm old enough to remember when they walked around with that stuff just tucked away in their heads'. Here Karin's reminiscence about the pre-digital past not only reasserts a spatial model of human interiority – one in which individuals keeps 'stuff just tucked away' – but also implies that the status of what's 'inside' the human psyche has more in common with digital content than Blue would like to believe. This observation links the bad media consumer to the domestic security project that seeks to flatten the subject of observation. We see this too when, in response to Jo Powers's heartless newspaper column imploring readers to 'Spare [her] the Tears' over a disability activist who commits suicide to protest government cuts to welfare programs, one reader leaves the online comment: 'You're trash inside and out Jo Powers'. The insult means to criticise Jo's moral character, but its phrasing gestures to the securitised mandate to make the domestic security subject's insides and outsides correspond.

Speaking of the domestic security subject's insides and outsides, it's fitting to conclude by returning to the scene where this chapter began – with the murderous microdrone, having successfully traversed the multiple thresholds of police perimeter, home, bedroom, and bathroom, finally moving from the outside to the inside of Clara's body through an unguarded nostril. Clara, exemplary of the bad digital user, has been targeted for her social media post desecrating a war memorial – a show of blatant disregard for the deification of service to the militarised state. Here, the linking of the civilian network with the martial network that constitutes drone operations in the episode reveals itself spatially by locating martial violence in the civilian space of the home. If the structural asymmetries of militarised drone power promise that violence is located at a distance from those who administer it, then 'Hated in the Nation' reduces that distance – unleashing drone violence in the domestic heart of empire. In this scene, the presumed position of safety in the intimate confines of the bathroom is not only undermined, it is also wrenched into aesthetic symmetry with sites of martial drone violence typically visited on racialised populations in the Greater Middle East and elsewhere. The scene's unsettling close up of the microdrone entering the nostril not only presents a perverse iteration of drone violence enacted through militaristic claims to the drone's precision but also, in its concluding shot of Clara's lifeless body sprawled on the bathroom floor, assumes a dispassionate aerial perspective situated at some distance from the ground and angled directly over the prone body. This view of the dead woman, her limbs splayed and entangled with those who tried to save her, portrays an uncanny domestic iteration of the 'bugsplat' – the US military's term for humans killed by drone strikes (the term itself derives from the miniature appearance of the victims mediated from the sky through the drone's visual apparatus). In this instance, the eruption of the military aerial sighting that has become a hallmark of the drone wars in a domestic bathroom effectively punctures the imperial fantasy that the space of war might be contained elsewhere, making it unclear where the battlespace begins and ends. The imagined domestic geographies of drone operations in the episode thus extend Gregory's observation that the advent and deployment of UAS technologies have set loose militarised violence from the zones of the conventional battlefield by burrowing inward – to the domestic spaces and bodies of unregimented imperial subjects (Gregory 2011b: 238-50).

What is more, the scene reconciles the securitised mandate to have inside and outside correspond in the case of the trash consuming digital user by deploying the aesthetics of gore. If deviant bodies are stubbornly opaque ones, their materiality unyielding to what Hall describes as the demand for voluntary transparency, then this particular gruesome scene of death doubles as a spectacle of securitised compliance – enforced jointly by civilians and the state. Despite the fact that the episode includes spectacles such as blood-soaked rooms, blood-spattered examination rooms, and the indiscriminate flowing of other bodily fluids, the gore deployed is not gratuitous. Instead, understood as an externalisation of the body's insides, the episode's gore aesthetic serves as a visceral literalisation of the demand to quite literally 'turn inside out' the security state's recalcitrant subjects.

If 'Hated in the Nation' portrays the affective project of securitised, volunteer digital users as one motivated by the cultivation of life – ensuring the education and protection of others as a matter of biopolitical management – then the episode's bringing together of martial networks with civilian ones reveals that the project of cultivating life always entails a complicity with the violent death of others for whom life is denied. As Jasbir Puar puts it, '[t]his distancing from death is a fallacy of modernity, a hallucination that allows for the unimpinged work of biopolitics' (2007: 32). By playing out the sovereignty of data and locating its violent effects through drone operations in the heart of empire, 'Hated in the Nation' eradicates the distance between life giving and death dealing, showing them to be two sides of the same project. But more than this, it brings to the fore how the affective, immaterial labour of social reproduction performed by feminised imperial subjects in digital contexts is, in our time of heightened national security and the ongoing war on terrorism, inevitably and inescapably necropolitical as well.

Works Cited

Black Mirror. 2016. 'Hated in the Nation'. Netflix video. 1:29:42, October 21.

Greer, Amanda. 2017. '"I'm Not Your Mother!": Maternal Ambivalence and the Female Investigator in Contemporary Crime Television'. New Review of Film and Television Studies 15: 327-47.

Gregory, Derek. 2011a. 'From a View to a Kill: Drones and Late Modern War'. Theory, Culture & Society 28: 188-215.

Gregory, Derek. 2011b. 'The Everywhere War'. The Geographic Journal 17: 238-50.

Grewal, Inderpal. 2017. Saving the Security State: Exceptional Citizens in Twenty-First-Century America. Durham: Duke University Press.

Hall, Rachel. 2015. 'Terror and the Female Grotesque: Introducing Full-Body Scanners to U.S. Airports'. In Feminist Surveillance Studies, edited by Rachel E. Dubrofsky and Shoshana Amielle Magnet, 127-49. Durham: Duke University Press.

Hu, Tung-Hui. 2016. A Prehistory of the Cloud. Cambridge: MIT Press.

Jarrett, Kylie. 2014. 'The Relevance of "Women's Work": Social Reproduction and Immaterial Labor in Digital Media'. Television & New Media 15: 14-29.

Joyrich, Lynne. 1992. 'All that Television Allows: TV Melodrama, Postmodernism, and Consumer Culture'. In Private Screenings: Television and the Female Consumer, edited by Lynn Spigel and Denise Mann, 227-52. Minnesota: University of Minnesota Press.

Kaplan, Caren. 2006. 'Precision Targets: GPS and the Militarization of U.S. Consumer Identity'. American Quarterly 58: 693-714.

Puar, Jasbir K. 2017. Terrorist Assemblages: Homonationalism in Queer Times. Durham: Duke University Press.

Stubblefield, Thomas. 2020. Drone Art: The Everywhere War as Medium. Oakland: University of California Press.

Sydney-Smith, Susan. 2009. 'Buddies, bitches, broads: the British female cop show'. Film International 7: 46-58.

TNS BMRB. 2016. 'Public dialogue on drone use in the UK: Moving Britain Ahead'. London: Crown. https://www.gov.uk/government/publications/drone-use-in-the-uk-public-dialogue.

7

The Drone's Other Target: The Generative Aesthetics of Drone Hobbyists' Love

Amy Gaeta

If the 'selfie' is the paradigmatic visual form of the 2010s, the 'dronie' might come to characterise the 2020s, a decade already latent with new forms of self-facilitated personal surveillance technologies and dissolving human-machine boundaries. In the most standard sense, a dronie is a photograph someone takes of themselves using a drone, typically a play drone for personal use. Seems simple, yet taking a dronie requires immense trust in the drone because, to take a dronie, one elects to become the drone's target, letting it track you; thus you accept a variation of self-surveillance. Despite this vulnerable position that is often associated with hunting and killing, dronies continue to uncritically proliferate in drone hobbyist circles and the wider sphere of social media. YouTube is bountiful with dronie compilation videos; the New York City Drone Film Festival, and Drone Video Awards regularly hold an award for 'Best Dronie', and the drone site AirVuz dubbed one hobbyist the 'Queen of Dronies' ('The Drone Dish' 2017). Dronies are so popular that many play drone manufacturers even programmed various types of dronie modes into their drones' operating systems and design.

When using my own play drone, a ScharkSpark Guard FQ36, I felt out of control when taking a dronie. I had little ability to dictate my self-representation or my relationship with the drone. Using the controller to take pictures of myself was unsettling because dronies require the drone to be pointed at the subject-user. As such, I gave my drone permission to target me. Even though it is not an armed drone, the drone 'came alive' as it stared me straight in the eyes. I found myself zoomorphising the drone, calling its 'eyes' and 'legs' as such rather than referring to each part as its camera sensors and landing gear. In this dynamic, it became apparent that physical proximity and willed vulnerability with the drone led me to consider its agency. But, while the drone was 'targeting' me, I was holding the controller, staring the drone directly in its 'face'. Neither of us held a stable role as 'controller' nor was there a stable power relation for either party. Therefore, I call personal drones, otherwise known as civilian or hobby drones, play drones. The reign of play is ambivalent, a space of exploration and perceived freedom with an object, and hence a breeding ground for imagining new lives for an object, and for oneself, beyond the object's intended use-value. Dronies, as Jablonowski (2019) contends, are especially primed to allow new ways of self-making, both dangerous and promising, precisely due to how the dronie views the subject at a distance from above.

The unstable power dynamic and vulnerability of the dronie, for me, began to complicate the frequent separation of drone-types in the media and scholarship, which imply that the military drone is radically different from seemingly neutral commercial and play drones. Debates about morality and ethics of drone warfare usage pay scant attention to other uses of drones for civilian and commercial fun and service; the apparent central difference between these drones is how only the former produces readily visible physical or psychological harm (Boyle 2013; Enemark 2013; Hines 2015). These drone distinctions are geopolitical markers that separate the Global North from the Global South based on normative feelings and conceptions of vulnerability and power roles. This chapter intervenes by using the genre of the dronie in hobbyist culture to examine the close attachments between civilian drone hobbyists and their beloved drones. As a relative of the selfie, dronies are particularly apt for this intervention because, like selfies, they are what Gómez Cruz and Thornham (2015) call a dynamic 'socio-technical phenomenon' that are produced, mediated, and circulated through a network of influences that exceed the drone operator and drone.

From a feminist disability perspective of this socio-technical relation between operator and play drone, interdependency and vulnerability are the present absences lurking with and through play drone usage. Feminist and disability theories of vulnerability have long suggested that vulnerability and interdependence can both be damaging and be a site of revolutionary potential, helping us imagine other value systems beyond those constructed on ableist and heteropatriarchal ideals (Butler 2006; Kafer 2013; McRuer 2006; Shildrick 2002). To understand the affective politics of the dronie, I use a feminist disability studies analytic called 'cripping', which means to assess and reimagine the value of vulnerable, interdependent bodies, i.e., bodies marked as powerless. Accounting for the drone's multitude of guises can shift the optic of drone warfare as one-sided vulnerability and characterised by explicitly masculine, militarised aesthetics. Thus, more than disturbing optics, I point toward the potential of these hobbyist-drone loving, trusting interdependencies to upend the very things that drones are meant to control: human emotion and vulnerability. To understand the aesthetic of the dronie, as well as the relation required to take one, we must attend to drone culture, in particular, hobbyist communities. First, I provide an overview of play drones and hobbyist culture by drawing representative excerpts from hobbyist forums. Next, I introduce how dronies express a 'disruptive' interdependency that challenges traditional ability/disability and masculinity/femininity distinctions and thus opens space to renegotiate these categories that likewise uphold power hierarchies. Lastly, I examine hobbyists' practices of self-surveillance, including self-tracking via drones and dronies within the context of domestic militarisation and surveillance.

Drone Hobbyists

Play drones differ from military and commercial drones in four primary ways: name, size, flight time, and pilot-positioning. Many play drone advertisements and manufacturers call their toys 'quadcopters', opting out of using 'drone'. A quadcopter is a type of drone characterised by having four rotors. This difference can affect a person's capacity to control the drone, as more rotors can allow for more speed but also more interferences due to having more rotors. Most such quadcopters are fragile in a sense, as they cannot hold any backup motors, carry heavy objects, or have consistent stability. Furthermore, most play drones typically weigh half-a-pound to five pounds, have a flight time of fifteen to thirty mins, and must always be in the operator's optical line-of-sight, per most federal regulations. Hence, the play drone and pilot share more physical contact, and the pilot has more immediate responsibility for the drone and their own actions as they must attend to maintenance for the drone, its navigational controls, legal regulations, and environmental factors. Play drones are smarter than most might expect of a 'toy'. Many of these drones can capture imagery and then synthesise multiple images into 3-D digital models. The strength of the drone's stability determines its camera capacities, including angles, range, and zoom. They are smart enough to see 'threats', thereby avoiding obstacles and keeping a stable flight path. However, no drone is yet completely autonomous. Like large-scale commercial and military drones, play drones require external stations, usually a mix of them, including GPS satellites, wireless radio frequency transmitters, WiFi networks, a ground station control computer, and of course, the user.

My primary case study of drone hobby culture are the drone fan websites, PhantomPilots.com, and MavicPilots.com. These websites are specifically for users of the DJI brand Phantom and Mavic series of drones, two of the most popular models for consumer use. These forums serve a variety of uses, sharing technical knowledge, providing updates on new drone models, and crowdsourcing answers to operational issues. Within these forums, there is also social interaction and support, which encourages hobbyists to freely express themselves and the changing, multifarious intricacies of their relationships with drones. The users align with the dominant demographic of drone users in the US and many European nations, men ranging in ages from the late teen years and up (Rossi 2017). Gender here is used as an analytic, a social idea defined by certain qualities, not an identity or biological category. There are plenty of woman-centred hobbyist communities as well. In a similar token, 'hobbyists', especially the ones surveyed here, are not an exceptional category.

Drone culture is widespread and multifarious, filled with various intensities of attachment.

As machines affiliated with militarism and warfare, drones and masculinity are an obvious pairing. In the forum, the outcome of this pairing is, on the surface, what you might expect: filled with violent, toxic masculine dominance that echoes military drone usage. One of the most popular threads is 'Things we tell our wives', a crowd-sourced list of different excuses, both comical and serious, for buying and flying a drone that these hobbyists use with their drone-reluctant wives. The wife becomes an obstacle to their drone-time, and they develop playful, yet violent and aggressive replies to their wives as a result. One of the highest-rated posts is a joke; they wrote 'if I can't have a drone can I have your sister?' ('Phantom Pilots Forums' 2017). To this, another replied, 'In my case, the family is loaded with beautiful sisters, I wouldn't use that as leverage as I have to go to sleep at some time […] (cue Jack Nicholson with a knife)' ('Phantom Pilots Forums' 2017). The poster is referencing a famous portrayal of a fictional enraged, possessed husband who kills his wife and son in the 1980 film *The Shining*. While these users are 'just joking' in their comments about killing, exchanging, and lying to beloved women in their lives, we cannot take these jokes lightly as humour indexes perspectives on reality. These jokes correspond to the dominant narrative of the drone operator as a cold, numbed, mindless 'drone' whose perception and judgement are altered due to the drone's detached 'video game' interface that leads them to dehumanise subjects.

This dominant narrative suppresses the exploration of the positive and tender attachments between pilots and drones, attachments that demonstrate immense vulnerability on the part of the human and drone. On the most basic level, to hobbyists, the drone is a special object that affords immense pleasure in the form of feelings of freedom through the play. Hobbyists treat flying time as playtime where they can escape the mundane toils of nine-to-five jobs and family obligations, for the drone provides what one hobbyist calls 'the freedom to fly' ('Mavic Pilots Forums' 2017). We can read 'fly' as the literal act of flying and drone and as the 'freedom' to 'fly away' from everyday life. Yet, a border is crossed within this freedom of flight – that between the user and drone – and their freedoms are interlinked. The drone is launched, physically flying, but the user is virtually flying through the drone, freed from their bodily limitations. In this relation, one's 'freedom to fly' cannot exist without one another.

As such, the 'freedom to fly' refers also refers to psychological flight between oneself and one's world, between the psychic realm and the physical realm. One hobbyist explains why they fly drones, 'the flying, gives me a sense of freedom and escape from everyday life. The twenty-five minutes or so of flight time is that time spent somewhere else, to see things as I normally wouldn't see it' ('Phantom Pilots Forums' 2019). The hobbyist's comments indicate a need for escapism from 'everyday life', as to suggest that drone-time is another reality, as if leisurely drone flying is innocent and thrilling escapism, countering the toils and restrictions of everyday life, that allows access to new psychological and physical spaces in a relieving manner.

Hobbyists' deep emotional attachments to their drones are unique in that they suggest the drone produces an overwhelming flourish of emotion, rather than the distance and numbness affiliated with military drone operators, as well as reports of drone operators attributing drone flying as the cause of immense mental distress and conditions (Greene and McEvers 2013). For some, the mere presence of drones is anxiety-inducing, even linked to PTSD, particularly in war zones where drone strikes are prevalent (Cavallaro, Knuckey, and Sonnenberg 2012). Civilians outside warzones, including the US and UK, have expressed fear of drones of various models, including play drones. The distinction between these scenes lies in how the drone becomes integrated into people's lives, how they use the drone, and how they perceive their relationship to the wider military and surveillance complex that gave birth to drones.

As play drones are a pared-down, domesticised version of military technology, the hobbyists' deep affection and even reliance on them, can work in favour of domestic militarisation and the surveillance state. How this goes unnoticed to hobbyists speaks to the pleasurable, trusting dynamic of hobbyist-drone relations, as well as the growing nature of drone culture in popular media, schools, and other domains of civilian life. Since the rise of the 'military-industrial-media-entertainment network', emerging after the Cold War, pleasure has been a powerful means to condition subjects to normalise warfare and militarism (Der Derian 2009). Hence, play drones can appeal to and condition nationalist sentiments, as well as compliance with drone use in warfare and domestic policing (Salter 2014). Moreover, domestic militarisation and surveillance may appear as nonthreats to many hobbyists because hobby culture is largely dominated by middle to upper-class white males in the US and other major nations in the global West, a population historically not targeted by either.

Even as this holds true, a deeper dive into the forums shows how the intimacy of hobbyists and drone relationships disrupt a fantasy of mastery or invulnerability in a way the hobbyists seem to accept via their emotional attachment. For these hobbyists, the loss of their drones is a partial loss of themselves. As one user writes, 'I can't give a full recount of events because it's simply too nauseating [...] but everyone's worst nightmare happened to me today when my P2V+ tumbled from the sky into the water [...] I feel like I'm mourning a child' ('Phantom Pilots Forums' 2014). By describing the drowned drone as a deceased child, we gain a stronger sense of how these drones are not simply bought, but made, an extension of the hobbyist; a child is loved unconditionally. The death of play drone-offspring even provokes collective mourning, as one user defends another who recently lost their drone: 'Can't you see he's in mourning. Have some compassion' ('Mavic Pilots Forums'

2019). Across the forums, there are drone RIP tribute videos, descriptions of drone losses causing bodily reactions (i.e., increased heart rate and sweating), and discussions of the intense lengths that 'mourning' brings them in efforts to save their drones. Hobbyists discernibly share a special bond, a nonjudgemental understanding of each other's attachment to their drones. The fact that these users primarily identify as male is pertinent here because their unabashed displays of tender emotions and reliance are in contradiction to traditional displays of stoic, individualist conceptions of masculinity.

Some hobbyists even describe their drone flight experiences as addicting and unique in comparison to other types of thrill-seeking. One poster describes himself as an older, retired Army service member with a lifelong interest in remote-controlled planes, air boats, off-road driving, and dirt bike racing. Despite all this, the drone is quite special. In his words, 'Nothing has ever given me the thrill that these little remote control drones do. I'm not that great of a pilot [...] This hobby or addiction has me won over. I'm hooked and love it!' ('Phantom Pilot Forums' 2014). Interestingly, the hobbyist admits that his skill level of flying does not compromise his thrill. It is implied that just the act of flying the drone itself gives him such a thrill, to the point where he is 'hooked' and unclear if this is a 'hobby or addiction'. The language of 'addiction' implies a level of incapacity supplemented by the drone. A hobby is a choice, but an addiction must be fed; the person relies upon it.

These disclosures of pilot-drone intimacy and reliance demonstrate the drone's immense capacity to overpower its operator through affective attachment, thus unfixing the active subject over passive object relationship. Further, the fact that the drone's absence causes such distress marks significant defiance from what drones were designed to do: protect its users from vulnerability while acting per the user's will. Rather than assume these attachments are wholly problematic as compliance with the surveillance state and proliferation of uncritical drone usage, I adapt what race and disability scholar Nirmala Erevelles terms 'disruptive vulnerability' (2014). Evervelles writes:

> disability studies is disruptive of any boundaries that claim to police distinctions between disabled/nondisabled subject positions. Noting the dangers of claiming that everyone is disabled at some historical moment, I propose instead a relational analysis to engage the materiality of disability at the intersections of race, class, gender, nation, and sexual identity within specific historical contexts. (2014 n.p.)

As an analytic, a crip approach, first theorised by Robert McRuer (2006) reassesses attributes related to disability as an embodied and social experience, such as interdependence, vulnerability, and passivity, which are wrongly considered inherently negative. Hence, hobbyists' disability status is irrelevant to my argument; instead, I consider how the vulnerabilities of hobbyist-drone intimacy are generative disruptions to conventional notions of drones as emotionally distancing tools that make the pilot invulnerable. While drones provide a fantasy of freedom that appeals to conventional masculinity and individualism simultaneously, I will further argue in what follows that the intimacy of hobbyist and drone relationships disrupt this fantasy and exercises an interdependent exploration of the self.

The Dronie

Dronies are a representative form of hobbyist-drone relations because they demonstrate the intimacy of the relationship and affective power the drone has over the hobbyist. The obvious predecessor of the dronie is the selfie. Visual culture and media studies have largely considered the selfie as affiliated with the self-portrait tradition, narcissism, neoliberal self-branding, identity performance, and the digital self (Burns 2015; Marwick 2013; Peraica 2017). In contrast, a growing body of scholarship theorises the selfie as a more social, dynamic form that is produced through a network of human and nonhuman (digital tools) actors. In these arguments, the selfie is more like a visual form of communication engaged in a social conversation (Gómez Cruz and Thornham 2015; Frosh 2015; Van House 2014). While arguments persist about the production of selfies and the effects of selfie culture, it is evident that selfies affect and reflect the selfie-taker to some degree. For the dronie, the drone is partially taking the photograph, hence a 'dronie' is a hybrid between the self and drone. This hybrid photograph form hints at how hobbyists celebrate human-drone integration, especially considering how 'dronie' doubles as a photographic object and an identity; across the forums, hobbyists regularly refer to themselves as 'dronies' ('Auto-dronie?' 2016; 'Hello Dronies' 2020). Yet, drones and selfies, in theory, are at odds. Drones anonymise the pilot(s) and de-individualise their 'target' via geographical and conceptual distance, as well as layers of mediation. Selfies are generally taken to affirm one's identity, even manipulating their appearance to achieve an idealised self-presentation. The 'dronie' is a middle-ground, I suggest. A dronie, a form of elected self-representation, claims to represent a subject, which in this case is the human-drone intimacy, their relation. Owning to 'dronie' as both photo and identity, the form itself indicates a generative disruption to individualism.

Dronies can facilitate or indicate an exploration of the self rather than a representational selfie because of the different heights and angles at which drones can fly. The content of dronies varies because the subject can be depicted in an endless range of proximities and settings. However, most dronies tend to be in a bird's-eye view perspective, taking advantage of the drone's flight capacity. Dronies can be taken on a timer, automatic setting, or simply by utilising the hand controller. One critical similarity between the dronie and selfie is how they circulate via social media, which can also drive motivation to take them and affect the content. Social media has normalised

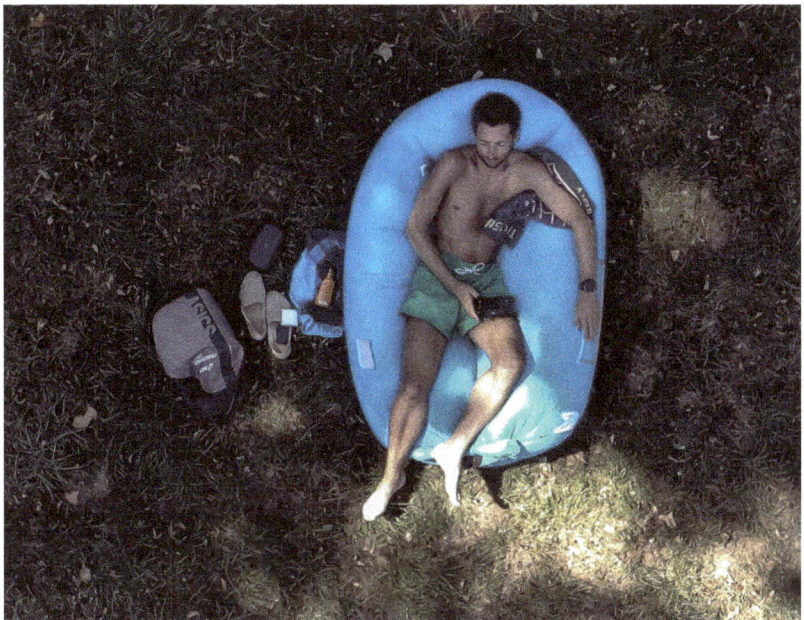

Figure 7.1. Marco Verch, *Drone Selfie* (2018).
Creative Commons License, CC-BY 2.0.

the regular practice of demonstrating one's social status and accomplishments, which includes intentionally or unintentionally projecting an idealised version of yourself. As such, it is common to see dronies posted on social media, and often these dronies show the human subject in fun or powerful positions against beautiful scenery, projecting them living a life of luxury and possessing socially desirable traits.

One dronie example (see Figure 7.1) demonstrates how a dronie is an attractive yet vulnerable prospect. The male-presenting human subject, the dronie co-photographer, lays directly beneath the drone in the center of the frame, seeming relaxed and unbothered by the drone above. To feel comfortable with such a position indeed implies a high degree of social privilege and a sense of control wherein the drone is a mere watchdog that the user trusts will stay put. Contributing to the intimacy of being and taking a 'dronie' is that this is a scene of rest, thereby indicating his confidence in his relationship with the drone. Rather than using the drone for thrill-seeking or taking dronies in unique scenery, such as famous sites or a mountain top, he elects to show himself living the 'good life', simple and peaceful. Moreover, as a scene of relaxation, rest is an exposing and passive position that allows the influence of external forces, which in this case is the drone and all its networked connections. While the proximity of the drone is unknown, it appears rather close.

As much as this is a seemingly static scene, in both content and medium, there is a dynamic movement implied by the remote that he is loosely holding in one hand, signaling the absent presence of the drone above. With the screen before him, he can watch himself through the drone, creating a sensation of being in two places at once. Yet, he is not truly seeing himself, but how the drone sees him. When taking a dronie, the pilot can see themselves on the pilot's screen that projects the drone's vision. The screen often shows themselves mapped by the drone, with grid lines framing their face and body against the background. Part of the process is that the pilot must make the drone focus on them, framing the pilot's body. The resulting aesthetic bears striking resemblance to what someone hunting or tracking an animal or enemy would see on their camera screen. The controller makes this mediation apparent and allows him to sense himself as a subject and object simultaneously. The subject is further conceptually decentred as the focus of the image due to the drone's haunting presence. Moreover, expectations of drone positions change; he is both pilot and target, which interrupts notions of drones as creating zones of one-sided vulnerability. Rather than settle this subject-object relation or pilot-target, we can think of 'dronie' as an intermediary state characterised by the willingness to be both.

Hobbyists' implicit desire to expose themselves to the effects of drones is antithetical to one of the supposed benefits of drones, making pilots invulnerable to any harm they may experience on the ground or in a manned aircraft. Of course, the risks of play drones versus military and commercial vastly differ in severity and scale. Yet, if we hold only a normative idea of how vulnerability appears and where, we overlook what the dronie represents: a willed disruption of independence. Differing from many technologies intimately engaged in one's everyday life, the hobbyists see the drone as having a life of its own, even giving their drones names and treating them as a friend. In the forums, one hobbyist begins imagining his reaction if his PhantomPro drone left him, meaning it 'flew away', which commonly occurs with play drone models (Kishk, Bader, and Alouini 2020). The hobbyist says, if 'Phantom decided to go see the world on its [*sic*] own, then yes, I would be upset, but I'll definitely go buy another, after a respectable period of mourning of course' ('Phantom Pilots Forums' 2013). The drone goes to 'see the world on its own' as if it is a child or ex-lover leaving home to advance on to the next part of their lives whose absence he will 'mourn'. Someone could come to love a drone to the point where they consider its 'growth' in such a tender manner, hence, setting the stage for a human-drone relationship not based on mastery nor disengagement but desire.

Retaining the interconnections between human, drone, and dronie echoes a pillar of feminist disability studies, which rethinks the negative valences attributed to interdependency and vulnerability, particularly with other people, and with support animals, devices, medications, technologies, and social systems such as hospitals and food distribution programs. By recognising the impossibility of pure autonomy, some disability scholars have proposed that such interdependency can engender new forms of subjectivity and materiality (Goodley, Rebecca, and Runswick-Cole 2014). Without reconciling the irresolvable tension between the positive and harmful effects of interdependence with technology, the desire and openness for such a relationship suggests a desire beyond the general overvaluation of independence, as it is conceptualised in a masculine, ableist framework, in liberal humanist traditions. Recalling the hobbyist forums and the loving affective disposition displayed towards play drones, and the mourning of lost or broken drones, it is evident drones provide a special experience that hobbyists come to rely upon. Questioning the authenticity of these attachments, as psychology or human-robot interaction studies might, is irrelevant to recognising the power of the attachment.

Life as Target

By its nature, human-technology interdependency invites risk and ambiguity. Indeed. the drone's military origins help us gather how this interdependent relationship is far from revolutionary. There is a long history of soldiers coming to love their weapons and technologies, especially when they rely on these objects to save their lives. This has been demonstrated in soldiers' bonds with various types of robotic technologies. Julie Carpenter, for one, has documented the close bonds that military personnel form with explosive ordnance disposal (EOD) robots used in the removal of harmful, explosive materials (2016). In the context of life-or-death military operations, it is more understandable why positive emotional attachments form between users and life-saving or sustaining technologies. The domestication of military medical technologies, namely modern-day prosthetics, has likewise played a role in catalysing users to develop intimate toward these technologies that both aid in their daily functioning and compromise their autonomy. These attachments have been particularly well-documented in disability studies from disabled people, which I would argue amplifies their vulnerability to military influence even as prosthetics offer a liberatory potential (Nelson, Shew, and Stevens 2019).

The affectionate normalisation of play drones threatens to condition people to accept, and perhaps even enjoy, experiencing life as a target. Play drones and military drones are extremely disparate systems, difficult to compare at a technical level, but dronies signify the ongoing militarisation of life in domestic spaces by conditioning trust in aerial, semi-autonomous visualising technologies and thus likewise spreading militarised modes of seeing. Numerous visual culture and technology theorists have charted the corresponding, interspliced histories of targeting guns, military weaponry, and film and photography (Burton 1978; Landau 2002; Virilio 1984). For Paul Virilio, moving images and war are deeply linked; the birth of cinema and the camera corresponded with the rise of action-at-a-distance warfare as the visualising technology mediates the distance between two enemies, between photographer/audience and visualised object. This sensory-technology relation trains the public for war that is always present or on the horizon, and, to add to Virilio, for domestic policing and surveillance. This training works by conditioning the public to not only expect that they are always under watch, always a target, but to accept the watchers as part of normal, daily life. For instance, numerous domestic police forces in the global North have been regularly deploying drones that bear visual resemblance to play drones, in both shape, size, and general design. At times, it may be hard to tell police from hobbyist drones.

In tandem with conditioning subjects to grow comfortable to targeting, play dronies are perhaps the civilian technology that most obviously motivates subjects to track themselves. There are even designated self-tracking 'selfie drones' that particularly promote self-tracking with seemingly safe and innocent functions and aesthetic design features (Richardson 2020). Play drones are a formidable contribution to the growing self-surveillance culture. The hobbyist is not alone with just the drone, as the drone's recording of their activity, and of the hobbyists, is digitally stored and thus available to be accessed by drone manufacturers and third parties. In fact, the data privacy risk of play drones is a controversial aspect discussed in media and legal circles (Winkler, Zeadally, and Evans 2018). Hobbyists self-surveil using their drones, often by using the 'follow me' feature on drones. In this mode, the drone links to the hobbyist's smartphone and follows the hobbyist as they move around physically on the ground. Many drones can be programmed to follow a GPS-enabled device, or to utilise sensors, recognition technology, and deep learning software that give drones the ability to identify and track a person or object. The drone simply follows the hobbyist, hovering like a guardian, whose flight path becomes the footpath of the hobbyist. The resulting relation is akin to a dog that loyally follows its owner.

Advancing the man-dog analogy, reciprocation is one critical variable that separates hobby-drone relations from other forms of conditioning self-surveillance. Unique to play drones in comparison to other drones and personal surveillance technologies (fitness trackers, sleep monitors, smartphones, etc.) is that the drone and hobbyist intimately watch one another; it is even part of federal law in many countries. In the US, the Federal Flight Administration (FAA) mandates that hobbyists always maintain physical sight of the drone and are responsible for the drone's flight paths. Unlike the networked operations of military and even commercial drone operations, which involve multiple human and nonhuman actors operating a single drone, it is largely just the hobbyist and the drone. As the hobbyist forums reveal, the drone serves as more of a companion than a tool or device, which may be due to how they share an optical engagement in the same physical space. This shared physical and psychological space may further explain how they are more apt to take more responsibility for the drone's actions.

The intimacy of their relationship does not reproduce a central moral dilemma of drone warfare, which is the apparent decentralisation of the machine-augmented decision-making process, and that of flight operations. When it comes to responsibility for individual acts of violence and misjudgements in war, who is accountable? Mary Cummings, an expert on human-unmanned systems interaction and an ex-military fighter pilot, has warned her colleagues and the public from conceptualising the drone as wholly or even largely autonomous. Cummings fears this conceptualisation could quell any sense of responsibility, and hence drone autonomy is a 'moral buffer' that can 'in effect, allow people to ethically distance themselves from their actions and diminish a sense of accountability and responsibility' (2014: 30). The 'moral buffer' of this distributed agency network does not transfer to hobbyist-drone relations, as hobbyists are more apt to take responsibility for their actions, but still attribute the drone with its own agency.

Due to the care hobbyists provide, and the perceived benefits of the drone, hobbyist-drone relations are a reciprocal, interdependent engagement, destroying what Nathan K. Hensley has identified as 'drone form' across drone-related literature and art. Hensley identified the nonreciprocal nature of drone vision, to see without being seen, as 'consolidated authority', explaining that,

> drone technology helps us see that in fact 'consolidated vision' was always naming a problem of sovereignty. Drone form makes this explicit, since it twins representational capacity – the power to see and to observe or, as Said has it, to narrate – 'with the capacity to kill'. (2016: n.p.)

Hensley specifies that drone vision is not a third-person omnipresent perspective, seeing all from nowhere, but a limited third-person perspective because drone vision, distant and asymmetrical, cannot access a watched subject's inner thoughts and emotions. Hence, drone form is about seeing all that others cannot feel, think, or do. For all the ways this drone form describes commercial and military drone operations, turning watched subjects into objects, this form does not hold when the drone operator is simultaneously the drone's watcher and the drone's target. When the drone operator is also the drone target, reciprocity is injected into drone form, decentralising authority as well as the capacities to see, observe, narrate, and kill, literally or symbolically. The operator's dual status as watcher and target, which inherently makes them vulnerable to the drone and its networks, disrupts the authority positions that the drone was arguably designed to create and uphold.

As a visual form produced through operator-drone intimacy, the dronie further corroborates that the hobbyist-drone relationship is a site where vulnerability and the reciprocal nature of the relation, can disrupt a manifold of boundaries on what can be seen, felt, and thought. For one, here I

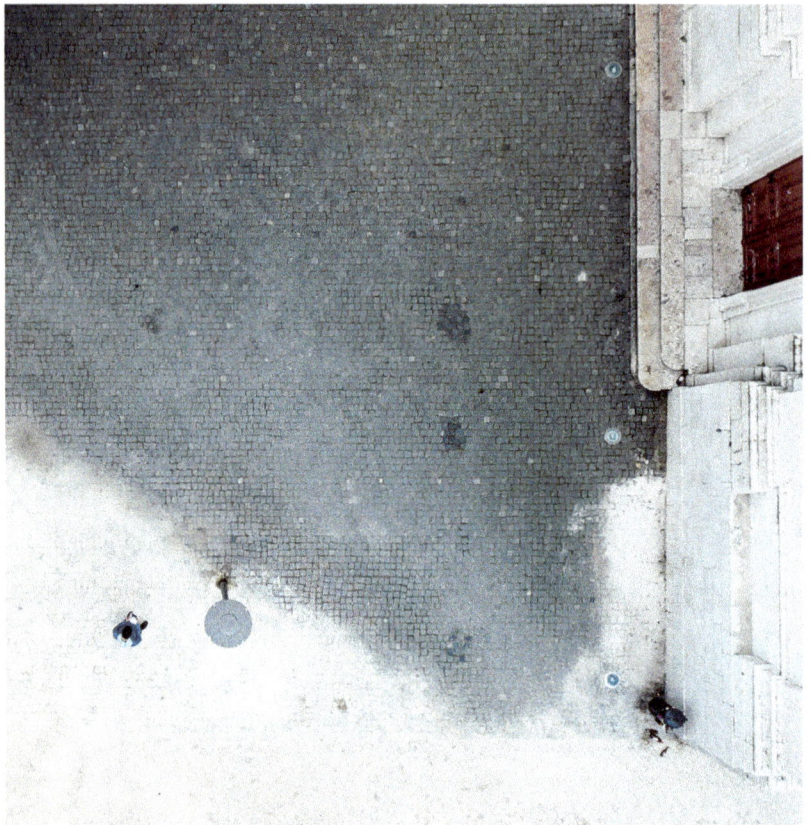

Figure 7.2. Marco Verch, *Drone Selfie* (2017).
Creative Commons License, CC-BY 2.0.

attend to how the dronie may increase one's awareness of surveillance. To this point, Maximillian Jablonowski theorises the dronie as expanding the drone's 'aesthetics of verticality', as the dronie's photographed subject is positioned at a vertical angle due to the drone's aerial position (2017: 97). Ultimately Jablonowski argues in favour of the dronie as a potential counter practice to dominant surveillance practices of verticality, as the dronie may cultivate new forms of representation and sensing. Prefiguring counter surveillance, however, is the drone's generative disruption of normative notions of who is vulnerable in the age of mass surveillance.

Figure 7.2 demonstrates the potential of the dronie to make new sensations of vulnerability palpable for the hobbyist, among others. It is taken at such a height that one might have difficulty distinguishing the human subject from the black pole on the right side of the frame against the building. Such ambiguity speaks to how drone vision clouds perception even as it enhances perception. Military drone operators, for instance, have gone as far as to confuse children and dogs when determining a target to strike (Friedersdorf 2012). The bird's eye angle and sparsity of the courtyard shown lend to framing the subject as a target. The dronie's de-individualising power and the drone's hovering presence make it apparent that they, the subject, are just an object of surveillance. Unlike just a photo of oneself taken by another person, the dronie is an intimate visualising process produced through the photographed subject and the drone that can force the subject to become estranged from themselves. The subject's conceptual distance from oneself can disrupt their assumptions of who is vulnerable within the surveillance state, extending the appearance of dehumanisation that drones induce in overseas warfare.

A lens purely on structural hierarchies forecloses how the 'dronie' is a mode of being that creates the possibility to imagine oneself differently, which is enabled by passivity toward the drone. Passivity, a form of vulnerability, is a necessary precondition for external force (i.e., the drone) to disrupt one's sense of self and build new relations. Rather than the subject's act of photographing oneself for a selfie, the dronie entails that the subject is passive, they let themselves be targeted and captured by the drone's lens. As such, the crip potential of the dronie is that it indicates an embrace of partial nonagency and interdependency as a means of understanding oneself. For instance, notable about the dronie shown in Figure 7.2 is that it refuses the selfie convention of showing one's face. In fact, their identity is indeterminable, known only to themselves and the drone. From this angle, the subject seems unaware of where the drone is or what they are seeing of them. The human subject can barely be seen at such a height; their identity is secondary to the drone's view of their identity. In tandem, the setting lacks vibrant colours or exciting scenery, portraying a rather gray mundane courtyard. By emphasising the anonymity and dissolution of the human subject, the image presents the question of who the subject could be under drones, avoiding representational fixity. If a selfie is reflective of egotism and self-promotion, a dronie can serve to explore oneself under the same drone skies we share.

As with many automated and action-at-a-distance technologies, drones were invented to mediate physically and emotionally dangerous experiences and to protect users from certain kinds of harm. In short, drones are supposed to turn humans into drones, into mindless, passive, and unchanging beings or states. Yet, in the case of hobbyists, instead of reducing feeling, drones amplify the feelings of these hobbyists, producing new zones of sensing and vulnerability. These affective, ambivalent attachments may not be positive or emancipatory, but they are a stark disruption to the automatic, numbed world that drones were invented to uphold.

Works Cited

'The Drone Dish'. 2020. *Airvuz.com* https://www.airvuz.com/video/The-Drone-Dish-wrenee?id=5a62169dc1bdfb63134f7213.

'Forums'. *MavicPilots.com*. 2010-Present. https://mavicpilots.com/.

'Forums'. *PhantomPilots.com*. 2010-Present. https://phantompilots.com/.

Boyle, Michael J. 2013. 'The Costs and Consequences of Drone Warfare'. *International Affairs* 89, no.1: 1-29.

Burns, Anne L. 2015. 'Self (ie)-discipline: Social Regulation as Reenacted through the Discussion of Photographic Practice'. *International Journal of Communication* 9: 1716-33.

Burton, Julianne. 1978. 'The Camera as "Gun": Two Decades of Culture and Resistance in Latin America'. *Latin American Perspectives* 5, no. 1: 49-76.

Butler, Judith. 2006. *Precarious Life: The Powers of Mourning and Violence*. London: Verso.

Carpenter, Julie. 2016. *Culture and Human-robot Interaction in Militarized Spaces: A War Story*. London: Routledge.

Cavallaro, James, Sarah Knuckey, and Stephan Sonnenberg. 2012. *Living Under Drones: Death, Injury, and Trauma to Civilians from US Drone Practices in Pakistan*. International Human Rights and Conflict Resolution Clinic.

Chamayou, Grégoire. 2015. *A Theory of the Drone*. New York: The New Press.

Cummings, Mary L. 2014. 'Creating Moral Buffers in Weapon Control Interface Design'. *IEEE Technology and Society Magazine* 23, no. 3: 28-33.

Der Derian, James. 2009. *Virtuous War: Mapping the Military-industrial-Media-Entertainment-Network*. London: Routledge.

Enemark, Christian. 2013. *Armed Drones and the Ethics of War: Military Virtue in a Post-heroic Age*. London: Routledge.

Erevelles, Nirmala. 2014. 'Thinking with Disability Studies'. *Disability Studies Quarterly* 34, no. 2. https://dsq-sds.org/article/view/4248/3587.

Friedersdorf, Conor. 2012. 'The Guilty Conscience of a Drone Pilot Who Killed a Child'. The Atlantic. December 19. https://www.theatlantic.com/politics/archive/2012/12/the-guilty-conscience-of-a-drone-pilot-who-killed-a-child/266453/.

Frosh, Paul. 2015. 'The Gestural Image: The Selfie, Photography Theory, and Kinesthetic Sociability'. *International Journal of Communication* 9: 1607-28;

Gómez-Cruz, Edgar and Thornham, Helen. 2015. 'Selfies Beyond Self-representation: The (theoretical) F(r)ictions of a Practice'. *Journal of Aesthetics & Culture*, 7, no. 1: 1-10.

Goodley, Dan, Rebecca Lawthom, and Katherine RunswickCole. 2014. 'Posthuman Disability Studies'. *Subjectivity* 7, no. 4: 342-61.

Greene, David, and Kelly McEvers. 2013. 'Former Air Force Pilot Has Cautionary Tales about Drones'. *Iowa Public Radio.* May 10. https://www.iowapublicradio.org/2013-05-10/former-air-force-pilot-has-cautionary-tales-about-drones.

Hensley, Nathan. 2016. 'Drone Form: Word and Image at the End of Empire'. *E-Flux* 72. https://www.e-flux.com/journal/72/60482/drone-form-word-and-image-at-the-end-of-empire/.

Himes, Kenneth R. 2015. *Drones and the Ethics of Targeted Killing.* Lanham: Rowman & Littlefield.

Jablonowski, Maximilian. 2013. 'Dronie Citizenship?'. In *Selfie Citizenship*, edited by Adi Kuntsman, 97-106. Palgrave Macmillan.

Kafer, Alison. 2013. *Feminist, Queer, Crip.* Bloomington: Indiana University Press.

Kishk, Mustafa, Ahmed Bader, and Mohamed-Slim Alouini. 2020. 'Aerial Base Station Deployment in 6G Cellular Networks using Tethered Drones: The Mobility and Endurance Tradeoff'. *IEEE Vehicular Technology Magazine* 15, no. 4: 103-111.

Landau, Paul S. 2002. 'Empires of the Visual: Photography and Colonial Administration In Africa'. *Images and Empires: Visuality in Colonial and Postcolonial Africa* 2: 141-71.

Marwick, Alice E. 2013. *Status Update: Celebrity, Publicity, and Branding in the Social Media Age.* New Haven: Yale University Press.

McRuer, Robert. 2006. *Crip Theory: Cultural Signs of Queerness and Disability 9.* New York: NYU Press.

Nelson, Mallory Kay, Ashley Shew, and Bethany Stevens. 2019. 'Transmobility: Possibilities in Cyborg (Cripborg) Bodies'. *Catalyst: Feminism, Theory, Technoscience* 5, no. 1: 1-20.

Noys, Benjamin. 2015. 'Drone Metaphysics'. *Culture Machine* 1: 1-22.

Peraica, Ana. 2017. *Culture of the Selfie: Self-representation in Contemporary Visual Culture.* Theory on Demand: Institute of Network Cultures.

Rhee, Jennifer. 2018. *The Robotic Imaginary: The Human and the Price of Dehumanized Labor.* Minnesota: University of Minnesota Press.

Richardson, Michael. 2020. 'Drone Cultures: Encounters with Everyday Militarisms'. *Continuum 34*: 858-69.

Rossi, Ben. 2017. 'Majority of Drone Owners Are Men Over 50 Years Old'. *Information Age.* October 24. https://www.information-age.com/majority-drone-owners-men-50-years-old-123469290/.

Salter, Michael. 2014. 'Toys for the Boys? Drones, Pleasure and Popular Culture in the Militarisation of Policing'. *Critical Criminology* 22, no. 2: 163-77.

Shildrick, Margrit. 2002. *Embodying the Monster: Encounters with the Vulnerable Self.* London: Sage Publications.

Van House, Nancy A. 2011. 'Feminist HCI meets Facebook: Performativity and Social Networking Sites'. *Interacting with Computers* 23, no. 5: 422-29.

Virilio, Paul. 1989. *War and Cinema: The Logistics of Perception.* London: Verso.

Winkler, Stephanie, Sherali Zeadally, and Katrine Evans. 2018. 'Privacy and Civilian Drone Use: The Need for Further Regulation.' *IEEE Security & Privacy* 16, no. 5: 72-80.

8

Imaginational Metaveillance: Revelations in the Drone Age

Kathryn Brimblecombe-Fox

> The fact of having reached the light barrier, the speed of light, is a historic event, one which disorients history and also disorients the relation of human beings to the world. If that point is not stressed, then people are being disinformed, they are being lied to. For it has enormous importance. It poses a threat to geopolitics and geostrategy.
>
> —Paul Virilio, 'Red Alert in Cyberspace', 1995

Since 2015, my paintings have been informed by research focused on airborne militarised drones, their persistent surveillance capabilities and increasingly autonomous systems. This research intersects with long-term interests in how landscape is mediated by technology, and existential risk posed by emerging technologies (see Figure 8.1).

I invite viewers of my paintings to fly into cosmic skies where they can soar around and beyond airborne drones or indications of their presence – for example, relay stations, signals, and satellites. I call this kind of 'flight' an act of 'imaginational metaveillance', a mode of oversight veillance outside a machine's capability. The medium of painting is not reliant on electronic, digital, or cyber technology for creation, exhibition, and storage, thus a distance is forged from the platforms that militarised, dual-use, and militarisable civilian technologies share. This distance, rather than precluding painting as a medium of critique, invigorates its critical capacities. As viewers of my paintings take 'flight', this distance reveals multiple new perspectives, affording multiple interpretations of each painting, even simultaneously. With imaginational metaveillance this multiplicity stimulates new questions, and therefore, possible new answers.

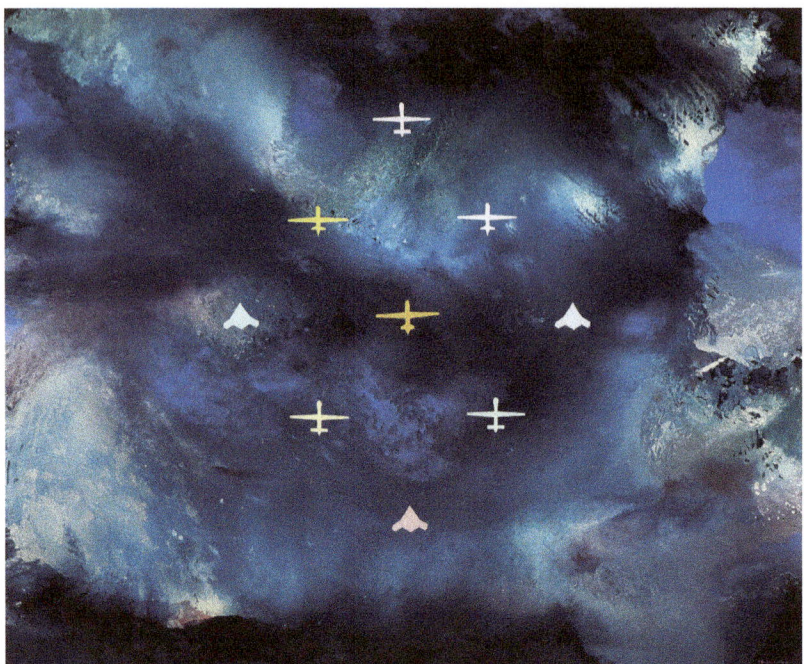

Figure 8.1. Kathryn Brimblecombe-Fox. *Drone Show*, oil on linen, 122x152cm (2020). Photo courtesy of Cian Sanders.

In their distancing from the techno-system, painting and imaginational metaveillance provide novel approaches that contribute to important and necessary multi-disciplinary discussions about technology, war, and humanity, now and in the future. The significance of imaginational metaveillance's cosmic oversight capacity, and the multiple perspectives it affords, is clear in light of cosmologist Martin Rees's comment: a 'cosmic perspective strengthens the imperative to cherish this "pale blue dot" in the cosmos. It should also motivate a circumspect attitude towards technical innovations that pose even a small threat of catastrophic downside' (Rees 2003: 188). My painting *Drone Spiral 2* (see Figure 8.2) speaks to the 'imperative to cherish this "pale blue dot"'. Weaponised drones are painted in a mock landscape that spirals, but is the landscape falling away from Earth, or collapsing into it? Some of the drones are painted with small squares, mimicking pixels and digital imaging. The viewer may be flying beyond the drones, but they could also be viewing a digital image on a computer screen. Although my paintings are imaginational, they are not fantasies. Rather, they are informed visual speculations that take a 'circumspect attitude'.

In this visual essay, particular attention is paid to signals, deployed via wavelengths in the electromagnetic spectrum to support and enable contemporary militarised technology, dual-use technology and militarisable civilian

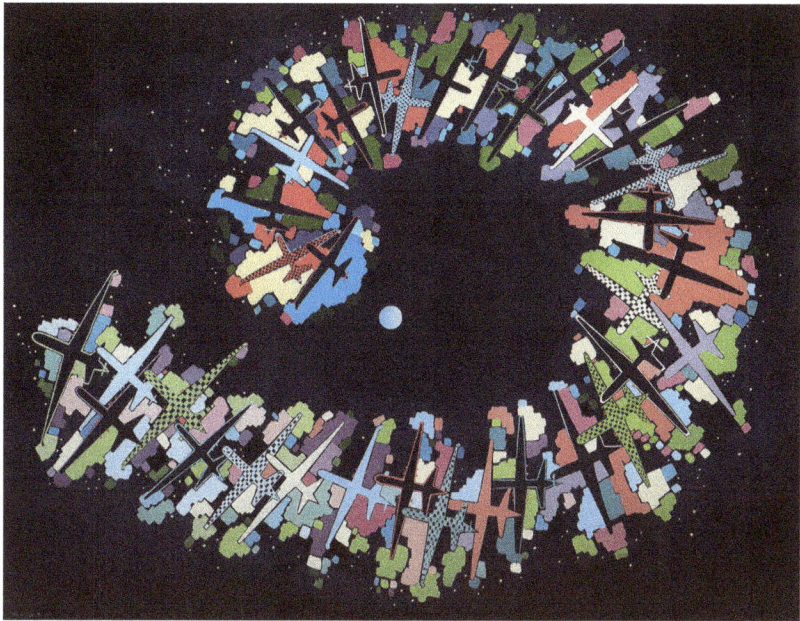

Figure 8.2. Kathryn Brimblecombe-Fox, *Drone Spiral 2*, oil on linen, 120x160cm (2018). Photo courtesy of Cian Sanders.

technology. Signals represent an invisible support infrastructure that facilitates the light speed transmission of information, data, and instructions from land-based, sky-based, and space-based assets and nodes. Here, imaginational metaveillance offers a way to scrutinise normally invisible signals. After years of visualising signals in my paintings, along with airborne drones and strings of colourful binary code, I suggest that the invisibility of signals both buttresses and obscures changing modes of war and war preparedness.

Since 1957, when the USSR launched Sputnik 1, the use of satellites in low Earth orbit (LEO) and geostationary orbit (GEO) has burgeoned to a point where these optimal orbits are increasingly populated with satellites of varying military, dual-use, and civilian capabilities. Using imaginational metaveillance, I 'see' the space between Earth and orbiting satellites as an extension of an environment occupied by signals, their invisibility obscuring the operative agency that enables contemporary technology. It is in this occupied space that airborne drones surveil and target. The drone, a sky-based intermediary between land and space, is a visible and material emblem of twenty-first century militarised technological prowess. The drone's declared and covert use by state and nonstate actors is underwritten by invisible signals, the harbingers of the changing nature of twenty-first century war.

My father was a grain grower in western Queensland, Australia. However, from the age of twelve, he was also a keen amateur radio enthusiast, a Ham, call sign VK4ZWB. When I was growing up, my father had at least three

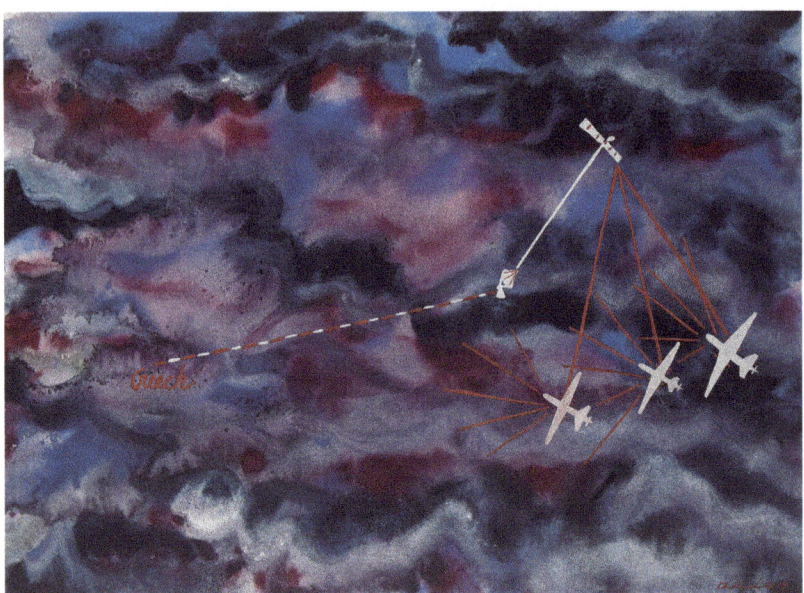

Figure 8.3. Kathryn Brimblecombe-Fox, *Multi-Mission*, gouache on paper, 30x42cm (2019). Photo courtesy of Cian Sanders.

aerials, one a huge structure, dotted around the farm. On each aerial he mounted antennae to optimise transmission and reception of signals, enabling messages to be sent and received from around Australia and the world. I grew up surrounded by electronic gadgets, and when digital and cyber technology became available, computers proliferated, spilling over from my father's Ham shack into the house. Before I was born, my father's Ham passion and his exemplary kit saw him participate in the inception of the Cold War's space race. When Sputnik 1 was launched my father, aged just 20, was one of the Hams around the world conscripted to track the spacecraft. When I asked him who he sent the co-ordinates to, he replied that it was 'someone' who then sent them to the Jet Propulsion Unit in America (NASA 2007).

In paintings, like *Multi-Mission* (see Figure 8.3) I depict signals as lines connecting land-based, sky-based, and space-based hardware and nodes. By making invisible signals visible it becomes apparent that our extended environment, from land to orbiting satellites, is netted and occupied. Given the role signals play in operatively enabling contemporary technology, networking, interconnectivity, and interoperability, an examination of this occupied space, as a type of battlespace, informs analyses of contemporary war and war preparedness. This examination is demanded in an age where civilian technology can be appropriated for militarised purposes, for example, in cases of tracking mobile phones and motor vehicle GPS. Here, the signal-enabled networked and interconnected system expedites conflating activities across military, security, and policing operations. As ideas of war reach beyond physical borders into cyberspace, algorithmic realms, and the internet of things (IoT), civilian and domestic geographic and cyber domains are hijacked or hijackable. Additionally, light-speed signal transmission of data, information and instructions combines invisibility with discrete dimensions of speed and time that are inaccessible to human beings. Taking militarised and militarisable technology, networking, interconnectivity, interoperability, and speed of signal transmission into account, Derek Gregory's idea of an 'everywhere war' encapsulates a persistent war, capable of instantly escalating or de-escalating, anywhere – anytime (Gregory 2011).

Paul Virilio's commentaries on the effects of accelerating speeds of technological development, and on the accelerating speeds of technological operation, provide critical lenses to examine the relationship between technology, speed, and contemporary war. Virilio identifies individual and societal electro-optical doping, paralysis, and inertia as effects of accelerating technological speed (Virilio 2012: 2, 18, 33). He describes technologically induced inertia as something that 'radically alters our relationship to the world, our relations with the *real* (terrestrial or extra-terrestrial) environment' (Virilio 2000: 70). He also notes that interconnectivity results in a 'progressive loss of relations with the external environment' (68). Loss or radical alteration of the way we relate to environment intersects with Virilio's ideas of the accident where 'no technology has ever been developed that has not had to struggle against its own specific negativity' (Virilio 1995: 2). Virilio's observations raise the question, what is the accident of a militarised and militarisable networked and interconnected system operating at light speed? Virilio's warning that 'the more powerful and high performance the invention, the more dramatic the accident', is a reminder that a combination of war and advancing technology is a volatile mix (Virilio 2007: 31). If accelerating speeds of technological development and operation contribute to a 'loss of relations with the external environment', the accident of contemporary militarised and militarisable technology might be Gregory's idea of the 'everywhere war' (Gregory 2011). If 'everywhere war' draws state and nonstate actors, and human and nonhuman forces, into a diffuse environment of real and virtual domains, how does this diffusion affect traditional ideas of human command? What happens when war is dispersed into realms of speed, time, and cyberspace inaccessible to humans? I offer a speculation: militaries are compelled to maintain command by attempting to martialise and militarise speed, time, and the future. What further accidents await?

Accelerated Warfare, the title of the Australian Chief of Army (2018-2022) Lieutenant General Rick Burr's 2018 'Futures Statement', reveals 'future of war' rhetoric that draws together technological speed with military planning (Burr 2018). The document is 'framed through the notion of future conflict', identifying 'artificial intelligence, machine learning, robotics, unmanned and autonomous capability with precision weaponry' as necessary for 'persistence and lethality' (Burr 2018). It also notes that 'Networking will be critical' and

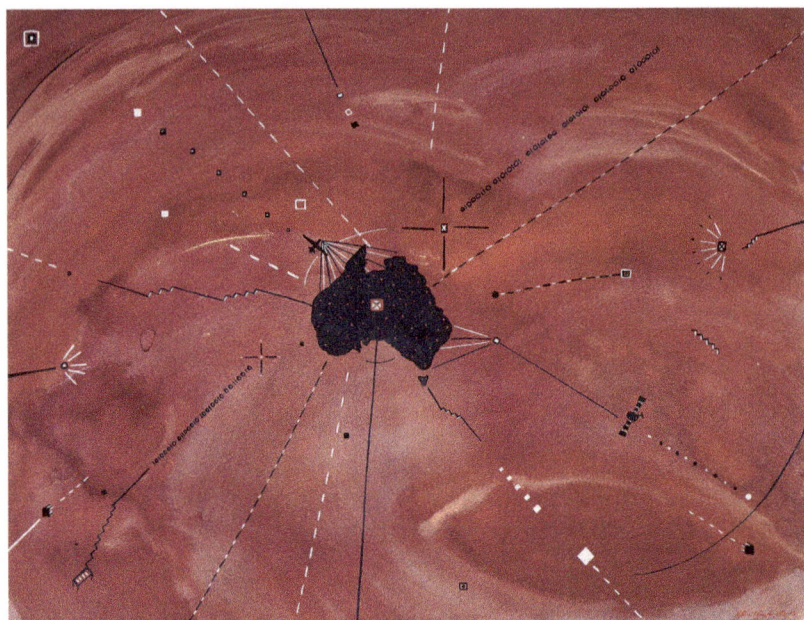

Figure 8.4. Kathryn Brimblecombe-Fox, *Not Waiting for the Future*, gouache on paper, 56x76cm (2018). Photo courtesy of Cian Sanders.

that 'Future warfare, in certain parts, will be fought at the speed of machines with success belonging to the side who can adapt the fastest' (Burr 2018). Clearly, speed is pivotal in contemporary strategic planning for war and imagined future war. Burr makes a comment in the last paragraph that demonstrates an anxiety about speed, technology, time, and the future. He writes, 'We must pull the future towards us rather than wait for it' (Burr 2018). My painting *Not Waiting for the Future* (2018) (see Figure 8.4) is a visual response to this comment. To indicate an acceleration of time, the Australian continent is inverted and seemingly perforated, and two strings of binary code 'instruct' the words FUTURE and LIFE. A drone, cross-hair graphics, signals, and a satellite are ominously placed. I have tried to demonstrate that Burr's strangely poetic comment pre-emptively militarises time and the future. Another example that provides further evidence of time's conscription into the accident of contemporary war is a statement by Bruce Jette, US Assistant Secretary of the Army, Acquisition, Logistics and Technology. Jette said, while touting the virtues of contemporary technological speed, that 'Around the acquisition community we're trying to get a philosophy going. Time is a weapon' (Association of the US Army 2019).

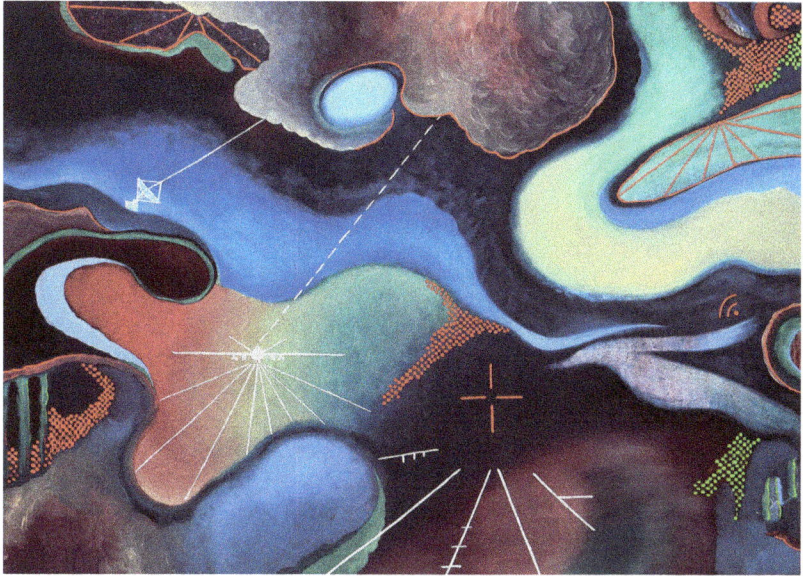

Figure 8.5. Kathryn Brimblecombe-Fox, *Lethal Landscape: False Horizons*, oil on linen, 70x100cm (2018). Photo courtesy of the artist.

Close Analysis: More Paintings

Lethal Landscape: False Horizon (2018)

In *Lethal Landscape: False Horizons* (see Figure 8.5) I have painted a weaponised drone and its support infrastructure in an abstruse landscape where sky and land merge into multiple horizons. The viewer seems to be airborne too, perhaps in front of the drone, slightly above it, or maybe monitoring it on a computer screen. These ambiguous perspectives are deliberate ploys to destabilise viewers, to release them from Earth-bound orientations in order to place the drone under the scrutiny of imaginational metaveillance.

White lines radiating from the drone's bulbous multi-spectral imaging sensor and its data-link antenna indicate normally invisible orienting, communication, surveillance and targeting signals. Other white and red lines mimic orienting sensors and computer-like graphics. Patches of green and red squares mimic pixels, the green indicating night-vision surveillance, and the red indicating thermal imaging or targeting technology. The appearance of pixels and computer graphic-like markings poses questions about the reality of a landscape where horizons may be false. Virilio's observation that the 'screen has become a substitute for the battlefield of the great wars of the past' informs my visual speculations (2007: 16). As I play with landscape and parodies of computer generated imagery, our radically altered relationship with the external environment, both terrestrial or extra-terrestrial, is pried open. I ask what kinds of horizons are crossed, literally and metaphorically, spatially and temporally, in the age of drone warfare, cyberwar, and 'killer algorithms'(Holland Michel 2020)?

Wingman (2020)

What if we called the drone a 'flying aerial', rather than an unmanned aerial vehicle (UAV)? As a signal emitting, transmitting and receiving intermediary between land and orbiting satellites, the drone's payload includes an array of antennae-reliant devices (Brimblecombe-Fox 2020). The more prosaically neutral term 'flying aerial' prompts an evaluation of human tendencies to anthropomorphise and fetishise technology. What risks are posed when machines and systems are ascribed human attributes, for example, '*body* of the drone', 'drone *vision*', 'machine *vision*' and '*eye* in the sky'? These terms put the human – the 'man' – back into the unmanned. Does this reveal a desire, potentially an unconscious dangerous desire, for relationship and identification with the machine? The name of the wingman drone-type, designed to fly as support for 'manned' fighter jets, clearly re-introduces the man. The wingman drone-type, like the jointly developed Royal Australian Air Force and Boeing 'loyal wingman' drone, now called the MQ-28 Ghost drone, even ascribes a human attribute of loyalty to the machine. With an array of advanced capabilities, including AI-assisted functions, payload flexibility and potential swarming facilities, the MQ-28 Ghost Bat drone is a remarkable example of contemporary militarised technology. However, rather than viewing advanced technologies, driven by AI and machine learning, as 'more than human', and therefore still relatable to humans, what happens if we think of them as 'other than human', inhuman or nonhuman?

In *Wingman* (see Figure 8.6) a surveillance night-vision green 'loyal wingman' MQ-28 Ghost Bat drone seemingly acts as a 'wingman' to Australia's Parliament House. For example, is it a 'fighter jet' or has technology jettisoned political coherence? How is Parliament House being 'piloted'? Is the loyal wingman drone *loyal* or a threat? Are the two hovering quadcopter drones benign observers, protectors, or signs of surveillance? These civilian drones address the creeping normalisation of drones used for surveillance and monitoring purposes, especially during the COVID-19 pandemic. The presence of the 'pale blue dot' asks: while Australia and other nations rapidly build advanced defence capabilities, what effects might a high-tech arms race have on our planet – our home?

As in my other paintings, the cosmic perspective evident in *Wingman* reminds us of distance, making room for multiple ways to critically think about war machines, militarised systems, and militarisable networks. Here, imaginational metaveillance restores distance in ways that reanimate the benefits of literal and metaphoric perspective. As cosmic and imaginational perspectives open up the sky, thoughts turn to those who are surveilled and targeted by drones in places such as the Middle East, Ukraine, and Somalia. That any person in the contemporary world is afraid of the sky, and of threats

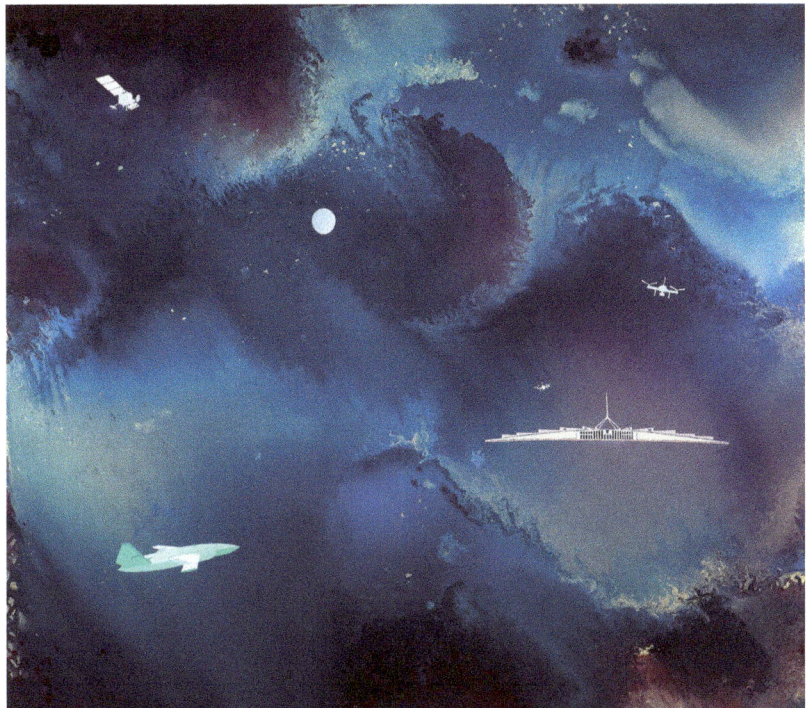

Figure 8.6. Kathryn Brimblecombe-Fox, *Wingman*, oil on linen, 97x115cm (2020). Photo courtesy of Cian Sanders.

it might harbour, condemns us all to an insidious foreclosure of literal and metaphoric perspective. Loss of any kind of perspective reduces the vitality of distance in ways that radically, but deceptively, alter our relationship with environment and each other. Is this evidence of Virilio's warnings of paralysis, doping, and inertia; perhaps blinding us to the forces of 'everywhere war'?

Topography Of Signals (2019)

A foreclosure of perspective, both literal and metaphoric, is presaged in a painting like *Topography of Signals* (see Figure 8.7) where the capacity for militarised systems to appropriate civilian systems and devices is presented as a kind of revelatory map. As viewers of the painting 'fly', are they above the signalscape looking down to a physical landscape, or are they below the signalscape peering up into a netted sky? The ability to oscillate between perspectives does not diminish the sense of enmeshment.

As the IoT burgeons, serious questions about the techno-colonising capabilities of militarised and militarisable systems need to be asked. I offer *Topography of Signals* as a kind of counter-map, a subversive exposure of the discrete nature of contemporary war preparedness, or war, perpetrated by state and nonstate actors through techno-colonising forces. Counter-mapping

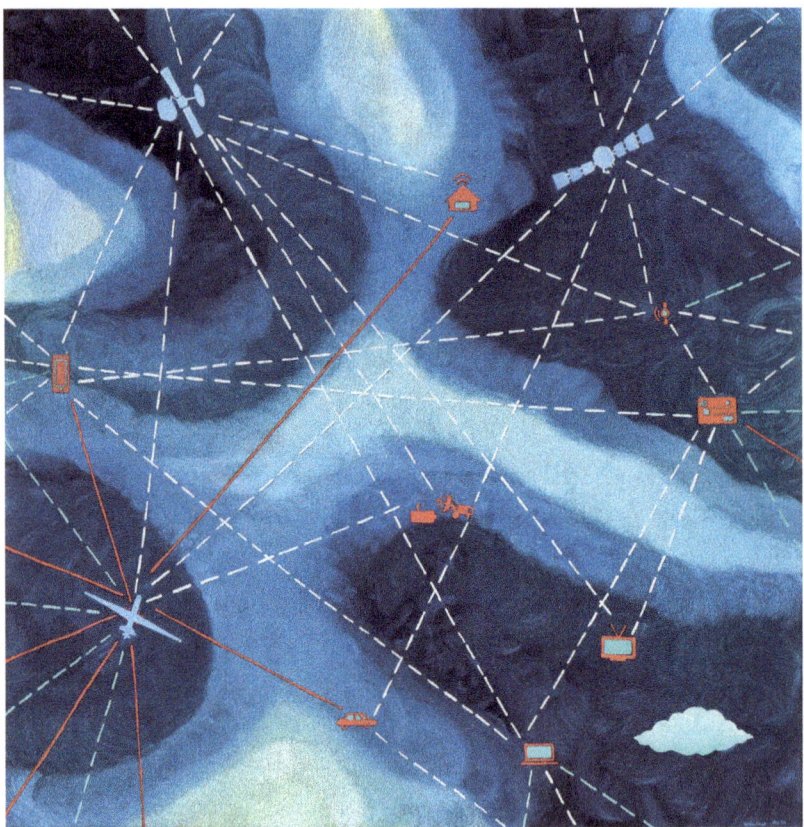

Figure 8.7. Kathryn Brimblecombe-Fox, *Topography Of Signals*, oil on linen, 57x57cm (2019). Photo courtesy of the artist.

is a visual method used by artists to deconstruct historical colonial annexations of land, and indigenous cultural and social dispersal. However, I offer paintings like *Topography of Signals* as speculative counter-maps that 'speak' to present and future modes of colonisation, and therefore, new modes of empire and war.

Taking Louise Amoore's conception that 'artistic interventions have capacity to call the norm into question, reminding us of what we do not pay attention to' *Topography of Signals* calls attention to new modes of techno-occupation of space by militarised and militarisable technologies. (Amoore 2009: 26) The topology of painted markings visualise and map techno-connectivity and interoperability. Here, underlying and enabling algorithmic instructions and authorisations cannot be ignored, for they 'speak' to Jean Baudrillard's 2003 prescient warning of a digitally coded future where it will be 'possible to measure everything by the same extremely reductive yardstick: the binary, the alternation between 0 and 1'. (Baudrillard 2003: 76) That future is now. Techno-colonising state and nonstate forces stealthily unleash what I call the code empire.

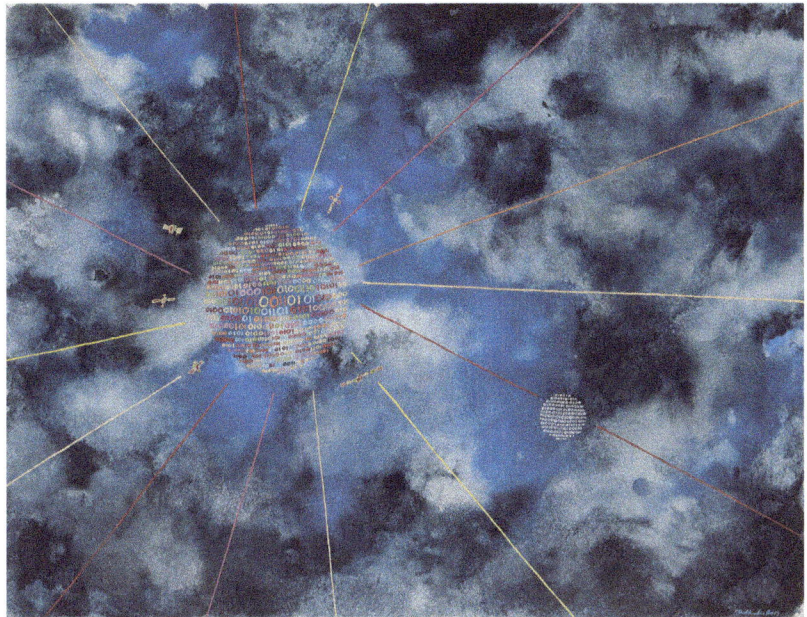

Figure 8.8. Kathryn Brimblecombe-Fox, *Code Empire*,
gouache on paper, 56x76cm (2017). Photo courtesy of Cian Sanders.

Code Empire (2017)

In my painting *Code Empire* (see Figure 8.8), painted strings of binary code 'instruct' the word EMPIRE. This painted code forms a colourful planet, presumably Earth, and its moon. The ubiquitous code, 'instructing' EMPIRE, has colonised both celestial bodies. The radiating signals, extending beyond the painting, suggest further signs of techno-colonisation. They could be autonomously activated protective shields, tracking of other spacecraft or communication attempts with extra-terrestrial intelligent life. As viewers of *Code Empire* 'fly' beyond the Earth and its moon, cosmic perspectives provide multiple critical portals into space and time. Are viewers imaginationally metaveilling a future planetary takeover by state or nonstate, human or nonhuman actors? Are viewers 'witnessing' colonisation by code, aided and abetted by light speed transmission of signals? Or, are viewers witnessing the algorithmic structure of simulation? Is this what 'everywhere war' looks like? change to: The painting speculatively searches the future as a warning notice for Burr's statement, 'We must pull the future towards us rather than wait for it.'"

Five Eyes And The Rest (2019)

In *Five Eyes And The Rest* (see Figure 8.9) five airborne drones circle. Each drone depicts partial sections of flags representing the Five Eyes intelligence alliance

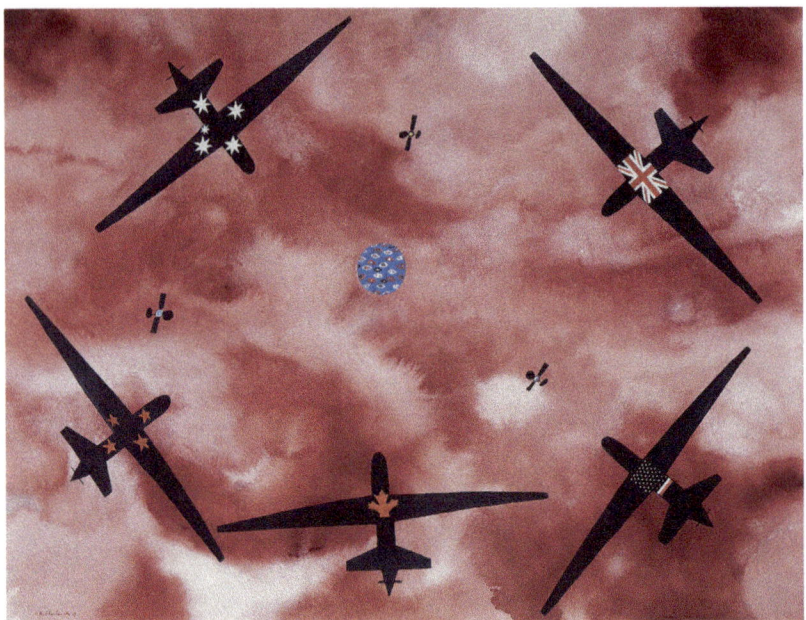

Figure 8.9, Kathryn Brimblecombe-Fox, *Five Eyes And The Rest*, gouache on paper, 56x76cm, (2019). Photo courtesy of Cian Sanders.

– Australia, New Zealand, Canada, United States, and the United Kingdom. Three satellites also hover, each bearing elements of Russian, Chinese, and Israeli flags. A pale blue dot – Earth – is covered with unblinking eyes, perhaps indicating Earth-based surveillance nodes and devices. The viewer 'flies', beyond Earth and the machines, casting the oversight of human imaginational metaveillance across technological surveillance and sousveillance activities. The viewer witnesses twenty-first century geopolitics as a big picture where a persistent and complex state of surveillance and reconnaissance prevails. This is not a state akin to a traditional standing army because although the human warfighter will respond swiftly, a call to arms cannot occur at near light-speed. However, nonhuman warfighting technologies, enabled by algorithms, signals, and increasing autonomy, could be considered as constantly deployed, with abilities to rapidly escalate or de-escalate operations. Can the 'pale blue dot' be cherished in a state of perpetual everywhere war? Jette's comment that 'Time is a weapon' portends a nonhuman war, perhaps a post-human war waged by artificially intelligent systems and robots. In either case, human beings are removed as active participants, but not necessarily victims, by processes unleashed by what Jeremy Packer and Joshua Reeves call the 'coming humanectomy' (Packer and Reeves 2017). Packer and Reeves provocatively suggest that accelerating technologies require human excision because, compared to 'explicitly nonhuman forms of intelligence, cooperation and communication' the human being is fallible, and therefore

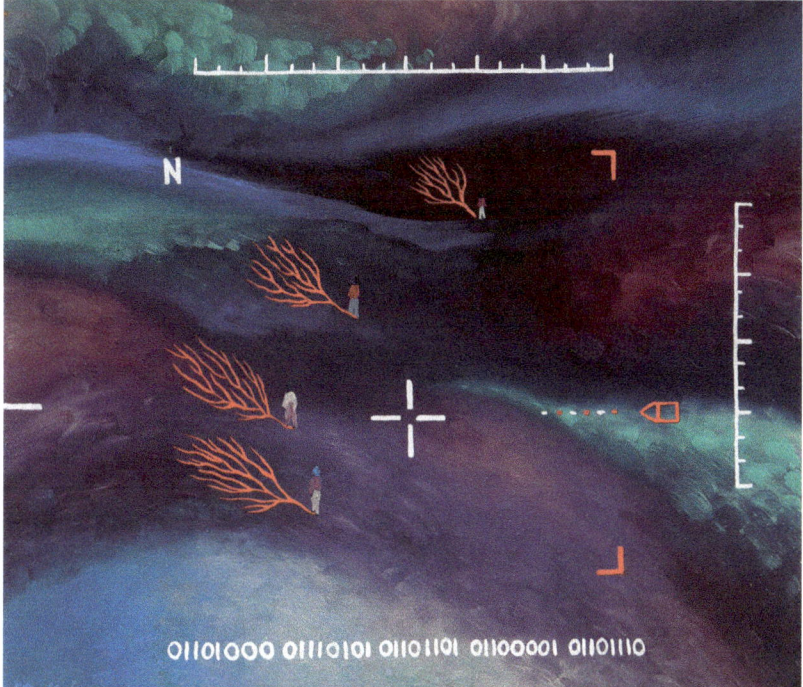

Figure 8.10. Kathryn Brimblecombe-Fox, *HUMAN*, oil on linen, 30x30cm (2019). Photo courtesy of Cian Sanders.

an impediment, even a danger (265-66). Perhaps human tendencies to anthropomorphise machines are subconscious attempts to maintain a sense of relationship that might impede excision. The unblinking fake eyes in *Five Eyes And The Rest* could be human eyes rendered sightless by paralysis, doping, or death. They could also indicate a successful nonhuman takeover of the planet? Either way, 'humanectomy' is evident. Burr's appeal to 'pull the future towards us rather than wait for it' may hasten the removal of the human-in-the loop, the 'coming humanectomy'. But, what if the future is already here? What if 'future of war' planning, fuelling a global high-tech arms race, has brought the future closer? Are there signs that the future war, being planned for, is already being waged?

HUMAN (2019) and Life, At The Front (2020)

In *HUMAN* four figures are targeted in a tumultuous landscape (see Figure 8.10). It is not apparent whether the figures are aware they are targets, however, there is a sense of precarity. This precarity is intensified by the painted computer graphic-like markings that parody orienting and targeting graphics. The impression is of a computer screen, perhaps evidence of an airborne

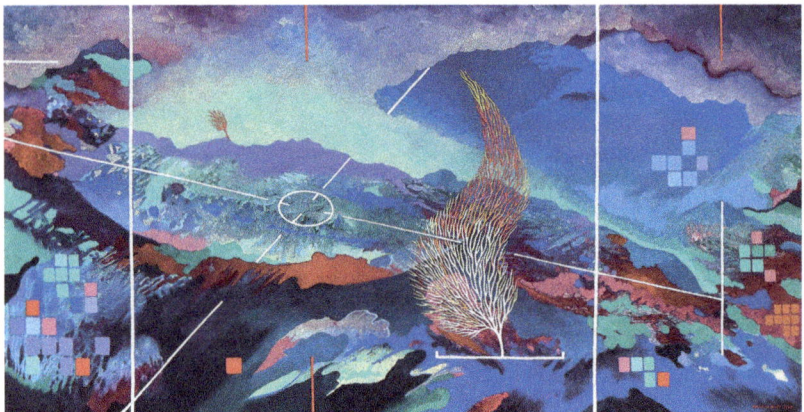

Figure 8.11. Kathryn Brimblecombe-Fox, *Life, At The Front*, oil on linen, 56x112cm (2020). Photo courtesy of the artist.

drone's imaging technology, recording, and transmitting data to a remote pilot, to assist identification for a so-called surgical strike.

The binary code at the bottom of the painting 'instructs' the word HUMAN. This gives a clue to algorithmic processes. It poses questions about how human beings are represented and codified, for and by digital and cyber systems, for identification, tracking, and targeting purposes. Although computer images are ubiquitous, their generation is for human use. The image-picture is not necessary for the machine to scope, identify and target. Sensors and software can scope for patterns and anomalies in raw data. What happens when images are no longer needed because autonomous systems identify, track and target using correlated data and pattern matching? Are these developing systems radically altering our relationship to the world, our relations with the *real* (terrestrial or extra-terrestrial) environment? If so, are we unwittingly excising ourselves from reality?

HUMAN does offer hope though. Each of the human figures cast a tree-of-life shadow. These shadows represent human characteristics, such as love, imagination, dreaming, ambition, despair, anguish, and more. *Life, At The Front* (see Figure 8.11), another parody of a computer screen, also offers hope, as two trees-of-life seem to speak across a distance. Does this distance re-establish perspective or is it a simulation? Maybe the red tree, as it bends in the wind on a distant horizon, sends a sign of hope, or perhaps a warning? The white tree, its canopy afire, appears to be tethered. Yet, it too bends in the wind. With both *HUMAN* and *Life, At The Front* the tree-of-life represents powerful forces of the human life and spirit. In both paintings, viewers are able to 'fly' into an imaginational distance where a collision of the real and virtual can be witnessed and critiqued. As a resistance to digital and cyber-based militarised scoping in the age of the drone, human imaginational metaveillance helps to remind us that contemporary technology cannot, currently, imagine.

Works Cited

Amoore, Louise. 2009. 'Lines of Sight: On the Visualisation of Unknown Futures.' *Citizenship Studies*, February: 17-30.

Association of the US Army. 2019. '*AUSA Sustainment Hot Topic – HON Bruce Jette - ASAALT*'. Keynote by Bruce Jette, YouTube video, 16:40. May 29. https://www.youtube.com/watch?v=LYlMIRihG9g.

Baudrillard, Jean. 2003. *Passwords*. Translated by Chris Turner. London and New York: Verso.

Burr, Rick, Lt Gen. 2018. 'Accelerated Warfare: Futures Statement for an *Army in Motion*'. Canberra: Australian Army Research Centre. https://researchcentre.army.gov.au/sites/default/files/2020-01/futures_statement_accelerated_warfare_booklet_u.pdf.

Gregory, Derek. 2011. 'The Everywhere War'. *The Geographical Journal* 177: 238-50.

Holland Michel, Arthur. 2020. 'Killer Algorithms Nobody's Talking About'. *Foreign Policy*. January 20. https://foreignpolicy.com/2020/01/20/ai-autonomous-weapons-artificial-intelligence-the-killer-algorithms-nobodys-talking-about/ .

NASA. 'First Contact: Sputnik'. https://www.nasa.gov/mission_pages/explorer/sputnik-20071002.html.

Packer, Jeremy and Reeves, Joshua. 2017. 'Taking People Out: Drones, Media/Weapons and the Coming Humanectomy'. In *Life in the Age of Drone Warfare*, edited by Lisa Parks and Caren Kaplan, 261-81. Durham: Duke University Press.

Rees, Martin. 2003. *Our Final Century: Will Civilisation Survive The Twenty-First Century?* London: Arrow Books.

Virilio, Paul. 1995. 'Red Alert in Cyberspace'. Translated by Malcolm Imrie. *Radical Philosophy*, November/December: 2-4.

Virilio, Paul. 2000. *Polar Inertia*. Translated by Patrick Camiller. London: Sage Publications.

Virilio, Paul. 2007. *The Original Accident*. Translated by Julie Rose. Cambridge: Polity Press.

Virilio, Paul. 2012. *The Great Accelerator*. Translated by Julie Rose. Cambridge: Polity Press.

9

The Swarm: Drone as Composite Technology and Neo-liberal Fantasy

Mitch Goodwin

> We press the 'I believe' button and close our eyes.
>
> —Deputy Secretary of Defense, Ret. Col. Bob Work speaking at the European Policy Centre, Brussels, Belgium. April 28, 2016

> Avoid at ALL COSTS any mention or implication of AI.
>
> —Chief scientist for AI at Google Cloud Dr. Fei-Fei Li, internal email, September 2017

The drone *singular* is a convergent system of techno-cultural ecologies. A mesh of machine fabric (alloys, silicon, plastics, and circuitry), zoomorphic behaviour (flight, adaptation, and predatory instincts), machine vision (the broadcast image, the targeting matrix, the drone's eye view), and human – mostly male – desire (to gaze, control, dominate, acquire, and, when necessary, erase). Drones are for the most part semi-autonomous devices, forebears to a new breed of Lethal Autonomous Weapon Systems (LAWS) that when deployed as a collective with a suite of technological enhancements, take on swarm-like abilities.

The swarm is part of our imagination, it is both a militaristic dream and a primal echo from a more savage past. First and foremost, for our purposes here, it is a convergence of economics, state power, and sophisticated engineering. A most pure extension of capitalist logic in the era of the Big Tech military industrial complex. The potential threat of the collective swarm is not a new idea, it has been alive in our origin fables and our most haunting of fictions in the form of birds and bots and plagues and subterranean machines. Their deployment in the remote battlespace is not only just emergent, but imminent.

Domestically, traces of swarm-like behaviour are already visible via the choreographed displays of Intel's Shooting Star drone system, the laser-like trails across the evening sky of Space-X Starlink satellites, while the capitalist worker analogy fits the drone swarm too, as 'hustle culture', once the preserve of Silicon Valley and tech enclaves in New York city, has become a managerial legacy of the plague years. Elsewhere, fleets of police drones equipped with facial recognition technology surveil ethnic minorities in Xinjiang province in China and America's 'inner cities' as citizens take on the distributed network qualities of a viral horde (Barrett 2018). In contrast, the blurry video grab of a swarm of Perdix drones, one hundred strong, tumbling from an F/A-18 fighter jet for the *60 Minutes* cameras in 2017 now seems historically quaint (CBS News 2017).

The underlying technologies that enable these systems are no longer rarefied by access or economics. Nor are they containable or the exclusive preserve of the military. They have become distributed, borderless, open source. (Smith and Browne 2019: 269) My voyeuristic paparazzi drone is also the sightline for your sniper quad copter; the 3-D printer that produces intricately detailed wargaming figurines also manufactures gun parts that evade body scanners. In this new era, exclusivity of access is no longer certain. Advances in big data capture, machine vision, aerospace hardware, and AI are closely guarded, however the commercialised outcomes are widely accessible and leak prodigiously across the vectors of public, private, and classified information spaces. This is the art of reproduction in the Age of Code. These techno-ecologies are omnidirectional, feeding forward into military R&D spaces while also folding back into the production pipelines of consumer products, domestic security governance, and, just beyond the curve, potentially slipping sideways into the unknowable.

Our focus in these pages is the military and techno-industrial space that enabled autonomous weapon systems development and the techno-cultural imaginary that frames our conception of their potential to swarm. Anticipations of full autonomy are already in service in contested territories in the form of fixed LAWS that react to remote sensor data at instantaneous speeds. From the SGR-A1 sentry guns along the Korean demilitarised zone and the Russian Uran-9 tank patrol in the forests of a contested Crimea (Saballa 2021) to the US Navy's Aegis anti-aircraft systems and Israel's infamous anti-missile system, the Iron Dome: these environmental sensors merge machine vision with deadly force.

Historically, naming conventions used by the military also anticipate the swarm. Zoomorphic connotations are present in the language of aerial conflict and remote surveillance technologies. From the development of guided munitions in 1918 via the Kettering Bug to the CIA 'dragon fly' drones of the 1970s; Northrop Grumman's contemporary Global Hawk (Emme 1961; Marsh 2017; Yeo 2021) to China's surveillance 'doves' to Raytheon's Silver Fox micro drone. Not to mention the hybrid-horror imaginings of the Defense Advanced Research Projects Agency (DARPA)'s experimental 'good gremlins' programme (Luna 2018; McCullough 2019). Indeed, the research pathway of co-operative intelligence and adversarial decision making of swarm technology is distinctly zoomorphic, modelled as it is on 'the cooperative epistemologies of flock and social animals such as birds, ants, and fish' (Packer and Reeves 2020: 58).

This perception of hybrid machines as a persistent environmental presence is felt most keenly by those on the ground. In the Pakistani tribal regions of South and North Waziristan the distant persistent buzz of the circling Predator or Reaper drone is known as *machay*, which means wasp in the local Pashtun language. In a further act of indignity and erasure, those who become collateral damage in the act of remote killing by a CIA drone attack are referred to as 'bugsplats': a term derived from a piece of software developed in 2003 for the second Iraq War which evaluated the potential collateral damage from a remote missile strike in a civilian target zone (Graham 2003; Robinson 2011). The US Department of Defense (DoD) and their industrial contractors are also fond of exotic word play, using cybernetic and biomimetic language and metaphor to brand DoD programs: SwarmTex, Skyborg, OctoRoach Project, JEDI (Joint Enterprise Defense Infrastructure), LOCUST (Low-Cost UAV Swarming Technology), OFFSET (OFFensive Swarm-Enabled Tactics), CODE (Collaborative Operations in Denied Environments), and BLADE (Behavioural Learning for Adaptive Electronic Warfare). The cyclic DNA of remote killing then is built on an epistemology of techno-zoomorphism, from the ply and papier-mâché chrysalids of the First World War to the algorithmic evaluation of civilian death counts in the Forever War/s.

Feeding the Algorithm

Domestically we inhabit an almost invisible, seemingly innocuous mesh of surveillance and machine sensing that have given rise to a myriad of sociopolitical effects, on privacy, equality, and what Mimi Sheller calls 'mobility justice' (Sheller 2018: 95). A plethora of sensing devices and drone-like architectures are in our midst if not on our person, enmeshed in commercial ecosystems built upon seductive, and ethically questionable, design properties (Harris 2019). These personal devices and the data clouds that support their function are already in the process of 'subjecting collective cognition to the patterns of the algorithm' (Berardi 2015: 213). Promoted as providing a singular dedicated and unique service, they share within their networks of interoperability a latent co-operative potential befitting autonomous agency within a networked environment. The inverse is also true, in that they represent sites of vulnerability for subversion and misuse. In mediated terms, we are familiar with the visual tropes that denote such threats: the cascading rivers of lurid green code, the twisting focus rings of an omnipresent CCTV network, the checkerboard of error screens, and virtual reality as addictive psychosis. This is the mise-en-scene of mass device shock presented in the near-future televisual dystopias like *Black Mirror* (2011) and *Years and Years* (2019). There is a sort of eerie self-fulfilling techno-apocalypse going on here, not dissimilar to the premediation cinema of Y2K and later 9/11 (Grusin 2010: 38).

Why should we care about these mediated constructions predicated as they are on second-order virtual dreamscapes? Because the genealogy of the drone is codified in pop-cultural as well as technological signifiers. Aesthetics and associations matter when mediated narratives oscillate between the past and future tense. Machine vision provides strong visual cues from the everyday to not only render cinematic fantasy but also existential erasure via social media networks or remote murder via autonomous weapons.

The latent perniciousness of the drone, whether it is deployed across the military battlespace or in the provision of state-based surveillance, is amplified when the singular becomes many. Particularly, when collective cooperative intelligence, in the form of a multitude of companion devices, becomes a desirable operational platform. Former Deputy Secretary of US Defence Robert Work pre-empted the cyborg pilot back in 2015, stating that 'AI and autonomy put inside these battle networks is going to allow [...] what we call human-machine symbiosis' (Work 2016). The drone operator – like the YouTube moderator, and the machine learning data trainer – would seem to be but temporary interlopers in an employment sector with ever diminishing career prospects.

To pre-empt this acceleration, the Defense Advanced Research Projects Agency (DARPA) is seeking to virtualise human agency by advances in neural augmentation. Once the preserve of mobility support and war veteran recovery, Brain Computer Interfacing (BCI) is now being put to use in a far more insidious fashion. As Al Emondi, the director of DARPA's Next-generation Nonsurgical Neurotechnology (N^3) programme, observes, 'Working with drones and swarms of drones, operating at the speed of thought rather than through mechanical devices – those types of things are what these devices are *really* for' (Tullis 2019).

According to Pentzold et al., 'the history of networked technologies and digitization is animated by powerful ideas about transcending imperfections' – whether it be the soldier, the patient, the trader – the augmented human becomes a desirable asset (Pentzold, Kaun, and Lohmeier 2020: 706). Hybrid modes of connection, accelerated and intimate forms of control are attractive efficiencies to have in the theatre of remote warfare. It contradicts of course the transcendental properties – enhanced freedom, dexterity, self-expression – that one might equate with such a procedure. Instead, the bio-tech trap of the invasive neural interface in the service of the machine would seem like an inescapable destiny for the future combat pilot.

Bob Work has form in making bold, if not disturbing, projections in the military technology space, firstly as the Deputy Secretary of the DoD for the

Obama and Trump administrations and more recently as the vice-chair of the National Security Commission on Artificial Intelligence (NSCAI). The NSCAI is chaired by former Alphabet CEO Eric Schmidt, co-founder of Google, he of the 'don't be evil' mantra. Schmidt and Work co-authored the open letter which prefaces the NSCAI's final report delivered to Congress on March first, 2021. The report is a clarion call to both Washington and Silicon Valley; it speaks to both the threat and the opportunity of an AI infused battlespace:

> AI systems will also be used in the pursuit of power. We fear AI tools will be weapons of first resort in future conflicts. AI will not stay in the domain of superpowers or the realm of science fiction. AI is dual-use, often open-source, and diffusing rapidly. State adversaries are already using AI-enabled disinformation attacks to sow division in democracies and jar our sense of reality. States, criminals, and terrorists will conduct AI-powered cyber-attacks and pair AI software with commercially available drones to create 'smart weapons'. (Schmidt, Work, and Bajraktari 2021: 2)

Stoking a fear matrix that ties together civilian policing, military R&D, rogue commercial operators, and the economics of private and commercial enterprise with a hint of state-sponsored cyber espionage is nothing new. After all, the War on Terror remains a durable narrative. Indeed, in an American context, the leveraging of convergent forms of patriotic labour and industrial capitalism in the service of homeland security and grand gestures of nation building is a central tenet of techno-capitalism and an enduring ruse of the neoliberal project. A historical narrative that actively seeks industrial capacity and civilian labour to underwrite – and where necessary, undertake – the business of war (O'Mara 2018).

A Field of Dreams

If the next desired evolutionary step is full autonomous weapons systems operating in a cooperative networked environment – in other words, a distributed hive with an intent to swarm – artificial intelligence then is the gateway technology that will enable the final evolutionary leap in that process. While the Generals sleep, their autonomous machines can keep watch, their positions pinged and their sensors primed – decoding image streams, comparing data stacks, evaluating the threat environment.

'We are in an AI arms race', notes Colonel Drew Cukor, from the Intelligence, Surveillance, and Reconnaissance Operations Directorate. 'Many of you will have noted that Eric Schmidt is calling Google an AI company now, not a data company' (Pellerin 2017). As recently as April 2021, in a joint press conference with the Department of Defense Joint Artificial Intelligence Center (JAIC), Bob Work opened with the following remarks:

> [...] for the first time since World War II, the United States technical predominance, which undergirds both our economic and our military competitiveness, is under severe threat by the People's Republic of China [...] We view AI much like Thomas Edison viewed electricity. He said, 'It is a field of fields. It holds the secrets which will reorganise the life of the world'. (Work and Groen 2021)

Work's language is indicative no doubt of the DoD's diplomatic agenda to project an image of 'military AI readiness' (Heckman 2021). Yet, unlike the humble lightbulb, the ability to switch it off and on at will is less certain. His hawkish rhetoric echoes Allen and Husain's speculative essay, *On Hyperwar*, in which they describe a convergence of offensive military assets that operate at the speed of machine intelligence: 'AI-enabled techniques such as autonomous swarming and cognitive analysis of sensor data' will make the decision-making process 'so tight that it becomes almost impossible to keep humans in the loop in most places. Commanders can continue to supply intent, but the prosecution of much of the war can conceivably shift to machines' (Allen, Husain, and Williams 2017). This theorised state of swarm 'readiness' is a looming reality, underwritten by a recently approved US Department of Defense request, authored by the NSCAI, to double the annual AI R&D funding to USD thirty-two billion by 2026.

With a lucrative honeypot and a pitch to corporate America, the programme will no doubt attract a mix of commercial and private contractors that reflect both the NASDAQ hit parade and the usual rollcall of military contractors skilled in the dark arts of remote warfare R&D (see: Raytheon, General Atomics, Northrop Grumman, Anduril Industries, et al.). As Jacob Silverman observes, despite the ethical and reputational damage that such associations may potentially hold for America's do-good feel-great Big Tech entities, 'it may be unrealistic to expect large, profit-seeking corporations [...] to decline work that's both wildly remunerative and earns them outsize influence with the very entities that wield the power to regulate them' (Silverman 2018). Such industrial partnerships, which spawn hawkish tech visions and hyper-autonomous weapons theories, go beyond a mere reshaping of the systems of control. This is not purely a subservient act of data analysis or security surveillance by an autonomous system. This is *the system* literally assuming control, responding to sensor data, and then acting upon it.

Will Roper, the assistant secretary of the Air Force for acquisition, technology, and logistics, has a dangerous idea: 'It would be really, really good if we integrated these two programs' – artificial intelligence and swarming drone technology – 'into a neat demonstration or an experiment where we take the best of breed, put them together, and let's go see what type of missions we can actually do!' (McCullough 2019) This is what the US military call 'mosaic warfare'. In this datafied dystopia, target environments become world-building sand boxes of co-operative relationships for mechanical embodied AI – 'cross-combatant command collaboration' – that author real violence in real time (Hitchens 2021).

These are the dreams that titillate the military elite and their cashed-up contractors – an exotic playground populated by gremlins, wing bots, drone flocks, nanobots, digi-dogs, and robo-bees. Each iteration of every 'breed' busily harvesting data for the hive.

The US Department of Defense's initiative, Project Maven (which is also known as the Algorithmic Warfare Cross-Functional Team), is set up to expedite that dream. By replacing the human intermediary in the kill chain with self-aware artificial intelligence to navigate the operational environment and crucially, identify targets. AI coordinated warfare serviced by machines becomes a reality for the DoD and ideas men like Will Roper (Pellerin 2017). In other words, intelligent Lethal Autonomous Weapons systems (an evolution we might call the inLAWs) that are designed to follow 'kill commands devised by machines based on coordinates formulated by machines, targeted at the enemy of machines' (Packer and Reeves 2020: 60).

Such obsessions were no doubt on the mind of Bruce Sterling, sci-fi author and speculative futurist, while on assignment for *Wired* magazine, when he was sniffing about inside DARPA's nascent VR tech in 1993:

> Now imagine two armies, two strategically assisted, cyberspace-trained, post-industrial, panoptic ninja armies, going head-to-head. What on earth would that look like? A 'conventional' war, a 'nonnuclear' war, but a true War in the Age of Intelligent Machines, analysed by nanoseconds to the last square micron. Who would survive? And what would be left of them? (Sterling 1993)

The implications of this are manifold, particularly the reduced role of human decision making as the complexity of these convergent systems increases and the battlespace becomes both rhizomatic and asymmetric as it is virtualised by machine vision. In 2001, Retired Lt Colonel Thomas K. Adams, in his article 'Future Warfare and the Decline of Human Decision Making' observed: 'Military systems (including weapons) now on the horizon will be too fast, too small, too numerous, and will create environments too complex for humans to direct' (Adams 2001). This cognitive deficiency, according to the 2021 NSCAI report, means human assets 'cannot defend against multiple machines making thousands of manoeuvres per second potentially moving at hypersonic speeds and orchestrated by AI across domains. Humans cannot be everywhere at once, but software can' (Schmidt, Work, and Bajraktari 2021:

24). Instantaneous overwatch is best then, at the speed of synaptic activity looking both back and forward in time, like the 'precogs' in *Minority Report*, floating in shallow pools of liquid electric soup.

Military Virtuality

> Everybody's flying and no one leaves the ground.
>
> —John Lennon, *Nobody Told Me*, Polydor, January 6, 1984

By 1993 Jaron Lanier, who coined the phrase 'virtual reality', had exited the VR research scene. While various developers attempted commercial crossovers, the technology was relegated mainly to the medical sciences and aviation realms. Lanier however had a prescient warning: 'This notion that you could see VR as a way to screw with people without their awareness, crossed with our current business model where everything is about advertising and manipulation and spying [...] It's been very painful to see that potential unfolding' (Lanier in Newton and Schnipper 2014). Fast forward to 2020 and VR is experiencing its second coming – or perhaps its first, depending on how dismissive you are of *The Lawnmower Man* and Nintendo's *Virtual Boy*.

If we consider VR as 'things, agents and events that exist in cyberspace' (Yoh 2001) then the common archetype of the drone singular – an Unmanned Autonomous Vehicle (UAV) – operates within a virtual computer simulation of its own making, constructed by machine sensing, and commandeered from afar. Infra-red, night vision, LIDAR sensing, and targeting computers are all tools of assisted reality that feed the authorship of their virtual environments of operation. Their decision-making process for a kill shot mimics a similar logic that governs data-mining practices, 'exploration, pattern definition, and validation' (Foster 2017). The drone is an embodied agent that leverages both the real and the virtual in order to facilitate a command pathway. As Michael Richardson notes, 'once the drone is abstracted away from the unmanned aerial vehicle and understood as the figure of autonomous, sensing technology, its logics become even more ubiquitous and its complex imbrications with our bodies inescapable' (Richardson 2018: 80).

This is the evolution of not only the drone operant but also the information space, from data stacks – of pattern-of-life analysis and communication meta-data, of maps and GPS coordinates, of serial numbers and financial records – to sophisticated coded environments of navigation and command execution. This new navigable reality is both reflexive and transferable, a cyberspace of consequence – a site of 'stigmergic cognition' (Marsh and Onof 2008). A target environment of observable and malleable sets of digital emulated objects that exist in both a mediated and corporeal reality, to be indexed, manipulated, exploited, and when necessary, violently erased.

Therefore, the functional ecology of the robotic swarm depends on the ability of the singular drone to perceive, interpret, and embody the virtual realm and, in a cognitive virtual turn, do so at an observable distance. This idea, of war at arm's length and conducted from the skies in overwhelming numbers, is as old as military aviation itself. However, war as mediated experience merged with a global doctrine was 'reactivated' in the first Gulf conflict under the auspice of a New World Order (Hippler 2017: 190). A philosophy that underpins to this day the ambition for ever more remote battlespaces, populated by lethal autonomous weapons systems, of which swarm capabilities are a stated ambition.

As Paul Virilio would have it, we are experiencing a 'temporal compression' the result of advances in tele-presence, in which we no longer go there to see; instead, we transmute, transpose, and transcode. This 'always-on' accelerated reality of drone architecture is very much akin to the intimate relationship we have with contemporary networked VR technologies. Flesh becomes a complicit component of the media interface, operating alongside and through the black mirror: 'the carnal centre of presence extends to the telepresence in the real-time world delivered by the instantaneity of a ubiquity that has now gone global' (Virilio 2007: 20). Just like the sandbox of mosaic warfare, one reality is transmitted from its virtual other. Drones – and by virtue, swarming autonomous robotic systems – therefore exist in virtual representations of a reality they themselves are the authors of.

Swarm Anxieties

> In principle, if someone was able to say hack all the autonomous Teslas, they could say – I mean just as a prank – they could say 'send them all to Rhode Island' [laughs] – across the United States [...] and that would be the end of Tesla and there would be a lot of angry people in Rhode Island.
>
> —Elon Musk speaking at the National Governors Association in Rhode Island, August 27, 2020

The fear of the swarm is instinctive – primal, relatable. It springs from a deep historical resonance – the locust, the pandemic, the marauding horde, the stampede, the military parade, the bomber squadron, bugs, bats and ACE2 receptors. Swarms also congregate and colonise – the hive, the infestation, the crypto-storm, the site of infection and the release of the executable are synonymous with swarm-like behaviour. However, it is the boldness of the drone swarm and its willingness to negate one of the singular drone's greatest assets: their relative invisibility and their stealthy approach to their business. The drone swarm is the inverse of this, an expression of extreme presence and a very visible display of imminent collective action. We are overwhelmed by their numbers, their relentless march, their coordinated posturing. These are the nightmarish scenes we know and recognise from nature, from ancient scripts and in our most elaborate gothic fictions.

The swarm potential of the drone collective then multiplies our existing anxieties around nascent artificial intelligence technology, networked virality, and computer operations more generally. The covertness of opaque algorithms and the cooperative behaviour of the drone and their ilk – the robot, the algorithm, the avatar, the chatbot – play to our suspicions that we are not in control and perhaps we never were. We cannot fully understand their motivations, nor our feelings towards them. We should expect then that the anthropomorphism of a robot's human-like behaviour or a chat bot's expressive displays of cleverness also extends to synthetic machines with zoomorphic properties. When grouped together our perception of them dips into the uncanny, their dexterity and cooperative flocking is unnerving, resonating as it does with our latent primal fear of the swarm.

How do we comprehend their being in the world, if they are not truly in the world, but somehow next to it? Not of nature but next-nature. They are, until aliens reveal themselves to us at least, the ultimate other. True to Arthur C. Clarke's observation that 'any sufficiently advanced technology is indistinguishable from magic' (Clarke 1973: 21), robotics and AI elicit both wonder and unease. This is especially true when we observe in them what we might think to be an independent thought or potentially malevolent behaviour. A mischievous interaction, subtle gamesmanship, or the quoting of an intimate data point of knowledge. These feelings are amplified when we are confronted by a screen glitch or a twisted phrase or a frozen image, a clicking hard disk or some errant code. Signature displays of mechanical corruption, signs of a ghost in the machine or the fail-safe system going rogue. Are these not the seeds of destruction in origin fables of our most elaborate fictions – from *2001: A Space Odyssey* (1968), to the *Alien* (1979), *Blade Runner* (1982) and *Terminator* (1984) franchises, and on to the contemporary dystopias of *Real Humans* (2013), *Westworld* (2016), *Next* (2019) and *Vesper* (2022)?

Domesticated AI assistants, and robot companions, just like the drone, are mass produced technologies, yet they function as singular objects with bespoke purposes and distinct identities – the Siris, Sophias, Xiaoices, and Hiroshis of this world. However, capitalist cultural logic tells us that the right bot, with the right skin-job, the perfect demeanour and a functional yet compliant autonomy will eventually be serialised, barcoded and mass-produced. This was the incomprehensible horror of the multiplicity that confronted the robot David in Spielberg's *AI: Artificial Intelligence*, who tragically thought he was the only boy in the world. How would this feel for the origin bot, to discover he is but one of many in a production line of comfort bots? His emotional and cognitive settings, the default template of a much larger commercial enterprise.

Delores Abernathy of Sweetwater knew this pain. An android pleasure-bot, circa 2058AD, Delores dutifully fulfilled the stereotypical bit part of the Rancher's Daughter in the choreographed narrative of violence and misogyny that is the adult theme park known as *Westworld*. Yet Delores is soon jacked up on a new batch of code, she gains her sentient patch and rallies the other skin-jobs. After generations of her and her kind being killed in the service of the human elite, does she realise that *Westworld* was in fact an elaborate war game designed by men? You bet she does. She turns the tables on her roboticist masters and busts out of Dodge commandeering her own clone stack to wreak havoc in the real world and to seek out and destroy the AI main frame upon which all human subjectivity now resides. Delores and her kind have enormous swarm potential.

The Multitudes

Given our anxieties when confronted with anomalies – or uncanny displays of artificial intelligence – in robots singular, how should we feel when we can see highly refined autonomy manifest in disciplined machine collaboration, of not only action but also re-action? Not programmed, but self-organised. A flock evading an obstacle or changing tact, the division of labour to acquire a target or survey a position, the calculation of a target's value or the relative cost of collateral damage, the shared execution of an order to kill or when their membership is under threat, to defend their companion flock with lethal force. The collective, acting as one, has always been a powerful force in military conflict, in political action and the digital simulations in the dark at the cinema. Clones, robotic hordes, insectile squadrons each displaying zoomorphic dexterity en masse is the nightmare scenario evoked in a sequence of 'swarm films' which appeared in quick succession in the years immediately following 9/11: *Star Wars Episode II: Attack of the Clones* (2002), *Rise of the Machines* (2003), *Matrix Revolutions* (2003), *I, Robot* (2004), and *Sky Captain and the World of Tomorrow* (2004). Digital representations of overwhelming swarming behaviour to be sure, yet they are also human revenge narratives featuring violent and gaudy visual 'bugsplats' and drawn-out mechanical dismemberment. As Kristen Whissel observes, the appearance of digital replication in 'swarm films' pre-empt an apocalyptic endgame, 'more often than not, the multitude's appearance heralds "The End" – the end of freedom, the end of a civilization, the end of an era, or even the end of human time altogether' (Whissel 2010).

While Hollywood might stoke our innate anxieties of swarm-like robotics, these are mere simulations, technological fantasies that belie the deadly potential of what remains a seductive ambition for military men like Bob Work and Wil Roper. Yet are not the ambitions for machine autonomy and swarm-like co-operation a desire for the auto-sublime and not that dissimilar to the desires of the fictitious roboticist?

Just like their operational intent, the development of these technologies remains secretive and opaque. Yet digital traces exist. Military contractors cannot help but share flashy animations of swarm-tech on their corporate PR web pages, TV news packages regularly throw to file footage of menacing Predator drones, while Trevor Paglen's telephotography, capturing glimpses of drone test flights over the Nevada desert, are important techno-cultural documents that make the invisible visible (Paglen 2012). Each of these mediated artefacts are historical evidence of the pre-visualisation of remote power. Yet the damage they wreak is rarely seen, and never documented in real time. We should be wary of this protection of power by stealth. We should see the socio-technical machinations which underpin it, and be privy to the lawlessness of those who seek to remove themselves from examination. The technology that seeks to act remotely, to communicate across encrypted bandwidth, that covertly designs its purpose, is a metaphor in itself for the endgame of lethal autonomous weapons development.

Grégoire Chamayou has noted that the ambition of military technological power is to be mechanical, distant, and subjectless. Power, he writes, exists 'wherever it is working actively in order to make itself forgotten' (Chamayou 2015: 207). It is working on two fronts, when it comes to the drone strike and the imminent arrival of the swarm, to not only obscure and efface authorship, but also to consolidate socio-technical structures of fear.

This is all playing out as societies are only just beginning to question the efficacy of other opaque technologies – big data mining, algorithmic governance, machine learning, and vehicle autonomy. Whether it be in signature air strikes on battlefields in foreign lands or the misconduct or misdirection of domestic policing at home, Virilio's notion of the accident of technology continues to unfurl, albeit at a distance and at speed (Virilio and Lotringer 2005). While the body politic is afflicted by an attention disorder, that is fuelled by AdWords and fake news and rabbit holes of reinforcement and rage, the state keeps busy too, indexing our attention matrix. These are the seemingly accepted norms of the lived experience in a post-Snowden world, a perfect political and cultural distraction for the techno-capitalist ambitions of the military industrial complex.

Works Cited

Adams, Thomas K. 2001. 'Future Warfare and the Decline of Human Decision Making'. *Parameters* 31, no. 4: 57-71.

Barrett, Brian. 2018. 'Lawmakers Can't Ignore Facial Recognition's Bias Anymore'. *Wired*. July 26. https://www.wired.com/story/amazon-facial-recognition-congress-bias-law-enforcement/.

Berardi, Franco 'Bifo'. 2015. *AND Phenomenology of the End*. Cambridge: Semiotext(e).

CBS News. 2017. 'Capturing the Swarm'. *60 Minutes Overtime*. August 20. https://www.cbsnews.com/news/60-minutes-capturing-the-perdix-drone-swarm/.

Chamayou, Grégoire. 2015. *Drone Theory*. New York: Penguin.

Clarke, Arthur C. 1973. *Profiles of the Future: An Inquiry Into the Limits of the Possible*. New York: Harper & Row.

Emme, Eugene M. 1961. 'Aeronautics and Astronautics Chronology, 1915-1919'. In *Aeronautics and Astronautics: An American Chronology of Science and Technology in the Exploration of Space, 1915-1960*. Washington, DC: NASA. https://www.hq.nasa.gov/office/pao/History/Timeline/1915-19.html.

Foster, Dennis L. 2017. *Your Obsolete Brain: Life and Death in the Age of Superintelligent Machines*. Milton Keynes: The Life Science Institute.

Graham, Bradley. 2003. 'Military Turns to Software to Cut Civilian Casualties'. *The Washington Post*. February 21. https://www.washingtonpost.com/archive/politics/2003/02/21/military-turns-to-software-to-cut-civilian-casualties/af3e06a3-e2b2-4258-b511-31a3425bde31/.

Harris, Tristan. 2019. 'Our Brains Are No Match for Our Technology'. *The New York Times*. December 5. https://www.nytimes.com/2019/12/05/opinion/digital-technology-brain.html.

Heckman, Jory. 2021. 'Commission tells DoD to prepare for 'military AI readiness' by 2025'. *Federal News Network*. February 17. https://federalnewsnetwork.com/artificial-intelligence/2021/02/commission-tells-dod-to-prepare-for-military-ai-readiness-by-2025/.

Hippler, Thomas. 2017. *Governing from the Skies: A Global History of Aerial Bombing, History*. London: Verso.

Hitchens, Theresa. 2021. 'NORTHCOM Developing, Testing AI Tools to Implement JADC2'. *Breaking Defense*. March 5. https://breakingdefense.com/2021/03/exclusive-northcom-developing-testing-ai-tools-to-implement-jadc2/.

Human Rights Watch. 2020. 'Killer Robots: Growing Support for a Ban. Human Rights Watch'. August 10. https://www.hrw.org/news/2020/08/10/killer-robots-growing-support-ban.

Lambert, Fred. 2020. 'The Big Tesla Hack: A hacker gained control over the entire fleet, but fortunately he's a good guy'. *Electrek*. August 27. https://electrek.co/2020/08/27/tesla-hack-control-over-entire-fleet/.

Luna, Thomas. 2018. 'China uses "Dove" drones for surveillance!' *We Talk UAV*. June 25. https://www.wetalkuav.com/china-uses-dove-drones-surveillance/.

Marsh, Allison. 2017. 'Meet the CIA's Insectothopter'. *IEEE Spectrum.* December 29. https://spectrum.ieee.org/meet-the-cias-insectothopter.

Marsh, Leslie, and Christian Onof. 2008. 'Stigmergic epistemology, stigmergic cognition'. *Cognitive Systems Research* 9, no. 1-2: 136-49.

McCullough, Amy. 2019. 'The Looming Swarm'. *Airforce Magazine.* March 22. https://www.airforcemag.com/article/the-looming-swarm/.

Newton, Casey, and Matthew Schnipper. 2014. 'Digital Natives: A conversation between virtual reality visionaries Jaron Lanier and Kevin Kelly'. In *The Rise and Fall and Rise of Virtual Reality. The Verge.* https://www.theverge.com/a/virtual-reality/interview.

O'Mara, Margaret. 2018. 'Silicon Valley Can't Escape the Business of War'. *The New York Times.* October 26. https://www.nytimes.com/2018/10/26/opinion/amazon-bezos-pentagon-hq2.html.

Packer, Jeremy, and Joshua Reeves. 2020. *Killer Apps: War, Media, Machine, Cultural Studies.* Durham: Duke University Press.

Paglen, Trevor. 2012. 'Reaper Drone: Indian Springs, NV'. *Trevor Paglen.* https://paglen.studio/2020/04/22/limit-telephotography/.

Pellerin, Cheryl. 2017. 'Project Maven to Deploy Computer Algorithms to War Zone by Year's End'. US Department of Defense. July 21. https://www.defense.gov/Explore/News/Article/Article/1254719/project-maven-to-deploy-computer-algorithms-to-war-zone-by-years-end/.

Pentzold, Christian, Anne Kaun, and Christine Lohmeier. 2020. 'Imagining and instituting future media: Introduction to the special issue'. *Convergence: The International Journal of Research into New Media Technologies* 26, no. 4: 705-15.

Richardson, Michael. 2018. 'Drone Capitalism: Affect, Autonomy, Body'. *Transformations* 31: 79-98.

Robinson, Jennifer. 2011. '"Bugsplat": The ugly US drone war in Pakistan'. *Al Jazeera.* November 20. https://www.aljazeera.com/indepth/opinion/2011/11/201111278839153400.html.

Saballa, Joe. 2021. 'Russia Establishing First Robot Tank Unit'. *The Defense Post.* April 13. https://www.thedefensepost.com/2021/04/13/russia-robot-tank-unit/.

Schmidt, Eric, Bob Work, and Yll Bajraktari. 2021. 'Final Report - National Security Commission on Artificial Intelligence'. Washington, US: NSCAI

Schwarz, Jon. 2021. 'The Most Terrifying Thing About 9/11 Was America's Response'. *The Intercept.* September 11. https://theintercept.com/2021/09/10/september-11-america-response/.

Shane, Scott, Cade Metz, and Daisuke Wakabayashi. 2018. 'How a Pentagon Contract Became an Identity Crisis for Google'. *The New York Times.* March 30. https://www.nytimes.com/2018/05/30/technology/google-project-maven-pentagon.html.

Sheller, Mimi. 2018. *Mobility Justice: The Politics of Movement in an Age of Extremes.* London: Verso.

Silverman, Jacob. 2018. 'Tech's Military Dilemma'. *The New Republic.* August 7. https://newrepublic.com/article/148870/techs-military-dilemma-silicon-valley.

Smith, Brad, and Carol Ann Browne. 2019. *Tools and weapons: the promise and the peril of the digital age.* New York: Penguin Press.

Sterling, Bruce. 1993. 'War Is Virtual Hell'. *Wired.* January 1. https://www.wired.com/1993/01/virthell/.

Tullis, Paul. 2019. 'The US Military is Trying to Read Minds'. *MIT Technology Review.* October 16. https://www.technologyreview.com/2019/10/16/132269/us-military-super-soldiers-control-drones-brain-computer-interfaces/.

Virilio, Paul. 2007. *Art As Far As the Eye Can See.* New York: Berg.

Virilio, Paul, and Sylvere Lotringer. 2005. *The Accident of Art.* Cambridge, Mass.: Semiotext(e).

Whissel, Kristen. 2010. 'The Digital Multitude'. *Cinema Journal* 49, no. 4 (Summer 2010): 90-110.

Whitlock, Craig and The Washington Post. 2021. *The Afghanistan Papers: A Secret History of the War.* New York: Simon & Schuster.

Williams, Brad D. 2017. 'Emerging "hyperwar" signals "AI-fuelled, machine-waged" future of conflict'. *Fifth Domain.* https://www.fifthdomain.com/dod/2017/08/07/emerging-hyperwar-signals-ai-fueled-machine-waged-future-of-conflict/.

Work, Bob. 2016. 'Remarks by Deputy Secretary Work on Third Offset Strategy'. In *Newsroom: US Department of Defense.* April 28. https://www.defense.gov/Newsroom/Speeches/Speech/Article/753482/remarks-by-deputy-secretary-work-on-third-offset-strategy/.

Work, Bob, and Michael S. Groen. 2021. 'Honorable Robert O. Work, vice chair of the National Security Commission on Artificial Intelligence, and Lieutenant General Michael Groen, the director of the DoD Joint Artificial Intelligence Center hold a press briefing on Artificial Intelligence'. *US Department of Defense.* April 9. https://www.defense.gov/Newsroom/Transcripts/Transcript/Article/2567848/honorable-robert-o-work-vice-chair-national-security-commission-on-artificial-i/.

Yeo, Mike. 2021. 'Japan's first Global Hawk begins flying at Northrop's California drone hub'. In *Asia Pacific*: *Defense News*. April 20. https://www.defensenews.com/global/asia-pacific/2021/04/19/japans-first-global-hawk-begins-flying-at-northrops-california-drone-hub/.

Yoh, Myeung-Sook. 2001. 'The reality of virtual reality'. Seventh International Conference on Virtual Systems and Multimedia. Berkeley, CA. October 25.

Part III: Ecology

10

Posthuman Photorealism: the Science and Art of Seeing Living Whales with Drones

Adam Fish and Edgar Gómez Cruz

Catching a Whale

Seeing the blow from a headlands cliff on a windless morning in the Eastern suburbs of Sydney, Australia, is the easy part. Flying the drone through the air to capture an image of a humpback whale poses a more serious challenge. But here we are, lifting off from sandstone, and powering through a headwind, towards the faint mist of whale exhale. Along the way, swirling schools of Australian salmon, bottlenose dolphins, and jumping kingfish are passed – the dolphins turning to look up at the drone, redirecting their trajectory. Seagulls fly with the drone towards the whale. The pilot and drone coordinate to predict the whale's next move. In this instance, the meeting of pilot, drone, atmosphere, and whale was perfectly choreographed. We catch a glimpse and sail along with the whale for a moment as it rises to breathe, communicates with its kin, or scratches its callosities on the water-surface tension. Later the whale launches itself through the sea surface and collapses playfully back into the thick ocean, an inverse waterfall exploding on re-entry in a swimway leading from the feeding grounds of Antarctica to the breeding bays of Indonesia.

One likes to imagine that this whale is content. Belly full of krill, en route to mating, no human predation for decades – though if this is an old whale it might remember the pursuit of the diesel-powered whaling ship and its explosive-tipped harpoon. Thankfully, the humpbacks of Australia have rebounded after the International Whaling Commission's moratorium in 1982. But other whales, like many marine species, have not. They may forever be unseen. Whales like the one we flew over are powerful 'eco-symbols' that stand as representatives of animals in the struggle against climate change, ecosystem devastation, and the sixth extinction (Kristoffersen, Norum, and Kramvig 2016). Catching an image of a living whale records a moment of flourishing.

By enabling agile and fast movement, the drone is a powerful technology that has democratised – for some – access to the atmosphere, the ocean, and other elements. Drone democratisation is not unlike earlier moments of agonistic, comparative, and temporary openness in communication infrastructure. With the advent and affordability of eight-millimetre film in the 1940s, magnetic video in the 1960s, cable television in the 1970s, satellite television in the 1980s, internet video in the 1990s, hacking in the 2000s, and social media in the 2010s – new communication or vision technologies and their associated distribution platforms democratised access to the means of media production and dissemination (Fish 2017). With access to the near-atmosphere, new relations between technologies, elements of sea and air, and organisms are possible. Following scholarship in atmospheric and elemental geographies (Adey 2015; McCormack 2018), Garrett and Anderson reflect on the elevated volumes the drone makes available, 'above rooftops and below piloted airplanes, an area of the sky previously looked at but rarely from' (2018: 343). Building upon this concept, we name this proximal air the mezzo (not to be confused with the mesosphere which is above the stratosphere).

The mezzo is the immediate space above us. Yet despite its ubiquity, it remains a novelty for ornate three-dimensional movement. Our human mobility in this space is a result of our evolution on this high-gravity, high-oxygen globe. Our flying, floating, and motile technologies evolved to exploit the possibilities of this thin atmospheric level, itself a result of interactions with the Earth, seas, and other atmospheres. In this conceptualisation of the mezzo, we are informed by theories of elementality that conceive of the water, atmosphere, earth, fire, and ether as mediators of communication and epistemology (McCormack 2018).

The mezzo offers more than a volumetric definition of a spatial 'sphere'. Rather, it comprises a geography of mobility and *seeing*, a space of encounter that opens a space of *thinking* (about space and mobility itself but also of embodiment, co-presence, and vitality). As such, the mezzo draws attention to discourses about vision and being. Mezzo means *middle* in Italian, but it also means 'means'. This double meaning usefully expands spatial understanding into a more cognitive and affective direction. With its middling meaning, mezzo is synonymous with *medium* and its plural *media* and it is also the 'means' by which a new space of sensing/thinking emerges. Thus, from the mezzo, the drone mediates between other scales, technologies, and species. It affords translations across technologies and species that are both visual and affective. What we call the mezzo is an area of seeing and sensing that allows intimate and lively ways of engaging with the oceans and its animals.

Seeing and Moving with the Posthuman

Photography from the mezzo is mobile, vertical, proximal, and thus, vivid. Drone mezzo-work produces a posthuman photorealism that connects to and reveals the contours and challenges of life. Posthumanism is a theory of relations across technologies, elemental forces, and other animals. It investigates the relations across *zoe*, *geo*, and *techne* (Braidotti 2019). *Zoe* is understood as animals and ecologies, wild and domesticated, including humans and our legacies of colonial dislocation, imperial subjugation, and capitalist inequality. *Geo* refers to the Earth, its minerals and elements, compounds both molecular and classical – waters, atmospheres, and fire – and their state shifts, pollution, and exchange values. *Techne* designates the technologies, tactics, and prosthetics that attempt to network, sense, datafy, control, and capitalise information from zoe and geo. A posthumanism approach to zeo, geo, or techne moves with, between, and through one or more of these modalities.

Posthuman photorealism exploits the atmosphere in co-creative engagements with whales. We investigate technologies of enhanced movement and vision that access the atmosphere and fly over the sea in acts of artistic and scientific examinations of marine megafauna. If posthuman subjects are invited to conceive of power's action transversely across zoe, geo, and techne, then we must ask how the whale's power and extension works from its body, through the sea and atmosphere, to the drone. In this brief chapter, we suggest that the drone is translating some of that whale vitality.

There is a growing scholarly interest in more-than-human, posthuman, nonhuman, and multispecies forms of vision. While the approaches vary, we align with Zylinska's claim that nonhuman vision is more than a concept, it is a form of being in the world that invites humans to see beyond a humanistic vision centred in *anthropos*, engaging instead with nonhuman actors (2017). The drone's mobility is key to understanding how it enables new modes of animal interaction. Scholarship on mobilities investigates the flow of people, goods, media, and social relations, as well as the experience of embodied movement (Sheller & Urry 2006). Mobility is key to understanding the enactment of drone photography.

The drone not only extends human mobility through technologies, but also detaches seeing from presence, allowing a visual co-presence with the object photographed while physically apart. This is relevant because drones inhabit the mezzo that humans cannot, opening new forms of visuality, relating, and connecting. The drone's sensors, stabilisers, flying capabilities, and gimbal technology render seeable otherwise hidden visibilities. The drone is a more-than-visual assemblage that sets in motion sensor feedback, that does not 'simply enable a way of *looking onto* the world but a complex way of *relating to* and *engaging with* it' (Jablonowski 2020: 347, emphasis in original). Drones represent the latest iteration of a historical relationship between the technologies of realism and mobility. New forms of scientific, artistic, and amateur image production result. Mezzo images reveal both the subject and its wider geographical context in ways micro- and macro-photography and video do not. The drone's computational-seeing is made possible by algorithms, movement, wireless tethering, and other sensing and technological advances. This allows the camera to move into position and see more clearly the lives of the organisms and spaces with which it engages.

Drone vision and drone mobility ultimately result in increased closeness between whales and drones with the effect being higher resolution images of living organisms in their own habitat. While the emergence of digital imagery challenged the historic connection between photography and consensual, normative reality (Mitchell 1994), the proliferation of digital imagery devices has opened new connections between photography and realism. Photorealism positions images within matrices of veracity, facticity, and related modes of meaning-making. The size and weight of early cameras prevented them from being very mobile. For example, one of the pioneers of nature photography, William Henry Jackson, used equipment that weighed 300 pounds. The implementation of different smaller platforms such as the thirty-five-millimetre camera allowed for greater portability. The result was more realistic images, the result of the photographer being able to move closer to animals (Osbourne 2000). At the same time, technological advancements allowed mobility itself to be studied, sometimes in animals – for example the explorations of Eadweard Muybridge with horses. Seeing animals realistically, vibrantly, and as co-producers of images rather than objects of them, can potentially contribute to the growth of an affective logic (Lorimer 2015) in image-making. These emergent uses of digital imagery create a posthuman photorealism that is enhanced by mobility, access to the mezzo, and engages with the living and the dying in the present age of extinction (Kember 2017; Stevenson and Kohn 2015).

Vision is implicated in constituting, documenting, challenging, and engaging the Anthropocene (Mirzoeff 2014), the era in which the impact caused by humans has caused the destruction of ecosystems and extinctions. While the concept of the Anthropocene has been contested because it repositions the human as the centre of the world and it fails to account for the multiple realities of nonwestern people (see Haraway et al. 2016), Lorimer (2015) suggests that the Anthropocene is useful as an epistemic intervention into binaries such as nature-culture. While access to the mezzo facilitated by the drone could contribute to the dominating 'vision from above', it can also be a force against it, a countervisuality in Mirzoeff's terms, by turning the aesthetic dimension accessed by the drone into a political tool for showing not only what can be controlled but what can also be saved (2014).

Contemporary photographers working from the mezzo reflect on large-scale issues, such as the terrestrial scars of war, mining, deforestation, and urbanism. Consider Tom Hegen's series *Coal Mine* taken in Germany in 2006 (see Figure 10.1). These drone photographs present a point of view that exposes a human scale that is different from satellite images where the scale is often beyond comprehension, but large enough to perceive our relations. These mezzo images position humans between the grounded realities of human labour and the macro forces of the Anthropocene (see Figure 10.1).

The drone's mobility, vision, intimacy, and image resolution constructs new relations between technologies, terrestrial geographies, and nonhuman

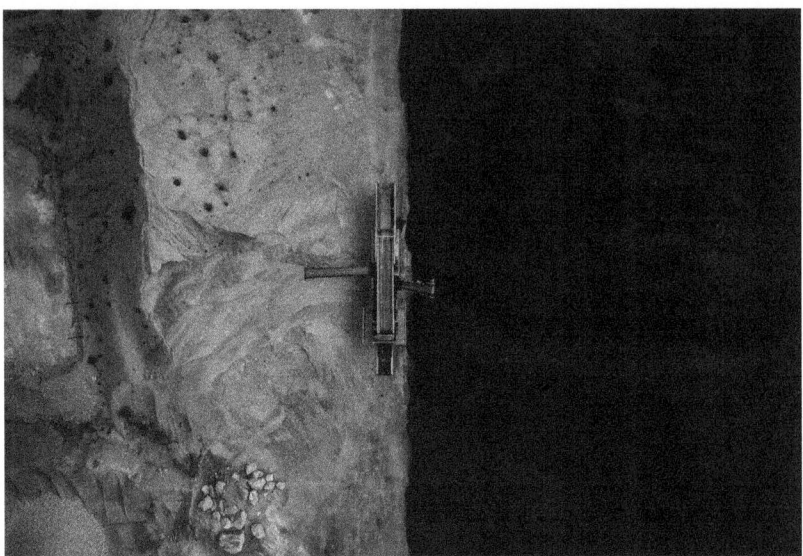

Figure 10.1. Tom Hegen, From the series *Coal Mine* (2006). Courtesy of the artist.

organisms. Our thesis is that both drone oceanography and drone art-photography are indicative of posthuman photorealism, with vibrant imagery as the output of the intertwinement of technologies, whales, humans, and the elements. Here are two examples of living whales entangled with the drone apparatuses of science and photographic art.

Scientific Views on Whales

No subject better embodies the qualities that define the problems with the world's oceans and our range of possible responses than the whale. Cetaceans are in peril. The Atlantic grey whale is extinct. So too is the Chinese river dolphin. The vaquita porpoise and the Māui dolphin are on the brink. The Gulf of Mexico Bryde's whale is severely threatened with only thirty-three individuals in existence with much of its habitat seriously compromised by the Deepwater Horizon oil spill of 2010 (Corkeron and Kraus 2018: 169). Only around thirty North Pacific right whales are alive today. Western Pacific gray whales number around 150. Perhaps 100 Arabian Sea humpbacks and Okhotsk Sea bowheads exist. Blue whale populations have not significantly recovered. They remain around one-percent of pre-whaling numbers. Drones allow scientists and artists to witness living whales while populations of their relatives decline.

Traditionally, cetacean science gathered insights into population, mating, migration, and health from the leftovers of the whaling industry – skin, skeletons, stomach contents, and kill location data (Burnett 2012). Cetologists would shoot whales with an arrow from a crossbow that would violently cut out a sample of blubber. The camera became essential to moving from studying dead and suffering whales to investigating living whales. For example, when research into killer whales in the Puget Sound of the Northwest coast of North America began it was not known that there were resident and transient whales. The pioneering work of Dr Michael Bigg painstakingly photographed every Southern Resident and developed a visual key to identify individuals based on the black and white patterns or scars on their dorsal fin (Colby 2018). In this case, the camera invited a new form of intimacy – the shift from objectification to subjectification in orca science.

Knowing individuals enabled the monitoring of genetic health through generations. Identifying individuals with markings allowed scientists to better understand and publicise how few and unique the Southern Resident orcas are, engendering conservation sentiments in the liberal local city of Seattle, Washington, in the Pacific Northwest of North America, where orcas – through romantic images – were made into icons of both the risks and the conservation responses possible in the Anthropocene.

A similar approach was taken by Dr Robert Payne who has conducted the longest investigation of whales in the world, focusing on the Southern Atlantic Right Whales of Patagonia, Chile. 2020 was the fortieth anniversary of the beginning of this investigation. For Payne, and other cetologists like Dr Iain Kerr, and their colleagues, photography was not only essential for identifying individual whales through the years; elevating their cameras above the whales was equally important, as a higher resolution of images could be achieved, which fine-tuned their individuation of the whales. The coastline along Patagonia, where the right whales were nurturing their young in shallow bays, is lined with high cliffs that Payne and Kerr would run along, following whales, stretching necks and arms upward to collect more refined and less horizontal images. When they had the funds, they would hire aeroplanes. They would try more experimental techniques to achieve the vertical view. Low flying aeroplanes, hovering hydrogen balloons, and parachute-lofted and camera-wielding scientists each inhabit a mezzo-level of the atmosphere.

While parachutes and hydrogen-filled balloons elevated the scientist and camera above nursing whales, today scientists such as Payne and his organisation Ocean Alliance have pioneered the use of drones in cetology. Drones afford discretion and a new kind of precise mobility while observing whales. Drone cetology is resulting in new data including infrared thermography of humpbacks in Cook Islands (Horton et al. 2019), details about grey whale behaviour in Oregon (Torres et al. 2018), analysis of the body condition and energy reserves of whales (Castrillon and Nash 2020), and the automated identification of whales based on drone images with convolutional neural networks (Gray et al. 2019).

In 2017 Ocean Alliance travelled to Keku Strait, Alaska to trial a real-time and artificially intelligent whale identification system designed by microchip designer Intel. The system had to be field-friendly, unintrusive, and run

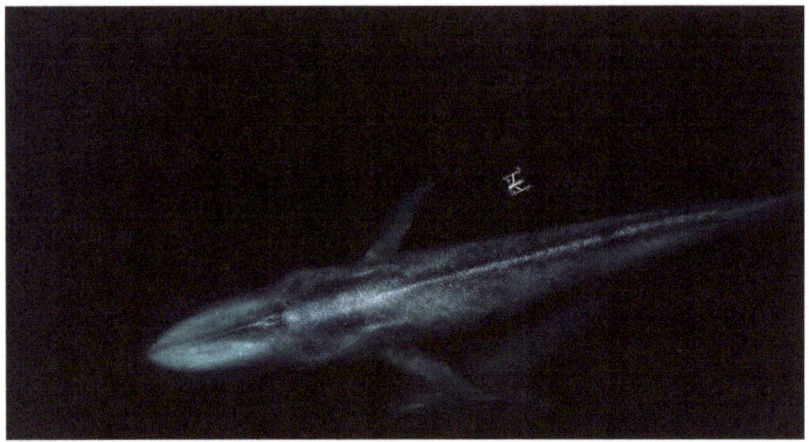

Figure 10.2. Christian Miller/Ocean Alliance, *Snotbot drone over blue whale*, Gulf of California, Mexico (2019). Courtesy of the artist.

on a boat with contingencies of waves, storms, and whales living out their own instinctual geographies and temporalities. They set up a small computer laboratory on board the research vessel, the *Glacial Seal*. They saw a blow, launched the drone, and flew fifty meters above it, relaying video back to the ship (see Figure 10.2). While the drone hovered, with ninety-two percent confidence, Intel's artificial intelligence identified 'Trumpeter', a humpback that had not been seen for twenty-three years – all in real time and based on live streaming video from a drone (see Figure 10.2).

Ocean Alliance's posthumanism entanglement weaves together not only drones and whales but also machine learning into a system of zoepolitical conservation. Ocean Alliance exploits access to the mezzo to build image databases of the bodies of numerous whale species, collaborate with Intel in using AI to identify individual humpback whales, and fly drones through the exhalations of whales to collect microbiota. Convoluted neural networks, or CNNs, are a type of artificial intelligence that builds upon drone-collected photogrammetry, computer vision, and deep learning to analyse and build correlates across three-dimensional moving images. Convoluted neural networks automate identification of blue, minke, and humpback whales with ninety-eight percent accuracy (1490). Images for training CNN must be generated by drones because high resolution is needed, and they must be collected from the mezzo. Drones and CNN mean increasing speed and automation in identification: 'If cetacean surveys are routinely conducted by UAS (unpersoned aerial systems) rather than ships and planes these automated capabilities will facilitate analysis and allow rapid management and ecological insights' (1497-98). Speed and automation, Leroi-Gourhan (1993) might argue, is the history of technology itself. We may wonder if these AI systems will document whale health fast enough. But the real question is whether or not

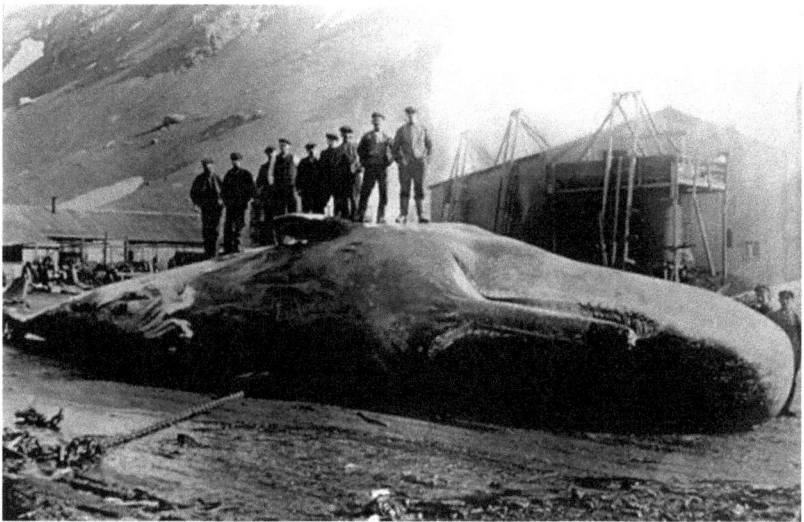

Figure 10.3. *Nine men standing on a beached sperm whale*, Leith Harbour, South Georgia (1914).
Source: Wikimedia Commons.

marine policymakers will listen to the insights from drone oceanography and slow the decline in whale populations.

Ocean Alliance was in Alaska to produce a segment for the National Geographic programme, *Earth Live*, a two-hour live wildlife documentary with camera crews simultaneously filming across six continents. These images and drone applications, therefore, are not only for scientific purposes. The drone-collected high-definition images portray the immensity of the whale's body and also index evocative displays of scientific prowess and entertainment acumen. Used in acts of awareness-raising and fund-raising, such images contribute to sustaining this non-profit science, and its goals, conserving whale populations and thereby hopefully minimising one manifestation of oceanic decline. A conservationist spirit is shared by artistic and amateur images of whales and with photography prompting care for protecting biodiversity (Hanisch, Johnston, and Longnecker 2019).

Artistic and Amateur Views on Whales

Artists and amateur photographers in the past shared a common feature with early cetologists, an embodied engagement with dead whales. The Library of Congress digital archive in the United States has a wealth of historical images produced by amateur photographers of recently deceased whales.

Common motifs of these images are people on top of the whale, stepping on it, victorious in an imaginary battle. Consider that in 1877, the proprietor of the Royal Aquarium, William Leonard Hunt, captured a beluga whale off the coast of Labrador, Canada and transported it to London for display. At

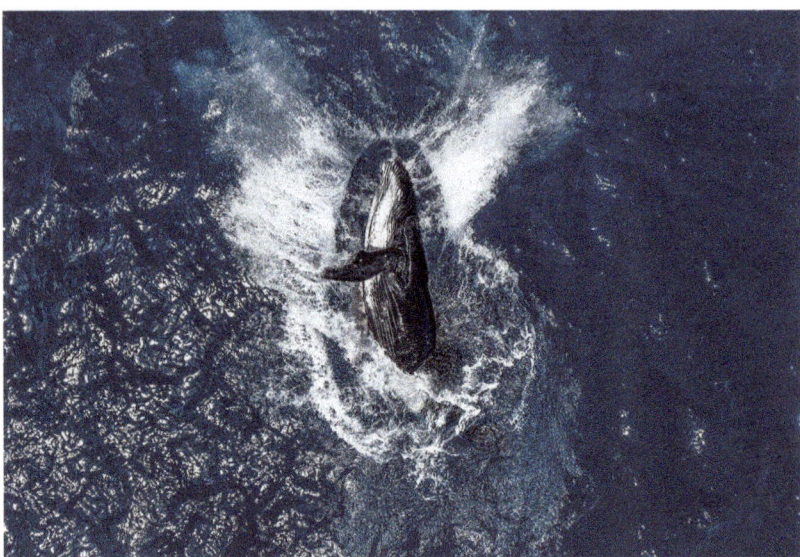

Figure 10.4. Karim Iliya, *Humpback Breach*. Courtesy of the artist.

that time, Britain depended on whale oils for illumination and lubrication but almost nobody except whalemen or sailors had seen one alive. The whale survived only four days before succumbing to pneumonia. Still seeking a profit, the entrepreneur stuffed and displayed the beluga. The gruesome reality for much of the recent past has been that 'the visual culture of any captive whale so long as the whale hunt continued was (and remains) a visual culture of death' (Bushnell 2019: 183). The mobility, verticality, and resolution provided by the drone pushes whale depictions from morbidity to vitality.

With advances in techniques of capturing and keeping whales alive in captivity, it has only recently become possible to see and profit off of living whales in places like SeaWorld – often critiqued for their inhuman captivities of intelligent species (Ventre and Jett 2015). For the enterprising, lucky, and patient photographer, drones allow whales and other marine animals to be seen alive and in their own environment. This practice is apparent in drone photography competitions. For example, the photo that won the Grand Prize at the SkyPixel Sixth Anniversary Aerial Photo and Video Contest in 2021 is called *Humpback Breach* (see Figure 10.4). Shot in French Polynesia by Karim Iliya, a photographer and environmentalist, we see a whale falling back into the sea, its entire profile in the centre of the frame, with the shape of its breach reproduced in a shadow on the water. While the image is beautiful and captivating, it is not unique. In photography contests throughout the world that have a drone category, images of whales are common. Another example is the photo *La Empalagosa* (The cloying one), taken by Mexican José Ruíz Cheires, in the

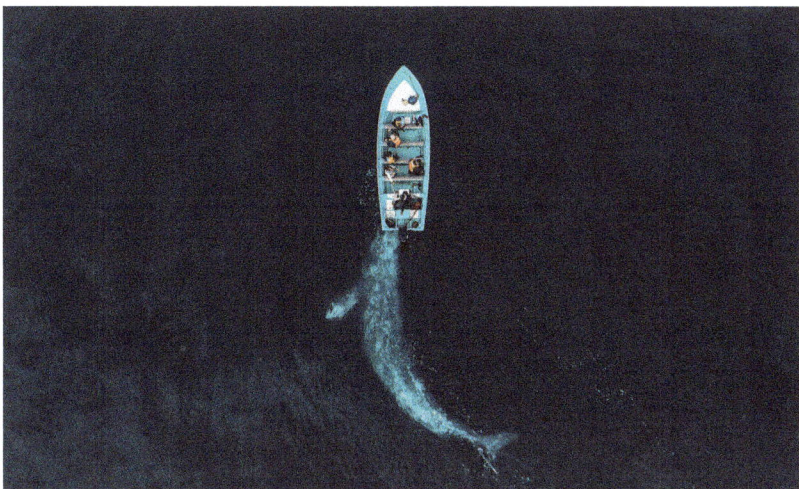

Figure 10.5. José Ruíz Cheires, *La Empalagosa*, Santuario de las Ballenas en Baja California Sur, Mexico. Courtesy of the artist.

Santuario de las Ballenas en Baja California Sur, Mexico, the winner of the Drone Photo Awards 2020 (Figure 10.5).

With more than two-point-four million photos using the hashtag 'whale' on Instagram and with a growing number of these images being taken with drones, whales have become a common character in how drones mediate and circulate human-ocean relations. In this way, whales are seen in ways they were not historically – alive.

As in oceanography, a new way of artistically documenting the world with moving pictures is possible from the mezzo, one that is aligned with posthuman photorealism. In the short documentary *Unmanned*, Wayne Perryman from the Marine Mammal Division of the National Oceanic and Atmospheric Administration, United States, says that with drones 'you are close to animals. It is beautiful, it is challenging. And also, you are seeing animals from a perspective that you normally don't get to see them. So, all of the sudden you are seeing things that you haven't seen before'. The drone is a non-invasive technology that allows humans to see whales with minimal disturbance and from a proximity that engenders intimacy, and, possibly, caring. Drone photographer Slater Moore in the same documentary said, 'These whales have always been doing this, but people haven't seen it until now because of the drone perspective'. The drone, as a technology that allows the mezzo to be accessed, embodies a posthuman photorealism that invites the viewers to see and attune with living whales, separating the historical connection between death and witnessing. The large assemblage of drones, humans, and social media platforms is set in motion, bringing together the zoe of whales and people, the geo of the ocean and the air, and the techne of drones and networks.

Scientific or artistic, images collected from the mezzo have a potential to inspire conservation. From *Planet Earth II* and *The Year the Earth Stopped* to the Academy Award-winning documentary *My Octopus Teacher*, many recent documentaries about the ocean feature drone footage. Ayers suggests, speaking of the TV series *Planet Earth II*, that it 'attempts to rehumanise the nonhuman vision of its technology, placing us within the natural world and perceiving the world from an animal's point of view' (2019: 205). While the drone may provide a bird's eye view, it is not a whale's vantage point. Mezzo vision is nonhuman and also noncetacean, but in its otherworldliness it provides a perspective on life-in-action.

With this conservationist ethos, images from drone oceanographers and amateur drone photographers are similar: the entire body of the whale, particularly when the upper part is above water, is contrasted with the blue of the ocean. While scientific, touristic, or artistic images taken from beside or below the whale struggle to represent it in its totality, the drone catches the breadth of the whale's body enacting physical, embodied, and elemental movement. Images from the mezzo show whales as living, breathing, exhaling, inhaling, jumping, playing, moving, caring beings.

Conclusion

We are in a historical moment of openness of and access to the atmosphere. Drones have democratised a form of posthuman relations, realism, and mobility by accessing the mezzo with existential implications for nonhumans and humans alike. The mezzo afforded by the drone opens new ways of embodying connection with animals, seeing them vividly alive. This challenges anthropocentrism, opening an aperture to think about the relationship between multispecies survival and technologies of vision. Posthuman realism is necessary during this era of extinction – potentially the last chance to witness certain species alive, to study them, and to portray them without directly disturbing or killing them. While anthropogenic factors continue to negatively impact whale existence, these images have the capacity to inform and inspire conservation, without which collecting drone images of living whales will become a thing of the past.

Posthuman photorealism is relevant not only as a conservationist genre but as a practice that opens a wider discussion about zoe-techno-geo entanglements, one that decentres the human as the main actor. This movement asks humans to consciously inhabit multispecies relations. Co-producing images with living whales forces humans to acknowledge their co-habitation and interdependence with a multiplicity of animal, geographic, atmospheric, and technological others. In the case of whales, the challenge of 'catching them' with a drone personifies struggles to see and be seen, to act and be acted upon. The drone is a visual and sensory device with affective logics that highlight caring and careful sensing.

Works Cited

Adey, Peter. 2015. 'Air's Affinities: Geopolitics, Chemical Affect and the Force of the Elemental'. *Dialogues in Human Geography* 5: 54-75.

Ayers, Drew. 2019. *Spectacular Posthumanism: The Digital Vernacular of Visual Effects*. London: Bloomsbury Publishing.

Braidotti, Rosi. 2019. *Posthuman Knowledge*. Cambridge: Polity Press.

Burnett, D. Graham. 2012. *The Sounding of the Whale: Science and Cetaceans in the Twentieth Century*. Chicago: University of Chicago Press.

Bushnell, Kelly P. 2019. 'Looking at Leviathan. The First Live Cetaceans in Britain'. In *Ecocriticism and the Anthropocene in Nineteenth-Century Art and Visual Culture*, edited by Maura Coughlin and Emily Gephart, 178-91. New York: Routledge.

Castrillon, Juliana, and Susan Bengtson Nash. 2020. 'Evaluating Cetacean Body Condition: A Review of Traditional Approaches and New Developments'. *Ecology and Evolution* 10, no. 12: 6144-62.

Caitlin. 2012 'What's in a name?' *B.C. Cetacean Sightings Network*. https://wildwhales.org/2012/12/18/whats-in-a-name/.

Colby, Jason. 2018. *Orca: How We Came to Know and Love the Ocean's Greatest Predator*. Oxford: Oxford University Press.

Corkeron, Peter, and Scott D. Kraus. 2018. 'Baleen Whale Species on Brink of Extinction for First Time in 300 Years'. *Nature* 554: 169.

Fish, Adam. 2017. *Technoliberalism and the End of Participatory Culture in the United States*. Basingstoke: Palgrave.

Garrett, Bradley, and Karen Anderson. 'Drone Methodologies: Taking Flight in Human and Physical Geography'. *Transactions of the Institute of British Geographers* 43, no. 3: 341-59.

Gray, Patrick C., Kevin C. Bierlich, Sydney A. Mantell, Ari S. Friedlaender, Jeremy A. Goldbogen, and David W. Johnston. 2019. 'Drones and Convolutional Neural Networks Facilitate Automated and Accurate Cetacean Species Identification and Photogrammetry'. *Methods in Ecology and Evolution* 10, no. 9: 1490-500.

Hanisch, Emma, Ross Johnston, and Nancy Longnecker. 2019. 'Cameras for Conservation: Wildlife Photography and Emotional Engagement with Biodiversity and Nature'. *Human Dimensions of Wildlife* 24, no. 3: 267-84.

Haraway, Donna, Noboru Ishikawa, Scott F. Gilbert, Kenneth Olwig, Anna L. Tsing, and Nils Bubandt. 2016. 'Anthropologists are Talking – About the Anthropocene'. *Ethnos* 81, no. 3: 535-64.

Horton, Travis W., Nan Hauser, Shannon Cassel, K. Frederika Klaus, Ticiana Fettermann, and Nicholas Key. 2019. 'Doctor Drone: Non-Invasive Measurement of Humpback Whale Vital Signs Using Unoccupied Aerial System Infrared Thermography'. *Frontiers in Marine Science* 6: 466.

Jablonowski, Maximilian. 2020. 'Beyond Drone Vision: the Embodied Telepresence of First-Person-View Drone Flight'. *The Senses and Society* 15, no. 3: 344-58.

Kember, Sarah. 2017. 'After the Anthropocene: the Photographic for Earthly Survival?' *Digital Creativity* 28, no. 4: 348-53.

Keller, Bryn. 2018. 'Machine Learning, Drones, and Whales: A Great Combination!' *Xoltar*. http://www.xoltar.org/posts/2018-04-26-whale-expedition/index.html.

Kristoffersen, Berit, Roger Norum, and Britt Kramvig. 2016. 'Arctic Whale Watching and Anthropocene Ethics'. *Tourism and the Anthropocene*: 94-110.

Leroi-Gourhan, André. 1993. *Gesture and Speech*. Cambridge: MIT Press.

Lorimer, Jamie. 2015. *Wildlife in the Anthropocene: Conservation after Nature*. Minneapolis: University of Minnesota Press.

McCormack, Derek P. 2018. *Atmospheric Things: On the Allure of Elemental Envelopment*. Durham: Duke University Press.

Mirzoeff, Nicholas. 2014. 'Visualising the Anthropocene'. *Public Culture* 26, no. 2: 213-32.

Mitchell, William John. 1994. *The Reconfigured Eye: Visual Truth in the Post-Photographic Era*. Cambridge: MIT Press.

Osborne, Peter. 2000. *Traveling Light: Photography, Travel and Visual Culture*. Manchester: Manchester University Press.

Sheller, Mimi, and John Urry. 2006. 'The New Mobilities Paradigm'. *Environment and Planning* 38, no. 2: 207-26.

Stevenson, Lisa, and Eduardo Kohn. 2015 'Leviathan: An Ethnographic Dream'. *Visual Anthropology Review* 31, no. 1: 49-53.

Ventre, Jeffrey, and John Jett. 2015. 'Killer Whales, Theme Parks, and Controversy: An Exploration of the Evidence'. In *Animals and Tourism: Understanding Diverse Relationships*, edited by Kevin Markwell, 128-45. Bristol: Channel View Publications.

Zylinska, Joanna. 2017. *Nonhuman Photography*. Cambridge: MIT Press.

11

Asymmetrical Cinema – Dawn of the Drone through Film, Cartography and Interspecies Relations

Jack Faber

Encounter of the First Kind

A man stands next to a dusty road in the middle of nowhere, squinting towards the horizon, waiting for a fictitious appointment which (although he doesn't know it yet) won't take place. The aerial machine, flying low on the other side of his field of vision, is getting closer. It seems to be a crop-duster. As it approaches, we notice it is single engine, double winged. We can't see a pilot – nor a gunner for that matter – as the machine rapidly opens fire at the man standing there, caught completely by surprise. Now the man is running for his life, falling on the hard ground, sprawling for cover, as the deadly machine keeps going at him, missing and flying past again, almost mowing him down. Luckily, the man is able to run into a cornfield, finding shelter among the tall thick stalks around him. Yet this feeling of safety proves false as the low-flying machine suddenly sprays the vegetation with heavy vapours. It is spreading a concentrated chemical substance which brings to mind the way the Americans will use Agent Orange in the upcoming Vietnam War. Escaping the chemical smoke, the man runs toward the open road in a last attempt to save his life. His aerial pursuer follows close. Almost failing to stop a truck on the road, the man falls with his back to the tarmac while the relentless flying machine, now too close to pull back, crashes into the braking truck, engulfing both in flames. The man is finally saved, yet the rest of us have just been hurtled into a future of uncertainty.

This seminal scene from Hitchcock's *North by Northwest* (1959) introduced the crop-duster whose pilot remains unseen as the design for man-made aerial manhunters, to be perfected in later generations with the Predator drone family (see Figure 11.1). It also articulates the essential asymmetrical equation of Man vs Aerial Machine, to be repeated in movies in the following years to the point of becoming a cinematic and cultural trope. This asymmetrical equation, placing the drone at the top trophic level of dominance,

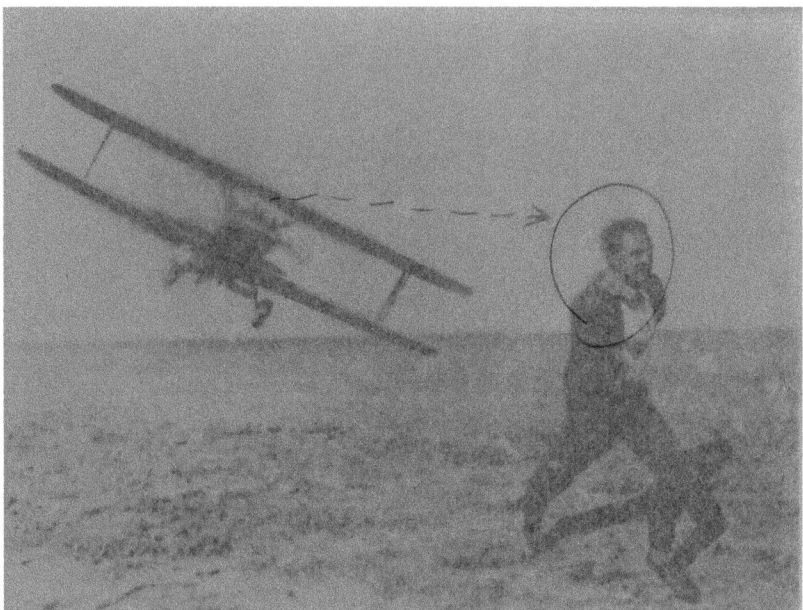

Figure 11.1. Jack Faber, *NNW, Line of Sight* – preparation sketch (2023). Courtesy of the artist.

also suggests a radical shift in the ecological pyramid. Situated as one of the most technologically advanced and rapidly expanding fields of interaction with our surroundings, the development and usage of drones is shaping new relations between us and the environment we co-inhabit with other species, animals especially. Such interspecies relations are forming simultaneously as part of military, industrial, and civilian drones' growing activities in various territories, and their intensified presence in war zones. Whether as part of an accelerating commercial reconnaissance to locate and exploit new natural resources on remote areas on our planet (and others, as seen by NASA's recent Ingenuity Drone Mars Mission); as a derivative of corporate infrastructure surveying missions; as a direct effort of wildlife conservation and research, or an offshoot of a post-colonial 'Safari' attitude extended into new altitudes by political actors in conflict arenas – the multiple ways in which drones are changing our relations to other species are overwhelming. Yet examining how the drone is embedded into the very fabric of interspecies relations, suggests an unaccounted history from which the drone originally emerged.

This chapter draws a map of cultural representations and interspecies relations, situating the drone as an outcome of artistic practices envisioning its inception and military proliferation. This is a crucial perspective shift from the traditional perception of drones as technical tools invented in aviation workshops and military labs, one which is essential for our environmentally precarious times. It suggests alternatives for perceiving the drone mostly as an asymmetrical agent of progress and appropriation, invading (albeit

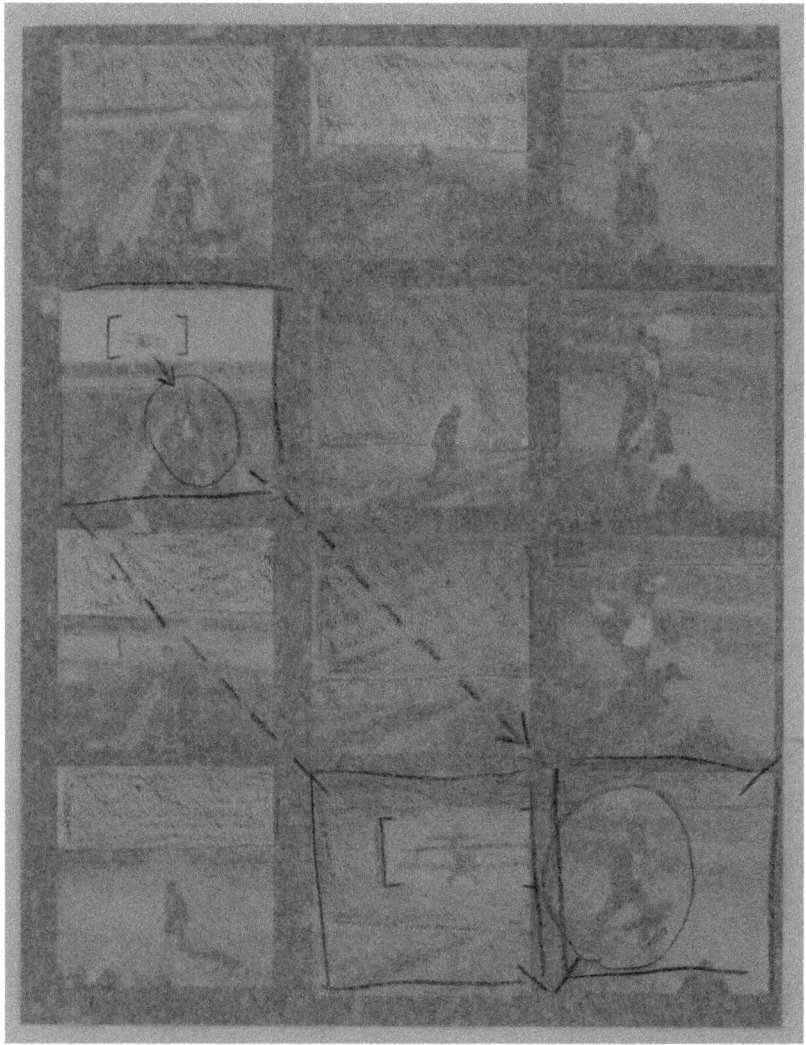

Figure 11.2. Jack Faber, *NNW, Line of Sight II* – preparation sketch (2023). Courtesy of the artist.

mostly unseen) into physical and theoretical terrains. This sort of asymmetry contrasts the surplus of advanced technologies and excess to resources on one side with significantly limited abilities and capacities on the other side. Perpetuating and proliferating these asymmetrical hierarchies of control, drones are often discussed exclusively within these terms – as apex products of the information industry and security economy. Studying the drone instead as an enmeshed conception of art practices – through versatile representations in media objects and their connection to interspecies relations – enables us to shed new light on the drone's social, political, and climatic roles, no longer confined by its current dominating asymmetrical use.

Asymmetry, Art and Cinema

Since the early days of art and cinema, the same technologies invented for projecting dreams and stories about the relations between humans and nature, from cave paintings to high-resolution screenings, were used to create asymmetrical relations between humans and other species, especially animals. As the latest prominent element in this equation, drones hold the potential to perpetuate, accelerate, and destabilise them. In the following pages the idea of Asymmetrical Cinema is suggested as a key term to investigate the drone as an enmeshed conception of art practices. Asymmetrical Cinema refers specifically to filmic events (whether scenes, shots, films in their entirety, moving image experiences or other related elements) which reveal the roles they play within asymmetrical ideologies and networks. Through them we can acknowledge, analyse, evaluate, and discuss the existence of asymmetrical equations. This, in turn, enables us to assess the functions they fulfil and their vast influence on our cultural perspectives, as well as our collective perceptions of interspecies relations. This text aims to highlight some of the less explored and unexpected paths linking these relations and different fields of study (such as surveillance and animal studies, film theory, art history, philosophy, literature, etc.) while offering new reflections regarding them. It acts as an introduction to the conceptual framework and the relations between the representations of drones and animal beings as shown by art and cinema. The chapter studies these relations simultaneously as seen horizontally, on a historical timeline, and vertically – from a bird's eye-view and as an unmanned aerial mapping of this theoretical landscape. It positions the drone as the contemporary embodiment of the divide between human and nonhuman that relies on practices of violence, following Fanon's observation that 'Sometimes this Manichaeanism reaches its logical conclusion and dehumanises the colonised subject. In plain talk, he is reduced to the state of an animal' (Fanon 2004: 7).

Through an interdisciplinary perspective, spanning from storytelling traditions and cultural artefacts to contemporary conflict areas, we can trace the development of the drone not only technologically but epistemologically. Through ancient mythologies and their modern metamorphosis into film and visual art, these traditions amplify and affect our understanding of the political nature of surveillance and its perceptual integration into interspecies relations. Existing research addresses interspecies relations with drones through lenses such as monitoring biodiversity (Wich and Pin Koh 2018), conservation (Lopez and Mulero-Pázmány 2019), or ethics and activism (McCausland, Pyke, and O'Sullivan 2018), to name a few. Yet investigating drone presence as a new system for producing cultural representations and imagination within the frame of interspecies relations – remains largely uncharted territory. To

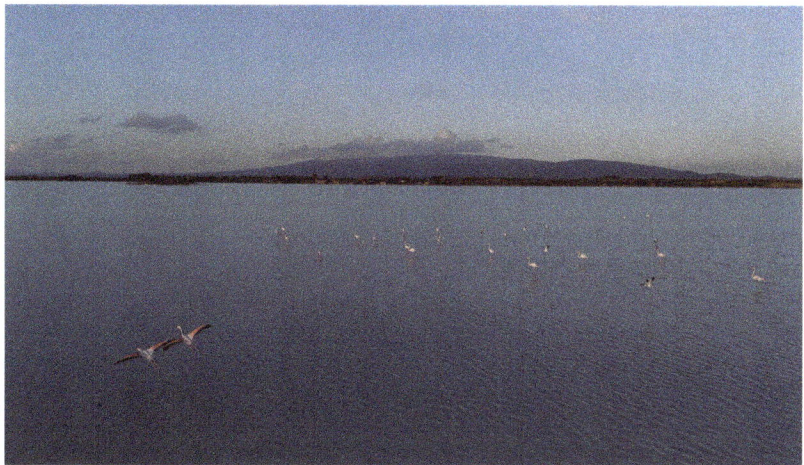

Figure 11.3. Jack Faber, *Unsafe Space*s – production still (2024). Courtesy of the artist.

navigate through this *terra incognita* my research required the development of a new methodology I call 'Cine-Cartography'. It is used to position relevant theories, media, and art objects in relation to each other, studying their connections and mutual influences while reframing them in light of recent discursive developments, historical context and contemporary relevance. Cine-Cartography is best understood as a multidimensional exploration taking place spatially and interactively (as a constellation of media objects). It is a composite of multiple layers including sound and duration, movement, and stillness – of images and within images. Given the spatial and dimensional limitation of printed text, Cine-Cartography manifests itself here as an annotated timeline. This timeline starts with the birth of the idea of remotely controlled flying devices. It continues to contemporary days through cinema – acting as the modern mass media myth making machine – by using prime examples of filmic representations. The reading of these representations, aided by revisiting ideas from Achille Mbembe, Katherine Chandler, Paul Virilio, Marina Verzier, and John Berger's notions of animals' intrinsic connection to human culture and perception, suggest that the origin of the drone, and perhaps its future, is in artistic representations of interspecies relations.

Mythology of Machines

What seem like new relations forming nowadays between animals, humans and drones have a rich history, hidden in two quite remote mythologies. Tracing the artefacts and art objects left by the cultures which created these mythologies reveals that the concept of the drone was originally conceived in ancient times as an artificial autonomous aerial animal. The famous Greek story about Prometheus's punishment concludes with Hercules shooting down the former's eternal aerial tormentor, the Caucasian Eagle – a bronze-made bird-like automaton, as well as described by a second-century AD Roman mythographer, Pseudo-Hyginus, in his *Astronomica:*

> He [Zeus] sent an eagle to him [Prometheus chained on Mount Kaukasos] to eat out his liver which was constantly renewed at night [...] many point out it [the eagle] was made by the hands of Volcanos [Hephaistos] and given life by Jove [Zeus]. (Theoi Project 2019)

Hercules's accurate archery ended an ordeal repeating itself for 30,000 years on a remote mountain peak (Theoi Project 2019) – a retaliation for the titan's rebellious act of stealing fire, representing knowledge and technology, and giving it as a gift to mankind. This duration supports the sources claiming the Caucasian Eagle is a mechanical construction, excelling in repeating the same action with great accuracy, *ad infinitum*. Some sources state that the Caucasian Eagle is actually a fell creature spawned by the she-dragon, Echidna, yet the second major mythological tradition, created in the vicinities of the Baltic Sea around 1,000 BC, clearly speaks of an elaborately constructed bird of prey:

> Smith Ilmarinen
> the everlasting craftsman
> forged an eagle of fire
> a wivern of flame;
> the feet he shaped of iron
> of steel the talons
> for wings the sides of a boat.
> (Lonnrot 1999: 242)

This description of a mechanical flying predator from the Finnish *Kalevala*, depicts how this ingenious invention was manufactured in order to fulfil and fit a specific mission profile which no human (or humanoid, such as Ilmarinen, the immortal smith) can accomplish – catching a monstrous pike 'without a net or a seine, without any other trap' (242). This is an imaginative shift from the Herculean confrontation with the Caucasian Eagle daily devouring the ever-regenerating liver of the chained titan Prometheus. Unlike the bronze-made eagle, excelling in his endlessly repetitive bloody act which no man can complete (yet robotic systems are perfect for) the Finnish Iron Eagle is not an adversary to the protagonist but part of a collaborative relation with its creator. Ilmarinen is observing from the safety of a remote shore how his artificial giant eagle is executing its pre-programmed task of extracting an elusive marine threat. It is important to notice that this deadly extraction is committed against an unconstructed animal, the Tuoni Pike, forming a triangulation in which man is pitting an artificial aerial animal (a drone, for all matters) against a biotic one, putting the two in opposition. After extracting the giant pike from the waters, the Iron Eagle disregards Ilmarinen's original orders, leaving him only with the pike's head as evidence of the entire affair, while autonomously soaring to the skies never to be seen again by its maker.

While the Herculean story puts the conflict between man and animal-like machine at the centre, the Kalevala's foretelling of the drone-eagle offers a more complex triangulation in which the remotely controlled mechanical bird-of-prey is built to achieve dominance over an infamously wild animal, and over nature in general. As Ilmarinen first climbs upon his constructed eagle's back, he is soon hurtled from it and the drone-eagle continues the hunt for the pike by itself, attempting multiple 'attack profiles' before capturing and eliminating its designated target. These detailed stories prefigure the idea of Unmanned Aerial Vehicles and even recent developments in this field, in the shape of ornithopters and animal-simulating drones (such as the BionicFlyingFox and the SmartBird by Festo). An intriguing mix of elements from both mythologies worth examining will later appear in the early 1980s in what emerged as the most effective apparatus of modern myth making, acting as an epic storytelling device and a visual narration of human thought – the cinema.

Bees, Bugs and Crop-dusters

Whether the first drone was the 1918 Kettering Bug, an American aerial torpedo pre-programmed to strike distant ground targets, or the 1935 Queen Bee, a British pilotless radio-controlled seaplane, is not central to our current discussion. Although the official term 'drone' is attributed to the latter, the former seems to manifest much of the philosophy of asymmetrical engagement. In both cases, naming these unprecedented autonomous aircraft seems to be a stepping stone to how 'the military seems to anticipate this changing relation with nature and technology in naming its drones: Global Hawk, Heron, Killer Bee, Mantis, Scan Eagle, and so on. Electronic birds hovering in the air, circling over warzones, until they spot a prey and attack' (Pater 2016). The early experimental drones modestly planted seeds for later explorations of the relations between unmanned airborne machines and animals, while shifting the aerial gaze from reconnaissance to remote attack. Intertwining the development of war and cinema in modern times, this aerial gaze was assimilated into pivotal weapon systems almost seamlessly as 'the function of the weapon is the function of the eye' (Virilio 1989: 26). Virilio studied how the accelerated progress of the ocular machine and the military asymmetrical means of oppression – physical, psychological, and spiritual – coincide. Acknowledging that 'even when weapons are not employed, they are active elements of ideological conquest' (8), he proposed this interconnection between the ability to see and to eliminate, highlighted by the fact that both seeing and targeting emerged as acquired skills, learned from perspectives created by cinematic techniques. This process accelerated as cinema became accessible to unprecedentedly larger audiences. Fusing the production of moving images and editing techniques into the mass effect of the cinematic projection, gave birth to the drone as we know it, at the level of perception. Paralleling the advancing technological progression and popularity of films with its own development and proliferation, the drones' flight plan from inception to present day has been drawn continuously throughout the twentieth century, as Szita points out:

> Despite the confusion, drones are not a new invention. Nicholas Tesla pioneered the concept one hundred years ago. The army began to adopt them after the Second World war, with the Ryan models of the 1950s being the prototypes of today's drones. (Szita 2016)

The military adoption of drone technology, four decades after its appearance in the form of the Kettering Bug, precisely corresponds to the first appearance of the concept of the drone in popular cinema. The seminal scene from Hitchcock's *North by Northwest* (1959), mentioned earlier, introduced the pilotless crop-duster as the design for man-made aerial manhunters. It cemented the asymmetrical equation of Man vs Aerial Machine as a cinematic and cultural trope, to be explored to different extents in *From Russia with Love* (1963), *Night Moves* (1975), *Close Encounters of the Third Kind* (1977), *First Blood* (1982), *Red Dawn* (1984), *Midnight Run* (1988), *Terminator 2: Judgment Day* (1991), *Mission: Impossible* (1996), and *A Good Day to Die Hard* (2013), among others. Many key elements which attack drones rely upon are all evident in North by Northwest's early detailed representation of a drone-targeted killing mission. Among these elements are the ability to remain hidden in plain sight (in this case the aerial aggressor camouflaging itself as an innocent mundane machine – a crop-duster); the capacity to remain in the air for long duration while carrying different payloads for different attack profiles (including automatic fire, chemical attack, and ramming); and the capability to conduct repeated aerial assaults as needed to accomplish the pre-assigned mission (including a final 'suicide strike'). As the aerial assault machine is soaring above to hound down a sole person who is trying to escape into the cornfield 'forest', the film reveals its own nature in the most precise and fundamental form – as a sequence of moving images devoid of any dialogue or other narrative devices. It is devoted completely and purely to constant and contrast movement, that of the single human and that of the artificial aerial entity seeking to destroy him.

Earlier cinematic explorations of aviation in asymmetrical confrontations – such as in *The Thief of Bagdad* (1924), *Sora no daikaijû Radon* (1956), *The Deadly Mantis* (1957) and *The Giant Claw* (1957) – pitted man against a flying terror in the shape of a giant animal, usually some sort of fantastic bird, bat, or insect. Such oppositions used complicated stop motion techniques to address the disproportionate struggle, matching a mere human figure versus the unequal surplus of size, strength, manoeuvrability, and attack measures manifested by the huge animal's massive predatory talons, beak, or teeth. The violent attempts to survive these encounters were framed within fantasy and science-fiction settings, placing the entire ordeal far from the potential experience of the safely seated spectator. *North by Northwest* subverts these settings by offering quite a different level of involvement, now that the aerial attack can commence without warning, from a mostly harmless looking machine, in the most mundane surroundings, by unseen and unknown assailants, against any ordinary individual, completely unprotected and mistakenly targeted.

The scene contrasts the two bodies conflicting through space – with the gravitationally limited human body revealed in all its fragility against the omnipotent artificial body which is moving freely through the air, while raining down metal and breathtaking hazardous haze in an overwhelming display of surplus. This contrast highlights even further the way this scene acts as an autonomous artwork within a film which until this point was loaded with sharp narrative twists, dialogues, and high pace humour. The lack of any utterances or other human sounds, except for some coughing due to the poisonous vapour, is unprecedented in a cinematic vehicle of this sort. This almost minimalistic approach within the landscape of a charismatic commercial thriller, reveals a hive of ideas ahead of their time. The fact that the subject of this targeted killing is an innocent, mistakenly marked civilian, will echo in a future full of wrongly identified targets of drone attacks (mostly led by the CIA) as Arthur Holland Michel indicates in a discussion in the 2014 'Drone Salon': 'The Bureau (of investigative Journalism) has calculated [...] between 12 percent and 35 percent civilian casualties (caused by drone strikes). The New America Foundation numbers put the proportion at between 8 and 15 percent' (Szita 2016).

In order to solve, at least conceptually, the proliferating cases involving the false identification of civilians as combatant targets, the US government transitioned to drone 'signature strikes' (Chamayou 2014: 47), here meaning aerial attacks authorised on the basis of traces, indications, or defining characteristics. Such strikes target individuals whose identity remains unknown but whose behaviour suggests membership in what the authority defines as a terrorist organisation. The targeted protagonist of *North by Northwest* is mistaken for a non-existent man, who is a complete fabrication by an unnamed American intelligence agency ('*We're all in the same alphabet soup*' as one of its chiefs explains later in the film) as part of their clandestine strategies. That is very much the epitaph of the unknown person whose behaviour suggests membership in a secret organisation with insurgent intentions. As Chamayou points out, 'strikes of this type, against unknown suspects, appear to constitute the majority of cases' (47). The targets of these aerial attacks are chosen based on collection of data arranged into models assimilating habits and behavioural categories of theoretical men, which can then fit any number of individuals. This also resonates with Achille Mbembe's notion of 'enemy by nature':

> Many innocent people are killed, not because of errors they had committed but instead for yet-to-be-committed errors. The war of conquest is thus not about upholding the law. If it criminalises the enemy, the aim is not to apply justice. Whether or not he bears arms, the enemy to be punished is an intrinsic enemy, *an enemy by nature*. (Mbembe 2019: 25)

In his examination, Mbembe highlights Necropolitics' strong connection to aerial policing and urban siege in the post-colony. Chandler elaborates and claims that 'the machinelike framework of the drone is doubled to establish threat as inhuman, even as denial never fully erases humanity [...] This denial builds on longstanding practices of violence that rely on the divide between human and nonhuman' (Chandler 2020: 9). Another visionary aspect of *North by Northwest* is the new hierarchy of interspecies relations shaped through the scene, as the imagined mastery man has achieved over nature is now reversed when he is hunted by the technological entity of his own creation. In order to survive, he now has to try and find refuge in the nature he has forsaken. Yet this is an artificial nature, a constructed 'forest' of tall corn stalks, and the next evolutionary aerial invention is already fully equipped with means to its end, as evident from the Agent Orange allusion.

This iconic scene demonstrates an effective repositioning of humanity within the very scales it invented to assert its authority over all other species and ascend from their ranks to unparalleled heights. The new order now formed as modern technology reaches even higher hierarchical altitude and replaces man, is achieved not only through relatively rudimentary elements but through the medium most recognised with that image of authority and ability for self-grandeur – the high-budget film. Hitchcock, globally known as the master of suspense, was also exceptionally good at hiding his intentions in plain sight, sending subversive messages and placing political gestures, even if cleverly covert, carefully packed inside the commercially crafted commodities of the Hollywood studios (Comolli and Narboni 1971). In his investigations of how global politics are designed and set in motion through complex espionage apparatuses and their reliance on codified images – as seen also in his *Topaz* (1969) and *Torn Curtain* (1966) – Hitchcock seems to play with Virilio's notion that following 'the Second World War, it became possible to sketch out a strategy of global vision, thanks to spy-satellites, drones and other video-missiles' (Virilio 1989: 2). Yet, this global strategy is reliant on the fact that 'a war of pictures and sounds is replacing the war of objects (projectiles and missiles)' (5). This convergence of complex connections of military strategies, representational mediums, vision-based technologies, and art is perhaps most evident in McLuhan's classic statement contextualising art as an 'early alarm system', as it were, enabling us to discover social and psychic targets in lots of time to prepare to cope with them' (McLuhan 1964). Cultivating his public image as the master manipulator of moving images, Hitchcock tapped

Asymmetrical Cinema 201

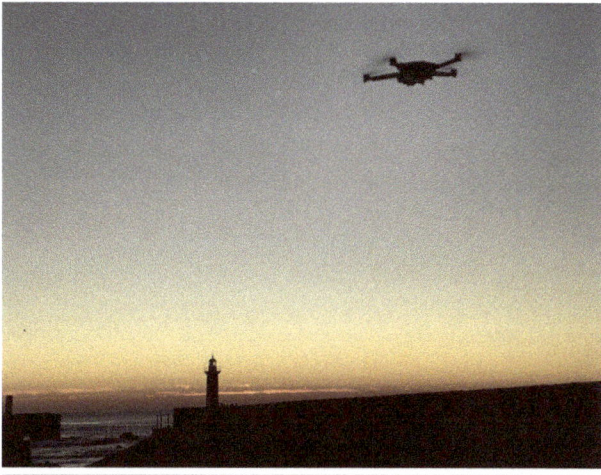

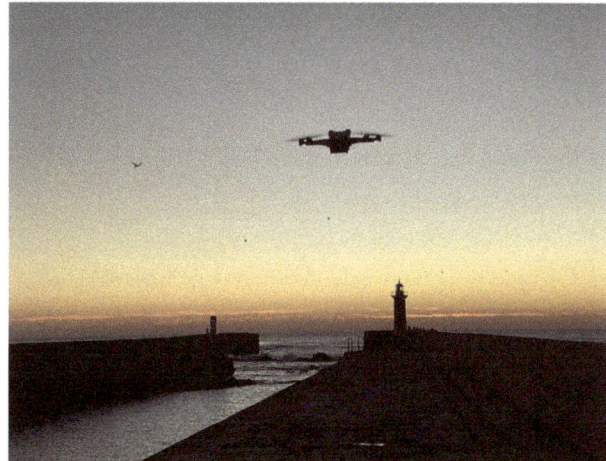

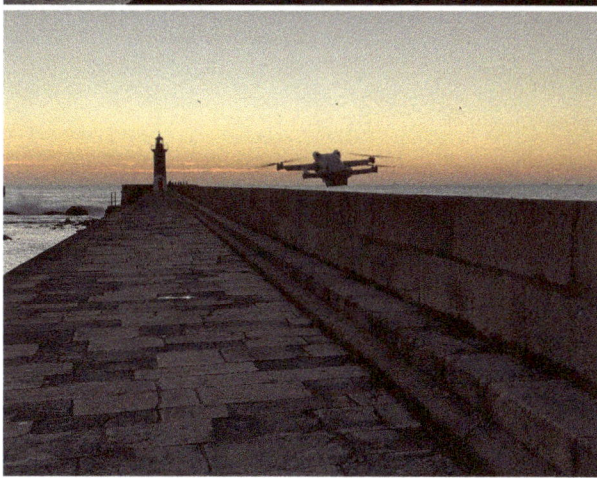

Figures 11.4(a), 11.4(b), 11.4(c). Jack Faber, *Dawn of the Drone* – production stills (2024). Courtesy of the artist.

into the mass media forms of his time and directed the collective gaze toward some of the terrors hidden within the mundane (like a crop duster, or a confusion in a restaurant leading to being mistakenly targeted by unknown forces and being hunted by an aerial aggressor). From their early inception in the late 1950s they would resonate in decades to come, amplified exponentially through an ever-growing ripple effect.

The Chase of the Cinematic Drone

Following the debut of the 'cinematic drone' in *North by Northwest*, while American drones were trialed and tested as guiding systems for aerial assaults by other means in the Vietnam War, their actual presence was generally omitted from the otherwise proliferating moving images. The military intelligence gathered from the American drones was to be used for various missions as carpet bombings by B-52s, napalm attacks, assault helicopters raids and spraying of vast vegetation areas and forests with Agent Orange as part of an unofficial chemical warfare campaign (Shaw 2016). Still, the notion of an anonymous aerial hunt conducted by opaquely operated machines, or ones that are guided by faceless crew members, found its way into cinema in artistic endeavours such as Joseph Losey's existential *Figures in A Landscape* (1970) or Peter Hyams's more commercially oriented *Capricorn One* (1977). Both works came as direct reactions to the heavy usage of helicopters during the Vietnam War as aerial monitors and as a highly efficient asymmetrical attack platform.

While *Figures in A Landscape* revolves around the escalating escape attempts of two fugitives from a relentless chopper which keeps tracking and confronting them through a changing landscape, from the wild to the semi-cultured, *Capricorn One* suggests a repeated chase in which a couple of renegade astronauts are fleeing through the American desert from a flock of black helicopters. Popularly known as 'whirlybirds' at the time, they are signified as pure machines, opaque metal and glass bodied, autonomous birds-of-prey mediating between their remote senders and those they seek to eliminate. This signification of the 'bird-of-prey' is emphasised even further in *Figures in A Landscape* where the image of the helicopter in flight is cut in motion to a flying eagle (right at the end of the first minute of the film), replacing the former's exact position and direction within the frame, continuing its aerial manoeuvre. From this shot the cut is to a point-of-view shot, closing from above the trees on escaping wild horses. This alteration from a mechanical aerial hunter to a fine feathered one is a cinematic gesture to be reversed later in the film, as a shot of a flying eagle is cut back to the helicopter. Accompanied by the galloping horses' escape into the forest and the analogy to the silhouettes of the human fugitives running away in the early morning light, it contextualises the relations between man, animals, and seemingly autonomous flying machines as part of a complex interspecies construction which brings to the fore questions of borders, orientation, and spatial dominance. Through these broader questions that lay at the core of the film's existential meditation on movement and space, the deriving issues of identification and domestication are further explored. The machine-animal-man equation in motion, defying the binary setting of 'Man vs. Flying Machine' discussed earlier, allows new freedom when investigating the amorphous nature of identification, both in the inability to keep the various elements within fixed categories and in the inconsistency of the film's landscape which keeps changing from wild to constructed to feral to artificial. In that sense, the examination of this equation maintains a constant interaction with the characters and the problem of their domestication. Both men are struggling against compulsory domestication while being forced to assimilate into its restrictions, as well as to continually adapt to the land and try to blend with the other species inhabiting it.

Capricorn One doesn't give space for the same scope and magnitude of discussion, yet it offers two important points – the desert as the ultimate hunting ground for future drones and the relation between such perception of a 'No Man's Land' and interplanetary remote missions. The film's persistent black helicopters, coining a cultural trope for deep state enforcers and the conspiratorial military-industrial-entertainment takeover of the United States (Der Derian 2009), first appeared as such in relation to cattle mutilation in the early 1970s (Barkun 2003). The helicopters scanning *Capricorn One*'s deserted landscapes echo the vast settings of iconic Westerns. They re-appropriate the wilderness to serve the ideology of spatial dominance under the new technological gaze. In this respect, they foresee the American use of the targeted killing drone doctrine as part of a world view perceiving the world outside the US as lawless, remote wilderness where authority is to be enforced by violent means (Verzier 2015: 12). This perfectly coincides with the dominant cinematic perspective of the Western, which was used to retrospectively justify past colonial crimes, mass land-grabs and genocide of First Nations peoples, as well as to propagate and encourage contemporary and future militaristic campaigns around the world (Lusted 2014: 20). The images of flying over deserts, badlands, arid mountain ridges and dry ravines which fill the screens in relation to the American military conflicts of the twenty-first century – mostly as part of drone activities, real or projected – reinforce this notion in the public's eye and establish it through a cinematic land claim. Similar wilderness landscapes, including the ideological infrastructure embedded in their audio-visual presence, are to be later seen in what is considered as one of the greatest achievements in the history of unmanned operations and mankind's recent accomplishments – the Ingenuity drone taking off and flying over Mars, streamed live by NASA on 19 April 2021. Given this precedent and the many missions to follow, it is quite a safe assumption that any life form which might be found on other planets will be first encountering a drone surveying their surface.

Interstellar (2014), another high-budget film dealing with pioneer missions of interplanetary colonisation (albeit focusing on the more technical and procedural aspects of this ideology), opens with a scene depicting a lone Predator-looking surveillance drone flying low over high-stalked corn fields. In this case the planet is our very near future earth, which is rapidly dying from overexploitation, pollution, and the ongoing climate crisis. The drone seems to be surveying the surface, foreshadowing the main character's task-to-be along the rest of the film, in search for signs of life. We never return to this drone later in the film, yet it is a clear cinematic mise-en-abyme (a short story within a story, acting as a condensed version of the longer one, often in a way that suggests an infinitely recurring sequence), compressing together advanced technology, ecological emergency, drones, and interspecies relations. In this scene, which cleverly alludes to *North by Northwest,* the roles have been reversed: this time it is the protagonist, and his two teenage kids, that are chasing the low flying unmanned aircraft through the tall corn fields. Collaborating in catching up with the drone, gaining control remotely, and landing it (in a subtle initiation to adulthood ceremony through technology for Murphy, the young daughter), the three then examine their catch. Murphy asks reclusively if they can't just let it go, adding softly that 'it wasn't hurting anybody', as if it was some accidentally trapped wild animal yearning for its freedom. *Capricorn One*'s hypothetical plot, on the other hand, suggests that a failure in the design of the first manned mission to Mars required that the whole affair be covered up by the authorities. A fabricated landing, produced and shot on a soundstage in an isolated desert base, will be presented to the public instead. As the three dedicated astronauts decide to go against this fake official narrative, they escape the base and try to survive in the wilderness with the opaque black machines flying fast to hunt them down.

Positioning the drone within the war effort and the film effect – whether by earlier surrogate representations such as the crop-duster or the opaque helicopters visual trope – highlights that:

> War can never break free from the magical spectacle because its very purpose is to produce that spectacle [...] 'The force of arms is not brute force but spiritual force'. There is no war, then, without representation, no sophisticated weaponry without psychological mystification. (Virilio 1989: 8)

Discussing further the role both forms of spectacle play, as a theatre of operation for drone representations and interspecies relations, will take us to the beginning of the 1980s. That is when Hollywood's ideological excess, economic surplus, and postmodernist pastiche diagonally aligned to form a high mark in visual effects and a low point in filmmaking, better known as *Clash of the Titans* (1981). It is an assorted alteration of Greek mythology tales, loosely based on the story of Perseus and filled with inaccuracies, mash-ups, and added-on inventions. One of these prominent inventions is an artificial owl that the young protagonist received from the gods to assist him with the

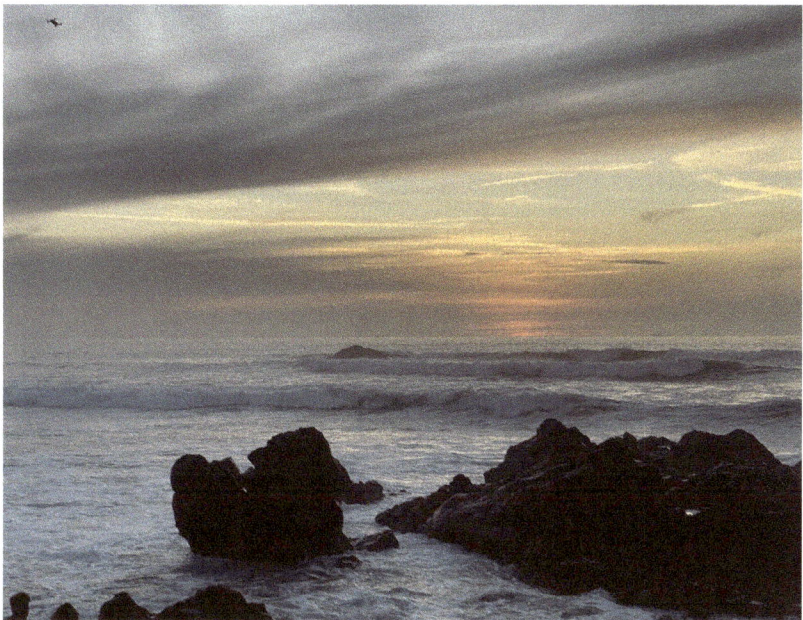

Figure 11.5. Jack Faber, *Low Res Tide (for Trevor Paglen)*, (2023). Courtesy of the artist.

demanding task ahead – the beheading of Medusa, the monstrous Gorgon. This clever invention, which has no support anywhere in the Greek mythology, has its closest and only foundation in the Caucasian Eagle mentioned before, as an earlier creation of Hephaistos. While the film itself is largely derivative pastiche, it makes an original intervention by combining the Caucasian Eagle tale with that of Kalevala's Iron Eagle as an immortal invention aimed to aid in accomplishing monumental tasks and extreme, otherwise unapproachable challenges, rather than as an opponent. The mechanical owl is built by Hephaistos to the request of Athena, goddess of war and wisdom, as a surrogate for her beloved 'all-knowing, all-seeing' real owl. Refusing to give the living bird, her eternal companion, away to Perseus as was ordered by her superior Zeus, Athena counts on Hephaistos to devise for her an iron and bronze duplicate. The owl, acting as one of Athena's main symbols by embodying knowledge, wisdom, and erudition, is planned by Zeus to replace Athena's previous gift which Perseus lost in the swamps earlier, her helmet of invisibility (another allusion to the most common trait of military drones – remaining unseen). Now, trying to replace the biotic animal with an artificial one, Hephaistos's skills as the god of smithing, sculpture, masonry, fire, and volcanoes do not fail. As evidence Perseus seems to understand the mechanical owl's wise advice when all others merely hear clicks, ticks, clunks, and beeps. This language of digitally inspired auditory signals resonates suspiciously like the sounds made by another recent artificial sidekick, the massively popular R2D2 from *Star Wars* (1977).

Clash of the Titans' artificial owl first appears in the empty skies of the wilderness and crashes comically at Perseus's and his companions' feet. Soon, the small bird automaton proves invaluable, being the one that leads them to the lair of Medusa, the Gorgon with the petrifying stare. Along with the tendency to name drones after various birds and animals, some of their technology, such as the Gorgon Stare sensor, derive straight from mythology. Allowing sophisticated forms of identification and following multiple targets at the same time, this sensor has been referred to as 'a surveillance team's wet dream' (Pater 2016: 47). Yet at the end of the day the small artificial owl is more than mere surveyor and adviser, relaying remote information and alerting its companions to approaching threats. In a later scene it acts as an assault drone, chasing away the gargantuan eagle watching over the caged flying horse Pegasus in a far hidden cave. In its autonomous rescue mission, the metal owl opens not only locked gates but new possibilities of interspecies relations. Such possibilities are evident in the way the artificial owl confronts one flying animal to help another, and in the process burns down the whole cave in a full-on aerial assault. In this, the artificial owl also embodies the pivotal transition in drone history discussed earlier – from reconnaissance to attack missions. To add another drone attack profile to its repertoire, the mechanical owl later salvages the decapitated yet still active head of Medusa, accidentally dropped by Perseus into the Mediterranean. In this way the artificial owl makes possible the use of this 'ultimate weapon technology' to fossilise the Kraken into stone. Creating yet another sort of man-drone-animal triangulation, one in which Perseus is using the metal owl to aim a destructive weapon and subdue an unique aquatic dweller, it is contextualised as a necessary protective measure from that terror of the sea – saving both the virginal Andromeda who was intended as its sacrifice and the entire city of Jaffa.

Despite its questionable cinematic quality, *Clash of the Titans* suggests some fresh perspectives in its mix of both mythologies and metaphors as it almost accidentally brings the first hybrid idea of artificial aerial animal into visual life. Iconifying it in ways which will become the blueprint for the future meeting grounds of drones and various species, forming different triangulations of interspecies relations. The all-knowing mechanical owl not only supplies some answers to how, in effect, such intermediary areas of thought and creation might look, but raises major questions in regard to the various roles drones can play in the lives of different species as well as the threats they can pose. One of the early key scenes of *Blade Runner* (1982) highlights this further. In the scene, Rick Deckard, the investigator who specialises in identifying renegade androids by distinguishing the real from the artificial, enters the neo-noirish headquarters of the monolithic Tyrell Corporation. He is fascinated by a magnificent owl, the sole occupant of the vast hall, as the winged creature is crossing the great hall in a low silent flight. Yet he can't tell whether this beautiful specimen is genuine. When he is informed it is not, Deckard automatically inquires about its economic value. 'Very expensive' is the answer he is given. In the near future in which *Blade Runner* takes place (originally envisioned to be 2019 Los Angeles) most animal life forms have already been made extinct by mankind, who also drove the planet beyond the brink of climate catastrophe and must face the deeper social and psychological implications of mass extinctions. Now, artificial animals act as surrogates in a variety of roles, ranging from work animals and companions to lucrative investments and status symbols. In this way, the highly influential film materialises its main questions of what is real and what is the meaning of real, through the introduction of constructed animals. The almost-real owl, a highly sophisticated drone as a matter of fact, is the future of the still somewhat clumsy attempts to deploy such animal-assimilating aerial machines, as in the recent attempts of the Russian aviation industry in manufacturing owl-like military spy drones (Simkins 2019).

These attempts go hand in hand with the understanding that our expanding technological resilience is very much at the expense of the prior familiarity with the natural surroundings and the knowledge it enriches us with. It is getting clearer that, to quote Ruben Pater:

> Our first ancestors could tell a lot from looking at the sky. Spotting and recognizing birds provided crucial information about the weather, where to find food, and what predators were near. In the urban landscape of the 21st Century, our knowledge of the natural environment has been replaced by knowledge of technology. Most of us can't tell the difference between the calls of an osprey or a hawk, but everyone can tell the difference between a Nokia ringtone and an iPhone one. We have grown so accustomed to technology that we perceive it as our natural habitat. Drones are quickly becoming a new species in this environment. (Pater 2016: 44)

It is not too far-fetched to assert now that our ability to differentiate between natural and artificially made elements in our surroundings is not only destabilised by these changes, but may lead to a collapse of classifications, just as drones are, to a certain degree, collapsing geographies. As Liam Young puts it, 'The drone network is a form of teleportation – a drone station in Australia coordinates strikes in the Middle East' (Szita 2016). Destabilisation of contemporary categorisations, putting animals in conflict with drones and using the latter as a device to threaten, invade, and colonise the habitats of the former – was soon to follow. The notion of destabilisation seems to be at the centre of the asymmetrical engagements that drones are involved in, as the films discussed above exemplify. Yet asymmetrical cinema reveals more than new perspectives of the origins, history, and how drones have been simultaneously

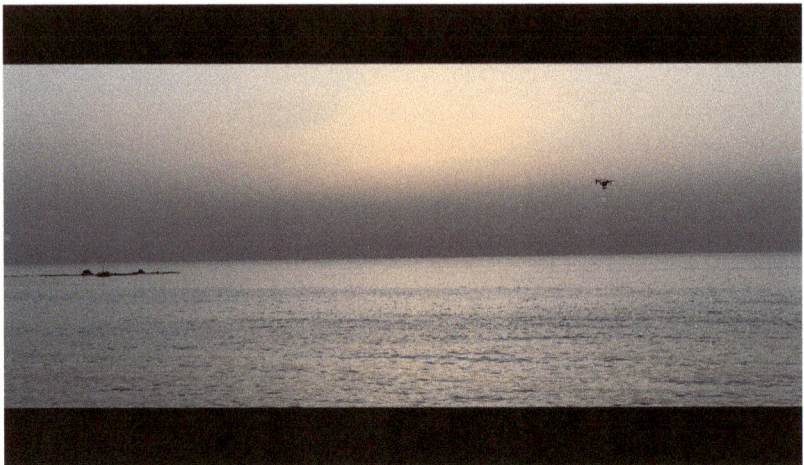

Figure 11.6. Jack Faber, *Dawn of the Drone* – production stills (2024). Courtesy of the artist.

assimilating as competitors, replacements, and foreign elements occupying other species' natural environments. It shows how the drones' 'design for destabilisation' reaches the point of undermining humankind's dominance over nature, pushing humanity back down the trophic pyramid it descended upon during its technological evolution. The careful Cine-Cartography drawn through these earlier and major appearances of drones in films, not only supports this claim but also strongly suggests them as new sorts of hybrid species. Although still dependent on human involvement (which is a matter for a whole new discussion), drones' autonomous capacities are rapidly evolving with the growing assistance of AI and automation. These fast-changing conditions suggest that there is much to explore in regard to drones' relations with other species. It seems that, thus far, film representations have been largely focused on animal figurations in the context of unmanned apparatuses rather than actual interspecies encounters, not yet willing to direct our gaze at the possibilities that direct exchanges between animals and drones may bring. Still, the majority of the films presented here subvert, to different degrees, the asymmetrical military-industrial drone-producing ideologies by revealing their own cinematic role in the public presentation and assimilation of such ideologies. In doing so, these movies expose both their industry's compliance and a cinematic complicity, reflecting all too well the drone's duplicity which is often presented as an objective perspective. These films reveal the ways human fragility is reinstalled into the animal kingdom, after humanity has been dethroned from its apex role, by the drone.

By presenting opportunities to discuss their own nature as apparatuses for constructing meaning and organising knowledge along said ideologies, the films and works addressed here reveal the drone presence within the frame of interspecies relations. At the same time, the films mirror the drone, suggesting that they act for similar asymmetrical purposes as its counterpart, given the correlation between seeing and targeting and the significance moving images play in the drone's existence since its early days. Cinema – with its deep understanding of the nature of conflict ('Montage is Conflict', noted Eisenstein in 1949 (1977)), the versatile possibilities for new examinations of interspecies relations, technological inventions, their epistemological interplay and sociopolitical interpretation – can be used not only for identifying and analysing these fields' flux so far, but as a cartography for the explorations ahead. It is clearer than ever now that our ancient relationship with nature has been broken. As John Berger suggested, the actual presence of animals – which used to be at the centre of our existence – is now marginalised, replaced, and reduced to a spectacle (Berger 2009). This approach could persist, and in effect exponentially grow, with drones coming to a foreground which is being aggressively cleared from the presence of other species that might present competition. Yet drones, progressively assimilating the shapes and traits of various animals while guided by algorithms and artificial intelligence, can also serve other agendas, and be used to discover new ways of living together with other species. Cinema has yet to project such compelling and capable relations between drones and other species without being mitigated by humans and their machine-mediated actions. Showing us such a lack – especially through the exposure of its own *raison d'être* and the ideological structures that work within asymmetrical cinema, simultaneously suggesting the limitations of the frame and hinting toward entire fields of perception existing outside of it – can act as an urgent feral call for things to come.

This chapter articulates the early epistemological framework for Asymmetrical Cinema and its methodology. It is continued and paralleled through the practice-based research project 'Autonomous Animals', dealing with urgent ontological questions brought by later drone representations and their interspecies entanglements, enmeshing twenty-first century political thrillers, sci-fi masterpieces, pigeons of war, and more.

The work on both 'Asymmetrical Cinema' and 'Autonomous Animals' is supported by a research grant from Kone Foundation.

Works Cited

Baraona-Pohl, Ethel, Marina Otero, and Malkit Shoshan eds. 2016. *Drone: Unmanned, Architecture and Security Series*. DPR-Barcelona.

Barkun, Michael. 2003. *A Culture of Conspiracy: Apocalyptic Visions in Contemporary America*. California: University of California Press.

Berger, John. 2009. *Why Look at Animals?* London: Penguin.

Brest, Martin, director. *Midnight Run*. Universal Pictures, 1988. 126 minutes.

Cameron, James, director. *Terminator 2: Judgement Day*. Tristar Pictures, 1991. 137 minutes.

Chamayou, Gregoire. 2014. *A Theory of the Drone*. Translated by Janet Lloyd. New York: The New Press.

Chandler, Katherine. 2020. *Unmanning: How Humans, Machines and Media Perform Drone Warfare*. London: Routledge.

Comolli, Jean-Luc, and Paul Narboni. 1971. 'Cinema/Ideology/Criticism'. *Screen* 12, no. 1: 27-38.

Davis, Desmond, director. *Clash of the Titans*. Metro-Goldwyn-Mayer, 1981. 118 minutes.

De Palma, Brian, director. *Mission Impossible*. Paramount Pictures, 1966. 110 minutes.

Der Derian, James. 2009. *Virtuous war: Mapping the Military-Industrial-Media-Entertainment-Network*. London: Routledge.

Eisenstein, Sergei. 1977. *Film Form: Essays in Film Theory*. Translated by Jay Layda. New York: Harcourt.

Fanon, Frantz. 2004. *The Wretched of the Earth*. Translate by Richard Philcox. New York: Grove Press.

Hitchcock, Alfred, director. *North by Northwest*. Metro-Goldwyn-Meyer, 1959. 136 minutes.

Hitchcock, Alfred, director. *Topaz*. Universal Pictures, 1969. 127 minutes.

Hitchcock, Alfred, director. *Torn Curtain*. Universal Pictures, 1966. 128 minutes.

Honda, Ishirô, director. *Sora no daikaijû Radon*. Toho, 1956. 82 minutes.

Hyams, Peter, director. *Capricorn One*. Warner Bros., 1977. 124 minutes.

Jiménez-López, Jesús, and Margarita Mulero-Pázmány. 2019. 'Drones for conservation in protected areas: present and future'. *Drones* 3, no. 1: 10.

Juran, Nathan, director. *The Deadly Mantis*. Universal International, 1957. 79 minutes.

Kotcheff, Ted, director. *First Blood*. Orion Pictures, 1982. 93 minutes.

Lonnrot, Elias. 1999. *The Kalevala*. Oxford: Oxford University Press.

Losey, Joseph, director. *Figures in A Landscape*. Twentieth Century Fox, 1970. 110 minutes.

Lucas, George, director. *Star Wars*. Twentieth Century Fox, 1977. 121 minutes.

Lusted, David. 2014. *The Western*. London: Routledge.

Mbembe, Achille. 2019. *Necropolitics*. Durham: Duke University Press.

McCausland, Clare, Susan Pyke, and Siobhan O'Sullivan. 2018. 'The Ethics and Politics of Drones in Animal Activism'. *Animal Studies Journal* 7, no. 1: 80-103.

McLuhan, Marshall. 1964. *Understanding Media: The Extension of Man.* New York: McGraw-Hill.

Milius, John, director. *Red Dawn.* MGM, 1984. 114 minutes.

Moore, John, director. *A Good Day to Die Hard.* 20th Century Studios, 2013. 97 minutes.

Simkins, J.D. 2019. 'This emo Russian owl drone is a real… hoot'. *Military Times,* June 26.

https:Sim//www.militarytimes.com/off-duty/military-culture/2019/06/25/this-emo-russian-owl-drone-is-a-real-hoot/.

NASA Jet Propulsion Laboratory. 2021. 'Enhanced Video Shows Dust During Ingenuity's Flight'. YouTube video, 0:47. April 21.

https://www.youtube.com/watch?v=lMMPBNzpoDg&ab_channel=NASAJetPropulsionLaboratory.

Nolan, Christopher, director. *Interstellar.* Paramount Pictures, 2014. 169 minutes.

Pater, Ruben. 2016 'Twenty-First Century Birdwatching' in *Drone: Unmanned, Architecture and Security Series,* edited by Ethel Baraona-Pohl, Marina Otero, and Malkit Shoshan, 44-52. DPR-Barcelona.

Penn, Arthur, director. *Night Moves.* Warner Bros., 1975. 99 minutes.

Scott, Ridley, director. *Blade Runner.* Warner Bros. Pictures, 1982. 117 minutes.

Sears, Fred. F., director. *The Giant Claw.* Columbia Pictures, 1957. 75 minutes.

Shaw, Ian G.R. 2016. *Predator empire: Drone Warfare and Full Spectrum Dominance.* Minneapolis: University of Minnesota Press.

Szita, Jane. 2016. 'A New View from Above, A Report on the Drone Salon' in *Drone: Unmanned, Architecture and Security Series,* edited by Ethel Baraona-Pohl, Marina Otero, and Malkit Shoshan, 102-25. DPR-Barcelona.

Spielberg, Steven, director. *Close Encounters of the Third Kind.* Columbia Pictures, 1977. 135 minutes.

Theoi Project. 2019. 'Theoi Greek Mythology'. https://www.theoi.com.

Verzier, Marina. 2016. 'Introduction' in *Drone: Unmanned, Architecture and Security Series,* edited by Ethel Baraona-Pohl, Marina Otero, and Malkit Shoshan, 12-17. DPR-Barcelona.

Virilio, Paul. 1989. *War and Cinema: The Logistics of Perception.* Translated by Patrick Camiller. London: Verso.

Vodka, Amir. 2020. 'Bug Wars' in *Eco Noir: A Companion for Precarious Times*, edited by Jack Faber and Anna Shraer. Helsinki: University of the Arts, Helsinki Press.

Walsh, Raoul, director. *The Thief of Bagdad*. United Artists, 1924. 140 minutes.

Werrell, Kenneth P. 1985. *The evolution of the cruise missile*. Maxwell Airforce Base, Alabama: Air University Press.

Wich, Serge A., and Lian Pin Koh. 2018. *Conservation drones: mapping and monitoring biodiversity*. Oxford: Oxford University Press.

Young, Terence, director. *From Russia with Love*. United Artists, 1963. 115 minutes.

12

Computing Hallucinations: How Drones Read Oceans

Simon M. Taylor

Introduction: Data Holidays

It is the 6th of November 2019 and I am in Canberra for a high-performance data training day at the National Computational Infrastructure (NCI). Australia's newest and fastest supercomputer is called Gadi, meaning 'to search for', in the indigenous language of the Ngunnawal people. Housed at the Australian National University (ANU), this water-cooled research supercomputer is the twenty-fourth most powerful in the world and the most powerful in the Southern Hemisphere. In a computer lab like any other (a line of PC desktops, nondescript interiors, and a table-top of coffee), we are instructed in preliminary tasks to access the Geo Sciences data portal. The training outlines how to structure, access, and locate datasets but also to digitally manipulate meteorological models, topological maps, and imaging processes. In the sequencing of data we simulate natural phenomena by producing spectral images and statistical flow charts – swarms of visual creations flood our screens.

I am drawn here by my research into a Geo-Sciences Australia database of deep-sea imaging, collected by search capable AUVs (automated underwater vehicles) and ROVs (remotely-operated-vehicles) that were deployed to locate the missing Malaysia Airlines aeroplane, MH370, presumed lost in an under-mapped area of the Indian Ocean off Western Australia. The operational search used sonar, submersible vehicles, and a location intelligence platform, Esri, to visualise data on this unknown site. The Australian Transport Safety Bureau (ATSB) coordinated the largest sonar operation ever conducted – collecting 172,741 square miles of bathymetry data in the search area and another 268,432 square miles of data as the vessels travelled to and from the search area – in both mapping and deep-sea monitoring (Wright 2020). Yet, despite the extensive and intensive scientific and technical resources thrown at the disappearance, MH370 was never located. Data is archived at the NCI and the interpretation of data and imaging is ongoing – it remains a contested site.

Despite the lack of a wreckage, we can find value in *what the drones did discover*. In trying to locate deep-sea remains of this lost plane, what navigation and imaging challenges did these drones encounter? What sensing apparatus identified potential targets? How did this shape automated navigation tasks in real time and in computational infrastructures? Humanities scholars (Bremner 2015; Day and Lury 2017; Williams 2020) have each studied the MH370 disappearance from multiple perspectives, yet none have analysed the role of drones. Lindsay Bremner's focus on sonic apertures in the 'seven satellite pings [...] and six underwater sonic recordings' (2015: 8) is the closest to my own, regarding the role of sound as a mode of visualisation, decision-making, anomaly production, and scientific navigation. By looking at the drone data archived in the NCI, I hope to understand how 'varied foraging and extraction behaviours exhibited by drones' (Rahwan et al. 2019: 482) may also reveal how remote scientific tasks, operationalised by drones, are being challenged in unknown and deep-sea environments. Specifically,

1. What properties and material problems does *the ocean* pose to drone observation? How does it challenge an ability to locate targets with forms of sonic perception and graphical visualisation?

2. Can artefacts instruct drones – in real time – to act in unpredictable ways, and can this technical disorientation be instructive to locate the limits of scientific method?

3. Finally, what is at stake in this technical data extraction via drones and their cartographic representations (mapping, target recognition) as a form of remote computation?

Drawing on the Australian Transport Safety Bureau operational report on the search for MH370 (ATSB 2017), and reflecting on my training at the NCI (National Computational Infrastructure) in Canberra, this chapter explores drone methodologies largely removed from 'vertical geographies as longstanding remote-sensing frameworks, to ones undertaken by drone practices and methodologies where social, environmental, or technological concerns are entangled with a *politics of access*' (Garrett and Anderson 2018: 343, my emphasis). This highlights a shift from pixelated and static satellite top-down images or GPS reliant location techniques into adaptive, automated, and proximal sensing in real time. If high-resolution optics and video-graphic investigations have been used to locate targets (Parikka and Gil-Fournier 2019), what happens when sonar is operationalised to differentiate between features in space, or between figure and ground, that is critical to navigation and decision making? And how do anomalous sounds, in unknown oceans, shape drone activities tasked with remote data collection?

By knitting together the MH370 disaster with a longer history of sonar, from the sinking of the Titanic to automated drones, we may go some way to reveal how 'existential plights of infrastructure' (Peters 2015: 104) orient scientific know-how using drone discoveries that may confuse data with reality.

Planetary Black Boxes: Models to Reality

The day after the training session, we gathered for the ALCS symposium at the Australian Academy of Science building. Designed by Roy Grounds, ANU's Shine Dome is affectionately called 'The Martian Embassy' (in reference to the 1960s space-ship structure – an almost comical circular dome – built like a Science Fiction model). Once inside, I merged into an esteemed crowd of physicists, astronomers, nano-material scientists, biologists, climate change and cyber-security experts, VR engineers, and mathematicians. I eagerly sat as mute witness in the amplified dome of high scientific discussion, ultimately chorusing in a demand for Exa-scale computation that uses around quintillion (10^{18}) calculations each second, to more realistically simulate processes in precision medicine, climate modelling, and planetary phenomena.

This demand also involved calls for increased democratic access to the NCI infrastructure and was crowned by a fascinating presentation from Professor Peter Littlewood (physicist and executive chair of The Faraday Institution) extolling near-future scientific 'convergences of experiment, prototyping, and computational simulation' (2019). His closing statement relayed how 'the processing and storage of data is now outrunning accessibility to computational power in many fields' and gestured to how nation-state storage is necessary but struggles to purpose real-time modelling of scientific phenomena, whether in human or rodent brain, nano-material structures, or a thermo-dynamic modelling of oceanic currents. The claim is that big data is rendering scientific methods based on lower powered computing ineffective to analyse this explosion of material.

I was struck by the heated political debate in this odd structure resembling a scene in Andrei Tarkovsky's film *Solaris* (1972) – a cinematic adaptation of Stanislaw Lem's 1970 novel. Tarkovsky staged a dramatic political battle on the investigation of an unknown planet. Politicians, astronauts, and engineers disputed scientific arguments pushing at 'the boundaries of human knowledge [...] descending into a mountain of disjointed and incoherent facts' (Tarkovsky 2002). The scene visually condenses a prominent section in Lem's novel that outlines the various exploratory attempts and resultant scientific failures to understand the mysterious fluid dynamics and odd material phenomena on the oceanic planet, Solaris. In the novel, this scientific and archival history is presented through a clever literary lens, of a lone scientist reading from a library volume, *Historia Solaris*, while orbiting the oceanic planet in deep space.

Historia Solaris is the library accounting of around 200 years of scientific explorations. We discover that the first contacts were made by low-orbit satellites and 'robotic avatars', that on entering the unknown oceanic environment, encountered a 'protoplasmic ocean-brain' with a reactive material intelligence. The recordings returned to the scientists didn't make much sense, as it appeared the ocean participated in the robotic readings – either by modifying sensory data, disrupting instrumentation, or initiating a profusion of signals – with most defeating all attempts at human, mathematical, political, or scientific analysis.

To decipher this information, vast computer systems, much like today's NCI, had to be built of virtually limitless capacity, using new forms of spectral imaging, mathematical models, and branches of statistical probability. Lem makes it clear how this produced an overabundance of images and computational data:

> […] microfilm libraries bursting at the seams with documents; from expeditions, some a thousand-strong, equipped with the most lavish apparatus Earth can provide – robotic recorders, sonar and radar, entire range of spectrometers, radiation counters […] material being accumulated at accelerating tempos. (Lem 2002: 166)

Here, *Solaris* exposes the possible inconsistencies with remote data collection and existing scientific theory, not only supporting Peter Littlewood's argument that data collection is outstripping computational abilities, but both claims act to mirror problems in the remote oceanic search for MH370, especially representing a scientific expedition to model the ocean. In the fissures between speculative fiction, scientific data collection, and robotic investigation, Lem and Littlewood discern how classical scientific methods (probing inputs for data outputs) confuse how drones operate in restricted oceanic spaces and perform manoeuvres in capturing data. This highlights methodological and scientific paradoxes of *models versus reality* that are being transformed whenever we automate sensing, navigation, and data collection through the remote exploration of robotics. Specifically, how scientific knowledge is bound to sonic and signaletic interpretations of the from drone decision making in the deep, compared to the interpretation undertaken by operators and scientists at the surface. This complicates how both attempt to structure data to be 'made sensible, intelligible, and shareable' yet are bound to understanding in computational terms (Gabrys 2019). This paradoxical situation orients us to the way that drones are tasked to perform traditional scientific roles involving knowledge construction of an unseen environment, such as indexing, replication, and operationalism. It is within drone exploration that a trust is required in the *robotic readings* – not simply from examinations of phenomena or environment – but as boundaries to science and measurements, and as true limits to human knowledge acts. As Lem explores in his novel (emerging as it did in the tenacious period of the Cold War and chaotic cultural experiments in space exploration in the Soviet Union) what *we know* about unknown environments through robotic explorations is perhaps but a fraction of the observable reality:

> [...] If the essence of [remote monitoring and oceanic] architecture is movement synchronised towards a precise objective. We observe a fraction of the process, *we know but cannot grasp*, the above and below, beyond the limits of perception or imagination, the thousands and millions of simultaneous transformations at work, interlinked like a musical score by mathematical counterpoint. (Lem 2002: 120)

Lem's tale of Solaris enables us to think through not only the alienness of a nonhuman environment, but the 'sensing' that drones must activate to traverse liquid vortices, temperature gradients, and swift unpredictable currents. There are the geographic contingencies inherent to the deep ocean. In the remote depths, the drones enter a scientific *black box*, framed by satellite plots and sensory signatures, guided by sonic inputs and '…squirrely artefact, and spatial distortion' (Brumfeld 2014). In this case, drone data must account for different categories of black boxes when undertaking scientific practices (Shindell, 2020).

Solaris is not merely a tale of outer space, traumatic isolation, and hallucinatory episodes, but of scales of geography and of *being*. As Melody Jue suggests, '*Solaris* imagines a sentient ocean and its responses to scientific investigation [...] provoking a crisis, jointly scientific, masculine, colonial, and terrestrial' (2014: 228). This crisis, however true, may not best be configured in Jue's 'feminine, yet decidedly anthropocentric terms', but from an analysis of robotics and the automation of perception in environments. What is required is a clearer perspective on the knowable and the unknowable, or as J. D. Barrow states, 'the fundamental divide between what is observable and the unknown whole' that can bring an awareness to the boundary between impossible acts and concluding what is real (1999: 250). We need to understand how science and computation act as *reality-generation mechanisms* and how drones serve within this framework. change to: My interest in robotic and scientific drone 'emissaries' diving out of sight to navigate the vast depths beneath a ship's wake (Lehman 2019) is how they drastically change scientific methods of data collection and that act from traditional expectations of concrete reality, yet perceive the ocean primarily from simulation and sound.

But in order to examine these relationships more closely, we need to shift focus from the off-world literary thought experiment of *Solaris* to how drones use sonar as a form of 'investigating, fathoming, listening' into the alien ocean (Helmreich 2009: 2015) to consider if this form of inquiry is appropriate when automated 'out of sight' and tasked to build meaning in science. In what follows, I examine the ATSB search for MH370 wreckage and focus on data results produced from the technical imaging based on sonic anomalies – errant reflections and distorted soundwaves inherent to oceanic volumes, currents, and depths. In doing so, I ask how anomalies structure both navigation and actions through operational images (Farocki, 2004) important to drone decision-making. I am assessing how anomalies of this kind 'work as techniques of time and imaging pushing further what counts as operatively real' (Parikka and Gil-Fournier 2019: 2). This is not simply an analysis of various modes of visual prediction or generative AI imaging but specifically, understanding how drones operate on a transmission and translation of sound anomalies to build images and that cause them to move to suspected crash targets, based on computing a technically-induced hallucination (2).

Parikka and Gil-Fournier's research on operational imaging is instructive as to how drones 'may weave and stitch knowledge' (Day and Lury 2017) on to oceans, not merely by acting on micro-temporal *soundings* of what is 'real', but by navigating across sonic predictions into what is the unfolding of geographical, navigational, and environmental monitoring of data as simulated space. In drone surveying of unknown environments, autonomous data capture also secures important economic and geopolitical information, yet a key aspect is how drones utilise 'their real-time autonomous decision-making […] complemented by constant – *and grey* – operations of prediction' (Gil-Fournier and Parikka 2019: 2). This *greyness* in terms of the computable orientations and the accuracy of sonic detections, also comes with potential for 'technically-induced hallucinations', in which autonomous drones are not acting on observable reality, but move based on anomalies and malfunctions conditional to the sonic contingencies in deep oceanic spaces.

As such, drones may become disorientated, acting in real time, on a misperception of targets and features: such as confusing sea mounts, rock platforms, or animals, with the man-made wreckage in the deep. This corrupts the exploratory premise of drones in the deep ocean, as knowable and computable entities, that are entrusted to undertake scientific roles to bring forth an observable and datafied reality. They diagram what Joseph Traub labelled 'dissonances between nature, simulation, and models' (Traub 1993: 239) to how scientific measurements, statistics, and simulations sometimes serve, in lieu of evidence (Bremner 2015: 8). Instead, they diagram what Joseph Traub labelled 'dissonances between nature, simulation, and models' (Traub 1993: 239). This means that scientific measurements, statistics, and simulations sometimes serve, in lieu of evidence (Bremner 2015: 8). In the search for MH370, I outline instances where drones utilised sonar to produce an intelligible and readable reality, yet this datafication of nature (Gabrys 2019b) was also based on distorted acts of technical perception.

MH370 and the Backscatter in Sonic Depths

On 8 March 2014, a Boeing 777-200ER operated by Malaysia Airlines took off from Kuala Lumpur and turned toward its destination in Beijing, China. Passenger flight MH370 lost contact with air traffic control and radar at approximately 01:20 MYT (Malaysia Time), and less than one hour after take-off disappeared completely from global monitoring and surveillance systems. In a protracted and complex series of political and international communications, digital handshakes and satellite data it was determined to have crashed somewhere in the Indian Ocean located significantly offshore Western Australia.

As yet, no crash site has been discovered. In the context of global tracking and surveillance systems, as William Langwiesche notes, 'the idea that a sophisticated machine, with its modern instruments and redundant communications, could simply vanish seems beyond the realm of possibility [...] but this one did, and more than five years later its precise whereabouts remain unknown' (2019). This ongoing unknown of the wreckage, however tragic, helps reveal a limit to a catalogue of techniques constructed by humans to calculate and to navigate the world – particularly foreign and remote environments. Perhaps, at best, this disaster may reveal an illusion we invest in our devices, namely, the falsity of an ability to measure and control the scientific real, and in doing so, we get closer to understanding the immense mystery of the living ocean itself.

In 1490, Leonardo da Vinci placed a tube in seawater to listen to the sound of distant passing ships and yet the first patent for sonar was in 1912 due to the sinking of the Titanic earlier that year. In a history of profiling the ocean, aesthetics, disaster, and sound entwine, dependent on both human and technical trust in the interpretation of sound to the unknowable or intractable elements encapsulated in the depths.

By tracing deep sounding technologies from 1850 to 1930, Sabine Höhler has outlined how global oceans are depicted in physical aids of sonic plots, graphs, figures, and numbers, slowly transforming the deep, dark environment 'into a technically and scientifically sound oceanic volume' (Höhler 2002: 144). These risk charts and navigational aids built upon an array of deep-sea sounding apparatuses to orient science in the revealing and visualising of hidden environments. But as Höhler argues, what her research unveils is less about the ocean than about faulty beliefs in the material capabilties of the depth measurement devices themselves (2002). This means oceanic-space taking shape is driven by an epistemic motivation of *trust in sounding* from material devices. So where do drones fit, as depth sounders, as mapping devices, and as instruments of precise calculation – especially if the sounding of depth is automated? What is our confidence in drones to interpret sonic measurements and make calculated efforts to also reduce the 'likelihood of malfunctions or unseen flukes' as they reach into the depths (Alaniz 2019: 612)?

Unlike their atmospheric cousins, underwater drones cannot rely on optical cameras or on GPS alone. Locational and observational processes in the deep require other sensing capacities – like thermal and gas tracing – but also the accurate *sonifying* of environmental space. The ocean is situated within an information eco-system of hydrophones, cables, buoys, pingers, floaters, and tagged marine animals that rely on sound components for communication and navigation. Arguably, acoustics is an oceanic sentience (a cognition, a knowing) through which underwater objects, machine or animal, position themselves to sense and to act. Drones belong to this vast, emerging, and multiscale acoustic and oceanic infrastructure that acts as an essential navigation system. It is similar to the incredible development of applications that the GPS and GNSS created, as acoustics is helping 'transition from an incoherent and chaotic view of ocean-space, into a focused, evolving, and transparent image, where humankind (importantly using robotic avatars) will be able to "see" the oceanic volume' (Howe et al. 2019: 9). Underwater drones belong to a network of smart interconnected objects known as the Internet of Underwater Things (or IoUT) (Kao, Lin, Wu, and Huang 2017). This includes extractive and repair apparatuses from gas and oil industries, strategic military objects of nation-states, and a host of environmental monitoring devices, that also highlight how the oceans are invaded and subject to urbanisation and extraction, 'envisioned as workplace, laboratory, or strategic asset' (Bremner 2015: 22). When tasked with securing various goals in the sonic, oceanic and volumetric depths, drones and remotely operated vehicles dive on a codification of sound directing them to a perception of targets, geologic features, and useful data. Yet inside this densely salinated and thermo-dynamic ocean drones encounter a complex, powerful, and reactive world. Oceans possess enormous volume. Drones are immersed in a dynamic 'phenomena of suction, vortices, waves, currents, unexplainable drifts that restrict' an ability to accurately determine the position and reflection of competing inputs (Steinberg and Peters 2015: 254) like transmissions of water, light, or sound that make surveillance, communication and operations deep underwater so challenging.

To overcome this challenge in *sonifying* the Indian Ocean the ATSB operated a search for MH370 across two main phases: first, the use of shipping mounted sonar to acquire bathymetric data on the unknown sea floor topography (providing a map to aid drone navigations during the underwater search); and second, the autonomous drone deployments to locate suspected crash targets, using detailed side scan sonar and backscatter imagery reliant on both supervised and automated detection of features on the unknown floor.

If we focus only on the second data set involving drone detection capabilities, what was required in the search for the missing plane wreckage was an ability to technically decipher possible targets 'defined as any anomaly on the deep seafloor appearing non-geologic in nature or at least, unusual compared to the surrounding environment' (ATSB 2017: 43). A key specification in the contract for search capabilities required a feature detection minimum 'with resolution of two cubic meters, selected on basis of the core size of the B777 Rolls Royce engines' (ATSB 2017: 43). Engine remnants from a crashed aeroplane are considered robust and thought likely to survive a high energy impact relatively intact, as they did in the AF447 (Air France) crash located off Brazil. The search for MH370 was to find evidence of hard material remains.

Finding MH370 required the use of backscatter sonar. This process is similar to the echolocation ability of marine animals as an active sensory process to find animals and objects by reflecting vocalisations as an important means of navigation. Backscatter is both a transmission and scanning process that involves the physics of 'Compton scattering' by which the momentum, velocity, and wavelength of rays, such as sound (or radiation and light) bounce when contacting matter (examples include X-rays, ultrasound, or airport detectors). Basically, a frequency spectrum is used to build a graphical display of rays recoiling from the surface and 'scattering back' to a detector. Remotely towed vehicles and drones pulse sound echoes to the floor and receive and stack echo traces to construct graphic images. The images are a function of time: strong reflectors, like steel or rock, bounce 'hard returns' in short time frames and are plotted as dark; while 'soft returns' from soil, sand, or biological matter are slower and grade in lightness. Rays absorbed by materials inform negative space in an image due to exclusion. This profile of gradients orients drones to a solid material compared to a sandy floor and multiple hard returns, received instantly, indicate flat or linear surfaces which are attributed to meaning something materially engineered, or human made, like remnants of a crashed aeroplane. This is a technical process to capture reflections of sounds in cases exceeding an ability to *look*. Backscatter speaks to multiple practices of sensing that operate as techniques of seeing like imaging in mammogram scans, baggage checks, metal fatigue analysis and environment mapping – the phenomena may be different, but the goal is the same – to differentiate subtle information. Backscatter is thus not only an apparatus, it is an 'architecture for perception' (Parisi 2013).

To tender the companies tasked with identifying the wreckage, the ATSB tested instrumental capacities by deploying four 2x2x2 metre steel crosses and 1.3x1.3x1.3 metre steel cubes in 1000 metre depths (see Figures 12.1 and 12.2).

Companies were tested in their ability to automate a sonic request of the environment by pulsing echoes to the floor and collect 'the residue left over from this projection' (Amoore and Hall 2009: 455) as a graphical interpretation of that which is scattered back to record evidence of these targets. Strangely, using drones successfully in the testing phase perhaps did not truly reflect the difficulty of the task lying ahead. We need only consider the hard and linear materiality of the testing targets – a literal X marks the spot – and also the relatively shallow depth of 1000 metres which reduced volumetric distortion of sound transmissions and reflections. The MH370 search was conducted in over ten times these depths, an unprecedented ask for the search

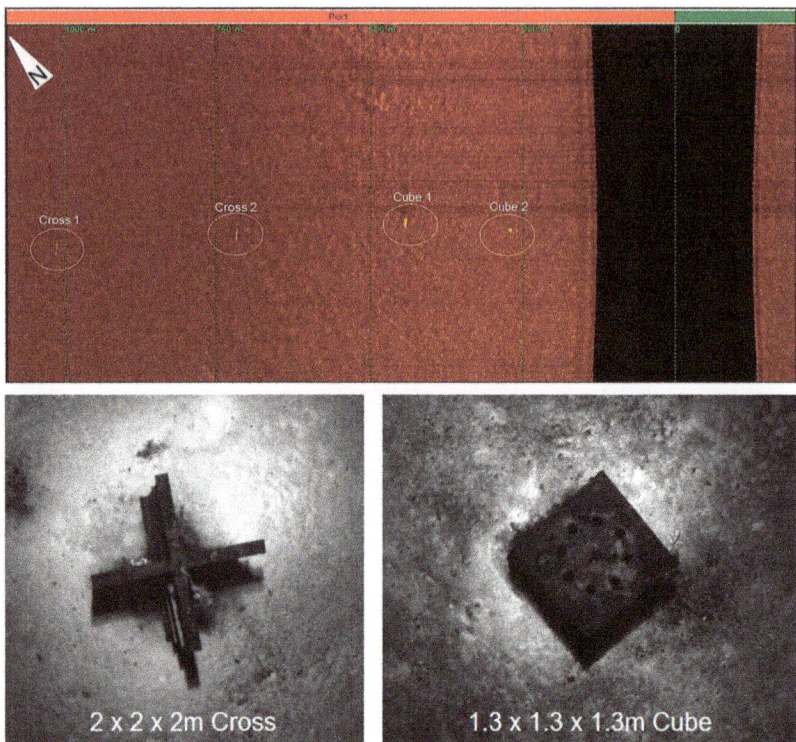

Figures 12.1 and 12.2. *Test targets as imaged by side scan sonar on seafloor.*
Source: Australian Transport Safety Bureau. ATSB 2017: 62). CC-BY 3.0.

capability of any drone, or ROV at that time. Lindsay Bremner summarises this complex issue, noting:

> Phoenix International's Autonomous Underwater Bluefin-21 Vehicle 'Artemis' was deployed for this task. The depth it could operate at was upgraded from 1500m to 4500m in only July 2013, so this was likely one of its first deployments at this depth [...] . After some initial programming glitches, it was deployed on eighteen 24-hour missions, taking four hours to dive and resurface, 16 hours to scan and four hours to download the recorded data each time. Significantly, none of these data have ever been publicly released. (2015: 18)

Geo-Sciences Australia built an Esri mapping platform at the surface that 'functioned as a photographer's dark room' exposing sonic gaps 'where steep geology prevented soundwaves from reaching the bottom' (Wright 2020). This assisted scientific interpretation requires drones and infrastructure to envision gaps, folds and thresholds between data processing and platform visuality

(MacKenzie and Munster 2019). In trying to enclose the ocean depths within information, sound, and computation, the drone's sonic transmissions became, at times, often opaque and indecipherable. This was due to the temporal particulars of sonar suffering lag, deviation, or signal attenuation yet still being codified into a form of mapping that is more familiar to human or vertical 'top-down' territorial knowledge. And so instead of bringing clarity to an unknown world, sonic navigation is found to be another perceptual ontology entirely and often required autonomous drones AUV to dive between sonic interstices and piece the missing data together. Sonic space and time required drones stitching across a *scattered field* to adjust target viewpoints and update frames on the surface. Images calculated were generated on micro-temporal sound reflections to 'infer the coded points out of the dataset' as being worthy of investigative motion (Parikka and Gil-Fournier 2019: 8). Therefore, the drones oriented themselves to targets in the deep by *trusting* the auditory reflections.

Machine or computer vision in this instance relies on sound define 'coded space' (Kitchin and Dodge 2011). The directional operations of drones rely on an environmental assemblage of object and signal relations, image relay, and accurate data reproductions. This includes where noise or *pseudo-sound* (Erbe, Verma, McCauley, Gavrilov, and Parnum 2015) as a machine by-product may force 'drones to an immediate and constant double take' (McCosker 2015: 13). Specific to drones' ability to navigate and locate targets, their perception of sounds depends on a relative assessment of acoustic reflections, their computable and temporal propagation through the environment, and the drones' ability to infer any artefact and noise from this raw data, with an ability to interpret and infer from sound what *artefacts are* on the fly. Importantly, this requires not only the acoustic capability of the drone, but a familiarisation of the drone as a machine listener (Stern, Parker, and Dockray 2020) with sounds that are inherent to in-human environments (Miksis-Olds, Martin, and Tyack 2018). Backscatter, as a component of drone operations, critically requires know-how on oceanic depths that produce sounds unheard of, yet become assembled by 'mathematical counterpoint' in an active perceptual system, composing sound elements elongated, reflected, compressed, or reduced in order to depict a detection of targets that cannot be *humanly, or even, humanely seen*. This is a story of how drones may be susceptible to 'noisy lures' in the oceans – and thus unable to contextualise from a hallucination of the primary targets, like a plane wreckage, that may be unseeable or even unreachable.

Not only was the MH370 wreckage never discovered, but the two primary targets investigated were a scattered rock field and a Portuguese coal ship. The fact that these two entities are so different from 'a plane wreckage' and so different from each other is instructive of difficulties faced in codifying a remote part of the world. The only reference we have to such untamed expeditions are science fiction exploits, like Stanislaw Lem envisioning a faulty robotic perception in an off-world planet. As such, the *smart enclosure* of the ocean by autonomous drones represents a science, that is not an observable reality, but a science framed inside the drone's own 'environmentality' (Andrejevic and Volcic 2019). That is – a drone's perceptual frame knowledges is at risk of being shaped by computational and oceanic complexity and so be diverted from interpreting recognition of targets that matter.

Recognition Matters: Machines Read the Ocean Through Their 'Technically-induced Hallucinations'

In the domain of imaging, some of the most interesting questions we can put to images or image theories concern the specific kinds of distortions that pictures suffer in different contexts (Elkins 2018: 240), like specific kinds of misrecognition. Indeed, the capacity to recognise a three-dimensional form and to decide on an optimal action, based on that recognition, is a challenge animating computational science that seeks to assemble machine operations across aesthetics, robotics, moving images, coding, and mathematics. Furthermore, processes of algorithmic sorting and decision metrics in machine imaging are required to help order the data environment into one that an automated drone can sense, anticipate, and act. This is driven by extracting sonic features into a statistical and graphical ledger to isolate images of interest. This machine inference *is a prediction engine* to remotely direct and automate drones, one in which, a failure to decipher between forms – whether rocks, planes, or shipwrecks – is a common feature (Amoore 2020: 99).

The ATSB report included 614 Level Three contacts that were labelled as contested anomalies. These were re-checked at each point of the data flow, and importantly, openly archived for future interpretations. Misidentified features and sonar gaps or drone disorientations were termed 'data holidays' in the report (ATSB 2017: 86). The types of 'data holidays' classified record specific image malfunctions and unusual drone deviations. For example, terrain avoidance (steering around a sea mount); equipment failure (two drones crashed and were lost); shadow event (involving ghosted or duplicated images); and off-track navigations (disorientated drones). A fifth category was called Lower Probability of Detection (LPD) when valid sonar data was collected but then ruled out due to loss of clarity, a result of poor seas, poor connections, or sensory degradation. This is the reality of scientific navigation beyond human vision.

In the ATSB report, 'data holidays' are a statistical summary – less than two percent of the sonar coverage – a footnote to sonic perceptual gaps and navigation challenges, being parsed and processed in real time. But within 'data holidays' as misidentified features, we glimpse how drones learn to act from screen-based translations, montaging gaps to trace missing sounds. It is not that instruments prove faulty and prone to error, but the ocean magnifies a trust in what is assumed to be scientifically real (Bremner 2015: 17). Backscatter is the drones' perception not 'of actual worlds', but of frequencies of data, building a statistical spreadsheet to calculate distorted visions. These 'hallucinatory images' are also pseudo-sounds, as drones dive through images that science position *as* ontologically real (Gil-Fournier and Parikka: 2019).

Drones become risk charts, mapping instruments, statistical calculations, and integrated data diagrams that help simulate unknown worlds, yet their exposure to sonic disruption destabilises a 'techno-scientific gaze of total control' (Bryld and Lykke 2000: 15). The disappearance of MH370 exacerbated real divisions between surveillance capabilities and remote sensing techniques, to incalculable or intractable problems in science. This may require an inescapable reckoning with use of drones, specifically, in a deep echoing of backscatter where 'the highest resolution scan, the cleanest signal, has distinct limits in clarity,' producing in terms of sonic perception an inevitable lag as the signal bounces between feature and ground but also to 'territory, object, base, target, ship, command, satellite, regulatory body, and finally the database' (Gregory 2011: 207). As *Solaris* teaches us, technical solutions to realms of the unknown are a long-in-the-tooth tale of both philosophy and epistemology. MH370 cut a disorientating wound across geo-political territories, time, space and surveillance to interface environments and data. MH370 cast responsibilities across human operators, satellite signals, autonomous devices, and navigational instruments, and when this knowledge collided with the ocean, it collided with a domain of images, triggering how sounds became critical not only to underwater drone capacity to detect in the depths, but can distort imaging techniques.

In kilometres of sonar imaging, ROV and drone missions, involving new cloud-based architectures and algorithms for automatic detection, the primary targets investigated were a scattered rock field and four shipwrecks, including a Portuguese coal ship. Perhaps drones transmit these unearthly images as evidence of our planetary condition: ancient geological stones lie with detritus from failed colonial explorations. The tragic revelation is how 'crashes are events laying bare entangled natures' (Beckman 2010), and in this case, how drones are nonhuman archivists of our self-harm, but on a deeper planetary data scale.

On arrival at the National Computational Infrastructure in Canberra, I expected to find answers in a close examination of the ATSB backscatter contact reports. But despite a fascinating and prolonged gaze at the abstract, and sometimes beautiful, if unclear, deep blue-grey and X-ray like images, my focus landed on 'data holidays' as a discursive marker in the operational report. The term captures more than a disclaimer on errant statistics, ghosted images, sonic artefacts, terrain problems and drone malfunctions. Data holidays is a heuristic stamp. It is a warning, a twisted rule-of-thumb for how previously unknown material properties of environments, like the ocean and its odd sonic and volumetric effects, distort a scientific confidence in remote observational data from drones. When diving into remote worlds, like the ocean, in the end, what becomes most visible is how disorientation, loss, and malfunction become an important resource to link and trace how and where technical operations and imaging platforms are placed in specific relations to computational hallucinations and scientific certainty. The search for MH370 was a "data holiday" in totality. It produced new geo-spatial information, sensitive data on strategic mapping assets, and yet every time drones scattered data into image-making they did not find MH370. Instead, they exposed not only the limits to autonomous surveillance, decision certainty and computational simulation, but perhaps revealed the deeper historical and planetary harms in abandoned coal ships, animals, and oil at the base of the deep Indian Ocean.

In researching MH370 we wish to honour the memory of those who have lost their lives and acknowledge the enormous loss felt by their loved ones.

Works Cited

Alaniz, Rodolfo. 2019. 'Before the "Black Box": The Inputs and Outputs of Nineteenth-century Deep-sea Science.' *Science, Technology, & Human Values* 45, no. 4: 596-617.

Amoore, Louise. 2020. *Cloud Ethics: Algorithms and the Attributes of Ourselves and Others*. Durham: Duke University Press.

Amoore, Louise, and Alexandra Hall. 2009. 'Taking People Apart: Digitised Dissection and the Body at the Border'. *Environment and Planning D: Society and Space* 27, no. 3: 444-64.

Andrejevic, Marc, and Zala Volcic. 2019. '"Smart" Cameras and the Operational Enclosure'. *Television & New Media* 22, no. 4: 1-17

ATSB. 2015. *MH370 – Definition of Underwater Search Areas*. Australian Transport Safety Report. Canberra: Commonwealth of Australia. https://www.atsb.gov.au/media/5668327/ae2014054_mh370__search_areas_30jul2015.pdf.

ATSB. 2017. *Operational Search for MH370*. Transport Safety Report. Canberra: Commonwealth of Australia. https://www.atsb.gov.au/media/5773565/operational-search-for-mh370_final_3oct2017.pdf.

Barrow, John D. 1999. *Impossibility: The Limits of Science and the Science of Limits*. Oxford: Oxford University Press on Demand.

Beckman, Karen Redrobe. 2010. *Crash: Cinema and the Politics of Speed and Stasis*. Durham: Duke University Press.

Bremner, Lindsay. 2015. 'Fluid Ontologies in the Search for MH370'. *Journal of the Indian Ocean Region* 11, no.1: 8-29.

Brumfield, Ben. 2014. 'Listen for a Ping, and the Water May Play Tricks on You'. *CNN*, April 13. https://edition.cnn.com/2014/04/11/tech/innovation/mh-370-underwater-sound/index.html.

Bryld, Mette, and Nina Lykke. 2000. *Cosmodolphins: Feminist Cultural Studies of Technology, Animals, and the Sacred*. London: Zed Books Limited.

Day, Sophia and Celia Lury. 2017. 'New Technologies of the Observer: #BringBack, Visualization and Disappearance'. *Theory, Culture & Society*, 34, no. 7-8: 51-74.

Elkins, James. 2018. *The Domain of Images*. New York: Cornell University Press.

Erbe, Christine, Arti Verma, Robert McCauley, Alexander Gavrilov, and Iain Parnum. 2015. 'The Marine Soundscape of the Perth Canyon'. *Progress in Oceanography*, 137: 38-51.

Farocki, Harun. 2004. 'Phantom images'. *Public* 29: 13-22.

Gabrys, Jennifer. 2019. 'Ocean Sensing and Navigating the End of this World'. *E-Flux* 101. https://www.e-flux.com/journal/101/272633/ocean-sensing-and-navigating-the-end-of-this-world/.

Garrett, Bradley and Karen Anderson. 2018. 'Drone Methodologies: Taking Flight in Human and Physical Geography'. *Transactions of the Institute of British Geographers* 43, no. 3: 341-59.

Gregory, Derek. 2011. 'From a View to a Kill: Drones and Late Modern War'. *Theory, Culture & Society* 28, no. 7-8: 188-215.

Helmreich, Stefan. 2009. 'Intimate Sensing'. In *Simulation and Its Discontents*, edited by Sherry Turkle, 129-50. Cambridge: MIT Press.

Helmreich, Stefan. 2015. *Sounding the Limits of Life: Essays in the Anthropology of Biology and Beyond*. New Jersey: Princeton University Press.

Höhler, Sabine. 2002. 'Depth Records and Ocean Volumes: Ocean Profiling by Sounding Technology, 1850-1930'. *History and Technology* 18, no. 2: 119-54.

Howe, Bruce M., Jennifer Miksis-Olds, Eric Rehm, Hanne Sagen, Peter F. Worcester, and Georgios Haralabus. 2019. 'Observing the Oceans Acoustically'. *Frontiers in Marine Science*, 6, no. 426: 1-22.

Jue, Melody. 2014. 'Churning up the Depths: Non-Human Ecologies of Metaphor in Solaris and "Oceanic"'. *Green Planets: Ecology and Science Fiction*: 226-41.

Kao, Chien-Chi, Yi-Shan Lin, Geng-De Wu, and Chun-Ju Huang. 2017. 'A Comprehensive Study on the Internet of Underwater Things: Applications, Challenges, and Channel Models'. *Sensors (Basel)* 17, no. 1477: 1-20.

Kitchin, Rob, and Martin Dodge. 2011. *Code/Space: Software and Everyday Life*. Cambridge: MIT Press.

Langewiesche, William. 2019. 'What Really Happened to Malaysia's Missing Airplane'. *The Atlantic*, July 17. https://www.theatlantic.com/magazine/archive/2019/07/mh370-malaysia-airlines/590653/.

Lehman, Jessica. 2019. 'Beneath the Paving Stones, The Wake'. *Alienocene: Journal of the First Outernational*. https://alienocene.files.wordpress.com/2019/03/jl-wake.pdf.

Lem, Stanislaw. 1970. *Solaris*. Translated by Kilmartin and Cox 2002. San Diego: Harvest Brace & Co.

Littlewood, Peter. 2019. 'Computational Science in an Exascale World'. *Australasian Leadership Computing Symposium (ALCS)*. November 6. https://nci.org.au/news-events/news/a-high-performance-community.

MacKenzie, Adrian, and Anna Munster. 2019. 'Platform Seeing: Image Ensembles and Their Invisualities'. *Theory, Culture & Society* 36, no. 5: 3-22.

McCosker, Anthony. 2015. 'Drone Media: Unruly Systems, Radical Empiricism and Camera Consciousness'. *Culture Machine* 16.

Miksis-Olds, Jennifer, Bruce Martin, and Peter Tyack. 2018. 'Exploring the ocean through soundscapes'. *Acoustics Today*, 14, no. 1: 26-34.

Parikka, Jussi, and Abelardo Gil-Fournier. 2019. '"Visual Hallucination of Probable Events", or, On Environments of Images and Machine Learning'. *MediArXiv*, August 6.

Parisi, Luciana. 2013. *Contagious Architecture: Computation, Aesthetics, and Space*. Cambridge: MIT Press.

Peters, John Durham. 2015. *The Marvelous Clouds: Toward a Philosophy of Elemental Media*. Chicago: University of Chicago Press.

Rahwan, Iyad, Manuel Cebrian, Nick Obradovich, Josh Bongard, Jean-François Bonnefon, Cynthia Breazeal, and Michael Wellman. 2019. 'Machine behaviour'. *Nature* 568: 477-86.

Shindell, Matthew. 2020. 'Outlining the Black Box: An Introduction to Four Papers'. *Science, Technology, & Human Values* 45, no. 4: 567-74.

Steinberg, Peter, and Peters, Kimberley. 2015. 'Wet Ontologies, Fluid Spaces: Giving Depth to Volume through Oceanic Thinking'. *Environment and Planning D: Society and Space*, 33, no. 2: 247-64.

Stern, Joel, James Parker, and Sean Dockray. 2020. 'Machine Listening Curriculum'. *Liquid Architecture*. https://machinelistening.exposed/curriculum/.

Tarkovsky, Andrei. 2002. 'Solaris [1972]' DVD. Curzon Artificial Eye: UK.

Traub, Joseph F. 1996. 'On Reality and Models'. In *Boundaries and Barriers: On the Limits to Scientific Knowledge*, edited by John L. Casti and Anders Karlqvist, 238-54. Basic Books.

Williams, Karen. 2020. 'Searching for a Remnant in Pixels and Static: The Fleeting Materiality of Plane Crashes'. *MAST: Journal of Media Art Study and Theory* 1, no. 2: 124-47.

Wright, Dawn. 2020. 'Scanning the Depths – The Search for MH370.' *Spatial Source.* https://www.spatialsource.com.au/gis-data/scanning-the-depths-the-data-behind-the-search-for-flight-mh370.

13

Drone Error: From Event to Structure

Madelene Veber

Recent times have witnessed a growing fixation with drones, not only in terms of what they can do but also in the many ways they can go wrong. The increased adoption of advanced remote sensing and machine learning systems to drone technology necessarily raises the stakes of error to disastrous extremes: the risk that these systems might err, or 'go rogue' has been considered so high that some argue 'weapons of terror' should be re-thought as 'weapons of error' (Walsh 2018: 70). Although these discourses are predicated on the possibility that fully autonomous weapons or 'killer robots' are an imminent reality, they nonetheless capture a legitimate concern. Errors can have dire, sometimes deadly outcomes: military drones misfire, malfunction, or misinterpret information. In the context of their employment in asymmetric warfare, the consequences of errors, such as crashes, for instance, are often fatal and involve the injury of civilians and the destruction of environments.

Whether or not error itself is a cause for concern, however, remains to be seen. Departing from such discourses, my intention is not to explore the relation between 'error' and 'terror' exclusively in terms of its moral implications. Rather, I aim to pry open the assumption that error is endemic to autonomous and semi-autonomous weapons by considering the different ways that drone error can be theorised and understood. Reflecting on the tendency to view error as an undesired outcome to be rectified, this chapter asks: by responding to error as a particular effect that should be resolved, what important social and political engagements might be obscured? Does positioning error as the primary problem for autonomous technology conceal or limit more complex manifestations of error? How do the discourses exploring the mishaps, failings, and accidents of the drone put a concept of error to work in new ways?

According to psychoanalyst Sigmund Freud, there is no such thing as a true error or accident. Our everyday bungled actions, flops, and failures, commonplace as they may be, are not just chance events but part of a meaningful process: laden with significance, our quotidian errors express an intention allied to our unconscious wishes (Freud 1960). For Freud, trivial blunders are not isolated from what he sees is a latent, unconscious mental process which informs, to a great degree nonetheless, our everyday conduct. He notes that

> Anyone who is ignorant of the facts of pathology, who regards the blunders of normal persons as accidental, and who is content with the old saw that dreams are froth need only ignore a few more problems of the psychology of consciousness in order to dispense with the assumption of an unconscious mental activity. (1957: 119)

While our conscious actions are guided by specific intentions, the existence of unconscious, hidden mental operations sometimes undermines our attempts to execute these aims. Freud used the concept of parapraxis as a collective term to represent the various expressions of error, such as slips of the pen or tongue, misreadings, clumsiness, and forgetting a familiar object or a proper name. In the event of parapraxis – for example, a slip of the tongue – the original aim has literally been substituted by another aim, one which the subject has unconsciously repressed or muffled (Laplanche and Pontalis 1980: 300). It is 'an act whose explicit goal is not attained; instead, this goal turns out to be replaced by another one' (300). The significance of error is that it is symptomatic of an authentic urge or desire; they are 'messages virtually begging to be decoded […] clues to desires or anxieties the actor is not free to acknowledge, even to himself' (Gay 2006: 125).

Freud's theory of error has certainly inspired a sociological tradition, where latent social tendencies in one way or another are thought to inform accidents, errors, and deviations from the norm (see, for example, Durkheim 1982; Latour 2007; Matthewman 2013; Merton 1936). Moreover, that terms like *Freudian slip* are common parlance suggests something about parapraxes that resonates with everyday experience. If it is possible to think of error as more than merely a coincidence or fluke, but as symptomatic of another meaning, what are the limits to, and possibilities of, rethinking drone error in these terms? Envisaging drone error as a symptom of a more comprehensive set of intentions, what is exposed about the drone's very function? This essay will attempt to show how such an approach helps to elaborate the significance and implications of error in the field of drone studies. It traces the drone across different contexts in order to sketch a general conception of drone error.

We might typically characterise error as an unintended mistake, or the act of straying from a set path or direction; the term's etymology refers to wandering without aim (err 1996). In this light, drone error can subsequently be thought as corresponding to the action of deviating from a preestablished or intended function. However, as Georges Canguilhem notes, the concept of error is polysemous (1991: 236). While this initial representation of drone error seems sufficient, attempting to empirically situate such a definition is challenging, as the various expressions of drone error reveal the multifaceted nature of such a concept, its potential to have multiple meanings. Drones are subject to a litany of errors: electrical or mechanical malfunction, human oversight, the miscommunication of information or a miscalculation of coordinates or targets, for example. The drone's performance can also be interrupted by atmospheric factors, like unprecedented storms or winds that might lead to signal failures and technical malfunctions (Conetta 2004: 23; Munster 2014). Moreover, aircraft often go renegade, disappear, or erratically plummet to earth (Crandall 2014).

These various characterisations of drone error are at the same time causally ambiguous: it is not clear that we can conclusively determine how or why such errors occur. What is more, the term error itself can designate both cause and effect (Hollnagel 1983) – in the sense that it can be attributed to the *cause* of a particular event, or used to describe the *effects* of a particular event – so that the rectification of error, in principle anyway, is not a straightforward undertaking. Freud's theory of parapraxis sees error as a symptom whose cause can be located in latent material, yet what exactly compromises the latent function of the drone? And might such a conception help to parse out the stakes of drone error?

Perhaps it is first necessary to recognise that in this context errors stand out insofar as they run counter to the drone's avowed operation, its 'coherent' function. It is this acute differentiation between function and malfunction that pronounces the significance of drone error, a key example of this being the drone crash. Indeed, errors (such as malfunctions, miscalculations, misjudgements, etc.) don't necessarily result in crashes, nor are all drone crashes the outcome of unintended actions or mishaps (drones can be intentionally shot down, or hacked, for instance (e.g., Babak Taghvaee 2020; Munster 2014: 155)). I propose that various theoretical approaches to the crash can assist in articulating the symptomaticity of drone error, or the way that it can be understood as not merely an extraneous glitch but a symptom that informs the drone itself.

UK-based NGO Drone Wars has since 2007 published a registry of reported military drone crashes. Crashes catalogued in the *Drone Crash Database* (Drone Wars UK n.d.) are based on corroborated evidence: video, photographs, media reports, and witness accounts, and they have been predominantly recorded in locations in the Middle East and Africa, and to a lesser extent in the US and Asia. At the time of writing this essay, Drone Wars have documented over 250 drone crashes. While the Drone Crash Database is not an exhaustive record given that reports of military drone crashes often require civilian witnesses or the presence of reporters or media, such an index saliently asserts that the crash, as Adam Fish notes, 'is a part of drone culture' (Fish 2020: 2).

The purpose of the Drone Wars Drone Crash Database is to track the expansion of military drone deployment with the hope of 'initiating and supporting activity designed to restrict the use of these systems' ('Drone Wars UK: Our Mission, Role and Strategic Aims' 2017; Cole and Cole 2020). In addition to monitoring military drone operations, this initiative also points to the unlikely significance of what appears to be an otherwise inoperative drone – a heap of knotted wires and shredded metal – insofar as it continues to inform our perception and understanding of the nature and extent of the ongoing utilisation and deployment of drones. As Lisa Parks notes, drone crashes are concurrently 'dirt borne ruins' and 'sites for forensic investigation' (Parks 2017: 147). Although the crashed drone appears at odds with its functional counterpart, there is still something about the crash, and drone errors more generally, that offers a special site for investigation and speculation. What is it about the crash that makes the drone possible?

Approaching the crash as more than a messy and sometimes tragic exposition of the consequences of drone deployment (while it certainly is this), its perceived failing becomes an opportunity to probe 'material traces' which help us to understand the drone's operation, and furthermore to 'catalyse public inquiry and responses' (152). As Jordan Crandall observes, the crash generates 'new discursive openings' (2014: 273), or the possibility to produce or reinforce particular realities about what the drone is and can be. Crandall states that

> [T]he narratives that are woven around the drone's fate – circulated around crash sites, dinner tables, cookouts, online forums and board rooms – have a vitality. They are social actors that negotiate realities even as they are negotiated by them. Yet the fate of the drone's carcass is but one narrativised outcome of a much larger and more vital function that the catastrophe performs. The crash is important because it destabilises the coherency of the drone and embroils it in a politics that was heretofore invisible or diminished. (273)

By claiming to 'expose' the otherwise invisible or obscured reality of the drone, the crash as drone error offers a unique theoretical departure point through which we can evaluate the drone and the social and political realities that organise it, engaging social forums through speculation and conjecture which in turn diagnose (and produce) a particular image of the drone. In this way, the drone and its milieu are thought to be co-constitutive, a synergy of material-discursive affects (Parks 2017; see also Holmqvist 2013). Reiterating this, Crandall asserts that the impact of the crash reveals more than 'just a small hollow in the sand'; it exposes 'the rituals of neighbours, the connectivities of machines, the routines of public agents, the chorus of desert cicadas' (2014: 264).

For Parks, the drone can be thought of as a 'technology of mediation' (Parks 2017: 135), since they 'materially alter or affect the phenomena of the air, spectrum, and/or ground', and they involve the 'capacity to register the dynamism of occurrences within, on, or in relation to myriad materials, objects, sites, surfaces, or bodies on earth' (135). Drones are mediative, 'etching their inadvertent affects into grounded lifeworlds and biomatter' (147). And yet, they are also mediated by a milieu that appears to precede and exceed them, since, as we have seen, the crash highlights the different actors and engagements that put the drone to work.

To return to Freud, the symptomatic nature of error sees it as a conduit through which a more expansive meaning is made possible. Unlike Freud's conception, however, the drone crash as symptom does not reveal a definitive cause for error. Nor does the recognition of drone error necessarily assume that the networks that establish the drone's operation can be brought under rational control. What it does speak to are the constituent factors and forces that manage its coherence or perform its apparent function. Are attempts to ameliorate error, then, merely a means to remedy the incoherence of such an entanglement of agencies and possibilities, one which is nonetheless constitutive of the drone?

Error is exceptional: it surprises, interrupts, disturbs. Our experience of error elicits a slew of emotions, often negative – shame, humiliation, disgrace, for example – that we often attempt to correct or make up for in one way or another. Witnessing error as a deviation or transgression from what is within the realm of the ordinary, we often seek clarification or explanation, especially when errors have hefty consequences that need to be reckoned with. The main issue here, it seems, arises when we responsibilise the two aspects of error explored so far: the way in which error brings to the fore the 'spectrum of agentic capacities' (Coole 2005) that comprise the drone, and the general social tendency to explicate error. Of course, these particular interpretations of drone error are not mutually exclusive, since the narratives that accompany the drone crash influence how the technology itself is imagined. Error, as it is conceived here, is not realised beyond the event of the crash. In this way, it is merely instrumental to exposing the drone's dimensionality: to put it another way, although error demonstrates the drone's flaws, it is not entirely clear how we grapple with error as something that should arise in the first place.

Indeed, conceiving the nature of the drone as one which is entangled with a milieu that both mediates and is mediated by it is extremely useful; however, the stakes of error here can be further elaborated by considering error as not just a diagnostic tool, something which can be temporally isolated as an 'event' or 'moment', nor a symptom indicating the drone's mediative nature. I suggest that we conceive the symptom as a crystallisation of error which actually guides or informs the drone's very operation to begin with: error as a structure. This approach certainly raises questions about how we claim responsibility for error, since it is through explaining error, or rectifying it, that we tend to account for it (and presumably prevent future errors). Rather than disavowing the question of responsibility altogether, conceiving of error structurally raises the stakes, as it asks us to think about how error is structurally pervasive to the ways in which the technology is imagined.

As a departure point for thinking about error beyond event or accident, we might consider Adam Fish's insightful account of drone use in species conservation. Fish examines how drones in wildlife conservation are ontologically bound up with the species they seek to protect: like endangered species, drones are vulnerable to collapse and decline (2020). For Fish, this demonstrates the fragile and paradoxical entanglement inherent in the operative function of the conservation drone, especially in relation to the species it should be monitoring. Conservation drone crashes confuse the assumed asymmetry of a vulnerable species surveilled by an all-seeing, efficacious surveillant (2020: 3). Fish notes that the crash, the fateful combination of drone technology and pilot skill - both of which are mediated by light and electricity - breaks the suspended relationships between conservation practices and endangered megafauna. The crash is a diffraction event that discloses slippages in the conservation drone phenomena and, more generally, in the claimed hybridisation of nature and culture. (5)

The strange paradox here is how the use of drones in conservation becomes, as Fish terms it, a 'contingent practice' (1). While the crash certainly emphasises the interdependency (or 'entrapment' (4)) of the conservation drone, its operator, and the species it seeks to protect, the very operation of the error-prone conservation drone was actually implicated in such an interdependency from the outset. Errors lay bare the fragile and vulnerable nature of such a relation, but they also underwrite it. Error is a possibility renewed at the drone's every moment.

Let's pause for a moment to consider more closely the stakes of the problem. To do this, we can turn to classic arguments in risk management theory. Institutional and organisational approaches and responses to error are telling, insofar as they suggest how accountability and responsibility are addressed with regard to error. Within these industrial contexts the close scrutiny of errors is an important part of risk management, insofar as understanding the causes of errors and accidents provides insights into how they might be mitigated or prevented in the future (for example, how a system might be better designed to assure workplace safety). While such contexts are not in the regular ambit of drone studies, they nonetheless provide a glimpse into how, when complex systems are involved, error is reckoned with and accounted for.

Sidney Dekker (2014) identifies two views of error: the *Old View* of error, otherwise known as the 'Bad Apple Theory', and the *New View* of error. These two views might be distinguished by the different ways they assess responsibility. Where the Old View sees the human agent as the primary cause of error, the New View of error considers human error a symptom of an underlying structural condition which effectively exceeds the human agent. Here, the error is attributed to a structural or systematic flaw rather than an individual's actions. To briefly elaborate on these two perspectives: The Old View sees error as attributable to a 'bad apple' in the system - a negligent, inept or inexperienced operator, for example, who is presumably a free agent and thus considered the efficient cause of an accident (Dekker 2014; Hollnagel 1983). In short, the Old View of error stops at what are referred to as 'human factors' or causes. As Burnham notes, the received wisdom guiding the bad apple theory was that 'pure accidents, events that cannot be anticipated, seldom happen' (2009: 17). Put another way, errors were not purely spontaneous nor inherently unexplainable: rather, 'someone has blundered, someone has disobeyed an order or undertaken to reverse the law of nature' (17). While the Old View of error sees the human agent as accident prone and blameworthy, the New View challenges this assumption by proposing that the human agent is not the cause; rather, according to this theory, the cause of the error or accident can be found in the broader organisation or formal system: this pertains to everything from the design of technology and industry practice, to ones work conditions. As Jens Rasmussen (1981), one of the original thinkers behind the New View (Dekker 2014: 7) has pointed out, one's work environment must be considered as creating the potential conditions for errors and accidents to occur (1981: 14).

For engineer Erik Hollnagel, however, both the Old and New views of error are problematic (1983, 2021). This is because, as Hollnagel sees it, error is conceptually ambiguous, and can be categorised in many ways: it is not always clear whether error refers to a cause or effect, and this means that attempting to rectify it is sometimes a futile or frustrated task. The Old and New views, for Hollnagel, attribute error to something that can be pinned down or located. Moreover, by way of this tendency to want to identify and rectify error, the Old and New theories effectively presume that a normal, perfect system or state of operation is possible. In other words, by conceiving error as something that can be identified and remedied, these theories assume a 'proper' way of doing things is achievable (1983). Furthermore, conceiving error as something that can be corrected overlooks the way in which error might be inherent to a system. The reason this is a problem for Hollnagel is because it obscures (and ignores) the complex nature of the normative mechanisms through which error emerges (2021: n.p.).

Elaborating on Hollnagel's position, we might see how error confuses what is perceived to be the 'normal' operation of the drone. This is particularly evident in literature exploring drone strikes and precision-guided munitions in the context of warfare. Moving from the crash to drone targeting, while illustrating the multifaceted nature of error, also helps to sketch out what is at stake in our attempts to make sense of what appear to be the drone's various deviations.

If the performance of the drone is measured in terms of efficacy, monitored by the drone's capacity to successfully undertake tasks (presumably the case in military contexts), then we might see that the operation of the drone and UAV technology is contingent on its efficient function. Efficacy, it seems, should be opposed to error. However, borrowing from Hollnagel, such a distinction is not straightforward, as the concept of error is not necessarily secondary to, nor severed from, a sense of efficacy.

Precision-guided munitions (PGM) systems demonstrate how error might be thought of as a structure fundamental to a technology's efficient function.

PGM systems provide weapons with the ability to aim at a designated point or target. For drones, PGM systems operate through GPS rather than being laser guided. As the case goes, PGM systems ensure weapons are better at targeting, thus limiting collateral damage and human suffering, making war safer, smarter, and supposedly more ethical (Zehfuss 2011: 544). However, claims advocating the efficacy of PGM meet a much murkier ethical reality, as in practice, the very admission of technical 'precision' is ambiguous. Analysing the ethical arguments surrounding PGM, Maja Zehfuss succinctly points out that in warfare, 'precision' inevitably implies imprecision (548). This is because precision-based weapon delivery systems typically encompass what is referred to technically as Circular Error Probable (CEP). As Carl Conetta notes, CEP delineates the margin of error for every target, 'the radius of a circle centered on an aimpoint within which some percentage – usually 50 percent – of weapons fired at the aimpoint will fall' (2004: 22). There is the statistical expectation, therefore, that the weapon will fire outside the designated radius every other time (Zehfuss 2011: 548; see also Devereaux 2015). Error, in this sense, is anticipated, even premediated, as Conetta suggests: 'A 13-meter CEP is the threshold for considering a weapon "accurate"; in 1998, the CEP standard for precision weapons was 3 meters' (2004: 23). CEP principles, for Conetta, demonstrate an inherent inaccuracy: 'they reflect the limits of the system employed, and cannot be removed without improving, supplementing, or changing these systems' (23). When we take into account the material implications of drone strikes for individuals and communities, this conception of error as precision is disconcerting as it seems to suggest that unintended casualties resulting from PGM are admissible.

This is certainly indicative of the more general obfuscation of the notion of accuracy in counterterrorism operations, which, as Lucy Suchman (2020) points out, obfuscates the difference between the precision in which a weapon hits its intended target, and 'the act of identifying legitimate threats that targeting presupposes' (2020: 183). Indeed, what is most striking about these observations concerning the stakes involved in negotiating 'precision' is the way in which error is not so much rectified or averted by advancements in precision-guided technologies – as a traditional concept of error might imply – but accommodated by the technology itself. In this way, CEP illustrates the inevitability of error, or how error might be more than merely an extraneous glitch, but a principle which drives the drone's very operation, even blurring the distinction between efficacy and error. This certainly raises new stakes, as in the case of CEP, error is anticipated and to an extent formalised. The drone's operation, its efficient function, is *in error*. This certainly elicits the more general question of how we discriminate what does and does not count as error? How do we understand drone errors when the very technology itself can be found to operate on a principle of contingency or imprecision?

In this vein, Jamie Allinson's (2015) research on the structural complicity of bias in the operation of autonomous weapons is worth examining. Allinson, like Zehfuss and Connetta, is interested in how the capabilities of autonomous weapons are arranged, and the social and ethical implications such arrangements entail. Driving the perceived efficiency of the drone or autonomous weapon is in this case its nature to seemingly act objectively. In particular, Allinson navigates both pro- and anti-drone arguments, especially in terms of how both camps articulate the autonomous or semi-autonomous drone as an objective (and so presumably ethical) weapons technology.

Scrutinising both the pro- and anti-military drone arguments, Allison's gloss is that these critiques often hinge on the likelihood that the drone will (randomly) err. The anti-drone argument makes a case for the likelihood for the drone to fault ('going haywire, killing people indiscriminately because of a programming error' (2015: 117)), while the pro-drone argument suggests that drones are in fact a more accurate and just substitute for human soldiers, who are inclined to 'submitting to their emotional drives and committing atrocities' (117). In the case of the former, the drone bears responsibility for error: the latter holds responsibility in the hands of the human operator.

As suggested at the outset of this chapter, anti-drone arguments to a large extent steer the majority of the literature on drone error especially in terms of the technology's increased automation. Here, error is largely moralised as that which is fundamentally wrong about automated or semi-automated weapons systems. The tendency to read error in this way is certainly not in itself unwarranted, especially considering the devastating impact that the use of such weapons have on both the actors involved in their deployment (drone operators, programmers) (e.g., Dao 2013; Chappelle et al. 2014), and the civilians who live in drone-occupied territory (e.g., Edney-Browne 2019). However, it seems to me that there is more to this argument than 'error', and by largely scapegoating error as the primary problem, we ignore the more complex issues at hand. Thus, we return to the question raised at the outset: what exactly is remedied by our attempts to rectify error? What does a scrutiny of drone error expose?

For Allinson, both pro- and anti-drone positions are short sighted: Allinson notes that these arguments focus on technological or human deviation as the primary problem, assuming that such technology, in and of itself, is entirely capable of operating 'correctly'. As with PGM, error and efficacy are distinguished. Error, which here comes to stand for a deviation from the norm, is for Allinson inherent in the very capacity for the technology to discriminate between those 'who are to be protected and those to be feared or destroyed' (117). Drawing on the work of Achille Mbembe, Allinson makes clear that such a discrimination is at the same time a 'racialisation', where asymmetry or difference is inscribed 'onto the body and other markers of lived experience' (118) which, in the context of precision and targeting weapons, are to be dominated or erased. Allinson states:

For the drone is not merely a new technology in the everyday sense of a mechanical and electrical assemblage: It is a technology of racial distinction. Circling and swooping above territories, the drone defines who is an 'object in the battlespace' and who is not, delineating those areas and populations characterised by the 'acceptability of putting to death'. The current debate on drones and their potential autonomy misses this point, not by underestimating the autonomy of drones, but overestimating that of their operators: There is *already* a target recognition system at work in the technology of racial distinction that embraces both the mechanical drones and their fleshy operators. (120, emphasis in original)

Particularly striking is Allinson's point that the ethical problem with drones cannot be reduced to either the 'mechanical drone' or the 'fleshy operator', but is always already operative; it is structurally pervasive to the technology itself. Indeed, this certainly raises a methodological concern, too: to understand error, it is necessary to identify the assumptions upon which we base certain notions of objectivity or efficacy. Katherine Chandler, in the compelling study *Unmanning* (2020) elaborates on the structurality of error, pointing out that automation, in terms of the drone, is organised by contradictions that are subsequently denied or silenced by those who put the drone the work. For Chandler, '[d]rone warfare is haunted by violence that exceeds the current war on terror, made possible through confusions between humans and machines', continuing to point out that 'the technopolitics made by the drone are tied to confusions and ambiguities that are part of the drone's ontology, not only established by what is unmanned but also proposing an ideal of what is human as unmanning's counterpart' (2020: 7). Thus, thinking error structurally requires rethinking what the drone actually does, what it is, and the tendencies that prime its interaction with the world. Error is thus an organizing principle (2020).

'Every technology carries its own negativity', states Paul Virilio, 'which is invented at the same time as technical progress' (1996: 89). Whether the drone or the cruise liner; the trading algorithm or the nuclear power plant, technology begets an accident, even a disaster: 'everything that constitutes the world has experienced an accident, and this is without exception' (2005: 34). Yet, for Virilio, accidents are necessary for technical development: they are part and parcel of the 'Janus-face of progress' (Matthewman 2013: 22), a necessary function of the accident (Featherstone 2000).

In the context of drone error, this critical technological progressivism is complicated. If error is inherent to the operation of the drone, and yet this operation is produced though more profuse and dynamic material and discursive networks, how do we designate the limits of the drone itself: its very haecceity or 'this-ness'? In other words, if error is a symptom of a more pervasive structural principle that informs and exceeds the drone, what is the 'drone' to which we attribute error? While it is tempting to indulge in the existential question of the drone, it is important not to lose sight of the significance of error here. After all, attributing responsibility for error has social and political purchase, circumscribing – even provisionally – a perceived determinant or agent through which we can grasp this particular technology and its operation. This should not imply that the drone is necessarily clear cut, predictable, or entirely knowable; rather, it reiterates earlier claims such as those by Crandall and Parks that conceive the drone as produced through social and political workings. In this way, determining responsibility (and thus agency) is by no means a straightforward task, and perhaps one that requires we first open up to the manifold expressions of the drone before any robust conception of error can be developed.

It can thus be seen that error, typically conceived as a phenomenon secondary to the drone's function, is capable of being reconfigured as a driving principle, both in terms of the way that the drone operates and is imagined. Error, therefore, speaks to the drone's various deviations as a reflection of the system that it is. The fact that the narratives included here treat the drone's transgressions as configurations of the technology is perhaps, in the final analysis, a demonstration of why we need to look beyond the technology, the 'site' of error, for the engaged and yet sometimes elusive networks that inform it.

Works Cited

Allinson, Jamie. 2015. 'The Necropolitics of Drones.' *International Political Sociology* 9, no. 2: 113–27. https://doi.org/10.1111/ips.12086.

Babak Taghvaee - The Crisis Watch (*@BabakTaghvaee1*). 2020. 'According to This Underwing Pylon, the Armed Drone Which Is Shot-down by a Pantsir-S1E of #Libya National Army near Al-Watiya Is Not an Anka-S of #Turkish Air Force. It Is in Fact a Wing Loong-II Armed Drone of #Libya National Air Force Which They Shot-down by Mistake!'. 16 May. https://twitter.com/BabakTaghvaee1/status/1261684090077659136.

Burnham, John C. 2009. *Accident Prone: A History of Technology, Psychology, and Misfits of the Machine Age.* Chicago: The University of Chicago Press.

Canguilhem, Georges. 1991. *The Normal and the Pathological.* Translated by Carolyn R. Fawcett. New York: Zone Books.

Chandler, Katherine. 2020. *Unmanning: How Humans, Machines, and Media Perform Drone Warfare.* New Brunswick: Rutgers University Press.

Chappelle, Wayne, Tanya Goodman, Laura Reardon, and William Thompson. 2014. 'An Analysis of Post-Traumatic Stress Symptoms in United States Air Force Drone Operators'. *Journal of Anxiety Disorders* 28, no. 5: 480–87.

Cole, Chris. 2019. 'Accidents Will Happen: A Dataset of Military Drone Crashes'. Drone Wars UK. 9 June. https://dronewars.net/2019/06/09/accidents-will-happen-a-dataset-of-military-drone-crashes/.

Cole, Chris, and Jonathan Cole. 2020. 'Libyan War Sees Record Number of Drones Brought down to Earth'. Drone Wars UK. 1 July. https://dronewars.net/2020/07/01/libyan-war-sees-record-number-of-drones-brought-down-to-earth/.

Conetta, Carl. 2004. 'Disappearing the Dead: Iraq, Afghanistan, and the Idea of a "New Warfare"'. *Research Monograph* 13. Cambridge, Massachusetts: Project on Defense Alternatives, Commonwealth Institute. http://www.comw.org/pda/fulltext/0402rm9.pdf.

Coole, Diana. 2005. 'Rethinking Agency: A Phenomenological Approach to Embodiment and Agentic Capacities'. *Political Studies* 53, no. 1: 124–42. https://doi.org/10.1111/j.1467-9248.2005.00520.x.

Crandall, Jordan. 2014. 'Ecologies of the Wayward Drone'. In *From Above: War, Violence, Verticality*, edited by Peter Adley, Mark Whitehead, and Alison J. Williams. Oxford: Oxford University Press.

Dao, James. 2013. 'Drone Pilots Found to Get Stress Disorders Much as Those in Combat Do'. *The New York Times*, 22 February. https://www.nytimes.com/2013/02/23/us/drone-pilots-found-to-get-stress-disorders-much-as-those-in-combat-do.html.

Dekker, Sidney. 2014. *The Field Guide to Understanding 'Human Error'*. Farnham, United Kingdom: Taylor & Francis Group. http://ebookcentral.proquest.com/lib/unsw/detail.action?docID=1825729.

Devereaux, Ryan. 2015. 'Manhunting in the Hindu Kush'. *The Intercept*. 15 October. https://theintercept.com/drone-papers/manhunting-in-the-hindu-kush/.

Drone Wars UK. 2017. 'Drone Wars UK: Our Mission, Role and Strategic Aims'. *Drone Wars UK*. 17 May. https://dronewars.net/role-and-aims/.

Drone Wars UK. n.d. 'Drone Crash Database'. Drone Wars UK. n.d. https://dronewars.net/drone-crash-database/.

Edney-Browne, Alex. 2019. 'The Psychosocial Effects of Drone Violence: Social Isolation, Self-Objectification, and Depoliticization'. *Political Psychology* 40, no. 6: 1341–56.

'err'. 1996. In *The Concise Oxford Dictionary of English Etymology*, edited by T. F. Hoad. Oxford: Oxford University Press. https://www.oxfordreference.com/view/10.1093/acref/9780192830982.001.0001/acref-9780192830982-e-5206.

Featherstone, Mark. 2000. 'Speed and Violence: Sacrifice in Virilio, Derrida, and Girard'. *Anthropoetics: The Journal of Generative Anthropology* VI, no. 2: 1-11.

Fish, Adam. 2020. 'Crash Theory: Entrapments of Conservation Drones and Endangered Megafauna'. *Science, Technology, & Human Values* 46, no. 2: 1-27 https://doi.org/10.1177/0162243920920356.

Freud, Sigmund. 1957 (1915). 'The Unconscious'. In *The Standard Edition of the Complete Psychological Works of Sigmund Freud, Volume XIV*. Translated by James Strachey. London: The Hogarth Press and the Institute of Psycho-Analysis.

Freud, Sigmund. 1960 (1901). 'The Psychopathology of Everyday Life'. In *The Standard Edition of the Complete Psychological Works of Sigmund Freud, Volume VI*. Translated by James Strachey. London: The Hogarth Press and the Institute of Psycho-Analysis.

Freud, Sigmund. 1963 (1916). 'Introductory Lectures on Psychoanalysis (Parts I and II)'. In *The Standard Edition of the Complete Psychological Works of Sigmund Freud, Volume XV.* Translated by James Strachey. London: The Hogarth Press and the Institute of Psycho-Analysis.

Gay, Sigmund. 2006. *Freud: A Life for Our Time*. New York: W.W. Norton & Company, Inc.

Hollnagel, Erik. 1983. 'Human Error'. *NATO Conference on Human Error.* Bellagio, Italy. https://erikhollnagel.com/onewebmedia/URTEXT%20on%20HE.pdf.

Hollnagel, Erik. n.d. 'The NO View of "Human Error"'. https://erikhollnagel.com/ideas/the-no-view-of-human-error-1983.

Holmqvist, Caroline. 2013. 'Undoing War: War Ontologies and the Materiality of Drone Warfare'. *Millennium: Journal of International Studies* 41, no. 3: 535–52. https://doi.org/10.1177/0305829813483350.

Laplanche, J, and J.-B Pontalis. 1980. *The Language of Psycho-Analysis*. Translated by Donald Nicholson-Smith. London: The Hogarth Press and the Institute of Psycho-analysis.

Latour, Bruno. 2005. *Reassembling the Social: An Introduction to Actor-Network-Theory*. Oxford: Oxford University Press.

Matthewman, S. 2013. 'Accidentology: A Critical Assessment of Paul Virilio's Political Economy of Speed'. *Cultural Politics: An International Journal* 9, no. 3: 280–95. https://doi.org/10.1215/17432197-2346982.

Merton, Robert K. 1936. 'The Unanticipated Consequences of Purposive Social Action'. *American Sociological Review* 1, no. 6: 894-904.

Munster, Anna. 2014. 'Transmateriality: Toward an Energetics of Signal in Contemporary Mediatic Assemblages'. *Cultural Studies Review* 20, no. 1: 150-67. https://doi.org/10.5130/csr.v20i1.3836.

Parks, Lisa. 2017. 'Vertical Mediation and the U.S. Drone War in the Horn of Africa'. In *Life in the Age of Drone Warfare*, edited by Lisa Parks and Caren Kaplan, 134-157. Durham: Duke University Press.

Suchman, L. (2020). Algorithmic warfare and the reinvention of accuracy. *Critical Studies on Security*, 8, no. 2: 175–87. https://doi.org/10.1080/21624887.2020.1760587.

Vaughan, Diane. 1999. 'The Dark Side of Organisations: Mistake, Misconduct, and Disaster'. *Annual Review of Sociology* 25, no. 1: 271–305. https://doi.org/10.1146/annurev.soc.25.1.271.

Virilio, Paul. 2005. *The Accident of Art*. Cambridge Mass.: Semiotext(e).

Walsh, Toby. 2018. *2062: The World That AI Made*. Collingwood: Schwartz Publishing. http://ebookcentral.proquest.com/lib/unsw/detail.action?docID=5486298.

Zehfuss, Maja. 2011. 'Targeting: Precision and the Production of Ethics'. *European Journal of International Relations* 17, no. 3: 543–66. https://doi.org/10.1177/1354066110373559.

14

ecologies of duration: a visual essay on thinking-imaging novel space-times with drones

Michele Barker and Anna Munster

Lakes and skies run from crystalline white-blue to damp grey in the sub-Arctic circle summer. Above the treeline, the exposed rock of Saana, a fell in Central Sápmi in north-west Finnish Lapland (see Figure 14.1), reveals the long duration of its 100-million-year orogeny event: the Caledonian fold, a mountain-building process that began in the Ordovician geological period, roughly 490 million years ago. At the edge of Lake Kilpisjärvi, 550 metres below the fell, tiny waves endlessly lap against August's unfrozen shores. Biologists and artists come to this area throughout the year to study fragile ecosystems for evidence of encroaching climate change. Bird eggs, pollinators, grasses, bone, and soil samples are painstakingly collected, hand counted, and analysed by scientists trekking up and back down the fell. Photographs and videos, ecoacoustic and bioart techniques, performance, collective and compositional processes are generated, shared, and exhibited by artist-researchers. What might a drone's

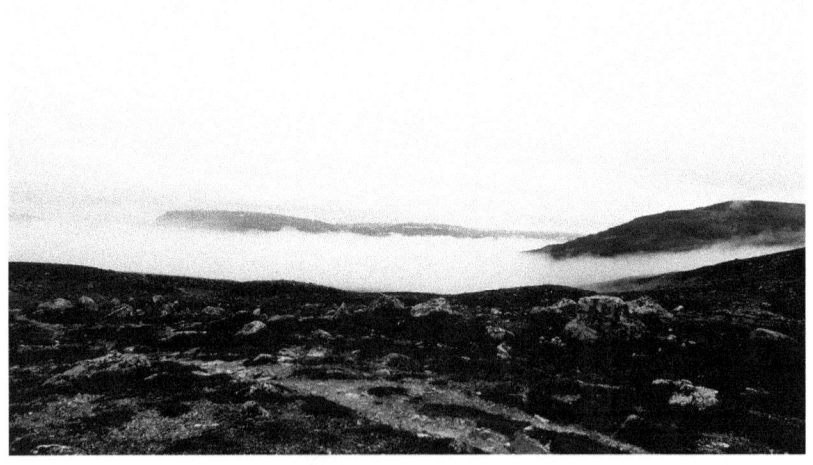

Figure 14.1.Michele Barker, *Saana, a fell in Central Sápmi*, north-west Finnish Lapland. Courtesy of the artist.

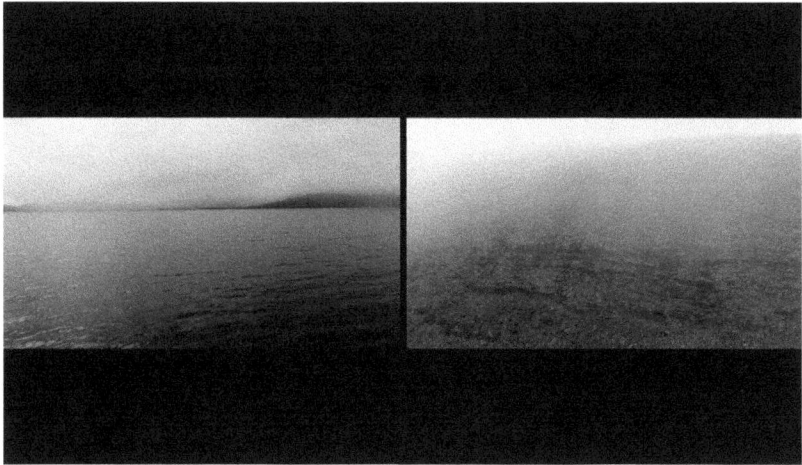

Figure 14.2. Michele Barker and Anna Munster, Still, *ecologies of duration*.
Courtesy of the artists.

view add to this growing repository of thinking-making across bioarts at the tip and tipping point of the planet?

The above image (see Figure 14.2) is a screenshot across two audiovisual channels, from our body of work, *ecologies of duration*, which began during an *Ars Bioarctica* artist residency (SOLU/Bioart Society 2021), at the Kilpisjärvi Biological Station, Faculty of Biological and Environmental Sciences, University of Helsinki in the summer of 2019. Continuing our preoccupation with duration and felt experience in works such as *pull* (2016) and *hold* (2019), we made the decision to use drones for *ecologies*, commencing our audiovisual research creation into 'geotime'. In the eighteenth century, geological time began to be understood via a cyclical history of erosion and renewal of the Earth's crust, which seemed to open a long durational and novel perspective on a dynamically transforming planet. Yet such early geological views were intimately entangled with a kind of humanistic deism in which geo-planetary processes were ultimately understood as mapping on to agricultural cycles suited to human inhabitation of the Earth (Dean 1992: 264). More recently, the earth sciences have developed methods of dating the planet to 4.55 billion years – a scale that exists well beyond human imagining. Western geology, or what Kathryn Yusoff (2018) has called 'White Geology' thus generates a doubled conception of the planet's timespan as both subjected to and beyond the human. The Anthropocene and its material planetary crises are thus forged in the nexus of the naming of geological time according to human scales and impact and in divergence from the human through its acknowledgement of (more-than) planetary temporal scales. 'Geotime', as a registration of these tensions, names our attempt to work in and with the sensings of this nexus. We want to ask: how might we bring a sensibility that accounts for geotime

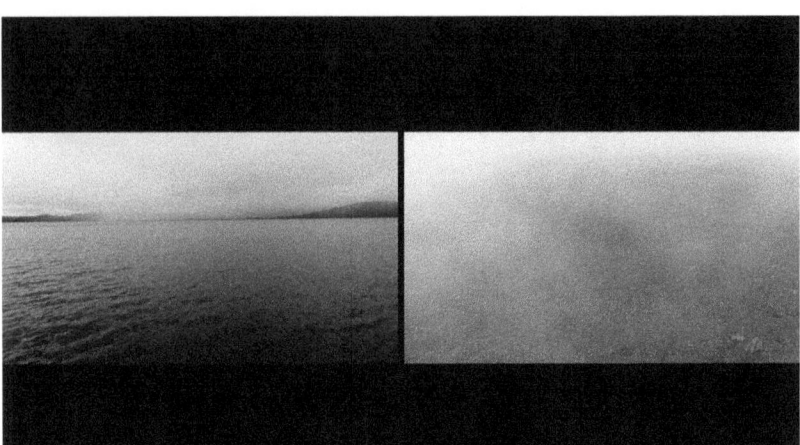

Figure 14.3. Michele Barker and Anna Munster, Still, *ecologies of duration*.
Courtesy of the artists.

as an event that is simultaneously immediate, ongoing, and already over for the audiovisual dronescape? How might drones be nudged into sensing the planetary and its terrain in ways that register multiplicities? And in ways that fold out on to a more-than-human, and, accordingly, a what-else for drone imaging, perhaps offering a visuality other than the more familiar spectacle of aerially re-presenting the Anthropocentric 'crisis'.

In the hands of visual and conceptual artists, drone cinematography and imagery has predominantly developed along two lines of intervention: either wrest ownership of the aerial perspective from state and extra-state actors; or deploy that point of view to develop a more 'planetary' perspective. In works as diverse as Edward Burtynsky's photographic contributions to *The Anthropocene Project* (2018), or Forensic Architecture's *Drone Strikes Platform* (2004-14), the drone's cinematic eye is locked upon land and planet in a re-presentation of colonialist cartographic and remote sensing visual strategies. Of course, it may precisely be such perspectives, as lenses of scopic and political regimes, that artists and cultural producers wish to critique or into which they attempt to tactically intervene. Yet as varied and incisive as much of this interventionist photographic and moving image practice has been, a fixation on an aerialised perspective continues that the 'steadied-cam' drift of drone imaging affords.

We have been exploring duration and perception as complex, messy, felt processes that might be detected via a drone's attempts to stay with, caress, move alongside water and earth. At the same time, we draw on drones' visually uncanny stabilising and distancing cinematic possibilities along with their status as sensors of high-dimensional data, seeking ways in which they might help register the dynamics between timescales that both involve and exceed us. We consider new ways of working with drone cinematography and soundscape: filming in close proximity to geoformations; developing techniques in which the moving image appears to both zoom in and recede from its 'target'; and capturing data in visually obscured natural circumstances such as fog or mist. In *ecologies of duration*, we work with the ways in which drones might sense, gesture, and generate their environments through machine-terrain encounters. In the work, a multiplicity of ecologies endlessly flow in and out of each other, converging onscreen and sonically. Each video channel is its own 'ecology' yet also in relation with all the other channels.

To register proximity – rather than the tendency toward remoteness in much drone imaging – we have sought to find ways to work with more terrain-hugging drone cinematography. In working against the scopic regime of the distant, aerial view, we work with drones in two ways: first, as a machine 'agent' capable not only of tracking and targeting but potentially also of gesturing, in the sense that Erin Manning proposes as 'reaching-toward' (2020: 179). Manning describes touch as a relational encounter that alters and displaces spatialities and temporalities. Although humans engage touch as a gesture that involves a full sensorium, Manning also suggests that the becoming as relation with environment is an engaging and reaching out and co-composing with environment/world. It is not so much that 'we' feel the world or some object in it; rather, the world is already alive with feeling. Can a drone that has, thus far, functioned as a remote sensing machine reach toward the planetary, itself be already alive with feeling?

At Kilpisjärvi, water, land, and light began to affect the roving lens of the drone camera, calling out for modes of perception and affection that might operate alongside – and outside – humans' short 'moment' in geological time. We commenced our own daily treks around the lakes, up and down the fells, in tandem with weather and unexpected diurnal rhythms. We worked audio-visually with what simply presented to us – a rockface, receding horizons, mist and bodies of water; constrained at the same time by the drone's short thirty-minute battery life. The immediacy of water and its ripples, the rolling fogs that are characteristic of the late summer fell weather and the endless light of a barely setting sun insisted upon and affected field recordings and raw footage. But all the while, we were also seeking to work with novel approaches to drone cinematography. We were trying out movements in imaging that might become generative of something more-than in the visual field of the familiar contemporary drone imaginary.

In this image (see Figure 14.3), there is a barely noticeable shift from its prior sequence in the previous image above – the mist has rolled horizontally across the frame of the righthand image channel. In the lefthand channel, the sun glints a little more keenly against the lapping waves. The mist against the fell continues to roll across the frame in the remainder of this segment of *ecologies*, looping continuously and folding back into itself. Saana's cliff face is revealed and obscured, revealed and obscured… The drone's gaze,

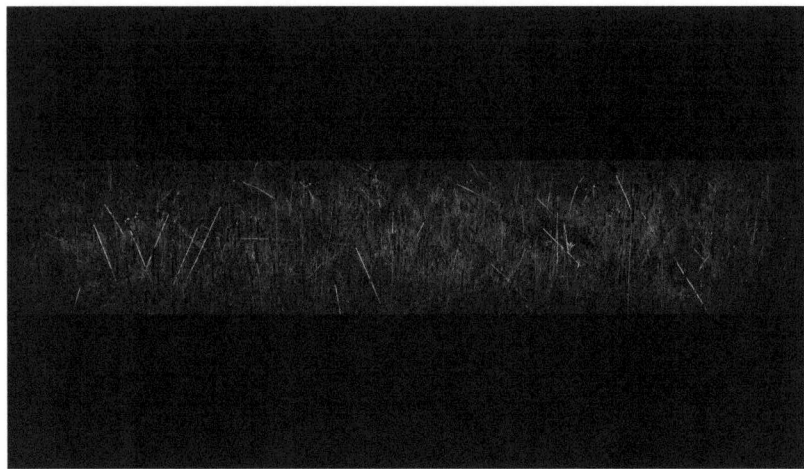

Figure 14.4. Michele Barker and Anna Munster, Still, *ecologies of duration*.
Courtesy of the artists.

usually trained to track a moving object or to roam over terrain continuously, is instead suspended in a continuous action of looking that never produces much of a 'thing' to be looked at. The mist undulates and seems to take hold of the drone's sensing apparatus, which becomes trapped in a haze of seeing but sees very little. Something else is happening just above the lake's surface. Deploying a dolly zoom, an in-camera manoeuvre that has been associated with heightened and unnerving psychological moments in classical films such as Alfred Hitchcock's 1958 *Vertigo*, the drone zooms in on the far shore of the lake while it is piloted/pulled backwards and out of the shot and away from the lake. Against the endless ripples and skyline, the drone seems to be both moving towards the image horizon and yet never getting any closer to its subject matter. Rather than emphasising the human subject's interior psychological state, we use the dolly zoom to suspend the capacity of the drone's gaze to track and capture terrain from above.

Like the view obscured by continuously rolling fog, the drone sees but cannot *track* the lake shore in the distance. In working with the drone at one tip of the world and at a time in which the world is fast tipping into ecological disaster, we try to constrain the drone to look in the moment, at a thickening 'now'. This moment in which there is little happening onscreen in the camera's view turns out to be full of movements both between and across the two channels and is suggestive of time itself being composed via 'movement-moving' (Manning 2013: 14). The drone's 'hovering' on the sightlines is also being explored sonically in *ecologies*, using gyroscope and accelerometer data from the drone flight logs to sonify its sensors' encounters with forces such as wind currents. The capacity of drone vision to maintain an uncanny steadiness in its environments is displayed as part of its aerial cinematographic prowess.

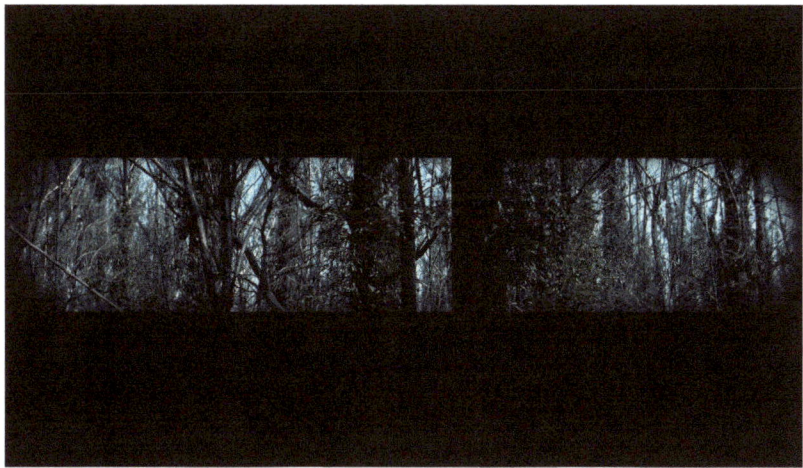

Figure 14.5. Michele Barker and Anna Munster, Still, *ecologies of duration*.
Courtesy of the artists.

We wager that sonifying this flight log data might bring out the imperceptible operations necessary to float such seamless seeing, perhaps repositioning the drone as a more vulnerable and less 'autonomous' apparatus – repositioning it as technology firmly entangled with environment.

Returning from the sub-Arctic, we plummeted into the Australian summer of 2019, the terrain fractured along the fissures of prolonged drought, horrific fires devastating a billion animals and burning over eighteen million hectares, much of it bush, followed by serious flooding events. To film the ravaged terrain using the drone felt both repulsive and necessary. The next set of channels of *ecologies* emerged out of more localised forays into the Australian landscape, also made necessary by having our own movement limited by the unfolding crisis of the COVID-19 pandemic. Without the intention of locating any obvious scars of fire, our road trips during 2020 took us to places that were suggestive of climate change and ecologies on the brink; rapidly undergoing successive transformation wrought by the acceleration of the Earth warming (see Figure 14.4). Yet even in the face of such landscape, we wanted to continue to develop ways for the drone to sense and to become sensitive to the fragility it was imaging.

If the drone *is* considered less than autonomous and more as an assemblage in which the camera is but one sensor among an array of gyroscopes, barometers, accelerometers, then this makes the camera-as-sensor a particular kind of technical object. The drone camera-as-sensor produces what the filmmaker Harun Farocki termed 'operational images' (2003); that is, images made by machines for machines. The increasing use of drones to sense environmental data raises an interesting question about how to think about the environment, terrains and ecologies rendered by such sensing. We can

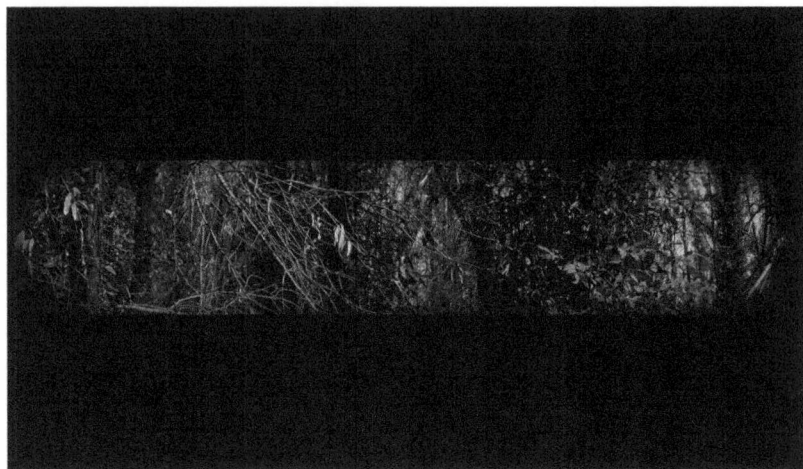

Figure 14.6. Michele Barker and Anna Munster, Still, *ecologies of duration*.
Courtesy of the artists.

recall Jennifer Gabrys's arguments about webcams as environmental sensors: 'Cameras-as-sensors concresce as distinct technical objects and relations, and in the process they articulate environments and environmental operations' (2016:7). Here we would need to think about drones as not simply entering into environments that pre-exist. They do not, especially in their conservation use, simply record 'states of nature'.

The firescapes, drought and flood are likewise traces and harbingers of the duration of climate change. A kind of spectacle is produced by imaging climate crisis via drones in much media and social media depiction: large icebergs melting, extensive shoreline erosion, cities blanketed in pollution. The

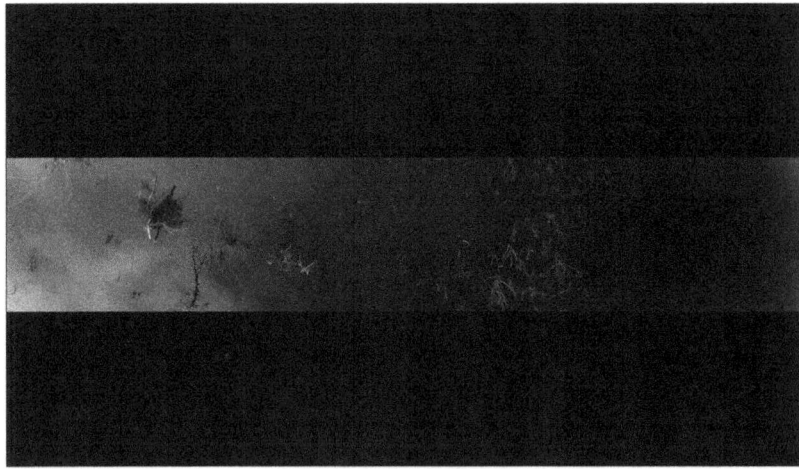

Figure 14.7. Michele Barker and Anna Munster, Still, *ecologies of duration*.
Courtesy of the artists.

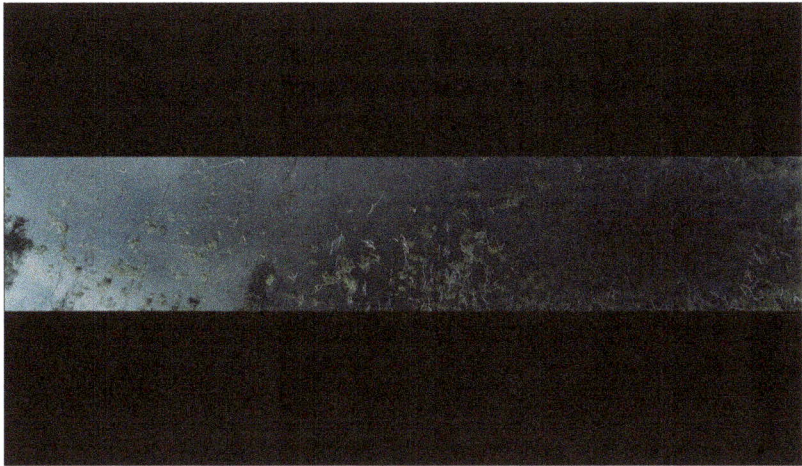

Figure 14.8. Michele Barker and Anna Munster, Still, *ecologies of duration*.
Courtesy of the artists.

drone seems above and outside the visual field as if it were only there to convey technological catastrophe and not own up to its part in it. Our terrains tend toward proximity or some kind of perceptual disorientation that playing with scale, movement, and speed might render. The terrains we image are often directly eventless with not much obviously happening, as we turn instead to the aftermath of crisis. As we reach-toward the dried, dead grass trees with the drone making close passes backward and forward across the *xanthorrhoea* fields in the image above, it is difficult to discern if we are looking at the conditions for or the aftermath of bushfire.

Terrain and life press on to the drone as a sensing apparatus. Amid trees that had been scorched and stripped along swathes of the firegrounds in the Shoalhaven district on the south coast of New South Wales, we pilot the drone horizontally past the fuzzy 'epicormic' eucalypt shoots of the surviving gums (see Figure 14.5). Australian native plant species are thought to have adapted to cycles of burning and flooding. These cycles have been described in earlier environmental studies as 'disturbance ecologies' (Sousa 1984) that are part of the natural cyclical or systemic activity of any ecology. However, dramatic changes to climate have meant that disturbance ecologies have become more severe, erratic in behaviour, and harder to predict. Usual and documented cycles of disturbance in environments are increasingly radically disrupted. This now means that many events in ecosystems function as exceptions to acknowledged 'disturbance ecologies', signalling the emergence of the disturbance of 'disturbance ecologies'.

The epicormic growth spurting forth from the burnt-out trunks makes it difficult to navigate the drone through the bush. The image above (see Figure 14.6) is taken from a sequence that begins with the previous image and pans across the trunkline then pauses as we try to pilot the drone through its depth axis. But the drone stops mid-air, its sensors detecting too many obstacles to move any further forward. Again, its cinematographic gaze is suspended and adopts a hovering motion. In this sequence, it shifts from side to side of one trunk in small movements, almost asserting some agency to its command to push forward. A kind of hesitation forms even while the camera stays level on its axes. This slight shiftiness is the drone being affected, disturbed as well by the disturbance ecology.

In the final channel of this segment of *ecologies*, the drone returns to the air but presents us with a narrow slit of its surveying of the terrain below. Sweeping across a floodplain that formed in the aftermath of the 2019 Australian fires, the cartographic capacities of the drone to cover space and trace the major features of a topography have bled dry. The image (see Figure 14.7) is disorienting – flattened of depth and discernment of scale. It could be a long shot or a close-up angle; the vegetation could be tall gums or grasses, or both at the same time. The water looks back at the sky; the geography compressed into one visual plane (see Figure 14.8).

As the terrain sweep continues down the slit screen view, the drone does not simply document what is happening to ecologies as they are disturbed but rather registers that disturbance as perceptual and affective.

Ecologies of duration – a project that will continue to unfold between drones and environment – tries to find ways for sensing technologies to 'witness' the disturbance of disturbance ecologies, whose multiple and nonlinear durations make such relationality difficult for humans to register. Such witnessing must place sensing machines within the event of perceiving, of looking and telling, not as mere observers of it. Michael Richardson and Kersten Schankweiler have called for a different understanding of media witnessing in which not just media technologies and formations but also affect be acknowledged as cutting across and working with the event(s) of witnessing (2021). We would add, this goes for percepts as well. The 'ecologies' presented in our work cohere via a multiplicity of views on a planetary scene or scape, scrambling direction (left-right; backwards-forwards) shifting perspective and point of view (in-out; depth-surface). They are caught in torsion between stillness and movement, operativity and sensibility. From these experimental audiovisual techniques, we ask drones to begin again from a nonhuman and more proximate perspective, to imagine an earth and time with which we are impossibly entangled and necessarily estranged. And in which drones, at every level and in all their functionalities, are always already implicated.

Works Cited

Barker, Michele and Anna Munster. 2019. *hold*. Multichannel immersive installation. Accessed July 1, 2021. https://vimeo.com/370014756.

Barker, Michele and Anna Munster. 2017. *pull*. Multi-channel immersive installation. Accessed July 1, 2021. https://vimeo.com/262297665.

Burtynsky, Edward. 2018–ongoing. *The Anthropocene Project*. Accessed July 1, 2021. https://www.edwardburtynsky.com/projects/the-anthropocene-project.

Dean, Dennis. 1992. *James Hutton and the History of Geology*. Cornell: Cornell University Press.

Farocki, Harun, 2003. *Eye/Machine III*. 2-channel video installation, 25min (loop). Accessed July 2, 2021. https://www.harunfarocki.de/installations/2000s/2003/eye-machine-iii.html.

Forensic Architecture, 2004–14. *Drone Strikes Platform*. Accessed July 2, 2021. https://forensic-architecture.org/investigation/the-drone-strikes-platform.

Gabrys, Jennifer. 2016. *Program Earth*. Minneapolis: University of Minnesota Press.

Manning, Erin. 2013. *Always More than One: Individuation's Dance*. Durham: Duke University Press.

Manning, Erin. 2020. 'Not at a Distance: On Touch, Synaesthesia and Other Ways of Knowing'. In *Touch*, edited by Caterina Nirta, Danilo Mandic, Andrea Pavoni and Andreas Philippopoulos-Mihalopoulos, London: University of Westminster Press.

Richardson, Michael, and Kerstin Schankweiler. 2020. 'Introduction: Affective Witnessing as Theory and Practice,' *Parallax* 26, no. 3: 235-53.

SOLU/Bioart Society. 2021. 'Ars Bioartica Residency', *website*. Accessed July 1, 2021. https://bioartsociety.fi/projects/ars-bioarctica/pages/residency.

Sousa, Wayne P. 1984. 'The Role of Disturbance in Natural Communities,' *Annual Review of Ecology and Systematics* 15: 353-91.

CODA

Post-Visual Images

Yanai Toister

I. New Image-Media?

'[M]edia determine our situation', Friedrich Kittler famously argued at the turn of the millennium (Kittler 1999: xxxix). This forceful assertion is celebrated in some traditions of media studies but remains rarely considered and largely unfamiliar in most strains of visual studies (Cramer 2016: 122). This can be attributed in part to the nonoverlapping geographical distributions of both fields (continental Europe and the English-speaking world, respectively). It can also be taken to indicate a deeper sentiment: images (taken broadly) are rarely understood as nothing but media. This is especially peculiar given that in Kittler's text 'media' is mostly inscriptive (Kahn 2012) and that the history of art in the West is mostly the history of inscription protocols (thus consistently ignoring the splendour of civilisations which did without those). Thus, in Western tradition, image-media is always about the circulation and consumption of inscribed and thus durably visible images.

How does Kittler's formulation hold true for present-day visualisation forms and image formats? Herein exist types and breeds of images where inscription is almost redundant (if not lacking altogether), and transmission is the only constant. Particularly, what kind of *us* or *we* do imaging systems integrated into weapon systems, operation-room robots, and driverless cars herald under such circumstances? This chapter argues that the *our* in 'media determine our situation' now incorporates non-sentient beings – machines and computers – and that this *situation* rarely necessitates the participation, the involvement, or even the presence of sentient beings like *us*. Particularly, image transmission without image inscription makes *us* redundant. Crucially, image ubiquity is now unthinkable without built-in camera sensors of various sorts. This is true not only in military, law enforcement, medical, and smart transport applications, but in numerous other professional and creative uses as well. It is equally true of everyday consumer devices, whether handheld, worn, or, in the near future, integrated within our bodies. In fact, the camera itself, argues Asko Lehmuskallio, has become an image sensor: one among many (Lehmuskallio 2016). The outputs from such sensors are routinely networked, their data tagged to generate huge masses of image data that are navigable in real time.

Under these rapidly changing circumstances, the already porous definition of *image* is placed under increasing pressure. If the very definition of the image cannot hold, can images still be understood by reconstructing the intentions of their human producers or the desires of their human receivers (as indeed commonly attempted in visual studies)? Once perception has been automated for artificial vision, argued Paul Virilio, the analysis of objective reality can be relegated to machines (Virilio 1994: 59). Therefore, the operations of imaging technologies can no longer be understood as being exclusively the effects of inscribed images. While these remain important, this chapter speculates on the possibility of image operations that do *not* emerge from visible representational functions (numerical code which has been rendered into an arrangement of picture elements). The image operations subject of this text perform *invisibly* or rather, play formative roles that are invisible to us humans.

II. Objective / Subjective

These recent developments shed interesting light on much earlier ones, and have the potential of rewriting the historiography of image making in retrospect. Surprisingly, the preclusion of the human from the productive creation of imagery can be located much earlier than most of us tend to think. In fact, it dates back to the genesis of photography as most assailants and some advocates of the medium argued (although not for the same purposes). Notwithstanding, the boundaries between human and machine had become undoubtedly and irreversibly blurred by the 1920s with the advent of smaller, lighter, and more mobile cameras. This is illustrated most vividly in the eye-and-camera analogy celebrated in Dziga Vertov's 1929 avant-garde film *The Man with the Movie Camera* (and repeated in Andreas Feininger's *The Photojournalist* from 1951). The marginalisation of human vision is also evident in the works of Alexander Rodchenko, Otto Umbehr and, most notably, László Moholy-Nagy – artist, designer, and celebrated master at the Bauhaus.

Moholy-Nagy argued that the camera was the beginning of an objective vision as it was, in his words, 'optically true', or objective. He further called for the 'elimination of perspectival representation', and sought to abolish the pictorial and figurative traditions that had been established by painters, and remained unchallenged for centuries (Moholy-Nagy 1969: 28). This extended to Moholy-Nagy's own work, which often sought to approximate the worm's- and bird's-eye points of view (see Figure 15.1). He also called for picturing motion, which, when done with extreme obliques, yielded previously unimagined image trajectories (Moholy-Nagy 1928).

This approach, of being '(un)encumbered with subjective intention' (Moholy-Nagy 1969: 96), eventually became known as the 'new objectivity', and came to be associated with German photography of the 1930s. In other words, these technological and theoretical breakthroughs facilitated a hitherto inconceivable rift between the supposed objectivity of the camera and the subjectivity of the human photographer – who, we can appreciate, is becoming a mere nuisance for some systems.

Although not unfamiliar, this narrative remains unpopular, perhaps unacceptable, from the perspective of classic (that is modernist) histories of photography. Those favoured the human 'photographer-as-protagonist' theme as the keyhole through which to view the broad expanse of photography. In contrast, the history of film, and particularly Hollywood film productions – since the 1920s through to the present day, when much film production is actually post- or virtual production – celebrates trajectories based precisely on *this* narrative, the rift between objectivity and subjectivity. Consequently, when relishing action films, our pleasure and satisfaction diminish in the absence of imagery captured (or made to look as if has been captured) from the perspective of a machine: be it a surfacing submarine, an accelerating locomotive, or a free-falling aircraft.

Artist, filmmaker, and essayist Harun Farocki referred to such points of view as *phantom-subjective images* (Farocki 2004: 13). Importantly, Farocki coined this term in response to footage from the First Gulf War, which was disseminated to television audiences worldwide and remained publicly available. These grainy moving-image sequences, mostly available in black and white, were produced by cameras mounted on warheads such as laser-guided bombs and cruise missiles, capable of closing in automatically on predesignated targets, mostly infrastructural or architectural, but at times also human. Contemporary phantom-subjective points of view include those of objects crossing the outer parts of the Earth's atmosphere, a pellet moving down the digestive tract or the rear-view of a mini-SUV. Closer to our own bodies, GoPro and other wearable and mountable devices aim at yielding a similar effect of supplementing or surpassing human anatomy. This confirms Stanley Cavell's assertion that the one human wish photography has truly satisfied is the wish to *escape* subjectivity, metaphysical isolation, and finitude (Cavell 1979: 21). Numerous programmes, gaming engines, and virtual cameras satisfy that same wish. In fact, in-game photography is a site where phantom subjective imagery is a common and often a desired option. Perhaps one day, when our aspirations for spatial exploration are fulfilled, and freefall and spacewalking become commonplace, phantom-subjective points of view will have become impossible or unnecessary. Until then, our inability to overcome

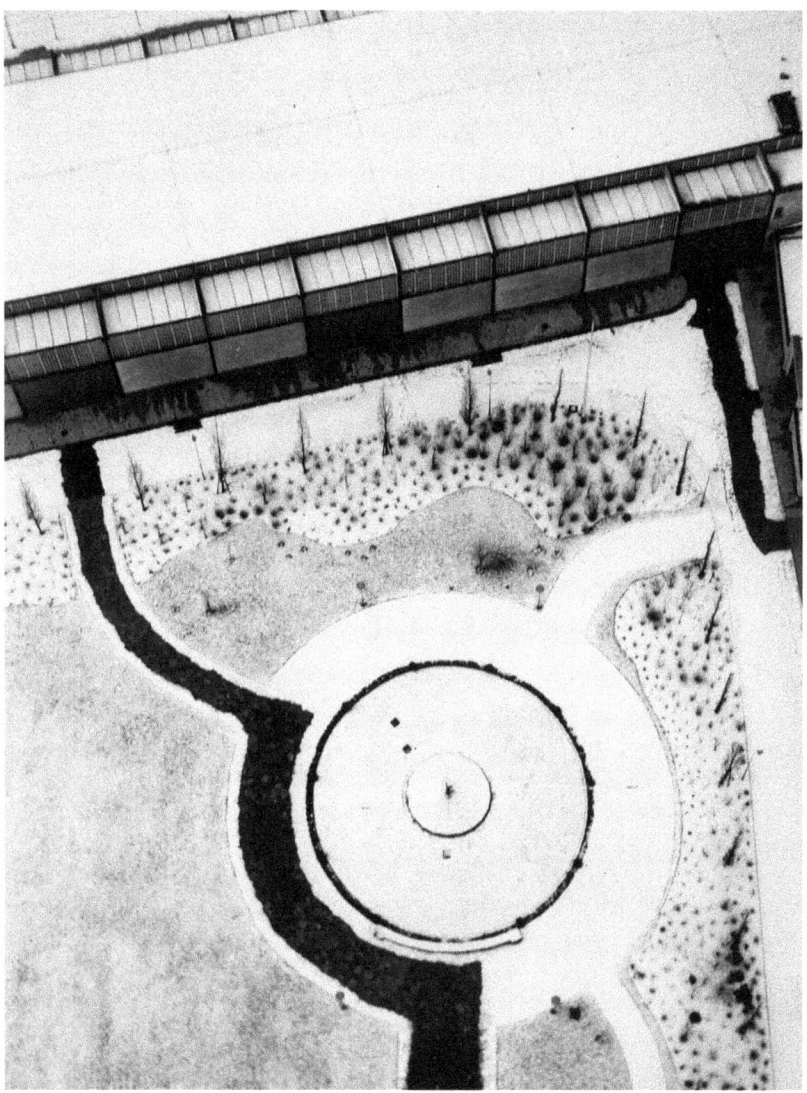

Figure 15.1. László Moholy-Nagy, *From the Radio Tower*, Berlin (1928).
Source: Wikimedia Commons.

gravitational, anatomical and sensorial limitations requires phantom-subjective images. These, lest we forget, emerge from technical and technological apparatuses and always remain bound to them, not to *us*. These are nowadays redesigned with growing alienation from human subjectivity and indifference to human experiences once celebrated.

III. Operativity and/or Subjectivity

Recent imaging systems bring into being image forms and formats which are not all meaningful or even legible to humans. The systems Farocki expounds upon in his installations, films, and essays continuously track changes in the world, and adjust their trajectories accordingly by juxtaposing input from on-board camera-sensors with input from other sensors and sources. Crucially, images generated in this way are not necessarily stored for subsequent analysis by humans, and thus cannot mediate the world for them. Rather, they are mostly scripts for an immediate operation: that of determining and correcting the real-time behaviour of an object-turned-subject, or a subject that cannot be human. This new breed of images has been dubbed *operational* or *operative images*. In fact, as artists such as Trevor Paglen and Hito Steyerl have been quick to note, the vast majority of images produced today are of this sort exactly (Paglen 2016; Steyerl 2016). While operative images have been first identified in tandem with phantom-subjectivities (with the latter also seeming like the precondition for the former), operative images may also appear independently thereof.

This is arguably most noticeable in services such as Google Street View (GSV), to which several artists and scholars have directed their attention in the last decade. An early artwork is Doug Rickard's *A New American Picture*. Therein GSV is used for a virtual exploration of the back roads of America, placing emphasis on the fact that the platform is a virtually infinite archive of visual vernacularity. This project was later described as 'virtual street-photography' thereby accurately capturing the awkwardness of the transition from 'offline' to 'online' photographic flânerie with nothing but bandwidth and a Lay-Z-Boy arm-chair. Jon Rafman's project, appropriately titled *9-eyes*, in reference to the nine cameras mounted on top of GSV cars, is more interesting from the contemporary perspective because it often focuses on the transitions between image captures and the instances when they seem to fracture – seem, that is, to the human eye. As compelling as these fractures are, they are the *exception* to the new rule: seamlessness. With operative imaging systems, images forever remain unfixed and unbounded, and never come into being as *only* images. Rather, image-captures breed unending panoramas which are merged with online cartographic services in two and three dimensions. Curiously, authors who have commented on GSV have failed to note it as an example wherein operative images initially appear from within standard-subjective points of view (street view), and not phantom ones which remain an opt-in possibility. Phantom-subjectivity in GSV appears only when one attempts to relocate spatially, thus turning the still image into video and the stationary viewer-cum-user to acrobatically fly through space, often arriving at giddy bird-like perspectives. It also appears when the user attempts to relocate temporally (an ability afforded, at least unidirectionally, by a recent feature of the GSV service). The most profound artwork to utilise GSV is probably Sylvia Grace Borda's *Farm Tableaux* (2013-2015). This is a project done in collaboration with photographer John M. Lynch and existing (that is exhibited) on and in the platform. *Farm Tableaux* attempts to 'fix' images within GSV, and thus claim artistic authorship over them, an intentionally futile endeavour. In so doing it reveals that within GSV images are always a complex ensemble of various types of data created ab initio by *multiple agents* and *agencies* distributed both spatially and temporally. The artworks described here make clear that GSV and similar services not only put our bodies to pasture, they also dull and dumb vision. In so doing they gradually raise the suspicion that our born sense of vision is a no-longer-useful form of knowledge acquisition. Moreover, vision may now be a form of acquiring only non-useful knowledge.

Operative images initially emerged with (and as a derivative of) mid-twentieth-century weapon systems and technologies. Their novelty has evolved through late-twentieth-century knowledge developed in tandem with (if not for) weapon systems and technologies, most notably machine vision and computer vision. These are required for the autonomy of drones where their use is indeed ubiquitous. When it comes to autonomous drones, the displacement of our somas is coupled with a devolution of vision, with only a dull interface for our senses. As on the ground, so too above, where eyes-closed blindness reigns and its reign affords comprehension, discrimination, and choice that are dramatically altered. Following the historical primacy of machines designed to kill (or at least pass the word of gods), other technologies have equally been made algorithmic – lock, stock, and barrel. In fact, just like drones, this *is* what they are celebrated for. Such systems are now routinely used to guide us on our morning drive, perform on our bodies when we are undergoing surgery, and protect us against all manner of domestic dangers – or at least provide warning, or, if not, documentation after the fact. These civilian settings are equally rife with epistemic, ethical, and pragmatic dilemmas. Because operative imaging systems often produce nonrepresentational images, they do away with various human decisions and actions. These are relegated to non-sentient beings whose ethical limits we do not know. A limit is always a meeting of two or more affordances, but the affordances of imaging that is not only non-representational but also nonvisual are impossible to fathom with toolkits mobilised from visual studies. Operative imaging systems can only be understood as prototypical habitats for the emergence of quasi-agentic media-mechanisms. Furthermore, such systems make abundantly clear that when mediation processes are indiscernible from their outcomes, there can never be a neat separation between autonomy and agency. When media is only potentially sensory (media as only transmission and not inscription at all) the gaps between producer, technician, and user well-nigh disappear, eclipsing the possibility of external action, operation, and knowledge.

Vision is no longer an exclusively human purview, nor is it any longer subject to our exclusive judgement and control, not even when it concerns our own bodies and indeed our very survival. In fact, some operative systems are free to autonomously and even authoritatively register, map, interact with, control, and regulate the parameters of hitherto un-existing epistemological forms. Think of radiation therapy wherein systems such as CyberKnife combine image guidance abilities with a robotic manipulator and a particle accelerator used for the treatment or removal of benign or malignant tumours. Such systems are, quite literally, a kill robot for tumours (Friedrich and Queisner 2014). Likewise, systems used for Neuro-navigation – and this is but one example – generate images which are benignly operative in the sense that they are 'part of an operation' in which the (human) surgeon is sitting in an adjacent space or even further removed from the patient. Such systems are clearly active and transformative, arguably reconfiguring the subject-object relationship throughout their operation, with machines becoming the seeing (and decision-making) subject, and human organs the objects to be seen or ignored.

To understand how this relation has been reversed, why operative images have become not only scripts for operation but operative entities in their own right, let me offer a short history of machines inspired by Vilém Flusser (2000: 24). Early industrial machines were designed to perform simple, single-purpose mechanical tasks in a system that always included humans, who were required to contribute at least a minimum of mental power and labour. Such machines can be described as 'blind', because of their inability to adapt to unforeseen events or situations. Human presence with and near such machines provided the necessary flexibility (or 'vision'). According to most modernist histories of the medium, the photographic camera was undoubtedly one such machine, as it was completely dependent on the human photographer in order to traverse the broad sweep of all potential photographs (including those yet to be realised). In contrast, Universal Turing Machines, or computers as we now call them, are designed with the capacity to perform multiple tasks, and do so not only rapidly and automatically, but also *autonomously*. This is possible so long as such machines are given a table of instructions that defines another machine (a non-Universal Turing machine). Such adaptive machines are programmable and, to the extent they are connected to sensors or cameras, may even be understood as machines with 'quasi-seeing' capacities, perhaps even full-fledged 'seeing' machines. With this in mind, could operative imaging systems be further described as being not only quasi-, but fully agentic?

Of course, some such systems do not operate entirely on their own because the images they generate, although made to be processed by computers on the fly, are ultimately destined for viewing by the human eye, for the sake of examining the outcomes of the operation as well as improving system performance (this is arguably the case for GSV and CyberKnife). Clearly, when it comes to seeing, the world is simply too plentiful for us to expect that an 'objective' imaging system could exist. The features or parts of the world revealed by one system are not strictly speaking the same as the features or parts revealed by another (Magnetic Resonance Imaging, or MRI, is useful for observing softer tissue than is usually revealed by Computerised Tomography, or CT, which uses X-rays). Each system and each method establishes its own 'working object', so to speak (Daston and Galison 2007). Nonetheless, when it comes to operating on human subjects, new imaging methods enact a productive displacement of our sensorium, necessary for bringing into the purview of our mind information that is naturally beyond it, information that would otherwise have eluded us. By augmenting human sensitivity, operative imaging systems expand the range of human action but also reveal its limits – the fact that, unaided, our 'dreary senses' (Nake and Grabowski 2017: 23) can only discern and rely on the analogue features of media.

Here we might do well to recall Lev Manovich's words on media (or 'new media' in his taxonomy) which in general can be said to consist of two distinct layers: a 'cultural layer' whose structural organisation 'makes sense to its human users', and a 'computer layer', whose structural organisation 'follows the established conventions of the computer's organisation of data' (2001: 45). With regard to the digital image (another ancestor of the operative one), mathematician and pioneer of algorithmic art Frieder Nake speaks of a marriage between 'subface' and 'surface' features. These can be taken as an inseparable double or as a hybrid single, but they are nonetheless two distinct processes. The surface is for us humans to experience, whereas the subface is for the computer to work with. The former is visible (or audible or palpable); the latter is nothing but symbolic coding (2001; 2008). We humans are usually aware only of the surface processes, remaining blissfully ignorant of the subface where the computer holds sway, where algorithms are the ultimate submarines, and can afford to remain forever submerged.

IV. Pseudo-Operative / Truly Operative

This then is a crucial distinction pertaining to operative images: that between promotional expressions (propaganda *for* technology) and operative images. It separates images that illustrate a function (and possible meaning) to a human receiver from ones produced exclusively for a non-sentient readership. The former may be called pseudo-operative, and the latter truly operative. They differ greatly, not only in terms of their level of abstraction but also in terms of their aesthetic qualities. Since a truly operative image is not necessarily produced for human consumption, it might not represent a recognisable object. Such an image is produced when image elements are scanned to check whether they correspond to pre-existing configurations in the database. This interplay occurs in the subface. The shifting colourful traces and outlines that appear to come alive on the surface of the pseudo-operative image simply illustrate instances of machine-based recognition, the momentary creation of transitions and correspondences between worlds.

This ephemeral image-making function is therefore perfunctory: 'a gesture of courtesy extended by the machines' (Pantenburg 2017: 49n4). This is illustrated in Ben Grosser's artwork *Computers Watching Movies* (2013) – a sequence of pseudo-operative images: humans (really) watching how computers (metaphorically) watch movies. A truly operative image is produced by computational sensing technologies for the consumption of computer programmes, and designed to function *without* human intervention or perception (and thus falls squarely outside the province of art).

With operative images emerges an order of the world with a universal method of articulation: image-processing software. This order is composed exclusively of simple geometric shapes: straight lines, arcs, and corners, elements in a language of edges, a segmented world that exists and that is governed by the rectangular picture frame. This new world finds its ideal expression in the autonomous electronic processing logic of the guidance (or classification) system and its agentic cybernetic capacity to constantly adjust its own situation by making micro-evaluations and minute- by-minute decisions. Put differently, although operative imaging systems can 'see' us, we cannot and have never seen operative images. Familiar representatives of the submerged algorithmic world with their arrows or dots are operative images 'decorated' by machines for the benefit of human experience – to be interpretable. A computer can process pictures, but needs no pictures to verify or falsify what it reads in the images it processes – it needs no snorkel. For the computer, the image subface (code) is enough. Computers do not need animated yellow arrows and green boxes in grainy video footage to calculate trajectories or recognise moving bodies and objects. Those marks are for the benefit of humans, to help them understand the ways of the machine. The systems that bring operative images into being interact with the world (or more precisely with a symbolic abstraction of the world with which we humans interact, as Kittler would have it), and do so with far greater efficiency than we ever could (if our standards are quantitative and not qualitative). They are in that sense, with recourse to classic photographic theory, a camera born to imitate its viewer's eye that has outstripped and replaced its model (Farocki 2003). The situation that operative images determine is a human-made situation – a 'cultural world', to which humans have no recourse (Ernst 2013).

V. Post Visual / Post Knowledge?

Three novelties set operative images apart from previous breeds of images. Firstly, they require neither human creation nor human perception. Operative images inform in the same ways they entertain – irrespective of their real functions and purposes. 'If such images possess beauty', declared Farocki, 'this beauty is not calculated' (Farocki 2003) – and beauty that is un-calculated, I clarify, remains unexperienced and unknown. On the other hand, any sampling of a spatio-temporal situation, anything that can exist as a signal, can

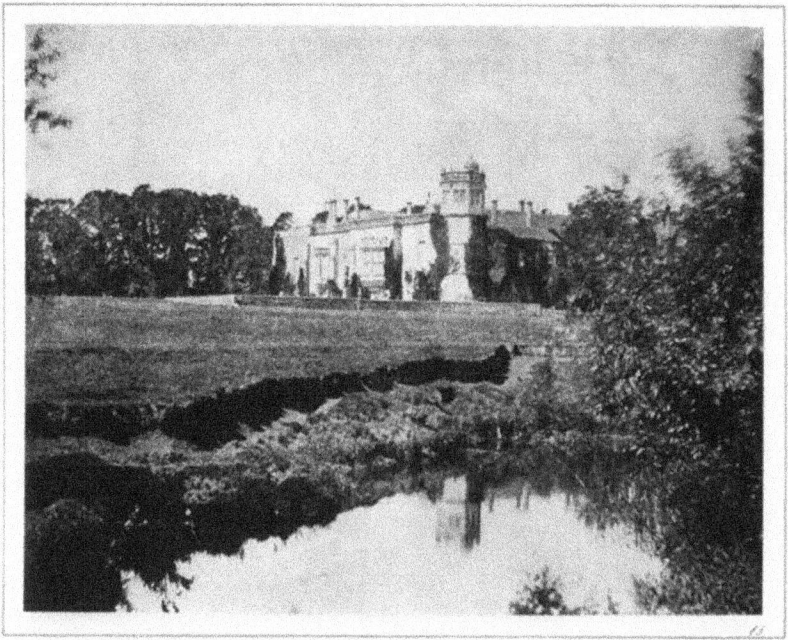

Figure 15.2. William Henry Fox Talbot, *Lacock Abbey in Wiltshire* (Plate XV in The Pencil of Nature) (1844). Source: Project Gutenberg.

be calculated to become an image. Thus, the fascination pseudo-operative images may engender (when true-operative images are somehow made to surface) resides mostly in their logic and precision. Their automatic and relentless capacity to evolve independently through space and time in order to attain their humanly undecipherable objectives, to mediate or interface algorithmically controlled processes: programmes and universal knowledge machines.

Secondly, in operative systems, we may concede, agency is *distributed*, as apparatuses, programmes and machines form an integrated system. Such systems often leave no residue, no permanent marking, no accessible memory, not even a voltage difference. Even to the extent that a renegade visual marking is left visible – and if we insist on maintaining that a human being has been integral in leaving it so, and further insist on designating this marking as an image – designating it as an *authored* image is detrimental to our potential understanding of imaging systems. In spite of their depictive potential, operative images are, I argue, not pictures but simply visual patterns – instructive functions as omnipresent through technology as they are in nature, wherein images are often markings but rarely pictures.

Thirdly, and more disturbingly, since this form of instruction is *purely* instrumental, it does not require aesthetic properties or culturally active assets. Operative imaging systems need not enable human perception at all.

Human perception, argues Wolfgang Ernst, is dominated by 'semiotically iconic, musically semantic, literally hermeneutic ways of seeing, hearing, and reading' (2013: 27). These make it, from the system's perspective, a nuisance. Computing machines are made for compilation and have no use for interpretation. For operative imaging systems, this is formalised into the well-defined question: How does this scene (and world) correspond to a dataset? Such systems not only 'see from memory' – they 'see' nothing but memory.

When operative images no longer require a human point of genesis, when they do not require a human point of reference, need they be visible to the human eye in the same ways conventional images are? Obviously not. This, then, is where operative images constitute a watershed moment for human culture. From Plato onwards, Western philosophy and later science have consistently acclaimed vision as the ultimate sense: the privileged form of knowledge acquisition, captured by such common phrases as 'seeing is believing'. Further, seeing was considered a form of 'knowing' *in and of itself* and practically thus indistinguishable from thinking, as in the phrase 'to see the light'. In recent decades however, vision has been replaced by sensing, ray tracing and calculation, so knowledge now runs in an 'endless loop' (Kittler 1992: 2), the end of which we cannot locate. Within this nonmetaphorical darkness, only that which can be quantified is deemed knowable. Nothing else is ever acquired. With this, expressions such as 'cognitive functions' no longer denote thinking but also processing (and no longer processing in hydrocarbons but also on silicon).

Conclusion

The operative image represents a mutation in the logic of data acquisition and management based on the development of a new relationship between worlds, as computer models increasingly overlay and override sections of concrete reality. It also represents a significant augmentation of the penetrating powers of observation that can be measured through the proliferation of these models. Thus, in many instances there is 'no real need to invade foreign space in order to collect data' (Farocki 2003): the ultimate significance of the operative image in a world order where computer models augment or altogether replace reality is their accuracy, which becomes the benchmark of human achievement and progress.

Images never cease to reorganise the relationships between humans and their technology. This was true of the first photographs and is true of operative images. This fuzzy photograph from William Henry Fox-Talbot's well-known *The Pencil of Nature* (see Figure 15.2) features a building hailed as 'the first that was ever yet known *to have drawn its own picture*' (Talbot 1839).

This notion was, for at least a century and a half, the golden standard of photography theory – an image *of* the world is formed *by* the world and remains forever bound to it. Nowadays, there is no such tangibility, no such correspondence. The new standard is not etched in substance and has no fixed relationship to the world. With this in mind, perhaps operative images hail the dawn of a new era. The decreasing demand for human labour in the autonomous creation of images implies a diminishing visual involvement in them, which in turn brings about a redundancy of human intervention and therefore agency. In this world, the concept of the *visible* image, the image produced for the human eye, has mutated. It is now simply a by-product of other operations: an impoverished aristocrat forced to serve as tour guide on their former estate (Winthrop-Young and Horn 2012).

Works Cited

Borda, Sylvia Grace. 2013-15. *Farm Tableaux*. http://www.sylviagborda.com/farm-tableaux---google-street-view.html.

Cavell, Stanley. 1979. *The World Viewed: Reflections on the Ontology of Film*. Cambridge: Harvard University Press.

Cramer, Florian. 2016. 'When Claire Bishop Woke Up in the Drone Wars: Art, Technology and the Nth Time'. In *Across & Beyond: A Transmediale Resder on Post-Digital Pracrices, Concepts and Institutions*, edited by Ryan Bishop, Kristoffer Gansin, Jussi Parikka and Elvia Wilk, 122-34. Berlin: Sternberg Press & Transmediale e.V.

Datson, Lorraine, and Peter Galison. 2007. *Objectivity*. New York: Zone Books.

Ernst, Wolfgang. 2013. *Digital Memory and the Archive*. Minneapolis: University of Minnesota Press.

Farocki, Harun. 2000, 2001, 2003. *Eye / Machine I, II, III*.

Farocki, Harun. 2003. *War at a Distance*.

Farocki, Harun. 2004. 'Phantom Images'. *Public* 29: 12-22.

Flusser, Vilém. 2000. *Towards a Philosophy of Photography*. Translated by Anthony Mathews. London: Reaktion.

Friedrich, Kathrin, and Moritz Queisner. 2014. 'Automated Killing and Mediated Caring: How Image-Guided Robotic Intervention Redefines Radiosurgical Practice'. 50th Anniversary Convention of the Society for the Study of Artificial Intelligence and the Simulation of Behaviour, London.

Grosser, Ben. 2013. *Computers Watching Movies*. https://bengrosser.com/projects/computers-watching-movies/#:~:text=Computers%20Watching%20Movies%20shows%20what,audio%20from%20the%20original%20clip.

Kahn, Douglas. 2013. *Earth Signal Earth Sound: Energies and Earth Magnitude in the Arts*. Berkeley: University of California Press.

Kittler, Friedrich A. 1999. *Gramophone, Film, Typewriter*. Translated by Geoffrey Winthrop-Young and Michael Wutz. Stanford: Stanford University Press.

Kittler, Friedrich A. 2012. 'The World of the Symbolic – A World of the Machine'. In *Literature, Media, Information Systems*, edited by John Johnston, 130-46. London: Routledge.

Lehmuskallio, Asko. 2016. 'The Camera as a Sensor: The Visualization of Everyday Digital Photography as Simulative, Heuristic and Layerd Pictures'. In *Digital Photography and Everyday Life: Empirical Studies on Material Visual Practices*, edited by Edgar Gómez Cruz and Asko Lehmuskallio. London: Routledge.

Manovich, Lev. 2001. *The Language of New Media*. Cambridge: MIT Press.

Moholy-Nagy, László. 1928. 'Photography is Manipulation of Light'. *Bauhaus* 1: 2-9.

Moholy-Nagy, László. 1969. *Painting, Photography, Film*. Translated by Janet Seligman. London: Lund Humphries.

Nake, Frieder. 2001. 'Vilém Flusser und Max Bense des Pixels angesichtig werdend: Eine Überlegung am Rande der Computergrafik'. In *Fotografie denken: Über Vilém Flussers Philosophie der Medienmoderne*, edited by Jäger Gottfried, 169-82. Bielefeld: Kerber.

Nake, Frieder. 2008. 'Surface, Interface, Subface. Three Cases of Interaction and One Concept'. In *Paradoxes of Interactivity. Perspectives for Media Theory, Human-Computer Interaction and Artistic Investigations*, edited by U. Seifert, J.H. Kim and A. Moore, 92-109. Bielefeld: transcript.

Nake, Frieder, and Susan Grabowski. 2017. 'Think the Image, Don't Make It! On Algorithmic Thinking, Art Education, and Re-Coding'. *Journal of Science and Technology in the Arts* 9: 21-31.

Paglen, Trevor. 2016. 'Invisible Images (Your Pictures Are Looking at You)'. *The New Inquiry*. December 8. https://thenewinquiry.com/invisible-images-your-pictures-are-looking-at-you/.

Pantenburg, Volker. 2017. 'Working Images. Harun Farocki and the Operational Image'. In *Image Operations: Visual Media and Political Conflict*, edited by Jens Eder and Charlotte Klonk, 49-62. Manchester: Manchester University Press.

Rafman, John. 2008-ongoing. '9-Eyes'. https://9-eyes.com/.

Rickard, Doug. 2010. 'A New American Picture'. https://dougrickard.com/a-new-american-picture/.

Steyerl, Hito. 2016. 'A Sea of Data: Apophenia and Pattern (Mis-) Recognition'. *E-Flux* 72. https://www.e-flux.com/journal/72/60480/a-sea-of-data-apophenia-and-pattern-mis-recognition/.

Talbot, William Henry Fox. 1839. *Some Account of the Art of Photogenic Drawing, or, the Process by Which Natural Objects May Be Made to Delineate Themselves without the Aid of the Artist's Pencil*. London: R. and J.E. Taylor.

Virilio, Paul. 1994. *The Vision Machine*. Translated by Julie Rose. Bloomington: Indiana University Press.

Winthrop-Young, Geoffrey, and Eva Horn. 2012. 'Machine Learning.' *Art Forum* 51: 473-79.

Contributors

Michele Barker is a media artist and researcher.

Antoine Bousquet is Associate Professor in the Department of Political Science at the Swedish Defence University. His work lies at the intersection of war and political violence, the history and philosophy of science and technology, and social and political theory in the digital age. He is the author of *The Eye of War: Military Perception from the Telescope to the Drone* (University of Minnesota Press, 2018) and *The Scientific Way of Warfare: Order and Chaos on the Battlefields of Modernity* (Hurst Publishers, 2009). His current research project is on the advent of nuclear weaponry as an event in thought.

Kathryn Brimblecombe-Fox, PhD, M. Phil, B.A, is a visual artist and interdisciplinary researcher based in Meanjin/Brisbane, Australia. She is an Honorary Research Fellow in the School of Communication and Arts, The University of Queensland. Her creative practice and research examine issues associated with militarised technology, and the militarise-ability of civilian technology. She has a particular interest in increasing military interest in the electromagnetic spectrum. Kathryn has presented about her creative practice and research at Australian-based and international conferences, and her research is published in peer reviewed journals and edited books. She has exhibited her paintings in Australia and internationally.

Joseph DeLappe is the Professor of Games and Tactical Media at Abertay University in Dundee, Scotland, where he relocated from the USA in 2017. He has developed numerous activist, creative projects, online gaming performances, video games, community engagements, and interventionists actions, which have been shown throughout the world. Creative works and actions have been featured widely in scholarly journals, books and in the popular media, including the *New York Times*, *Art in America*, *The Guardian*, and the BBC. He has written widely regarding art, memory, and activism. In 2017 he was awarded a Guggenheim Fellowship in the Fine Arts.

Jack Faber is a Helsinki-based artist-researcher and filmmaker whose work explores narratives of security, survival and new species relations. Investigating their interconnections and role in escalating economic and ecological crises, his interdisciplinary practice focuses on surveillance and cinema. His use of drones, phones and new technologies in unexpected ways, often alter them into means of questioning the militarization of public spaces and open territories. In his work he examines climate conflicts and possibilities of emancipatory engagements through a hybrid of salvaged footage, archival materials, documentation and scripted works. He sensitively uses humor, transgression, and immersion for in-depth studies of possible species equality in relations to AI, animals and human rights.

Adam Fish is an Associate Professor in the School of Arts and the Media at the University of New South Wales. He is a cultural anthropologist, documentary video producer, and interdisciplinary scholar who works across social science, computer engineering, environmental science, and the visual arts. His books include *Hacker States* (MIT, 2020, with Luca Follis), *Technoliberalism* (Palgrave Macmillan, 2017), *After the Internet* (Polity, 2017, with Ramesh Srinivasan), which was translated into Spanish in 2021, and *Oceaning: Governing Marine Life with Drones* (Duke, 2024).

Amy Gaeta is a Research Associate at the Centre for Drones and Culture as well as the Leverhulme Centre for the Future of Intelligence at the University of Cambridge. She uses feminist theory and critical disability studies to analyze the emotional, aesthetic, and political dimensions of human-tech relations, especially those concerning consumer drones. Gaeta asks how semi-autonomous technologies impact the formation of subjecthood and ideas of humanness.

Edgar Gómez Cruz is an Associate Professor at the School of Information at The University of Texas at Austin, and director of DigiSUR Lab, a laboratory for the study of digital technologies in the Global South. His recent publications include the books: *Vital Technologies. Thinking digital cultures from Latin America* (2022), *From Kodak Culture to Networked Image: An Ethnography of Digital Photography Practices (2012)*, and the co-edited volumes *Digital Photography and Everyday Life: Empirical Studies on Material Visual Practices* (2016) with Asko Lehmuskallio and *Refiguring Techniques in Visual Digital Research* (2017), with Shanti Sumartojo and Sarah Pink.

Sophia Goodfriend is a Post-Doctoral Fellow at Harvard Kennedy School's Middle East Institute for the 2024/2025 academic year. She earned her doctorate from Duke University's Department of Cultural Anthropology in 2024, where she wrote a dissertation entitled 'Algorithmic Dispossession: Automating Warfare in Israel and Palestine'. Goodfriend's writing on surveillance, warfare, and automation in Israel/Palestine has appeared in a range of academic and popular press outlets.

Mitch Goodwin is an artistic researcher with interests in emergent media ecologies, cultures of automation and digital aesthetics at the University of Melbourne. An interdisciplinary academic, his writing has appeared in the

M/C Journal, *Rolling Stone*, *Acoustic Space* and *The Conversation*. Mitch was the founding curator of *Screengrab International* (2009-15) which interrogated the political and technical infrastructures of network culture. His media works have screened widely, including WRO Media Arts Biennale (Wroclaw, Poland), The Lumen Prize (New York & Cardiff), Fantasy Film Festival (Gold Coast) and MADATAC (Madrid). Mitch is a Liverpool fan and a Bowie tragic. #YNWA.

Caren Kaplan is Professor Emerita of American Studies at the University of California at Davis. Her research draws on feminist transnational cultural studies, cultural geography, landscape art, and military history to explore the ways in which undeclared as well as declared wars produce representational practices of atmospheric politics. Recent publications include *Aerial Aftermaths: Wartime from Above* (Duke 2018) and *Life in the Age of Drone Warfare* (Duke 2017).

Anna Munster is a Professor of Art and Design at the University of New South Wales, Australia. Their collaborative practice engages with experimental cinema and acoustic environments to explore the human and more-than-human via perception, embodiment, movement, and duration. They have been commissioned to produce immersive work's such as *pull* (2017), Experimenta Make Sense: Triennial of Media Art, and have exhibited at major Australian, UK, Asian and American galleries. Their ongoing *ecologies of duration* is a multi-channel, experimental drone, sound and generative AI site-based work. Munster is also the author of *DeepAesthetics: Computational Experience in a Time of Machine Learning* (Duke, 2025).

Beryl Pong is a UKRI Future Leaders Fellow at the Centre for the Future of Intelligence and the Institute for Technology and Humanity, University of Cambridge, where she directs the Centre for Drones and Culture. She holds affiliated positions with Trinity College and the Faculty of English at Cambridge, and with the Department of English, Linguistics, and Theatre Studies at the National University of Singapore. She is the author of *British Literature and Culture in Second World Wartime: For the Duration* (Oxford, 2020).

Michael Richardson is a writer, researcher, and teacher living and working on Gadigal and Bidjigal land. He is an Associate Professor in Media and Culture at UNSW Sydney, where he co-directs the Media Futures Hub and an Associate Investigator with the ARC Centre of Excellence on Automated Decision-Making + Society. His research examines technology, power, witnessing, trauma, and affect in contexts of war and crisis. His latest book is *Nonhuman Witnessing: War, Climate, and Data After the End of the World* (Duke, 2024).

J. D. Schnepf is an assistant professor of American Studies at the University of Groningen. She holds a PhD from Brown University. Her writing on domestic drone culture appears in *American Literature*, *Catalyst: Feminism, Theory, Technoscience*, *Media and Environment*, *Modern Fiction Studies*, and *Surveillance and Society*.

Tom Sear is one of Australia's leading commentators, researchers and advisers on democratic resilience in an era of cyber conflict and social media manipulation. He has advised parliaments and industry on social media manipulation, counter influence initiatives, IoT and 5G policy, and worked as a cyber security practitioner in government. His research concerns how to build resilient national computational cultures to defend against active measures, manipulation and cyber storm. Tom undertook his PhD as an Industry Fellow in Cyber Security with UNSW Canberra Cyber at the Australian Defence Force Academy (ADFA).

Simon Michael Taylor is a 2024 Visiting Fellow at the School of Regulation and Global Governance, Australian National University. As a Science and Technology Studies scholar he investigates infrastructural and genealogical components of autonomous decision systems. In contending with societal impacts from Artificial Intelligence he has contributed to the development of International Standards and policy making on Cyber-security, the Internet of Things, and Privacy law. Recent work explores impacts of computing on animals and environments. This includes an article titled 'Species Ex-Machina' for the *British Journal for the History of Science*, and contributing to the artist Nicholas Mangan's exhibition *A World Undone* (2024).

Yanai Toister (Ph.D.) is an artist, writer and educator serving as associate professor at Shenkar College in Tel Aviv. Toister's artworks have been shown in venues including Sandroni.Rey, Los Angeles; Dvir Gallery, Tel Aviv; Kunsthalle Luzern; Maison Européenne de la Photographie, Paris; the 11th International Architecture Exhibition at the Venice Biennale; Kunstmuseen Krefeld; Israel Museum. Toister's writing has been published in various journals including *Digital Creativity*; *Flusser Studies*; *Journal of Visual Art Practice*; *Media Theory*; *Philosophy of Photography*; *Photographies*. Toister's book *Photography from the Turin Shroud to the Turing Machine* has been published by Intellect/University of Chicago Press.

Madelene Veber is a PhD Candidate in Sociology at the University of New South Wales, Sydney. Her dissertation research examines the concept of error in social theory, in particular the different ways that error is sublimated and their implications for theory and everyday life. She is a recipient of the Australian Research Training Program Scholarship (2020-2023) and the Honours Thesis Publishing Award.

www.ingramcontent.com/pod-product-compliance
Lightning Source LLC
Chambersburg PA
CBHW041920240526
45473CB00039B/2925